THE MAJOR LANGUAGES OF WESTERN EUROPE

THE MAJOR LANGUAGES OF WESTERN EUROPE

EDITED BY
BERNARD COMRIE

ROUTLEDGE
London

First published as part of
The World's Major Languages in 1987 by
Croom Helm Ltd

Reprinted with revisions and additional material in 1990 by
Routledge
11 New Fetter Lane, London EC4P 4EE

British Library Cataloguing in Publication Data
Available on request

ISBN 0–415–04738–2

Typeset in 10 on 12pt Times by Computype, Middlesex
Printed and bound in Great Britain by Mackays of Chatham

Contents

Preface

The text of this book has been extracted from that of *The World's Major Languages* (Routledge, 1987). The aim of that book was to make available information on some fifty of the world's major languages and language families, in a form that would be accessible and interesting both to the layman with a general interest in language and to the linguist eager to find out about languages outside his or her speciality. Not all of those interested in major languages of the world, however, have an interest that includes all parts of the world, and it therefore seemed advisable to publish portions of the original text in a series of paperbacks — *The Major Languages*. Readers interested in only one part of the world now have access to discussion of those languages without having to acquire the whole volume.

Perhaps the most controversial problem that I had to face in the original volume was the choice of languages to be included. My main criterion was admittedly, a very subjective one: what languages did I think the reader would expect to find included? In answering this question I was, of course, guided by more objective criteria, such as the number of speakers of individual languages, whether they are official languages of independent states, whether they are widely used in more than one country, whether they are the bearers of long-standing literary traditions. These criteria often conflict — thus Latin, though long since deprived of native speakers, was included because of its immense cultural importance — and I bear full responsibility, as editor, for the final choice.

The notion of 'major language' is obviously primarily a social character-isation, and the fact that a language was not included implies no denigra-tion of its importance as a language in its own right: every human language is a manifestation of our species' linguistic faculty and any human language may provide an important contribution to our understanding of language as a general phenomenon. In the recent development of general linguistics, important contributions have come from the Australian Aboriginal lan-guages Walbiri (Warlpiri) and Dyirbal (Jirrbal). Other editors might well have come up with different selections of languages, or have used somewhat different criteria. When linguists learned in 1970 that the last speaker of Kamassian, a Uralic language originally spoken in Siberia, had kept her language alive for decades in her prayers — God being the only other speaker of her language — they may well have wondered whether, for this person, *the* world's major language was not Kamassian.

Contributors were presented with early versions of my own chapters on Slavonic languages and Russian as models for their contributions, but I felt it inappropriate to lay down strict guidelines as to how each individual chapter should be written, although I did ask authors to include at least some material on both the structure of their language and its social background. The main criterion that I asked contributors to follow was: tell the reader what you consider to be the most interesting facts about your language. This necessarily meant that different chapters highlight different phenomena, e.g. the chapter on English the role of English as a world language, the chapter on Arabic the writing system, the chapter on Turkish the grammatical system. But I believe that this variety lent strength to the original volume, since within the space limitations of what is quite a sizable book it would have been impossible to do justice in a more comprehensive and homogeneous way to each of over 50 languages and language families.

The criterion for dividing the contents of the original volume among the four new books has been my assessment of likely common and divergent interests: if the reader is interested in language X, then which of the other major languages of the world is he or she likely to be most interested in? In part, my decisions have been governed by consideration of genetic relatedness (for instance, all Romance languages, including Rumanian, are included in *The Major Languages of Western Europe*), in part by consideration of areal interests (so that *The Major Languages of The Middle East, South Asia and Africa* includes the Indo-Iranian languages, along with other languages of the Middle East and South Asia). Inevitably, some difficulties arose in working out the division, especially given the desire not to have too much overlap among volumes, since a reader might want to acquire more than one of the paperback volumes. In fact, the only overlap among the volumes is in the Introduction, substantial parts of which are the same for all volumes, and in the fact that the chapter on Indo-European languages is included in both of the European volumes (given that most of the languages of both western and eastern Europe are Indo-European).

Editorial support in the preparation of my work on the original volume was provided by the Division of Humanities of the University of Southern California, through the research fund of the Andrew W. Mellon Professorship, which I held during 1983–4, and by the Max Planck Institute for Psycholinguistics (Nijmegen, The Netherlands), where I was a visiting research worker in the summer of 1984. I am particularly grateful to

Jonathan Price for his continuing willingness to consult with me on all details of the preparation of the text.

Bernard Comrie
Los Angeles

Abbreviations

abilit.	abilitative	conj.	conjunction
abl.	ablative	conjug.	conjugation
abstr.	abstract	conjv.	conjunctive
acc.	accusative	cont.	contemplated
acr.	actor	cop.	copula
act.	active	cp	class prefix
act.n.	action nominal	crs.	currently relevant state
adj.	adjective	Cz.	Czech
adv.	adverb	Da.	Danish
Alb.	Albanian	dat.	dative
Am.	American	dbl.	double
anim.	animate	decl.	declension
aor.	aorist	def.	definite
Ar.	Arabic	dent.	dental
Arm.	Armenian	deriv. morph.	derivational morpheme
art.	article	de-v.	deverbal
Ashk.	Ashkenazi(c)	dir.	direct
asp.	aspirated	disj.	disjunctive
AT	actor-trigger	Dor.	Doric
athem.	athematic	drc.	directional
aux.	auxiliary	DT	dative-trigger
Av.	Avestan	du.	dual
ben.	beneficiary	dur.	durative
BH	Biblical Hebrew	d.v.	dynamic verb
BN	B-Norwegian	E.	Eastern
Boh.	Bohemian	Eng.	English
BP	Brazilian Portuguese	ENHG	Early New High German
Br.	British		
BT	beneficiary-trigger	EP	European Portuguese
c.	common	erg.	ergative
Cast.	Castilian	ex.	existential-possessive
Cat.	Catalan	f.	feminine
caus.	causative	fact.	factive
cc	class concord	foc.	focus
Cent.	Central	Fr.	French
cl.	class(ifier)	fut.	future
clit.	clitic	g.	gender
comp.	comparative	gen.	genitive

ger.	gerund(ive)	neg.	negative
Gk.	Greek	NHG	New High German
Gmc.	Germanic	nm.	nominal
Go.	Gothic	NN	N-Norwegian
gr.	grade	nom.	nominative
GR	Gallo-Romance	noms.	nominalisation
gutt.	guttural	NP	New Persian
H	High	nt.	neuter
Hier. Hitt.	Hieroglyphic Hittite	Nw.	Norwegian
Hitt.	Hittite	O.	Oscan
hon.	honorific	OArm.	Old Armenian
IE	Indo-European	obj.	object
imper.	imperative	obl.	oblique
imperf.	imperfect(ive)	OBs.	Old Burmese
inanim.	inanimate	Oc.	Occitan
incl.	inclusive	OCS	Old Church Slavonic
indef.	indefinite	OE	Old English
indic.	indicative	OFr.	Old French
indir.	indirect	OFri.	Old Frisian
infin.	infinitive	OHG	Old High German
inst.	instrumental	OIc.	Old Icelandic
intr.	intransitive	OIr.	Old Irish
inv.	inversion particle	OIran.	Old Iranian
irr.	irrational	OLat.	Old Latin
It.	Italian	OLith.	Old Lithuanian
IT	instrument-trigger	ON	Old Norse
i.v.	intransitive verb	OP	Old Persian
L	Low	opt.	optative
lab.	labial	OPtg.	Old Portuguese
Lat.	Latin	orig.	original(ly)
Latv.	Latvian	OS	Old Saxon
LG	Low German	OV	object–verb
lig.	ligature	p.	person
lingu.	lingual	pal.	palatal
lit.	literally	part.	participle
Lith.	Lithuanian	pass.	passive
loc.	locative	pat.	patient
m.	masculine	PDr.	Proto-Dravidian
MBs.	Modern Burmese	perf.	perfect(ive)
ME	Middle English	pers.	person
med.	medio-passive	PGmc.	Proto-Germanic
MH	Middle Hebrew	PIE	Proto-Indo-European
MHG	Middle High German	PIt.	Proto-Italic
mid.	middle	Pkt.	Prakrit
MidFr.	Middle French	pl.	plural
ModE	Modern English	Po.	Polish
ModFr.	Modern French	pos.	position
MoH	Modern Hebrew	poss.	possessive
Mor.	Moravian	prep.	preposition
MP	Middle Persian	prepl.	prepositional
n.	noun	pres.	present
necess.	necessitative	pret.	preterit

prim.	primary	st.	standard
prog.	progressive	su.	subject
pron.	pronoun	subj.	subjunctive
PT	patient-trigger	sup.	superlative
Ptg.	Portuguese	s.v.	stative verb
Q	question	SVO	subject–verb–object
rat.	rational	Sw.	Swedish
recip.	reciprocal	tap.	tense/aspect pronoun
refl. pron.	reflexive pronoun	tg.	trigger
rel.	relative	them.	thematic
rep.	reported	Tk.	Turkish
res.	result	Toch.	Tocharian
Ru.	Runic	top.	topic
Rum.	Rumanian	tr.	transitive
Rus.	Russian	transg.	transgressive
Sard.	Sardinian	t.v.	transitive verb
SCr.	Serbo-Croat	U.	Umbrian
sec.	secondary	v.	verb
Seph.	Sephardi(c)	v.n.	verbal noun
sg.	singular	vd.	voiced
S-J	Sino-Japanese	Ved.	Vedic
Skt.	Sanskrit	VL	Vulgar Latin
Slk.	Slovak	vls.	voiceless
SOV	subject–object–verb	VO	verb–object
Sp.	Spanish	voc.	vocative
spec.	species	VSO	verb–subject–object

* The asterisk is used in discussion of historical reconstructions to indicate a reconstructed (non-attested) form. In synchronic discussions, it is used to indicate an ungrammatical item; (*X) means that inclusion of X makes the item ungrammatical; *(X) means that omission of X makes the item ungrammatical.

In the chapters on the Romance languages, capitals are used to represent Latin or reconstructed Proto-Romance forms.

INTRODUCTION

Bernard Comrie

1 Preliminary Notions

How many languages are there in the world? What language(s) do they speak in India? What languages have the most speakers? What languages were spoken in Australia, or in California before European immigration? When did Latin stop being spoken, and when did French start being spoken? How did English become such an important world language? These and other similar questions are often asked by the interested layman. One aim of the volumes of *The Major Languages* series is to provide answers to these and related questions, or in certain cases to show why the questions cannot be answered as they stand. The chapters concentrate on an individual language or group of languages, and in this Introduction I want rather to present a linking essay which will provide a background against which the individual chapters can be appreciated.

After discussing some preliminary notions in this section, section 2 of the Introduction provides a rapid survey of the languages spoken in western Europe today. Since the notion of 'major language' is primarily a social notion — languages become major (such as English), or stop being major (such as Sumerian) not because of their grammatical structure, but because of social factors — section 3 discusses some important socio-linguistic notions, in particular concerning the social interaction of languages.

1.1 How Many Languages?

Linguists are typically very hesitant to answer the first question posed above, namely: how many languages are spoken in the world today? Probably the best that one can say, with any hope of not being contradicted, is that at a very conservative estimate some 4,000 languages are spoken today. Laymen are often surprised that the figure should be so high, but I would emphasise that this is a conservative estimate. But why is it that linguists are not able to give a more accurate figure? There are several different reasons conspiring to prevent them from doing so, and these will be outlined below.

One is that many parts of the world are insufficiently studied from a linguistic viewpoint, so that we simply do not know precisely what languages are spoken there. Our knowledge of the linguistic situation in remote parts of the world has improved dramatically in recent years — New Guinea, for instance, has changed from being almost a blank linguistic map to the stage where most (though still not all) of the languages can be pinpointed with accuracy: since perhaps as many as one fifth of the world's languages are spoken in New Guinea, this has radically changed any estimate of the total number of languages. But there are still some areas where uncertainty remains, so that even a detailed index of the world's languages such as Voegelin and Voegelin (1977) lists several languages with accompanying question marks, or queries whether one listed language might in fact be the same as some other language but under a different name.

A second problem is that it is difficult or impossible in many cases to decide whether two related speech varieties should be considered different languages or merely different dialects of the same language. With the languages of Europe, there are in general established traditions of whether two speech varieties should be considered different languages or merely dialect variants, but these decisions have often been made more on political and social grounds rather than strictly linguistic grounds.

One criterion that is often advanced as a purely linguistic criterion is mutual intelligibility: if two speech varieties are mutually intelligible, they are different dialects of the same language, but if they are mutually unintelligible, they are different languages. But if applied to the languages of Europe, this criterion would radically alter our assessment of what the different languages of Europe are: the most northern dialects and the most southern dialects (in the traditional sense) of German are mutually unintelligible, while dialects of German spoken close to the Dutch border are mutually intelligible with dialects of Dutch spoken just across the border. In fact, our criterion for whether a dialect is Dutch or German relates in large measure to social factors — is the dialect spoken in an area where Dutch is the standard language or where German is the standard language? By the same criterion, the three nuclear Scandinavian languages (in the traditional sense), Danish, Norwegian and Swedish, would turn out to be dialects of one language, given their mutual intelligibility. While this criterion is often applied to non-European languages (so that nowadays linguists often talk of the Chinese languages rather than the Chinese dialects, given the mutual unintelligibility of, for instance, Mandarin and Cantonese), it seems unfair that it should not be applied consistently to European languages as well.

While native speakers of English are often surprised that there should be problems in delimiting languages from dialects — since present-day dialects of English are in general mutually intelligible (at least with some familiarisation), and even the language most closely related genetically to English, Frisian, is mutually unintelligible with English — the native speaker of English would be hard put to interpret a sentence in Tok Pisin, the English-based pidgin of much of Papua New Guinea, like *sapos ol i karamapim bokis bilong yumi, orait bai yumi paitim as bilong ol* 'if they cover our box, then we'll spank them', although each word, except perhaps *i*, is of English origin ('suppose all ?he cover-up-him box belong you-me, all-right by you-me fight-him arse belong all').

In some cases, the intelligibility criterion actually leads to contradictory results, namely when we have a dialect chain, i.e. a string of dialects such that the adjacent dialects are readily mutually intelligible, but dialects from the far ends of the chain are not mutually intelligible. A good illustration of this is the Dutch-German dialect complex. One could start from the far south of the German-speaking area and move to the far west of the Dutch-speaking area without encountering any sharp boundary across which mutual intelligibility is broken; but the two end points of this chain are speech varieties so different from one another that there is no mutual intelligibility possible. If one takes a simplified dialect chain A – B – C, where A and B are mutually intelligible, as are B and C, but A and C are mutually unintelligible, then one arrives at the contradictory result that A and B are dialects of the same language, B and C are dialects of the same language, but A and C are different languages. There is in fact no way of resolving this contradiction if we maintain the traditional strict difference between language and dialects, and what such examples show is that this is not an all-or-nothing distinction, but rather a continuum. In this sense, it is impossible to answer the question how many languages are spoken in the world.

A further problem with the mutual intelligibility criterion is that mutual intelligibility itself is a matter of degree rather than a clearcut opposition between intelligibility and unintelligibility. If mutual intelligibility were to mean 100 per cent mutual intelligibility of all utterances, then perhaps no two speech varieties would be classified as mere dialect variants; for instance, although speakers of British and American English can understand most of one another's speech, there are areas where intelligibility is likely to be minimal unless one speaker happens to have learned the linguistic forms used by the other, as with car (or auto) terms like British *boot, bonnet, mudguard* and their American equivalents *trunk, hood, fender*. Conversely, although speakers of different Slavonic languages are often unable to make full sense of a text in another Slavonic language, they can usually make good sense of parts of the text, because of the high percentage of shared vocabulary and forms.

Two further factors enter into the degree of mutual intelligibility between two speech varieties. One is that intelligibility can rise rapidly with increased familiarisation: those who remember the first introduction of American films into Britain often recall that they were initially considered difficult to understand, but increased exposure to American English has virtually removed this problem. Speakers of different dialects of Arabic often experience difficulty in understanding each other at first meeting, but soon adjust to the major differences between their respective dialects, and Egyptian Arabic, as the most widely diffused modern Arabic dialect, has rapidly gained in intelligibility throughout the Arab world. This can lead to 'one-way intelligibility', as when speakers of, say, Tunisian Arabic are more likely to understand Egyptian Arabic than vice versa, because Tunisian Arabic speakers are more often exposed to Egyptian Arabic than vice versa. The second factor is that intelligibility is to a certain extent a social and psychological phenomenon: it is easier to understand when you want to understand. A good example of this is the conflicting assessments different speakers of the same Slavonic language will often give about the intelligibility of some other Slavonic language, correlating in large measure with whether or not they feel well-disposed to speakers of the other language.

The same problems as exist in delimiting dialects from languages arise, incidentally, on the historical plane too, where the question arises: at what point has a language changed sufficiently to be considered a different language? Again, traditional answers are often contradictory: Latin is considered to have died out, although its descendants, the Romance languages, live on, so at some time Latin must have changed sufficiently to be deemed no longer the same language, but a qualitatively different language. On the other hand, Greek is referred to in the same way throughout its attested history (which is longer than that of Latin and the Romance languages combined), with merely the addition of different adjectives to identify different stages of its development (e.g. Ancient Greek, Byzantine Greek, Modern Greek). In the case of the history of the English language, there is even conflicting terminology: the oldest attested stages of English can be referred to either as Old English (which suggests an earlier stage of Modern English) or as Anglo-Saxon (which suggests a different language that is the ancestor of English, perhaps justifiably so given the mutual unintelligibility of Old and Modern English).

A further reason why it is difficult to assess the number of languages spoken in the world today is that many languages are on the verge of extinction. While it has probably been the case throughout mankind's history that languages have died out, the historically recent expansion of European population to the Americas and Australia has resulted in a greatly accelerated rate of language death among the indigenous languages of these areas. Perusal of Voegelin and Voegelin (1977) will show a number of languages as 'possibly extinct' or 'possibly still spoken', plus an even greater number of languages with only a handful of speakers — usually of advanced age — so that a language may well be dying out somewhere in the world as I am writing these words. When a language dies, this is sometimes an abrupt process, such as the death of a fluent speaker who happened to have outlived all other speakers of the language; more typically, however, the community's facility with the language decreases, as more and more functions are taken over by some other language, so that what they speak, in terms of the original language of the community, is only a part of that language. Many linguists working on Australian Aboriginal languages have been forced, in some cases, to do what has come to be called 'salvage linguistics', i.e. to elicit portions of a language from someone who has neither spoken nor heard the language for decades and has perhaps only a vague recollection of what the language was like.

1.2 Language Families and Genetic Classification

One of the basic organisational principles of this volume, both in section 2 of the Introduction and in the arrangement of the individual chapters, is the organisation of languages into language families. It is therefore important that some insight should be provided into what it means to say that two languages belong to the same language family (or equivalently: are genetically related).

It is probably intuitively clear to anyone who knows a few languages that some languages are closer to one another than are others. For instance, English and German are closer to one another than either is to Russian, while Russian and Polish are closer to one another than either is to English. This notion of similarity can be made more precise, as is done for instance in the chapter on the Indo-European languages below, but for the moment the relatively informal notion will suffice. Starting in the late eighteenth century, a specific hypothesis was proposed to account for such similarities, a hypothesis which still forms the foundation of research into the history and relatedness of languages. This hypothesis is that where languages share some set of features in common, these features are to be attributed to their common ancestor. Let us take some examples from English and German.

In English and German we find a number of basic vocabulary items that have the same or almost the same form, e.g. English *man* and German *Mann*. Likewise, we find a number of bound morphemes (prefixes and suffixes) that have the same or almost the same form, such as the genitive suffix, as in English *man's* and German *Mann(e)s*. Although English and German are now clearly different languages, we may hypothesise that at an earlier period in history they had a common ancestor, in which the word for 'man' was something like *man* and the genitive suffix was something like *-s*. Thus English and German belong to the same language family, which is the same as saying that they share a common ancestor. We can readily add other languages to this family, since a word like *man* and a genitive suffix like *-s* are also found in Dutch, Frisian, and the Scandinavian languages. The family to which these languages belong has been given the name Germanic, and the ancestor language is Proto-Germanic. It should be emphasised that the proto-language is not an attested language — although if written records had gone back far enough, we might well have had attestations of this language — but its postulation is the most plausible hypothesis explaining the remarkable similarities among the various Germanic languages.

Although not so obvious, similarities can be found among the Germanic languages and a number of other languages spoken in Europe and spreading across nothern India as far as Bangladesh. These other languages share fewer similarities with the Germanic languages than individual Germanic languages do with one another, so that they are more remotely related. The overall language family to which all these languages belong is the Indo-European family, with its reconstructed ancestor language Proto-Indo-European. As is discussed in more detail in the chapter on Indo-European languages, the Indo-European family contains a number of branches (i.e. smaller language families, or subfamilies), such as Slavonic (including Russian and Polish), Iranian (including Persian and Pashto), and Celtic (including Irish and Welsh). The overall structure is therefore hierarchical: the most distant ancestor is Proto-Indo-European. At an intermediate point in the family tree, and therefore at a later period of history, we have such languages as Proto-Germanic and Proto-Celtic, which are descendants of Proto-Indo-European but ancestors of languages spoken today. Still later in history, we find the individual languages as they are spoken today or attested in recent history, such as English or German as descendants of Proto-Germanic and Irish and Welsh as descendants of Proto-Celtic. One typical property of language change that is represented accurately by this family-tree model is that, as time goes by, languages descending from a common ancestor tend to become less and less similar. For instance, Old English and Old High German (the ancestor of Modern German) were much closer to one another than are the modern languages — they may even have been mutually intelligible, at least to a large extent.

Although the family-tree model of language relatedness is an important foundation of all current work in historical and comparative linguistics, it is not without its problems, both in practice and in principle. Some of these will now be discussed.

We noted above that with the passage of time, genetically related languages will grow less and less similar. This follows from the fact that, once two languages have split off as separate languages from a common ancestor, each will innovate its own changes, different from changes that take place in the other language, so that the cumulative effect will be increasing divergence. With the passage of enough time, the divergence may come to be so great that it is no longer possible to tell, other than by directly examining the history, that the two languages do in fact come from a common ancestor. The best established language families, such as Indo-European or Sino-Tibetan, are those where the passage of time has not been long enough to erase the obvious traces of genetic relatedness. (For language families that have a long written tradition, one can of course make use of earlier stages of the language, which contain more evidence of genetic relatedness.) In addition, there are many hypothesised language families for which the evidence is not sufficient to convince all, or even the majority, of scholars. For instance, the Turkic language family is a well-established language family, as is each of the Uralic, Mongolian and Tungusic families. What is controversial, however, is whether or not these individual families are related as members of an even larger family. The possibility of an Altaic family, comprising Turkic, Mongolian, and Tungusic, is rather widely accepted, and some scholars would advocate increasing the size of this family by adding some or all of Uralic, Korean and Japanese.

The attitudes of different linguists to problems of this kind have been characterised as an opposition between 'splitters' (who require the firmest evidence before they are prepared to acknowledge genetic relatedness) and 'clumpers' (who are ready to assign languages to the same family on the basis of quite restricted similarities). I should, incidentally, declare my own splitter bias, lest any of my own views that creep in be interpreted as generally accepted dogma. The most extreme clumper position would, of course, be to maintain that all languages of the world are genetically related, although there are less radical positions that are somewhat more widely accepted, such as the following list of sixteen stocks, where a stock is simply the highest hierarchical level of genetic relatedness (just as a language family has branches, so families would group together to form stocks): Dravidian, Eurasiatic (including, inter alia, Uralic and Altaic), Indo-European, Nilo-Saharan, Niger-Kordofanian, Afroasiatic, Khoisan, Amerind (all indigenous languages of the Americas except Eskimo-Aleut and Na-Dene), Na-Dene, Austric (including Austro-Asiatic, Tai and Austronesian), Indo-Pacific (including all Papuan languages and Tasmanian), Australian, Sino-Tibetan, Ibero-Caucasian (including Basque and Caucasian), Ket, Burushaski — this schema still operates, incidentally, with two language isolates (Ket and Burushaski), i.e. languages not related to any other language, and retains a number of established language families as distinct (Dravidian, Indo-European, Nilo-Saharan, Niger-Kordofanian, Afroasiatic, Khoisan, Australian, and Sino-Tibetan).

While no linguist would doubt that some similarities among languages are due to genetic relatedness, there are several other possibilities for the explanation of any particular similarity, and before assuming genetic relatedness one must be able to exclude, at least with some degree of plausibility, these other possibilities. Unfortunately, in a great many cases it is not possible to reach a firm and convincing decision. Let us now examine some of the explanations other than genetic relatedness.

First, two languages may happen purely by chance to have some feature in common. For instance, the word for 'dog' in Mbabaram, an Australian Aboriginal language, happens to be *dog*. This Mbabaram word is not, incidentally, a borrowing from English, but is the regular development in Mbabaram of a Proto-Australian form something like *gudaga* (it is usual to prefix reconstructed forms with an asterisk). If anyone were tempted to assume on this basis, however, that English and Mbabaram are genetically related, examination of the rest of Mbabaram vocabulary and grammar would soon quash the genetic relatedness hypothesis, since there is otherwise minimal similarity between the two languages. In comparing English and German, by contrast, there are many similarities at all levels of linguistic analysis. Even sticking to vocabulary, the correspondence *man* : *Mann* can be matched by *wife* : *Weib, father* : *Vater, mother* : *Mutter, son* : *Sohn, daughter* : *Tochter*, etc. Given that other languages have radically different words for these concepts (e.g. Japanese *titi* 'father', *haha* 'mother', *musuko* 'son', *musume* 'daughter'), it clearly can not be merely the result of chance that English and German have so many similar items. But if the number of similar items in two languages is small, it may be difficult or impossible to distinguish between chance similarity and distant genetic relatedness.

Certain features shared by two languages might turn out to be manifestations of language universals, i.e. of features that are common to all languages or are inherently likely to occur in any language. Most discussions of language universals require a fair amount of theoretical linguistic background, but for present purposes I will take a simple, if not particularly profound, example. In many languages across the world, the syllable *ma* or its reduplicated form *mama* or some other similar form is the word for 'mother'. The initial syllable *ma* enters into the Proto-Indo-European word for 'mother' which has given English *mother*, Spanish *madre*, Russian *mat'*, Sanskrit *mātā*. In Mandarin Chinese, the equivalent word is *mā*, while in Wiyaw (Papua New Guinea) it is *mam*. Once again, examination of other features of Indo-European languages, Chinese and Wiyaw would soon dispel any possibility of assigning Chinese or Wiyaw to the Indo-European language family. Presumably the frequency across languages of the syllable *ma* in the word for 'mother' simply reflects the fact that this is typically one of the first syllables that babies articulate clearly, and is therefore interpreted by adults as the word for 'mother'. (In the South Caucasian language Georgian, incidentally, *mama* means 'father' — and 'mother' is *deda* — so that there are other ways of interpreting baby's first utterance.)

Somewhat similar to universals are patterns whereby certain linguistic features frequently cooccur in the same language, i.e. where the presence of one feature seems to require or at least to foster the presence of some other feature. For instance, the study of word order universals by Greenberg (1963) showed that if a language has verb-final word order (i.e. if 'the man saw the woman' is expressed literally as 'the man the woman saw'), then it is highly probable that it will also have postpositions rather than prepositions (i.e. 'in the house' will be expressed as 'the house in') and that it will have genitives before the noun (i.e. the pattern 'cat's house' rather than 'house of cat'). Thus, if we find two languages that happen to share the features: verb-final word order, postpositions, prenominal genitives, then the cooccurrence of these features is not evidence for genetic relatedness. Many earlier attempts at establishing wide-ranging genetic relationships suffer precisely from failure to take this property of typological patterns into account. Thus the fact that Turkic languages, Mongolian languages, Tungusic languages, Korean and Japanese share all of these features is not evidence for their genetic relatedness (although there may, of course, be other similarities, not connected with recurrent typological patterns, that do establish genetic relatedness). If one were to accept just these features as evidence for an Altaic language family, then the family would have to be extended to include a variety of other languages with the same word order properties, such as the Dravidian languages of southern India and Quechua, spoken in South America.

Finally, two languages might share some feature in common because one of them has borrowed it from the other (or because they have both borrowed it from some third language). English, for instance, borrowed a huge number of words from French during the Middle Ages, to such an extent that an uncritical examination of English vocabulary might well lead to the conclusion that English is a Romance language, rather than a Germanic language. The term 'borrow', as used here, is the accepted linguistic term, although the terminology is rather strange, since 'borrow' suggests a relatively superficial acquisition, one which is moreover temporary. Linguistic borrowings may run quite deep, and there is of course no implication that they will ever be repaid. Among English loans from French, for instance, there are many basic vocabulary items, such as *very* (replacing the native Germanic *sore*, as in the biblical *sore afraid*).

Examples from other languages show even more deep-seated loans: the Semitic language Amharic — the dominant and official language of Ethiopia — for instance, has lost the typical Semitic word order patterns, in which the verb precedes its object and adjectives and genitives follow their noun, in favour of the order where the verb follows its object and adjectives and genitives precede their noun; Amharic is in close contact with Cushitic languages, and Cushitic languages typically have the order object-verb, adjective/genitive-noun, so that Amharic has in fact borrowed these word orders from neighbouring Cushitic languages.

It seems that whenever two languages come into close contact, they will borrow features from one another. In some cases the contact can be so intense among the languages in a given area that they come to share a significant number of common features, setting this area off from adjacent languages, even languages that may happen to be more closely related genetically to languages within the area. The languages in an area of this kind are often said to belong to a sprachbund (German for 'language league'), and perhaps the most famous example of a sprachbund is the Balkan sprachbund, whose members (Modern Greek, Albanian, Bulgarian (with Macedonian), Rumanian) share a number of striking features not shared by closely related languages like Ancient Greek, other Slavonic languages (Bulgarian is Slavonic), or other Romance languages (Rumanian is Romance). The most striking of these features is loss of the infinitive, so that instead of 'give me to drink' one says 'give me that I drink' (Modern Greek *ðos mu na pjo*, Albanian *a-më të pi*, Bulgarian *daj mi da pija*, Rumanian *dă-mi să beau*; in all four languages the subject of the subordinate clause is encoded in the inflection of the verb).

Since we happen to know a lot about the history of the Balkan languages, linguists were not deceived by these similarities into assigning a closer genetic relatedness to the Balkan languages than in fact holds (all are ultimately members of the Indo-European family, though from different branches). In other parts of the world, however, there is the danger of mistaking areal phenomena for evidence of genetic relatedness. In South-East Asia, for instance, many languages share very similar phonological and morphological patterns: in Chinese, Thai and Vietnamese words are typically monosyllabic, there is effectively no morphology (i.e. words do not change after the manner of English *dog, dogs* or *love, loves, loved*), syllable structure is very simple (only a few single consonants are permitted word-finally, while syllable-initially consonant clusters are either disallowed or highly restricted), and there is a phonemic tone (thus Mandarin Chinese *mā*, with a high level tone, means 'mother', while *mǎ*, with a falling-rising tone, means 'horse'), and moreover there are a number of shared lexical items. For these reasons, it was for a long time believed that Thai and Vietnamese were related genetically to Chinese, as members of the Sino-Tibetan family. More recently, however, it has been established that these similarities are not the result of common ancestry, and Thai and Vietnamese are now generally acknowledged not to be genetically related to Chinese. The similarities are the results of areal contact. The shared vocabulary items are primarily the result of intensive Chinese cultural influence, especially on Vietnamese. The tones and simple syllable structures can often be shown to be the result of relatively recent developments, and indeed in one language that is incontrovertibly related to Chinese, namely Classical Tibetan, one finds complex consonant clusters but no phonemic tone, i.e. the similarities noted above are neither necessary nor sufficient conditions for genetic relatedness.

In practice, the most difficult task in establishing genetic relatedness is to distinguish between genuine cognates (i.e. forms going back to a common ancestor) and those that are the result of borrowing. It would therefore be helpful if one could distinguish between those features of a language that are borrowable and those that are not. Unfortunately, it seems that there is no feature that can absolutely be excluded from borrowing. Basic vocabulary can be borrowed, so that for instance Japanese has borrowed the whole set of numerals from Chinese, and even English borrowed its current set of third person plural pronouns (*they, them, their*) from Scandinavian. Bound morphemes can be borrowed: a good example is the agent suffix *-er* in English, with close cognates in other Germanic languages; this is ultimately a loan from the Latin agentive suffix *-ārius*, which has however become so entrenched in English that it is a productive morphological device applicable in principle to any verb to derive a corresponding agentive noun.

At one period in the recent history of comparative linguistics, it was believed that a certain basic vocabulary list could be isolated, constant across languages and cultures, such that the words on this list would be replaced at a constant rate. Thus, if one assumes that the retention rate is around 86 per cent per millennium, this means that if a single language splits into two descendant languages, then after 1,000 years each language would retain about 86 per cent of the words in the list from the ancestor language, i.e. the two descendants would then share just over 70 per cent of the words in the list. In some parts of the world, groupings based on this 'glottochronological' method still form the basis of the only available detailed and comprehensive attempt at establishing genetic relations. It must be emphasised that the number of clear counter-examples to the glottochronological method, i.e. instances where independent evidence contradicts the predictions of this approach, is so great that no reliance can be placed on its results.

It is, however, true that there are significant differences in the ease with which different features of a language can be borrowed. The thing that seems most easily borrowable is cultural vocabulary, and indeed it is quite normal for a community borrowing some concept (or artifact) from another community to borrow the foreign name along with the object. Another set of features that seem rather borrowable are general typological features, such as word order: in addition to the Amharic example cited above, one might note the fact that many Austronesian languages spoken in New Guinea have adopted the word order where the object is placed before the verb, whereas almost all other Austronesian languages place the object after the verb; this change occurred under the influence of Papuan languages almost all of which are verb-final. Basic vocabulary comes next. And last of all one finds bound morphology. But even though it is difficult to borrow bound morphology, it is not impossible, so in arguments over genetic relatedness one cannot exclude *a priori* the possibility that even affixes may have been borrowed.

2   Languages of Western Europe

Europe, taken here in the traditional cultural sense rather than in the current geographical sense of 'the land mass west of the Urals', is the almost exclusive preserve of the Indo-European family. This family covers not only almost the whole of Europe, but also extends through Armenia (in the Caucasus), Iran and Afghanistan into Soviet Central Asia (Tadzhikistan), with the easternmost outpost of this strand the Iranian language Sarikoli, spoken just inside China. Another strand spreads from Afghanistan across Pakistan, northern India and southern Nepal, to end with Bengali in eastern India and Bangladesh; an off-shoot from northern India, Sinhalese, is spoken in Sri Lanka, and the language of the Maldives is the closely related Maldivian.

In addition, the great population shifts that resulted from the voyages of exploration starting at the end of the fifteenth century have carried Indo-European languages to many distant lands. The dominant languages of the Americas are now Indo-European (English, Spanish, Portuguese, French), as is the dominant language of Australia and New Zealand (English). While in some countries these languages are spoken by populations descended primarily from European settlers, there are also instances where a variety of the European language is spoken by a population of a different origin, perhaps the best known example being the creolised forms of European languages (especially English, French and Portuguese) spoken by the descendants of African slaves in the Caribbean. It should be noted that these population shifts have not led exclusively to the spread of European languages, since many languages of India, both Indo-European and Dravidian, have also extended as a by-product, being spoken now by communities in the Caribbean area, in East Africa and the South Pacific (especially Fiji).

Western Europe is even more solidly Indo-European than is the continent as a whole, indeed the western half of the continent is almost exhaustively divided between two branches of Indo-European, Germanic in the north and Romance (technically a sub-branch of Italic) in the south; while the Celtic languages were once spoken over a much wider area, they are now restricted to parts of Europe's western fringe (parts of Wales, Brittany, Ireland and Scotland). The only indigenous non-Indo-European language still spoken on the western European mainland is Basque, a language isolate, with no established genetic relations to any other language. It is spoken in the Pyrenees on both sides of the French-Spanish border. Basque is perhaps most noted for its ergative construction, whereby instead of having a single case (nominative) for both subjects of intransitive verbs and subjects (agents) of transitive verbs, with a different case (accusative) for objects (patients) of transitive verbs, Basque uses one case (absolutive) for both intransitive subjects and objects of transitive verbs, and a different case (ergative) for subjects of transitive verbs, as in the following sentences from the Labourdin dialect:

Martin ethorri da. 'Martin came.'
Martinek haurra igorri du. 'Martin sent the child.'

In the first sentence, *Martin* is intransitive subject, and stands in the absolutive (no inflection); in the second sentence, *Martin-ek* is transitive subject, and therefore stands in the ergative (suffix *-ek*), while *haurra* 'child' is transitive object, and therefore stands in the absolutive, with no inflection.

Finally, the Semitic branch of the Afroasiatic family is represented in Europe by Maltese, spoken on the Maltese islands between Sicily and North Africa.

3   The Social Interaction of Languages

As was indicated in the Preface, the notion of 'major language' is defined in social terms, so it is now time to look somewhat more consistently at some notions relating to the social side of language, in particular the social interaction of languages. Whether a language is a major language or not has nothing to do with its structure or with its genetic affiliation, and the fact that so many of the world's major languages are Indo-European is a mere accident of history.

First, we may look in more detail at the criteria that serve to define a language as being major. One of the most obvious criteria is the number of speakers, and certainly in making my choice of languages to be given individual chapters number of speakers was one of my main criteria. However, number of speakers is equally clearly not the sole criterion.

An interesting comparison to make here is between Chinese (or even more specifically, Mandarin) and English. Mandarin has far more native speakers than English, yet still English is generally considered a more useful language in the world at large than is Mandarin, as seen in the much larger number of people studying English as a second language than studying Mandarin as a second language. One of the reasons for this is that English is an international language, understood by a large number of people in many different parts of the world; Mandarin, by contrast, is by and large confined to China, and even taking all Chinese dialects (or languages) together, the extension of Chinese goes little beyond China and overseas Chinese communities. English is not only the native language of sizable populations in different parts of the world (especially the British Isles, North America, Australia and New Zealand) but is also spoken as a second language in even more countries, as is discussed in more detail in the chapter on English. English happens also to be the language of some of the technologically most advanced countries (in particular of the USA), so that English is the basic medium for access to current technological developments. Thus factors other than mere number of speakers are relevant in determining the social importance of a language.

Indeed, some of the languages given individual chapters in this series have relatively few native speakers. Some of them are important not so much by virtue of the number of native speakers but rather because of the extent to which they are used as a lingua franca, as a second language among people who do not share a common first language. Good examples here are Swahili and Malay. Swahili is the native language of a relatively small population, primarily on the coast of East Africa, but its use as a lingua franca has spread through much of East Africa (especially Kenya and Tanzania), and even stretches into parts of Zaire. Malay too is the native language of relatively few people in western Malaysia and an even smaller number in Indonesia, but its adoption as the lingua franca and official language of both countries has raised the combined first and second language speakers to well over a hundred million. In many instances, in my choice of languages I have been guided by this factor rather than by raw statistics. Among the Philippine languages, for instance, Cebuano has more native speakers than Tagalog, but I selected Tagalog because it is both the national language of the Philippines and used as a linga franca across much of the country. Among the Indonesian languages, Javanese has more native speakers than Malay and is also the bearer of an old culture, but in terms of the current social situation Malay is clearly the dominant language of this branch of Austronesian. A number of other Indo-Aryan languages would surely have qualified for inclusion in terms of number of speakers, such as Marathi, Rajasthani, Panjabi, Gujarati, but they have not been assigned individual chapters because in social terms the major languages of the northern part of South Asia are clearly Hindi-Urdu and Bengali.

Another important criterion is the cultural importance of a language, in terms of the age and influence of its cultural heritage. An example in point is provided by the Dravidian languages, where Telugu actually has more speakers than Tamil; Tamil, however, is the more ancient literary language, and for this reason my choice rested with Tamil. I am aware that many of these decisions are in part subjective, and in part dangerous: as I emphasised in the Preface, the thing furthest from my mind is to intend any slight to speakers of languages that are not considered major in the contents of this volume.

Certain languages are major even despite the absence of native speakers, as with Latin and Sanskrit. Latin has provided a major contribution to all European languages, as can be seen most superficially in the extent to which words of Latin origin are used in European languages. Even those languages that have tried to avoid the appearance of Latinity by creating their own vocabulary have often fallen back on Latin models: German *Gewissen* 'conscience', for instance, contains the prefix *ge-*, meaning 'with', the stem *wiss-*, meaning 'know', and the suffix *-en* to form an abstract noun — an exact copy of the Latin *con-sci-entia*; borrowings that follow the structure rather than the form in this way are known as calques or loan translations. Sanskrit has played a similar role in relation to the languages of India, including Hindi. Hebrew is included not because of the number of its speakers — this has never been large — but because of the contribution of Hebrew and its culture to European and Middle Eastern society.

A language can thus have influence beyond the areas where it is the native or second language. A good example to illustrate this is Arabic. Arabic loans form a large part of the vocabulary of many languages spoken by Islamic peoples, even of languages that are genetically only distantly related to Arabic (e.g. Hausa) or that are genetically totally unrelated (e.g. Turkish, Persian and Urdu). The influence of Arabic can also be seen in the adoption of the Arabic writing system by many Islamic peoples. Similarly, Chinese loan words form an important part of the vocabulary of some East Asian languages, in particular Vietnamese, Japanese and Korean; the use of written Chinese characters has also spread to Japan and Korea, and in earlier times also to Vietnam.

It is important to note also that the status of a language as a major language is far from immutable. Indeed, as we go back into history we find many significant changes. For instance, the possibility of characterising English as the world's major language is an innovation of the twentieth century. One of the most important shifts in the distribution of major languages resulted from the expansion of European languages, especially English, Spanish, Portuguese, and to a lesser extent French as a result of the colonisation of the Americas: English, Spanish and Portuguese all now have far more native speakers in the New World than in Britain, Spain or Portugal. Indeed, in the Middle Ages one would hardly have imagined that English, confined to an island off the coast of Europe, would have become a major international language.

In medieval Europe, Latin was clearly the major language, since, despite the lack of native speakers, it was the lingua franca of those who needed to communicate across linguistic boundaries. Yet the rise of Latin to such preeminence — which includes the fact that Latin and its descendants have ousted virtually all other languages from southwestern Europe — could hardly have been foreseen from its inauspicious beginnings confined to the area around Rome. Equally spectacular has been the spread of Arabic, in the wake of Islamic religious zeal, from being confined to the Arabian peninsula to being the dominant language of the Middle East and North Africa.

In addition to languages that have become major languages, there are equally languages that have lost this status. The earliest records from Mesopotamia, often considered the cradle of civilisation, are in two languages: Sumerian and Akkadian (the latter the language of the Assyrian and Babylonian empires); Akkadian belongs to the Semitic branch of Afroasiatic, while Sumerian is as far as we can tell unrelated to any other known language. Even at the time of attested Sumerian inscriptions, the language was probably already approaching extinction, and it continued to be used in deference to tradition (as with Latin in medieval Europe). The dominant language of the period was to become Akkadian, but in the intervening period this too has died out, leaving no direct descendants. Gone too is Ancient Egyptian, the language of the Pharaohs. The linguistic picture of the Mediterranean and Middle East in the year nought was very different from that which we observe today.

Social factors and social attitudes can even bring about apparent reversals in the family-tree model of language relatedness. At the time of the earliest texts from Germany, two distinct Germanic languages are recognised: Old Saxon and Old High German. Old Saxon is the ancestor of the modern Low German (Plattdeutsch) dialects, while Old High German is the ancestor of the modern High German dialects and of the standard language. Because of social changes — such as the decline of the Hanseatic League, the economic mainstay of northern Germany — High German gained social ascendancy over Low German. Since the standard language, based on High German, is now recognised as the standard in both northern and southern Germany, both Low and High German dialects are now considered dialects of a single German language, and the social relations between a given Low German dialect and standard German are in practice no different from those between any High German dialect and standard German.

One of the most interesting developments to have arisen from language contact is the development of pidgin and creole languages. A pidgin language arises from a very practical situation: speakers of different languages need to communicate with one another to carry out some practical task, but do not speak any language in common and moreover do not have the opportunity to learn each other's languages properly. What arises in such a situation is, initially, an unstable pidgin, or jargon, with highly variable structure — considerably simplified relative to the native languages of the people involved in its creation — and just enough vocabulary to permit practical tasks to be carried out reasonably successfully. The clearest examples of the development of such pidgins arose from European colonisation, in particular from the Atlantic slave trade and from indenturing labourers in the South Pacific. These pidgins take most of their vocabulary from the colonising language, although their structures are often very different from those of the colonising language.

At a later stage, the jargon may expand, particularly when its usefulness as a lingua franca is recognised among the speakers of non-European origin, leading to a stabilised pidgin, such as Tok Pisin, the major lingua franca of Papua New Guinea. This expansion is on several planes: the range of functions is expanded, since the pidgin is no longer restricted to uses of language essential to practical tasks; the vocabulary is expanded as a result of this greater range of functions, new words often being created internally to the pidgin rather than borrowed from some other language (as with Tok Pisin *maus gras* 'moustache', literally 'mouth grass'); the structure becomes stabilised, i.e. the language has a well defined grammar.

Throughout all of this development, the pidgin has no native speakers. The next possible stage (or this may take place even before stabilisation) is for the pidgin to 'acquire native speakers'. For instance, if native speakers of different languages marry and have the pidgin as their only common language, then this will be the language of their household and will become the first language of their children. Once a pidgin has acquired native speakers, it is referred to as a creole. The native languages of many inhabitants of the Caribbean islands are creoles, for instance the English-based creole of Jamaica, the French-based creole of Haiti, and the Spanish- and/or Portuguese-based creole Papiamentu (Papiamento) of the Netherlands Antilles (Aruba, Bonaire and Curaçao). At an even later stage, social improvements and education may bring the creole back into close contact with the European language that originally contributed much of its vocabulary. In this situation, the two languages may interact and the creole, or some of its varieties, may start approaching the standard language. This gives rise to the so-called post-creole continuum, in which one finds a continuous scale of varieties of speech from forms close to the original creole (basilect) through intermediate forms (mesolect) up to a slightly regionally coloured version of the standard language. Jamaican English is a good example of a post-creole continuum.

No pidgin or creole language has succeeded in gaining sufficient status or number of speakers to become one of the world's major languages, but pidgin and creole languages provide important insights into the processes that arise from natural language contact. And while it would probably be an exaggeration to consider any of the world's major languages a creole, it is not unlikely that some of the processes that go to create a pidgin or a creole have been active in the history of some of these languages — witness, for instance, the morphological simplification that has attended the development from Old English to Modern English, or from Latin to the modern Romance languages.

A few centuries ago, as we saw above, it would have been difficult to predict the present-day distribution of major languages in the world. It is equally impossible to predict the future. In terms of number of native speakers, it is clear that a major shift is underway in favour of non-European languages: the rate of population increase is much higher outside Europe than in Europe, and while some European languages draw some benefit from this (such as Spanish and Portuguese in Latin America), the main beneficiaries are the indigenous languages of southern Asia and Africa. It might well be that a later version of this series would include fewer of the European languages that are restricted to a single country, and devote more space to non-European languages. Another factor is the increase in the range of functions of many non-European languages: during the colonial period European languages (primarily English and French) were used for most official purposes and also for education in much of Asia and Africa, but the winning of independence has meant that many countries have turned more to their own languages, using these as official language and medium of education. The extent to which this will lead to increase in their status as major languages is difficult to predict — at present, access to the frontiers of scholarship and technology is still primarily through European languages, especially English; but one should not forget that the use of English, French and German as vehicles for science was gained only through a prolonged struggle against what then seemed the obvious language for such writing: Latin. (The process may go back indefinitely: Cicero was criticised for writing philosophical treatises in Latin by those who thought he should have used Greek.) But at least I hope to have shown the reader that the social interaction of languages is a dynamic process, one that is moreover exciting to follow.

Bibliography

The most comprehensive and up-to-date index of the world's languages, with genetic classification, is Grimes (1988), which supersedes Voegelin and Voegelin (1977). A recent valuable work on genetic classification of the world's languages is Ruhlen (1987).

References

Greenberg, J. H. 1963. 'Some Universals of Grammar with Particular Reference to the Order of Meaningful Elements', in J. H. Greenberg (ed.), *Universals of Language* (MIT Press, Cambridge, Mass.), pp. 73–112

Grimes, B. F. (ed.). 1988. *Ethnologue: Languages of the World* (11th edition) (Summer Institute of Linguistics, Dallas)

Ruhlen, M. 1987. *A Guide to the World's Languages, Volume 1: Classification* (Stanford University Press, Stanford)

Voegelin, C. F. and F. M. 1977. *Classification and Index of the World's Languages* (Elsevier, New York)

1 INDO-EUROPEAN LANGUAGES

Philip Baldi

1   Introduction

By the term *Indo-European* we are referring to a family of languages which by about 1000 BC were spoken over a large part of Europe and parts of southwestern and southern Asia. Indo-European is essentially a geographical term: it refers to the easternmost (India) and westernmost (Europe) expansion of the family at the time it was proven to be a linguistic group by scholars of the eighteenth and nineteenth centuries (the term was first used in 1813). Of course modern expansion and migrations which have taken Indo-European languages to Africa, Hawaii, Australia and elsewhere around the world now suggest another name for the family, but the term *Indo-European* (German *Indogermanisch*) is now well rooted in the scholarly tradition.

Claiming that a language is a member of a linguistic family is quite different from establishing such an assertion using proven methods and principles of scientific analysis. During the approximately two centuries in which the interrelationships among the Indo-European languages have been systematically studied, techniques to confirm or deny genetic affiliations between languages have been developed with great success. Chief among these methods is the comparative method, which takes shared features among languages as its data and provides procedures for establishing proto-forms. The comparative method is surely not the only available approach, nor is it by any means foolproof. Indeed, other methods of reconstruction, especially the method of internal reconstruction and the method of typological inference, work together with the comparative method to achieve reliable results. But since space is limited and the focus of this chapter is Indo-European and not methods of reconstruction, we will restrict ourselves here to a brief review of the comparative method using only data from Indo-European languages.

When we claim that two or more languages are genetically related, we are at the same time claiming that they share common ancestry. And if we make such a claim about common ancestry, then our methods should provide us with a means of recovering the ancestral system, attested or not. The initial

Table 1.1: Some Basic Indo-European Terms

A. NUMERALS	*one*	*two*	*three*	*four*
Skt.	éka-	dvá, dváu	tráya-	catvára-
Gk.	oînos 'ace'	dú(w)o	treîs	téttares, téssares
Lat.	ūnus	duo	trēs	quattuor
Hitt.		dā-	*trijaš (gen.)	
Toch. A		wu	tre	śtwar
B		we	trai	ś(t)wär
OIr.	oïn, ōen	dāu, dō	trī	ceth(a)ir
Go.	ains	twai	þreis	fidwōr
OCS	inŭ	dŭva	trĭje	četyre
Lith.	víenas	dù	trỹs	keturì
Arm.		erku	erek'	č'ork'
Alb.	një	dü	tre, tri	katër

B. ANIMAL NAMES	*mouse*	*wolf*	*cow*	*sheep*
Skt.	múṣ-	vŕ̥ka-	gó-	ávi-
Gk.	mûs	lúkos	boûs	ó(w)is
Lat.	mūs	lupus	bōs	ovis
Hitt.				
Toch. A			ko	
B			kau	
OIr.		olc 'evil'	bō	ōi
Go.	mūs	wulfs OIc. kȳr OHG	ouwi
OCS	myšĭ	vlŭkŭ	gumŭno 'threshing floor'	ovĭca
Lith.		viĺkas Latv.	gùovs Lith.	avìs
Arm.	mukn		kov	hoviw 'shepherd'
Alb.	mī	ulk		

C. BODY PARTS	*foot*	*heart*	*eye*	*tongue*
Skt.	pád-		ákṣi-	jihvá
Gk.	poús (gen. podós)	kardíā	ópsomai 'I will see'	
Lat.	pēs (gen. pedis)	cor (gen. cordis)	oculus	lingua
Hitt.	pat-	kard-		
Toch. A	pe		ak	käntu
B	pai		ek	kantwo
OIr.	īs 'below'	cride	enech	teng
Go.	fōtus	haírtō	augō	tuggō
OCS	pěšĭ 'on foot'	srĭdĭce	oko	językŭ
Lith.	pãdas 'sole'	širdìs	akìs	liczùvis
Arm.	otn	sirt	akn	lezu
Alb.	(për)posh 'under'		sü	

D. KINSHIP TERMS	*mother*	*father*	*sister*	*brother*
Skt.	mātár-	pitár-	svásar-	bhrátar- 'member of a brotherhood'
Gk. (Dor.)	mátēr	patér	éor (voc.) (Dor.)	phrátēr <
Lat.	māter	pater	soror	frāter
Hitt.				
Toch. A	mācar	pācar		pracar
B	mācer	pācer		procer
OIr.	māthir	athir	siur	bräth(a)ir
OIc.	mōðir Go.	fadar	swistar	brōþar
OCS	mati		sestra	bratrŭ, bratŭ
Lith.	mótė 'woman'		sesuõ	brólis
Arm.	mayr	hayr	k'oyr	ełbayr
Alb.	motrë			

	five	*six*	*seven*	*eight*	*nine*
	páñca	šáṭ-	saptá-	aṣṭá(u)	náva-
	pénte, pémpe	héks	heptá	oktô	enné(w)a
Hier.	quïnque	sex	septem	octô	novem
Hitt. <	paⁿta		šipta-		
	pëñ	säk	ṣpät	okät	ñu
	piś	ṣkas	ṣuk(t)	okt	ñu
	côic	sê	secht	ocht	noï
	fimf	saíhs	sibun	ahtau	niun
	pçtï	šcstï	sedmï	osmï	devçtï
	penkì	šcši	septynì	aštuonì	devynì
	hing	vec'	evt'n	ut'	inn
	pesë	gjashtë	shtatë	tetë	nëntë

	pig	*dog*		*horse*	
	sūkará-	śván-		áśva-	
		hûs		kúōn	híppos
		sūs		canis	equus
		ku		yuk	
	suwo	ku		yakwe	
		cū		ech	
	swein	hunds	OE	coh	
	svinija				
Latv.	suvêns, sivêns Lith.	šuō (OLith.)		cšvà, ašvà, 'mare'	
	'young pig'	šun			
	thi				

Table 1.1 continued over.

Table 1.1 cont'd:

E. GENERAL TERMS	*full*	*race, kind*	*month*	*die, death*
Skt.	pūrṇá-	jána-	mā́s-	mṛtá-
Gk.	plérēs	génos	mḗn	ámbrotos 'immortal'
Lat.	plēnus	genus	mēnsis	mortuus
Hitt.				merta
Toch. A			mañ	
B			meñc	
OIr.	lān	gein 'birth'	mī	marb
Go.	fulls	kuni	mēna, mēnōþs	maúrþr
OCS	plŭnŭ		měsęcĭ	mīrǫ, mrěti
Lith.	pilnas		ménuo	miřti
Arm.	li	cin 'birth'	amis	
Alb.	plot		muai	

demonstration of relatedness is the easy part; establishing well-motivated intermediate and ancestral forms is quite another matter. Among the difficulties are: which features in which of the languages being compared are older? which are innovations? which are borrowed? how many shared similarities are enough to prove relatedness conclusively, and how are they weighted for significance? what assumptions do we make about the relative importance of lexical, morphological, syntactic and phonological characteristics, and about directions of language change?

All of these questions come into play in any reconstruction effort, leaving us with the following assumption: if two or more languages share a feature which is unlikely to have arisen by accident, borrowing or as the result of some typological tendency or language universal, then it is assumed to have arisen only once and to have been transmitted to the two or more languages from a common source. The more such features are discovered and securely identified, the closer the relationship.

In determining genetic relationship and reconstructing proto-forms using the comparative method, we usually start with vocabulary. Table 1.1 contains a number of words from various Indo-European languages which will demonstrate a common core of lexical items too large and too basic to be explained either by accident or borrowing. A list of possible cognates which is likely to produce a maximum number of common inheritance items, known as the basic vocabulary list, provides many of the words we might investigate, such as basic kinship terms, pronouns, basic body parts, lower numerals and others. From these and other data we seek to establish sets of equations known as correspondences, which are statements that in a given environment X phoneme of one language will correspond to Y phoneme of another language *consistently* and *systematically* if the two languages are descended from a common ancestor.

In order to illustrate the comparative method we will briefly and selectively choose a few items from tables 1.1 and 1.2, restricting our data to fairly clear cases.

old		vomit
sána-	'last	vámiti
hénos	year's'	eméō
senex		vomō
sen		
sineigs	OIc.	vāma 'sickness'
sēnas		vémti
hin		

	mouse		mother		nine
Skt.	mū́s-		mātár-		náva
Gk.	mūs	(Dor.)	mā́tēr		enné(w)a
Lat.	mūs		māter		novem
Go.	mūs	OIc.	mōðir	Go.	niun

	dead		dog		race, kind
Skt.	mṛtá-		śvā́n-		jána-
Gk.	ámbrotos 'immortal'		kúōn		génos
Lat.	mortuus		canis		genus
Go.	maúrþr 'murder'		hunds		kuni

	'I am'		vomit		old
Skt.	ásmi		vámiti		sána-
Gk.	eimí		eméō		hénos 'last year's'
Lat.	sum		vomō		senex
Go.	im	OIc.	vāma 'sickness'	Go.	sineigs

We will first look only at the nasals m and n. Lined up for the comparative method they look like this:

	mouse	mother	nine	dead	dog	race, kind	I am	vomit	old
Skt.	m-	m-	-n-	-m-	-n	-n-	-m-	-m-	-n-
Gk.	m-	m-	-nn-	-m(b)-	-n	-n-	-m-	-m-	-n-
Lat.	m-	m-	-n-	-m-	-n-	-n-	-m	-m-	-n-
Gmc.	m-	m-	-n-	-m-	-n-	-n-	-m	-m-	-n-

Before we begin reconstructing we must be sure that we are comparing the appropriate segments. It is clear that this is the case in 'mouse', 'mother', 'dog', 'race, kind', 'I am', 'vomit' and 'old', but less clear in 'nine' and 'dead'. What of the double n in Gk. *enné(w)a*? A closer look reveals that *en-* is a prefix; thus, the first n is outside the equation. Similarly with *ámbrotos* 'immortal': the *á-* is a prefix meaning 'not' (=Lat. *in-*, Go. *un-*, etc.), and the b results from a rule of Greek in which the sequence *-mr-* results in *-mbr-*, with epenthetic b (cf. Lat. *camera* > Fr. *chambre*). So the m's do indeed

Table 1.2: Inflectional Regularities in Indo-European Languages

A. Examples of Verb Inflection

	I am	*he, she is*
Skt.	ásmi	ásti
Gk.	eimí	estí
Lat.	sum	est
Hitt.	ešmi	ešzi
Toch. A		
B		ste
OIr.	am	is
Go.	im	ist
OCS	jesmŭ	jestŭ
OLith.	esmì	ēsti
Arm.	em	ē
Alb.	jam	është

B. Examples of Noun Inflection

tooth

	Skt.	Gk.	Lat.	Go.	Lith.
Sg.					
nom.	dán	odṓn	dēns	*tunþus	dantìs
gen.	datás	odóntos	dentis	*tunþáus	dantiḗs
dat.	daté	odónti	dentī	tunþáu	dañčiui
acc.	dántam	odónta	dentem	tunþu	dañti
abl.	datás		dente		
loc.	datí				dantyjè
inst.	datā́				dantimì
voc.	dan	odṓn	dēns	*tunþu	dantiē
Pl.					
nom.	dántas	odóntes	dentēs	*tunþjus	dañtys
gen.	datā́m	odóntōn	dentium	tunþiwē	dantũ
dat.	dadbhyás	odoũsi	dentibus	tunþum	dantìms
acc.	datás	odóntas	dentēs	tunþuns	dantìs
abl.	dadbhyás		dentibus		
loc.	datsú				dantysè
inst.	dadbhís				dantimìs
voc.	dántas	odóntes	dentēs	*tunþjus	dañtys

C. Examples of Pronoun Inflection

I, me

	Skt.	Gk.	Lat.	Hitt.	Go.	OCS
nom.	ahám	egṓ	ego	uk	ik	azŭ
gen.	máma(me)	emoũ(mou)	meī	ammēl	meina	mene
dat.	máhyam(me)	emoí(moi)	mihī	ammuk	mis	mĭně(mi)
acc.	mā́m(mā)	emé(me)	mē(d)	ammuk	mik	mene(mę)
abl.	mat		mē(d)	ammēdaz		
loc.	máyi			ammuk		mĭně
inst.	máyā					mŭnojǫ

C. Examples of Pronoun Inflection – *continued*
    you (sg.)

	Skt.	Gk.	Lat.	Hitt.	Go.	OCS
nom.	tvám	sú	tū	zik	þu	ty
gen.	táva(te)	soú(sou)	tuī, tīs	tuēl	þeina	tebe
dat.	túbhyam(te)	soí(soi)	tibī	tuk	þus	tebě(ti)
acc.	tvám(tvā)	sé(se)	tē(d)	tuk	þuk	tebe(tę)
abl.	tvát		tē(d)	tuēdaz		
loc.	tváyi			tuk		tebě
inst.	tváyā					tobojǫ

Note: Forms in parentheses are enclitic variants.

align, leaving us with a consistent set of *m* and *n* correspondences:

m : m : m : m   n : n : n : n
⟵⟶   ⟵⟶

These alignments represent the horizontal or comparative dimension. Next we 'triangulate' the segments, adding the vertical, or historical dimension:

Finally, after checking all the relevant data and investigating their distributional patterns, we make a hypothesis concerning the proto-sound. In these two cases there is only one reasonable solution, namely **m* and **n*:

At this stage of the analysis we are claiming that **m* > (develops into) *m* and **n* > *n* in the various daughter languages.

Neat correspondences such as these are more the exception than the rule in historical-comparative linguistics. It is far more common to find sets in which only a few of the members have identical segments. But the method of comparative reconstruction, when supplemented with sufficient information about the internal structure of the languages in question, can still yield replicable results. Consider the following data from table 1.1, supplemented by some additional material:

	six	old	race, kind (gen. case)	be
Skt.	ṣáṭ	sána-	jánasas	ástu 'let him be!'
Gk.	héks	hénos 'last year's'	géneos (génous)	éō (ð) 'I might be'
Lat.	sex	senex	generis	erō 'I will be'
Go.	saíhs	sineigs (OCS	slovese 'word')	ist 'he/she is'

We are concentrating here on the correspondences which include *s*, *h*, and *r*. In 'six' and 'old' we have the set *s* : *h* : *s* : *s* initially (cf. also 'seven' and 'pig'). In final position we find Ø : *s* : *s* : *s* in 'six' and 'old' (cf. also 'one', 'three', 'mouse' and 'wolf', among others). And in medial position we have *s* : Ø : *r* : *s* in 'race, kind' (gen.) and 'be'. What is or are the proto-sound(s)?

A brief look at the languages in question takes us straight to *s for all three correspondences. *s > *h* in Greek initially (weakens), and disappears completely medially, yielding a phonetically common pattern of *s* > *h* > Ø (cf. Avestan, Spanish). Final Ø in the Sanskrit examples is only the result of citing the Sanskrit words in their root forms; the full nominative forms (as in the other languages) would contain *s* as well (e.g. *jánas*, *sánas*, etc.). And the medial Latin *r* is the result of rhotacism, whereby Latin consistently converts intervocalic *s* to *r* (cf. *es*- 'be', *erō* 'I will be'; (nom.) *flōs* 'flower' (gen.) *flōris*).

From these few, admittedly simplified examples we see that the comparative method, when supplemented by adequate information about the internal structure of the languages in question and by a consideration of all the relevant data, can produce consistent and reliable reconstructions of ancestral forms. It is with such methods that Proto-Indo-European has been reconstructed.

2 The Languages of the Indo-European Family

The Indo-European languages are classified into eleven major groups (ten if Baltic and Slavonic are considered together as Balto-Slavonic). Some of these groups have many members, while some others have only one. Of the eleven major groups, nine have modern spoken representatives while two, Anatolian and Tocharian, are extinct.

2.1 Indo-Iranian
The Indo-Iranian group has two main subdivisions, Indo-Aryan (Indic) and Iranian. The similarities between the two subdivisions are so consistent that there is no question about the status of Indo-Iranian intermediate between Proto-Indo-European and the Indic and Iranian subgroups. The Indo-Aryan migrations into the Indian area took place some time in the second millennium BC.

2.1.1 Indo-Aryan (or Indic)
(See Chapter 1 of *The Major Languages of The Middle East, South Asia and Africa*, edited by Bernard Comrie (Routledge, 1990).)

2.1.2   Iranian
(See Chapter 5 of the same book.)

2.2   Hellenic
(See Chapter 6 of *The Major Languages of Eastern Europe*, edited by Bernard Comrie (Routledge, 1990).)

2.3   Italic
(See p. 170ff.)

2.4   Anatolian
The Anatolian languages were unknown to modern scholars until archaeological excavations during the first part of this century in Boğazköy, Turkey, yielded texts which were written primarily in Hittite, the principal language of the Anatolian group. The texts, which date from approximately the seventeenth to the thirteenth centuries BC, were written in cuneiform script and contained not only Hittite, but Akkadian and Assyrian as well. Decipherment proceeded quickly and it was claimed by B. Hrozný in 1915 that the Hittite in the texts was an Indo-European language. It was later shown that Hittite contained a large number of archaic features not found in other Indo-European languages, which resulted in revised reconstructions of the proto-language. Now totally extinct, the Anatolian group contains, in addition to Hittite, Luwian, Palaic, Lydian and Lycian, the last three surviving only in fragments.

2.5   Tocharian
Around the turn of this century a large amount of material written in an unknown language was discovered in the Chinese Turkestan (Tarim Basin) region of Central Asia. The language represented in these texts is now known as Tocharian, and is unquestionably of the Indo-European group. The documents are chiefly of a religious nature, but also contain commercial documents, caravan passes and medical and magical texts. There are two dialects of Tocharian: Tocharian A, also known as East Tocharian or Turfan, and Tocharian B, also known as West Tocharian or Kuchean. The texts found in Chinese Turkestan are all from the period AD 500 to 1000, so this language has not played the same role as other twentieth-century discoveries like Hittite and Mycenaean Greek in the shaping of reconstructed Proto-Indo-European.

2.6   Celtic
The Celtic languages are largely unknown until the modern period, though it is clear from inscriptional information and place and river names that Celtic languages were once spread over a fairly wide section of Europe in the pre-Christian era. The Celtic languages are commonly classified into two groups: the Goidelic or Gaelic group, made up of Irish, Scots Gaelic and the extinct

Manx, and the Brythonic or Brittanic group, made up of Welsh, Breton and the extinct Cornish. The oldest records of Celtic are some sepulchral inscriptions from the fourth century AD, and Old Irish manuscripts which date from the late seventh to early eighth century AD.

Many specialists believe that the Celtic and Italic languages have a remote relationship intermediate between the disintegration of Proto-Indo-European and the establishment of the separate Celtic and Italic groups. The 'Italo-Celtic' topic recurs periodically in Indo-European studies.

2.7   Germanic
(See p. 58ff.)

2.8   Slavonic
(See Chapter 1 of *The Major Languages of Eastern Europe*.)

2.9   Baltic
This highly conservative group of Indo-European languages has played a significant role in Indo-European studies. Despite the fact that the oldest useful recorded material from Baltic dates from the mid-fourteenth century AD, Baltic has preserved many archaic features, especially in morphology, which scholars believe existed in Proto-Indo-European.

Only two Baltic languages are spoken today, Lithuanian and Latvian (or Lettish). Many others are now extinct, including Semigallian, Selonian, Curonian, Yotvingian and Old Prussian. Old Prussian is the most important of these; it became extinct in the early eighteenth century, but provides us with our oldest written documentation of the Baltic group.

The Baltic languages are considered by many specialists to be in a special relationship with the Slavonic languages. Those who follow such a scheme posit a stage intermediate between Proto-Indo-European and Baltic and Slavonic called Balto-Slavonic.

2.10   Armenian
Spoken now predominantly in Soviet Armenia, Armenian was probably established as a language by the sixth century BC. The first records of the language are from the fifth century AD, and it shows considerable influence from Greek, Arabic, Syriac and especially Persian. In fact, so extreme is the foreign influence on Armenian that it was at first thought to be a radical dialect of Persian rather than a language in its own right. Written in an alphabet developed in the fifth century, the language is quite conservative in many of its structural features, especially inflectional morphology and, by some recent accounts, consonantal phonology.

2.11   Albanian
The remote history of Albanian is unknown, and although there are

references to Albanians by Greek historians in the first century AD, we have no record of the language until the fifteenth century. Much influenced by neighbouring languages, Albanian has proven to be of marginal value in the reconstruction of Proto-Indo-European. There are two principal dialects of Albanian: Gheg, spoken in the north and in Yugoslavia, and Tosk, spoken in southern Albania and various colonies in Greece and Italy.

In addition to these eleven major groups, there remain a number of 'minor' Indo-European languages which are known only in fragments, glosses, inscriptions and other unpredictable sources. Though there is some dispute about the Indo-European character of some of these languages, scholars generally agree on the following as Indo-European: Ligurian (Mediterranean region), Lepontic (possibly affiliated with Celtic), Sicel (possibly affiliated with Italic), Raetic, Thraco-Phrygian (frequently connected with Armenian and Albanian), Illyrian (especially prevalent along the Dalmatian coast), Messapic (with uncertain Italic or Albanian connections), and Venetic (probably connected with Italic). None of these languages exists in sufficient material detail to be of systematic value in the reconstruction of Proto-Indo-European.

3   The Structure of Proto-Indo-European

There have been many attempts to reconstruct Proto-Indo-European from the evidence of the daughter languages. The discoveries of Hittite, Tocharian and Mycenaean Greek in this century have modified the data base of Indo-European studies, so it is not surprising that there have been frequent changes in views on Proto-Indo-European. Also, there have been a refinement of technique and an expansion of knowledge about language structure and language change which have modified views of the proto-language. In this section we will briefly review past and present thinking on Proto-Indo-European phonology, and we will then discuss commonly held positions on the morphological and syntactic structure of the proto-language.

3.1 Phonology

3.1.1 Segmental Phonology
The first systematic attempt to reconstruct the sound system of Proto-Indo-European was by A. Schleicher in the first edition of his *Compendium der vergleichenden Grammatik der indogermanischen Sprachen* in 1861. Using the sound correspondences worked out by his predecessors, Schleicher proposed the consonant system as in table 1.3 (from the 1876 ed., p. 10). Schleicher's vowel system was based primarily on the pattern found in Sanskrit whereby 'basic vowels' are modified by strengthening processes

Table 1.3: Schleicher's Reconstructed System

	unaspirated		aspirated	spirants		nasals	r
	vls.	vd.	vd.	vls.	vd.	vd.	vd.
gutt.	k	g	gh				
pal.					j		
lingu.							r
dent.	t	d	dh	s		n	
lab.	p	b	bh		v	m	

which the Indian grammarians called *guṇa* 'secondary quality' and *vṛddhi* 'growth, increment'. By these processes a basic three-vowel system is changed by the prefixation of *a* as follows (1876:11):

Basic Vowel	First Increment	Second Increment
a	a + a → aa	a + aa→ āa
i	a + i → ai	a + ai → āi
u	a + u → au	a + au→ āu

This system is not identical to the Sanskrit system; it is, however, patterned on it.

Schleicher's system soon gave way to the model proposed by the Neogrammarians, a group of younger scholars centred at Leipzig who had quite different views about Proto-Indo-European, and about language change generally, from their predecessors. The Neogrammarian system is embodied in the classic work of K. Brugmann, as in table 1.4 (1903:52).

Brugmann's system is much more elaborate than Schleicher's in almost every respect: there are more occlusives, more fricatives, diphthongs, etc. But probably the most significant difference is in the vowel system. Brugmann proposes a six short, five long vowel system which is much more like that of Greek or Latin than that of Sanskrit. This change was brought about by the discovery that a change had taken place whereby Sanskrit collapsed PIE *ĕ, *ŏ, *ă into ă (cf. Lat. *sequor*, Gk. *hépomai*, Skt. *sáce* 'I follow' (*e*); Lat. *ovis*, Gk. *óis*, Skt. *ávi-* 'sheep' (*o*); Lat. *ager*, Gk. *agrós*, Skt. *ájra-* 'field, plain' (*a*)). From this it could be seen that Sanskrit was not to be considered closest to the proto-language in all respects.

The Neogrammarian system, which in modified form still finds adherents today, was put to the test by the theories of Saussure and the findings of Kuryłowicz and others. Based on the irregular behaviour of certain sounds in the daughter languages, Saussure proposed that Proto-Indo-European had contained sounds of uncertain phonetic value which he called 'coefficients sonantiques'. According to Saussure, these sounds were lost in the daughter languages but not before they left traces of their former presence on the sounds which had surrounded them. For example, there is no regular explanation for the difference in vowel length between the two

Table 1.4: Brugmann's Reconstructed System

Consonants

Occlusives:	p	ph	b	bh	(labial)			
	t	th	d	dh	(dental)			
	k̂	k̂h	ĝ	ĝh	(palatal)			
	q	qh	g	gh	(velar)			
	qu̯	qu̯h	gu̯	gu̯h	(labio-velar)			
Fricatives:	s	sh	z	zh	þ	þh	ð	ðh	(j)
Nasals:	m	n	ñ	ŋ				
Liquids:	r	l						
Semi-vowels:	i̯	u̯						

Vowels (Brugmann 1903:67, 89, 122-38)

A.	Vowels:	e	o	a	i	u	ə	
		ē	ō	ā	ī	ū		
B.	Diphthongs:	ei̯	oi̯	ai̯	əi̯		eu̯	ou̯	au̯	əu̯
		ēi̯	ōi̯	āi̯			ēu̯	ōu̯	āu̯	
C.	Syllabic Liquids and Nasals:	l̥	r̥	m̥	n̥	ñ̥	ŋ̥	
		l̥̄	r̥̄	m̥̄	n̥̄	ñ̥̄	ŋ̥̄	

forms of Gk. *hístāmi* 'I stand' and *stătos* 'stood'. Saussure theorised that originally the root had been **steA* (A = a coefficient sonantique). The A had coloured the *e* to *a* and had lengthened it to *ā* in *hístāmi* before disappearing. The major changes ascribed to the action of these sounds include changing *e* to *o*, *e* to *a* and lengthening preceding vowels.

This new theory, based on abstract principles, was put to use to explain a wide range of phonological and morphological phenomena in various Indo-European languages. It came to be called the 'laryngeal theory', since it is thought that these sounds may have had a laryngeal articulation. Proposals were made to explain facts of Indo-European root structure, ablaut relations (see section 3.2.2) and other problems. Many proposals concerning the exact number of laryngeals, and their effects, were made. Some scholars worked with one, others with as many as ten or twelve. It remained an unverifiable theory until 1927, when Kuryłowicz demonstrated that Hittite preserved laryngeal-like sounds (written as *ḫ* or *ḫḫ*) precisely in those positions where Saussure had theorised they had existed in Proto-Indo-European. Some examples: Hitt. *ḫanti* 'front': Lat. *ante*; Hitt. *ḫarkiš-* 'white': Gk. *argés*; Hitt. *palḫiš* 'broad': Lat. *plānus*; Hitt. *meḫur* 'time': Go. *mēl*; Hitt. *u̯aḫanzi* 'they turn': Skt. *vāya-* 'weaving'; Hitt. *newaḫḫ-* 'renew': Lat. *novāre*.

The empirical confirmation that Hittite provided for Saussure's theories led to a complete reworking of the Proto-Indo-European sound system. We may take the system proposed by W. Lehmann as representative of these developments as in table 1.5 (1952:99):

Table 1.5: Lehmann's Reconstructed System

Obstruents:	p	t	k	kʷ
	b	d	g	gʷ
	bʰ	dʰ	gʰ	gʷʰ
		s		
Resonants:	m	n		
	w	r	l	y
Vowels:		e	a	o	ᵉ
	i·	e·	a·	o·	u·
Laryngeals:		x	γ	h	ʔ

There are many differences between Lehmann's system and that of Brugmann. Note in particular the postulation of only one fricative, s, the lack of phonemic palatals, diphthongs, voiceless aspirates and shwa. These were all given alternative analyses, partly based on the four laryngeals which Lehmann assumed.

Recent criticisms of the Lehmann system (and others of its generation) centre on the typological naturalness of the overall system. While faithful to the comparative method, such a system seems to be in conflict with known patterns of phonological structure in attested languages. One problem lies in

Table 1.6: Szemerényi's Reconstructed System

Obstruents:	p	pʰ	b	bʰ
	t	tʰ	d	dʰ
	(k'	k'ʰ	g'	g'ʰ?)
	k	kʰ	g	gʰ
	kʷ	kʷʰ	gʷ	gʷʰ
	s	h		

Resonanants: y w
m n
l
r

Syllabic Liquids and Nasals: ṇ   ṃ   ṇ̄   ṃ̄
ḷ   r̥   ḹ   r̥̄

Vowels and Diphthongs:

i		u	ī		ū		
e ə o			ē	ō		ei oi	eu ou
a			ā			ai	au

One to three laryngeals

the presence of the voiced aspirate stops without a corresponding series of voiceless aspirates. A principle of typological inference stipulates that the presence of a marked member of a correlative pair implies the presence of the unmarked member of that pair.ⱼThus $bh \supset ph$. And as T. Gamkrelidze puts it (1981:591): 'Reconstructed systems should be characterized by the same regularities which are found in any historical system.'

Partly in response to such objections (which had been voiced earlier by both Jakobson and Martinet), O. Szemerényi proposed the system in table 1.6 (1980:142). Pursuing the dicta of typological structure and dependency, many scholars have recently begun a new approach to Indo-European sound structure. The focus of the new work has been the obstruent system of Proto-Indo-European, which has long presented problems to Indo-European scholars. Chief among the problems are the following:

(a) The traditional system without voiceless aspirates is in violation of certain markedness principles. But the solution of Szemerényi (and the Neogrammarians) to have a voiceless aspirated series only begs the question, since only one language (Sanskrit) has the four-way distinction of voiced/voiceless, aspirated/unaspirated. Thus the elaborate Proto-Indo-European system seems to rely far too heavily on Sanskrit, and is unjustified for the other groups.

(b) There has always been a problem with *b. It is extremely rare, and those few examples which point to *b (e.g. Lith. *dubùs*, Go. *diups* 'deep') are by no means secure.

(c) There are complicated restrictions on the cooccurrence of obstruents in Proto-Indo-European roots (called 'morpheme' or 'root structure' conditions) which are only imperfectly handled with traditional reconstructions. They are that a root cannot begin and end with a plain voiced stop, and a root cannot begin with a plain voiceless stop and end with a voiced aspirate, or vice versa.

(d) Plain voiced stops as traditionally reconstructed almost never occur in reconstructed inflectional affixes, in which Proto-Indo-European was rich. This is a distributional irregularity which canot be explained under the traditionally reconstructed system.

(e) It has long been a curiosity to Indo-European scholars that both Germanic and Armenian underwent similar obstruent shifts (the Germanic one came to be celebrated as 'Grimm's Law', and forms the backbone of much pre- and post-Neogrammarian thinking on sound change):

'Grimm's Law' and the Armenian Consonant Shift

PIE					Gmc.				Arm.			
*p	t	k	k^w	>	f	þ	h	h^w	h(w)	th	s	kh
*b	d	g	g^w	>	p	t	k	k^w/k	p	t	c	k
*bh	dh	gh	gh^w	>	b	d	g	g^w/g	b	d	z(j)	g

In the new reconstruction of the obstruent system, the pattern in the occlusives is based on a three-way distinction of voiceless stops/voiced aspirates/glottalised stops (see Hopper 1981, Gamkrelidze 1981, Gamkrelidze and Ivanov 1984). The traditional plain voiced stops are now interpreted as glottalised stops (ejectives).

Typologically Reconstructed Obstruents

	I *Glottalised*	*II* *Voiced Aspirates/* *Voiced Stops*	*III* *Voiceless Aspirates/* *Voiceless Stops*
Labial	(p')	b^h/b	p^h/p
Dental	t'	d^h/d	t^h/t
Velar	k'	g^h/g	k^h/k
Labio-velar	k'w	g^{wh}/g^w	k^{wh}/k^w

The allophonic distribution of these segments has been a matter of some debate, and indeed each Indo-European language seems to have generalised one allophone or another, or split allophones, according to differing circumstances.

This new system provides phonetically natural solutions to the five problems posed above:

(a) The system with the three-way distinction above violates no naturalness condition or typological universal. In fact, it is a system found in modern Armenian dialects. Under this view, Indo-Iranian is an innovator, not a relic area.

(b) The near absence of *b now finds a simple solution. In systems employing glottalised stops, the labial member is the most marked. Thus this gap, unexplained by traditional views, is no longer anomalous.

(c) The complicated morpheme structure restrictions turn out to be fairly simple: two glottalised stops cannot occur in the same root; furthermore, root sounds must agree in voicing value.

(d) The absence of plain voiced stops in inflections turns out to be an absence of glottalics in the new reconstruction. Such a situation is typologically characteristic of highly marked phonemes such as glottalised sounds (Hopper 1981:135).

(e) Under the new system the parallel Germanic and Armenian consonant 'shifts' turn out to reflect archaisms rather than innovations. All the other groups have undergone fairly regular phonological changes which can be efficiently derived from the system just outlined.

As Bomhard has insightfully pointed out (1984), we must recognise different periods in the development of the various Indo-European groups.

Thus any attempt to arrive at an airtight, uniform reconstruction of Proto-Indo-European fails to recognise the unevenness of the records and the fact that some of the languages undoubtedly split off from Proto-Indo-European long before others did. This is especially true with Hittite, whose extreme archaism suggests that if it is not a 'sister' of Proto-Indo-European, it is at least a daughter that split off from Proto-Indo-European long before the latter started to disintegrate. It is for these reasons that Proto-Indo-European phonology continues to be a matter of debate.

3.1.2   Ablaut

In the oldest stages of Proto-Indo-European, verbs and probably nouns as well were differentiated in their various classes by a modification of the root-vowel rather than by the addition of suffixes to invariant bases, which we find predominating in later stages of the language. This type of vowel modification or alternation is known as 'ablaut' or 'vowel gradation'.

Vowel gradation patterns were based on the interplay of both vowel quality (qualitative ablaut) and vowel quantity or length (quantitative ablaut). The main alternations were between the basic root-vowel, usually *e*, called the 'normal grade', alternating with *o* ('*o*-grade'), zero (Ø) ('zero-grade') and lengthening plus change (lengthened *ō*-grade). In what follows I will treat the two ablaut types separately, though it should be emphasised that this is one system, not two. They are separated here because the daughter languages typically generalised either the qualitative or quantitative system, or eliminated ablaut altogether.

Qualitative Ablaut

The primary qualitative relations were based on the vowels *e* ~ *o* ~ Ø (*ei* ~ *oi* ~ *i*; *er* ~ *or* ~ *r̥*; *en* ~ *on* ~ *n̥*, etc.). Different forms of a morpheme were represented by different ablaut grades. This system is rather well

	e-grade		*o-grade*		*Ø-grade*	
Gk.	pét-omai	'I fly'	pot-ế	'flight'	e-pt-ómēn	'I flew'
Gk.	ékh-ō	'I have'	ókhos	'carriage'	é-skh-on	'I had'
Lat.	sed-eō	'I sit'	sol-ium (<*sod-ium)	'throne'		
Lat.	reg-ō	'I rule'	rog-us(?)	'funeral-pyre'		
Lat.	teg-ō	'I cover'	toga	'a covering'		
Gk.	leíp-ō	'I leave'	lé-loip-a	'I left'	é-lip-on	'I left'
Lat.	fīdō (<*feidō)	'I trust'	foedus	'agreement'	fidēs	'trust'
Gk.	peíth-ō	'I persuade'	pé-poith-a	'I trust'	é-pith-on	'I persuaded'
Gk.	dérk-omai	'I see'	dé-dork-a	'I saw'	é-drak-on	'I saw'
Gk.	pénth-os	'grief'	pé-ponth-a	'I suffered'	é-path-on	'I suffered'

represented in Greek, but is recoverable in nearly every Indo-European language to one degree or another. (Note: $e \sim o \sim \emptyset$ alternation is not the only series, nor does this account consider the many interactions between vowel length and quality.)

Quantitative Ablaut

Quantitative ablaut patterns are based on the alternations of 'normal', 'lengthened', and 'reduced' varieties of a vowel, e.g. $o : \bar{o} : \emptyset; e : \bar{e} : \emptyset; a : \bar{a} : \emptyset$. While represented vestigially in a wide number of Indo-European languages, (cf. Lat. $p\bar{e}s$, gen. $pedis$ 'foot'; $v\bar{o}x$ 'voice, $voc\bar{o}$ 'I call'; Gk. $pat\acute{e}r$, $patr\acute{o}s$ (gen.), $pat\acute{e}ra$ (acc.) 'father'), the quantitative system is most systematically represented in Sanskrit. This is the system which the Indian grammarians described in terms of $gu\d{n}a$ and $v\d{r}ddhi$ increments (though in a different order). Quantitive vowel alternation, in conjunction with the qualitative type, provided an important means of morphological marking in Proto-Indo-European, providing a basis for distinguishing different grammatical representations of a morpheme.

Normal Grade (=guṇa)	Lengthened Grade (=vṛddhi)	Reduced Grade
$pát$-ati 'he falls'	$p\bar{a}t$-áyati 'he causes to fall'	papt-imá 'we fell'
kar-t̥- 'doer'	$k\bar{a}r$-yá 'business'	k̥r-tá- 'done'
$de\acute{s}$-á- $(e < ai)$ 'region'	$dai\acute{s}$-ika- $(ai < \bar{a}i)$ 'local'	$dí\acute{s}$- 'region, direction'

3.1.3 Accent

Because of the widely different accentual patterns found in the daughter languages, reconstructing the accent of Proto-Indo-European is a hazardous undertaking. Developments in all the descendant groups except for Sanskrit and Greek seem to be innovative, thus forcing us to rely heavily on our interpretations of accent in these two languages.

The best accounts of Proto-Indo-European accent suggest that it was a pitch accent system. Every word (except clitics, which were unaccented) had one and only one accented syllable which received high pitch accent. The accent was 'free' in that it could fall on any syllable in a word, its specific position being conditioned by morphological considerations; accent was one means of marking grammatical categories in Proto-Indo-European. (For a parallel, cf. Eng. $rébel$ (n.): $rebél$ (v.); $cónflict$ (n.): $conflíct$ (v.).)

For example, some noun cases are typically accented on the inflections, while others are accented on the root for 'foot'. Here we see that the nominative and accusative cases, the so-called 'strong cases', have root accent, while the genitive and dative (and instrumental) have inflectional accent, indicating that accent is interacting with case markers to indicate grammatical function.

Root/Inflectional Accent (Nouns)

	Gk.	Skt.
nom.	poús	pā́t
acc.	póda	pā́dam
gen.	podós	padás (gen./abl.)
dat.	podí	padé
		padí (loc.)

Similarly, some verbal forms are accented on roots, some on inflections:

Root/Inflectional Accent (Verbs)

	Pres.	Perf.	Perf. Pl.	Part.
Skt. 'turn'	vártāmi	vavárta	vavṛtimá	vṛtanáḥ
OE 'become'	weorþe	wearþ	wurdon	worden

The original nature of the Sanskrit accent in the various morphological categories is confirmed by the evidence of Germanic, which, though it has root-initial accent throughout, treated certain obstruent forms differently (þ, ð (d)) depending on whether the accent originally preceded (þ) or followed (ð (d)) the sound in question (Verner's Law). For further evidence, cf. the following forms for 'point out, show':

Skt. didéśa (1st sg. perf.): OE tāh OHG zeh (<*dedóika)
 didiśimá (1st pl. perf.): tigon zigum (<*dedikmé)

3.2 Morphology
As we mentioned in the preceding discussion, the unevenness of historical records and huge chronological gaps among many of the languages (e.g. 3,000 years between Hittite and Lithuanian) pose special problems for the reconstruction of phonology. These same problems exist in the reconstruction of morphology, perhaps even more dramatically because of the much larger inventory of morphological elements. Many of the older, well-documented languages, especially Latin, Greek and Sanskrit, have very complex morphologies: they have well-developed case systems in nouns, adjectives and pronouns; they have finely marked gender and number categories with fixed concord relations. In the verb they have elaborate systems of tense, voice, mood and aspect, as well as number markers and even gender concord in some forms, all marked with complex morphological formatives.

Many Indo-European languages reflect this complex morphology to one degree or another: Baltic, Slavonic, Celtic, Armenian and, in part, Tocharian, in addition to Latin, Greek and Sanskrit. But many of the other languages of which we have adequate records show much less morphological complexity, with fewer formal categories and distinctions; and it is not only the modern ones. Hittite, Germanic, Tocharian (in part) and Albanian do not agree with the other groups in morphological complexity.

What does the analyst do? Traditionally, scholars have reconstructed the largest composite system which the data allow. Thus reconstructed Proto-Indo-European has assumed all the features of the attested languages. When a particular language shows a given feature, this is evidence for the prior existence of that feature. And when a given language does not show that feature, it is assumed that the feature has been lost, or that it has merged with another feature in that language. This preference for over-differentiated proto-systems reflects a methodological bias on the part of linguists (and not only Indo-Europeanists) to postulate rules of loss or deletion from full forms rather than to assume rules of accretion or addition from impoverished forms. In short, it is easier to assume a specific something and make it disappear than it is to assume nothing and specify when it develops into a specific something.

The fact is that the highly complex morphological systems of Sanskrit, Greek, Latin, Baltic and Slavonic must have come from somewhere! There is no justifiable reason to assume that Proto-Indo-European emerged full-blown with no history of its own. We must keep this in mind as we proceed.

3.2.1 Nominal and Pronominal Morphology

Traditionally, Proto-Indo-European is considered to be an inflecting language which uses case markers to indicate grammatical relations between nominal elements and other words in a sentence, and to indicate gender and number agreement between words in phrases. Of all the Indo-European languages, Sanskrit has the most detailed nominal morphology. It has eight cases (nominative, vocative, accusative, genitive, ablative, dative, locative and instrumental), three genders (masculine, feminine and neuter), and three numbers (singular, plural and dual). No other Indo-European language has such detailed nominal morphology: Old Church Slavonic, Lithuanian and (by some accounts) Old Armenian have seven cases, and Latin has six. But Greek, Old Irish and Albanian have only five; Germanic has only four, and Hittite may have had as few as four. In gender categories most of the groups have the three mentioned above, but Hittite and a few others have no such system, nor is there any reason to believe they ever did. The same is true with number: Sanskrit, Greek and Old Irish, for example, show the three-way singular/plural/dual distinction, and there are apparent relics of it in Latin and Hittite. Do we assume that it was lost in those groups which do not show it, or do we assume that it never developed in those languages?

This is not the place to debate the history of Indo-European noun inflection or the philosophy of reconstruction. So, following Shields (1981) we will give a brief chronological overview of what *might* have been the developmental stages in the prehistory of Proto-Indo-European. In this way one might be able to imagine how various languages might have broken off from the main stock during the formation of Proto-Indo-European. We must not think of Proto-Indo-European as a single monolithic entity, uniform and dialect-free, which existed at a certain time in a single place before it began to disintegrate. Rather, we must recognise that this language was itself the product of millennia of development. As Ivanov puts it (1965:51):

> Within the limits of the case systems of the Indo-European languages it is possible to distinguish chronological layers of various epochs beginning with the pre-inflectional in certain forms of the locative and in compound words ... right up to the historical period when the case systems were being formed ... Between these two extreme points one must assume a whole series of intermediate points. (Quoted from Schmalstieg 1980:46.)

Shields postulates the following five stages in the development of Proto-Indo-European:

Stage I. In this, the formative period of the language, Proto-Indo-European might have been an isolating language, like Chinese, in which words were monosyllabic roots and there was no complex morphology. At this point there was probably no distinction between nouns and verbs, and no agreement or concord. The lack of agreement or concord in compounds like Gk. *akrópolis* (not **akrápolis*) 'high or upper city' and *logopoiós* (not **logompoiós*) 'prose-writer' attests to this stage. Gender was based on a distinction between animate, inanimate and natural agents.

Stage II. During this period Proto-Indo-European became an ergative system, i.e. one in which the subject of a transitive verb is in a different case from the subject of an intransitive verb, and in which the object of a transitive verb is in the same case as the subject of an intransitive verb (in English it would be something like *I* (subject) *see* (trans.) *her* (object), but *her* (subject) *falls* (intrans.)). Evidence for this stage comes from noun inflection patterns in different gender categories in various languages, as well as occasional irregular subject patterns in some languages in which oblique cases serve as subjects. At this time there were only two cases, the agent case in $*\emptyset$ or $*r$, and the absolutive case in $*N$. Through the development of a concord relationship between verbal suffixes and noun suffixes, Proto-Indo-European starts to develop into a nominative/accusative language.

Stage III. The oblique cases start to develop, primarily from the fusion of adverbs and particles onto noun stems. Nominative and vocative functions become generalised, and gender distinctions start to develop. As the ergative marker develops into a generalised subject marker, the language changes into a nominative/accusative type, where the subjects of transitive and intransitive verbs are the same (cf. Eng. *He sees Bill*: *He falls*).

Stage IV. Dative, instrumental, locative and genitive/ablative functions start to emerge as separate entities. The dual number starts to develop, and the gender distinction (found in Hittite) based on the animate/inanimate distinction first appears. Gender and number agreement within phrases as well as concord between nouns and verbs becomes fixed. This is now close to traditionally reconstructed Proto-Indo-European.

Stage V. This is a period of highly accelerated dialect division, and the beginning of the disintegration of Proto-Indo-European. New endings and formal markers develop within various groups, with formal and functional differentiations of case forms. The feminine gender emerges.

The preceding summary, based on Shields's 1981 speculations, provides us with a brief but provocative account of the prehistory of Proto-Indo-European. We will now proceed to a discussion of the traditional system as reconstructed in the nineteenth and twentieth centuries. This system represents one, surely very late, stage of Proto-Indo-European from which some, but not all of the daughter languages descended. In this context it has validity as the most probable system based on the comparative method.

Proto-Indo-European nouns and adjectives were inflected in three genders, three numbers and eight cases. Through a comparison of the various languages we arrive at the following reconstruction of case endings (Szemerényi 1980:146):

Reconstructed Case Endings

	Sg.	*Pl.*	*Du.*
Nom.	-s, -Ø	-es	
Voc.	-Ø	-es	-e, -ī/-i
Acc.	-m/-m̥	-ns/-n̥s	
Gen.	-es/-os/-s	-om/-ōm	-ous? -ōs?
Abl.	-es/-os/-s; -ed/-od	-bh(y)os, -mos	-bhyō, -mō
Dat.	-ei	-bh(y)os, -mos	-bhyō, -mō
Loc.	-i	-su	-ou
Inst.	-e/-o, -bhi/-mi	-bhis/-mis, -ōis	-bhyō, -mō

These endings represent a composite set of possibilities for the Proto-Indo-European noun; no single form reflects them all. The structure of the noun was based on the following scheme: a *root*, which carried the basic lexical meaning, plus a *stem*, which marked morphological class, plus an *ending*, which carried grammatical information based on syntactic function. Thus a word like Lat. nom. sg. m. *lupus* (OLat. *lupos*) 'wolf' would be *lup + o + s*. Generally we recognise consonantal and vocalic stem nouns. Some examples of consonantal stems are **ped* 'foot' (Skt. *pád-*, Gk. (gen.) *podós*, Lat. (gen.) *pedis*); **edont-/*dont-/*dent-* 'tooth' (Skt. *dánt-*, Gk. (gen.) *odóntos*, Lat. (gen.) *dentis*; **ĝhom-* 'man' (Lat. *homo*, Go. *guma*); **māter* 'mother' (Skt. *mātár-*, Gk. *mḗtēr*, Lat. *māter*); **gonos/*genos-* 'race' (Skt.

(gen.) *jánasas*, Gk. (gen.) *géneos* (< **génesos*), Lat. (gen.) *generis* (< **genesis*)).

To illustrate some of the vocalic stems we may cite the *i*-stem form **egnis/ *ognis* 'fire' (Skt. *agní-*, Lat. *ignis*) or **potis* 'master' (Skt. *páti-*, Gk. *pósis*, Lat. *potis*); an *-eu-* diphthongal stem like **dyeu-* 'sky, light' (Skt. nom. *dyáus*, Gk. *Zeús*, Lat. *diēs*, *-diūs*); and finally the *o*-stem **wḷkʷos* 'wolf ' (Skt. *vṛka-*, Gk. *lúkos*, Lat. *lupus*).

The Proto-Indo-European adjective followed the same declensional pattern as the noun. Adjectives were inflected for gender, number and case, in agreement with the nouns which they modified. Some adjectives are inflected in masculine, feminine and neuter according to m. *-o* stem, f. *-ā* stem and nt. *-om* patterns, as in **newos*, **newā*, **newom* 'new' (cf. Skt. *návas*, *návā*, *návam*, Gk. *né(w)os*, *né(w)ā*, *né(w)on*, Lat. *novus*, *nova*, *novum*). Other adjectival forms have identical masculine and feminine forms, but separate neuter (cf. Lat. *facilis, facile* 'easy'), and still others have all three identical in some cases (cf. Lat. *ferens* 'carrying' (< **ferentis*)).

Adjectives were compared in three degrees, as in English *tall*, *taller*, *tallest*. Comparative forms are typically derived from positive forms through the suffixation of **-yes*, **-yos* (cf. Lat. *seniōr* 'older' (*senex*), Skt. *sánya* 'older' (*sána-*), and with **-tero-* (cf. Gk. *ponērós* 'wicked', comp. *ponēróteros*). Superlatives are often found with the suffixes *-isto-* and *-samo-*, though there are others. Some examples: Gk. *béltistos*, Go. *batista* 'best', Skt. *náviṣṭha-* 'newest' (*náva-*). For **-samo-*, cf. Lat. *proximus* 'nearest', *maximus* 'greatest', OIr. *nessam* 'next'. As with Gk. *béltistos*, Go. *batista*, adjectival comparison was occasionally carried out with suppletive forms, cf. Lat. *bonus*, *melior*, *optimus* 'good, better, best'.

Proto-Indo-European distinguished many different types of pronouns. A short sample of personal pronouns is given in table 1.2. Pronouns followed the same general inflectional patterns as nouns, though they have their own set of endings for many of the case forms, except personal pronouns, which are almost entirely different from nouns and did not mark gender. In addition to the personal pronouns 'I/we', 'you/you' (**eĝ(h)om*, *eĝō/*wei*, **ṇsmés*; **tū*, **tu/*yūs*, **usmés*), Proto-Indo-European also had demonstrative pronouns with the form (m.) **so*, (f.) **sā*, (nt.) **tod* and **is*, **ī*, **id*. These also served the function of third person pronouns in many of the Indo-European languages. The first of these is represented in Skt. *sa*, *sā*, *tad*, Go. *sa*, *so*, *þata* and Gk. *ho*, *hē*, *tó*. The latter Proto-Indo-European demonstrative forms are represented in Lat. *is*, *ea*, *id* and in various forms in Sanskrit and Germanic such as Skt. nom. sg. nt. *id-ám*, acc. sg. m. *im-ám*, f. *im-ám̐*, and Go. acc. sg. *in-a*, nom. pl. m. *eis*, acc. pl. *ins*.

Interrogative and relative pronouns are also well represented, though it is not possible to reconstruct a single relative. From a PIE (anim.) **kʷis*, (inanim.) **kʷid*, which had either interrogative or indefinite meaning, we find Lat. *quis*, *quis*, *quid*, Gk. *tís*, *tís*, *tí*, Hitt. *kwis*, *kwit*, Skt. *kás*, *ká*, *kim*, and a number of variants of this stem with interrogative or indefinite meaning. In Italic, Tocharian, Hittite, Celtic and Germanic the root *$k^w is$, *$k^w id$ also functioned as a relative pronoun (as does Eng. *who*). In Indo-Iranian, Greek and Slavonic a different form *yos, *$y\bar{a}$, *yod served the relative function (cf. Skt. *yás*, *yǎ*, *yád*, Gk. *hós*, *hě́*, *hó*). There is also a recoverable reflexive form *sew-, *sw (OCS *sę*, Lat. *se*, Go. *si-k*).

3.2.2   Verb Morphology

The Proto-Indo-European verb presents the analyst with many of the same problems as the noun. The various daughter languages show wide variation in formal categories and inflectional complexity; some of the ancient classical languages, especially Greek, Latin and Sanskrit, have highly diversified formal structure characterised by intricate relations of tense, mood, voice and aspect. Others, like Hittite and Germanic, have fairly simple morphological systems with few formal distinctions. We can contrast formal complexity by the following simple chart.

Verbal Categories

	Voices	*Moods*	*Tenses*
Greek	3	4	7
Sanskrit	3	4	7
Hittite	2	2	2
Gothic	2	3	2

As with the noun, we may take several paths to a reconstructed system. We can propose a full Proto-Indo-European system with losses and syncretisms in Hittite and Gothic, we may propose a simple Proto-Indo-European system with additive, accretionary developments in Greek and Sanskrit, or we may assume different periods of development and break-off from the parent language. Accepting this final alternative in effect prohibits us from reconstructing a single system which will underlie the others, but this is surely the most reasonable course. All we can do, then, is to present one version, surely quite late, of the Proto-Indo-European verbal system as traditionally reconstructed, recognising that many unanswered questions remain which are outside the scope of this chapter.

The classical reconstruction of the Proto-Indo-European verbal system posits two voices, four moods and from three to six tenses. In addition, there were person and number suffixes and a large number of derivational formatives by which additional categories were formed. The verb structure is as follows:

Voice refers to the relationship of the subject to the activity defined by the verb, i.e. whether the subject is agent, patient or both. In Proto-Indo-European there were two voices, active and medio-passive. An active verb is one in which the subject is typically the agent, but is not directly affected by the action (e.g. *John called Bill*). Medio-passive is a mixed category which includes the function of middle (= reflexive) and passive. When the subject of the verb is both the agent and the patient, the verb is in the middle voice (e.g. Gk. *ho paĩs loúetai* 'the boy washes himself', Skt *yájate* 'he makes a sacrifice for himself'). When the subject of the verb is the patient, but there is a different agent, the verb is in the passive voice (e.g. Gk. *ho paĩs loúetai hupò tẽs mētrós* 'the boy is washed by his mother'). In general, the various Indo-European languages generalised either the middle or the passive function from the Proto-Indo-European medio-passive. For example, in Sanskrit the middle function dominates, the passive being late and secondary. In Greek the middle and passive are morphologically identical in all but the future and aorist tenses, with the middle dominating. Italic and Celtic have mostly passive use, though there are ample relics of the middle in deponent verbs like Lat. *loquitur* 'he speaks', OIr. *-labrathar* 'who speaks', as well as Lat. *armor* 'I arm myself', Lat. *congregor* 'I gather myself', and others. Germanic has no traces of the middle, and Hittite has a medio-passive with largely middle function.

Mood describes the manner in which a speaker makes the statement identified by the verb, i.e. whether he believes it is a fact, wishes it, doubts it or orders it. In Proto-Indo-European there were probably four moods: indicative, optative, conjunctive (known more commonly as subjunctive), and imperative. With the indicative mood the speaker expresses statements of fact. Indicative is sometimes marked by a vowel suffix (thematic class) and sometimes not (athematic class), e.g. Skt. *rud-á-ti*, Lat. *rud-e-t* 'he cries' (thematic); Skt. *ás-ti*, Lat. *es-t* 'he is' (athematic). The optative mood is used when the speaker expresses a wish or desire, and is also marked by a vowel which depends on the vowel in the indicative, e.g. OLat. *siet*, Gk. *eíē*, Skt. *syất* 'let him be'. The conjunctive is used when the speaker is expressing doubt, exhortation or futurity. Its theme vowel depends on the vowel of the verb in the indicative, though it is commonly with *e/o* ablaut. Some examples are Lat. *erō* 'I will be', *agam*, *agēs* 'I, you will/might drive', Gk. *íomen* 'let us go'. The final mood is the imperative, which is used when the speaker is issuing a command. The imperative was formed from the bare verbal stem, without a mood-marking vowel as with the other three. Imperatives are most common in the second person, though they are found in the first and third as well. Examples are (second person) Gk. *phére*, Skt. *bhára*, Lat. *fer* 'carry' (sg.) and *phérete*, *bhárata*, *ferte* (pl.). There were other imperative suffixes as well which need not concern us here.

Tense refers to the time of the action identified by the verb. The original Proto-Indo-European verb was probably based on aspectual rather than temporal relations (aspect refers to the type of activity, e.g. momentary, continuous, iterative, etc.), but traditionally these have been interpreted as tenses. We usually identify three tense stems, the present, the aorist and the perfect. The present identifies repeated and continuing actions or actions going on in the present (= imperfective aspect): Lat. *sum*, Gk. *eimí*, Skt. *ásmi* 'I am', or Lat. *fert*, Gk. *phérei*, Skt. *bhárati* 'he carries'. The aorist stem (= perfective aspect) marks actions that did or will take place only once, e.g. Gk. *égnōn* 'I recognised', Skt. *ádāt* 'he gave', Gk. *édeikse* 'he showed', Skt. *ánāiṣam* 'I led'. The final stem is the perfect stem (= stative aspect), which describes some state pertaining to the subject of the verb. Examples are Skt. *vḗda*, Gk. *oĩda*, Go. *wáit* 'I know'.

The exact internal structure of the various tense systems is extremely complicated. A number of formal types exist, including stems characterised by ablaut, reduplication, prefixation (augment), infixation and a wide variety of derivational suffixes. An interesting fact is that though tense was not directly and explicitly marked in Proto-Indo-European, most of the daughter languages generalised tense as the defining characteristic of their respective verbal systems.

In addition to the tense, voice and mood categories, the Proto-Indo-European verb carried at the end of the verbal structure a set of endings which indexed first, second or third person and singular, plural or dual number. There were different sets of endings for different voices, tense stems and moods. Here we list only the principal 'primary' and 'secondary' endings; they are identical except for the final *-i*, an earlier particle which marks the primary endings. These endings were originally used with specific tenses and moods, but have been largely generalised in the daughter languages

Verbal Endings

	Primary	*Secondary*
1st sg.	-mi (Skt. bhárāmi)	-m (Lat. sum)
2nd sg.	-si (Skt. bhárasi)	-s (OLat. ess)
3rd sg.	-ti (Skt. bhárati)	-t (Lat. est)
3rd pl.	-nti (Skt. bháranti)	-nt (Lat. sunt)

We can schematise the overall structure of the Proto-Indo-European verb as follows:

The Structure of the Indo-European Verb

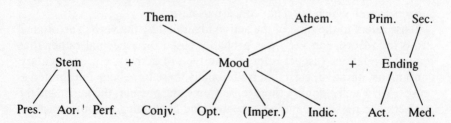

A few examples:

Lat.	am	ā	s	'you love'	(Pres. indic. 2nd pers. sg. act.)
	am	ē	s	'you might love'	(Pres. subj. 2nd pers. sg. act.)
	am	ā	ris	'you are loved'	(Pres. indic. 2nd pers. sg. pass.)
	am	ē	ris	'you might be loved'	(Pres. subj. 2nd pers. sg. pass.)
Gk.	paideú	ei	s	'you teach'	(Pres. indic. 2nd pers. sg. act.)
	paideú	ē	s	'you might teach'	(Pres. subj. 2nd pers. sg. act.)
	paideú	oi	s	'may you teach'	(Pres. opt. 2nd pers. sg. act.)
Skt.	bhár	a	ti	'he carries'	(Pres. indic. 3rd pers. sg. act.)
á	neṣ		vahi	'we two led ourselves'	(Aor. indic. 1st pers. du. mid.)
	sunu		yắma	'we might press'	(Pres. opt. 1st pers. pl. act.)

Besides the finite verb forms which we have been discussing, Proto-Indo-European also made use of a number of derivative forms which were non-finite, i.e. they did not stand as independent tensed predications. We include here a number of infinitive forms, which were originally noun forms in various oblique cases (mostly accusative and dative) and became reanalysed as part of the verbal system: cf. Skt. *dātum* (acc.), *dātavē* (dat.) 'to give'. There were also participial formations represented in most of the languages from Proto-Indo-European formations in *-nt-* (e.g. Go. *bairands*, Skt. *bháran-*, Lat. *ferens* 'carrying'), as well as others in *-wes-* (cf. Skt. *vidvás-* 'knowing'), *meno-* (cf. Gk. *hepómenos* 'following'), and *-to-* (cf. Lat. *amātus* 'loved'). These secondary formations, as well as a number of others such as gerunds, gerundives, supines and other verbal nouns, are widely represented and used throughout the Indo-European family.

3.3 Syntax

The reconstruction of syntax has lagged far behind the reconstruction of the phonological, morphological and lexical structures of Proto-Indo-European. This is initially surprising in light of the central role played by syntax and syntactic theory in modern linguistics. There are many reasons for this lag. Among them are the following:

(a) The lack of native speakers. Modern linguistics draws its data from the speech and intuitions of native speakers, but of course a reconstructed language has no such data source.

(b) The abstractness of syntax. Phonological, morphological and lexical units are far more concrete units than rules or patterns of syntax. Fewer theoretical notions are required in order to isolate concrete units, whereas in syntax, nothing exists pretheoretically. Syntax is an abstract set of principles, requiring abstract theories before even data organisation can begin.

(c) The structure of the descendant languages. The Indo-European daughter languages are of a highly inflecting type, and carry out a great deal of their 'syntax' in morphological expressions. Consider the difference between (1) and (2) in English:

(1) The boy sees the girl.
(2) The girl sees the boy.

The Latin equivalents to these sentences can have the words arranged in any order without affecting the agent/patient relations:

(1')	i	Puer	puellam	videt.
		Boy	girl	sees
	ii	Puellam	puer	videt.
		Girl	boy	sees
	iii	Videt	puer	puellam.
		Sees	boy	girl
			etc.	

(2')	i	Puella	puerum	videt.
		Girl	boy	sees
	ii	Puerum	puella	videt.
		Boy	girl	sees
	iii	Videt	puella	puerum.
		Sees	girl	boy
			etc.	

From these few examples we can readily see that the morphology/syntax division in inflected languages is quite a different matter from the same division in a language like English.

(d) The data. The Indo-European languages on which the reconstruction of Proto-Indo-European is based are simply not uniform enough to allow a straightforward account of syntactic patterns. The problem is no greater, and no less, than that found in phonology and morphology.

We will move now to a brief and highly selective review of some major features of Proto-Indo-European syntax. Because the citation of examples is extremely complicated, I will limit the data to the bare minimum.

3.3.1 Word Order

Late Proto-Indo-European was most likely a subject–object–verb (SOV) language with attendant adjective + noun (*good boy*), genitive + noun (*John's hat*), standard + marker + adjective (*John than bigger*) order, postpositions (*the world over*), and the preposing of relative clauses (*the who I saw man*). The reconstruction of these structural patterns is based on principles of typological inference developed largely by W. Lehmann (e.g. 1974), who extended the concepts of word order harmony formulated by J. Greenberg (1963) to historical syntax. According to these principles, there are major structural configurations in languages which are harmonious or compatible with each other. They take the form of statements like the following: if a language has some property P, then it will also have some property Q. For example, if a language is SOV in its basic sentence pattern, it will also have postpositions; if it is SVO, it will have prepositions.

Lehmann has put such 'implicational universals' to work in the reconstruction of Proto-Indo-European word order patterns. For example, Hittite, Vedic Sanskrit and Tocharian are SOV; Latin is predominantly SOV (Homeric Greek is apparently alternately SVO/SOV). Concentrating on Hittite, we find that it has postpositions and adjective + noun order, and dominant genitive + noun and relative clause + noun order. This seems to be ample evidence for an SOV Proto-Indo-European, a conclusion which is augmented by the existence of SOV-harmonic forms in otherwise SVO languages like relic postpositions in Slavonic and Baltic, as well as large numbers of formulaic postpositions in the Italic languages which, though they are mostly SOV, become SVO by the time of Vulgar Latin. The archaic-like nature of the frozen postpositions in Latin *mēcum* 'with me', *tēcum* 'with you' (not *cum mē, *cum tē, as expected; cf. *cum puellā* 'with the girl') or English expressions like *the world over* can be taken as evidence for early SOV structure, even in languages which show a move toward SVO structures. Discovering such patterns and drawing inferences for reconstruction depends crucially on the assumption that such marked structures as the Latin postpositions are indeed archaisms and not innovations.

There has been much criticism of the typological approach to syntax. For one thing, it has been noted that inflected languages have much freer word order possibilities than do languages like English, which rely on word order for marking grammatical function. According to this view, the word order issue is a false one, since word order serves mainly secondary functions like marking topic or focus relations

Another problem with the typological approach is the fact that the pure types are very rare (in the Indo-European family only Celtic is consistent, and it is VSO!). But the typological method has a built-in escape: languages which are internally inconsistent, like English with its SVO but adjective + noun structures, are said to be in transition from one type to another; the process is not yet complete. This begs the issue, because languages are always in such a transitional state. In other words, Greenberg's observations should be regarded as interesting tendencies and frequentalia, and should not be elevated to the status of explanatory devices. Furthermore, there is ample evidence that such implicational universals do not serve as reliable predictors of future syntactic change in a language.

Finally there is the matter of method. Typological inferences often are based on data being used in two directions, viz. if a language is SOV, one expects postpositions. And if a language is SVO but a stray postposition is found, one assumes that it must have been SOV at one time. There is also the issue of 'marked' vs. 'unmarked' structures. Determining that a language is SOV or SVO when both are present in the data requires a judgement that one of the structures is more natural, more basic, more regular than the other. The problem with ancient languages with no native speakers is that judgements about marked/unmarked structures often reduce to simple frequency counts, and this is not adequate.

3.3.2 Ergative–Nominative/Accusative Structure

It is clear from the daughter languages that late Proto-Indo-European was of the nominative/accusative type. That is, the agent of the verb was inflected in the nominative case, and the patient or goal was inflected in the accusative: cf. Lat. *Marc-us amat puell-am* 'Marcus loves the girl'. But as we saw in our discussion of early Proto-Indo-European noun morphology, there is significant evidence that Proto Indo European was at one time of the ergative type, i.e. a language in which the subject of a transitive verb is in a different case from the subject of an intransitive verb. There are many instances throughout the early Indo-European languages of agents in the genitive case: cf. OArm. *ēr nora* (gen.) *hraman aŕeal* 'he (of him) had received a promise', Lat. *attonitus serpentis* 'astonished by the serpent'. There are other cases where the real object of a verb of perception is in the accusative while the producer of the perceived act is in the genitive: cf. Skt. *vácam* (acc.) *śṛṇóti* 'he hears a voice' vs. *devásya* (gen.) *śṛṇóti* 'he hears a god'. These agentive genitives may at one time have been the subjects of intransitive verbs with genitive agents, as would be found with ergative languages. As Proto-Indo-European developed its complex nominal and verbal morphology, these genitives were reinterpreted as objects of transitive verbs and are now considered simply irregular formations. Schmalstieg (esp. 1980) has found traces of ergative syntax in a number of Indo-European dialects.

3.3.3 Some Syntactic Characteristics of Proto-Indo-European

Proto-Indo-European made use of a simple phrase structure principle by which the verb was the only obligatory constituent of a sentence. The subject of the verb was in the nominative, the object in the accusative and a number of other grammatical functions were served by the remaining cases. Verb structures could be expanded with case expressions of time, place-to, place-in, place-from, goal, possession and a number of other qualifiers. Conjunction of both noun phrases and other constituents was possible, including sentence conjunction. Simple sentences could be extended by the use of cases, adverbs and particles to indicate circumstance, purpose, result or manner. Particles were used to introduce different types of clauses (e.g. subordinate, interrogative, relative, co-ordinate). The modality of a sentence, as well as tense and aspect, were expressed inflectionally, though they may have been originally marked only by particles. Finally, there is evidence for a well-developed noun-compounding system, represented chiefly by Sanskrit.

As a final note to the structure of Proto-Indo-European, it may be useful to take a brief look at a version of a reconstructed Proto-Indo-European sentence. This sentence is from Lehmann and Zgusta's (1979:462) reinterpretation of Schleicher's famous Indo-European fairy tale, which was written in 1868.

Owis		ek̂wōskʷe			
Sheep		horses-and			
Gʷərēi	owis,	kʷesyo	wl̥hnā	ne	ēst
Hill-on	sheep,	of whom	wool	not	is
ek̂wōns	espek̂et,	oinom	ghe	gʷr̥um	
horses	he-saw,	one	emph. prt.	heavy	
woĝhom	weĝhontm̥,	oinomkʷe	meĝam		
load	pulling,	one-and	great		
bhorom	oinomkʷe	ĝhm̥enm̥	ōk̂u	bherontm̥	
burden	one-and	man	swiftly	carrying.	

'The sheep and the horses

On a hill, a sheep which had no wool saw horses, one pulling a heavy load, one carrying a great burden and one (carrying) quickly a man.'

4 Aspects of Proto-Indo-European Culture and Civilisation

When we reconstruct a proto-language, we are by implication also reconstructing a proto-culture and civilisation. But linguistic evidence alone is not sufficient to provide a complete picture of a proto-culture; it must be supplemented by information from archaeology, history, folklore, institutions and other sources. The question 'Who were the Proto-Indo-Europeans?' has been studied ever since the Indo-European family was established. Where was their homeland, when were they a unit, and what was the nature of their culture?

Many different areas of the world have been suggested for the Proto-Indo-European homeland. Central Asia was an early favourite because of the strong Biblical tradition that this was the home of mankind; the Baltic region, Scandinavia, the Finnic area, Western Europe, the Babylonian Empire, southern Russia, the Mediterranean region and a number of other places have been advanced as possibilities. The reason such a wide variety of views exists lies not only in the complexity and ambiguity of the issues, but also in the trends of the times and the prejudices of individual investigators, many of whom have been motivated by racial or ethnic considerations rather than scientific method. For example, many of the early researchers, lacking the insights of modern anthropology, believed that the obviously strong and warlike Indo-European people could only have been blond, blue-eyed Aryans who must have originated in Northern Europe, and not Asia or the Baltic region, for example. Such a confusion of the matters of race, culture and language, fuelled by religious prejudice and scientific immaturity, produced the many speculations on the homeland issue.

A famous argument about the homeland was made by Thieme (1953, summarised in 1958). Using the word for 'salmon' *laḱs (Eng. lox < Yiddish laks), Thieme argued that these fish fed only in the streams of northern Europe in the Germano-Baltic region during Indo-European times. Since *laḱs is recoverable with the meaning 'salmon' in Germanic and Baltic and 'fish' in Tocharian, this distribution suggests a northern homeland. In Indo-Iranian a form Skt. lakṣá 'one hundred thousand' is interpreted by Thieme as an extension of the uncountable nature of a school of salmon. Thieme concludes that the existence of this root in Indo-Iranian and Tocharian, where salmon are unknown, confirms the Germano-Baltic region as the original homeland.

Thieme uses similar argumentation with the reconstructed words for 'turtle' and 'beech tree'. There is a botanical beech line where the beech flourished about 5,000 years ago, as well as an area which defines the limits of the turtle at the time. Finding these roots in a number of Indo-European languages where the physical objects are unknown suggests the north European region again.

Of course the problem with such argumentation is that the botanical evidence for the beech line of 5,000 years ago is not conclusive. Also, it is well known that speakers frequently transfer old names to new objects in a new environment, as American speakers of English have done with the word robin. Thus the root *bhāgo- may have been used to designate trees other than the beech in some dialects.

This brief review provides us with some background to consider current thinking on the 'Indo-European Problem' (Mallory 1973). The most widely held view is that of M. Gimbutas, who has argued in a number of research articles (e.g. 1970) that the Proto-Indo-European people were the bearers of the so-called Kurgan or Barrow culture found in the Pontic and Volga steppes of southern Russia, east of the Dnieper River, north of the Caucasus, and west of the Ural mountains. The Kurgan culture (from Russian kurgan 'burial mound') is typified by the tumuli, round barrows or 'kurgans', which are raised grave structures from the Calcolithic and Early Bronze Age periods. Evidence from the Kurgan archaeological excavations gives clear evidence of animal breeding, and even the physical organisation of houses accords with the reconstructed Proto-Indo-European material. For example, Go. waddjus 'wall' is cognate with Skt. vāya- 'weaving', which reflects the wattled construction of walls excavated from the Kurgan sites.

Kurgan culture is divided into three periods, beginning in the fifth millennium BC. The Indo-Europeanisation of the Kurgan culture took place during the Kurgan II period, roughly 4000–3500 BC. Kurgan sites from this period have been found in the north Pontic region, west of the Black Sea in the Ukraine, Rumania, Yugoslavia and Eastern Hungary. During the Kurgan III period (c. 3500–3000 BC), Kurgan culture spread out across Central Europe, the entire Balkan area and into Transcaucasia, Anatolia and northern Iran. Eventually, it also spread into northern Europe and the upper Danube region. During the final period, Kurgan IV, waves of expansion carried the culture into Greece, West Anatolia and the eastern Mediterranean.

According to Gimbutas, the archaeological evidence attesting to the domesticated horse, the vehicle, habitation patterns, social structure and religion of the Kurgans is in accord with the reconstruction of Proto-Indo-European, which reflects a linguistic community from about 3000 BC.

In a recent work (Renfrew, 1987) it has been proposed that the older Indo-European languages were spoken as early as the seventh millenium BC in eastern Anatolia, and that they spread from there gradually throughout Europe through the introduction of farming. This view, which is based primarily on the archaeological record and a demographic model of processual spread, fits with the independently formulated linguistic speculations of Gamkrelidze and Ivanov (1984), who place the original Indo-Europeans in the same region, though a few millenia later.

Salient lexical items which give insight into Proto-Indo-European culture can be cited. In the remaining space we will note those items which are particularly useful in developing a view of Proto-Indo-European culture. *Physical Environment.* Words for day, night, the seasons, dawn, stars, sun, moon, earth, sky, snow and rain are plainly recoverable. A number of arboreal units have been identified and successfully reconstructed. Words for horse, mouse, bear, wolf, eagle, owl, turtle, salmon, beaver, otter, dog, cattle, sheep, pig, goat, wasp, bee and louse can also be reliably postulated. It is interesting that no single word for river or ocean can be established.

Family Organisation and Social Structure. According to Friedrich (1966:29), Proto-Indo-European culture had patriarchal, patrilocal families that probably lived in small houses and adjacent huts. Villages were small, distant and presumably exogamous. There is excellent evidence for patriliny, and cross-cousin marriage was probably not permitted. Kinship terms are reconstructible for father, mother, brother, sister, son, daughter, husband's in-laws and probably grand-relatives. The word for husband means 'master' and the wife was probably 'a woman who learns through marriage'. Evidence for Proto-Indo-European patriarchal kinship comes not only from the lexicon, but also from epic songs, legal tracts and ethnological sources from the various ancient Indo-European languages.

There is widespread evidence of a word for tribal king, giving some indication that government was established.

Technology. The Indo-European languages confirm the technological advancements of the proto-culture. Evidence from farming and agricultural terms indicates small-scale farmers and husbandmen who raised pigs, knew barley, and had words for grain, sowing, ploughing, grinding, settlement and field or pasture. We can also safely reconstruct words for arrow, axe, ship, boat, gold, wagon, axle, hub and yoke, showing a rather advanced people with knowledge of worked metals and agriculture.

Religion and Law. From lexical, legal and other sources we find clear indications of a religious system among the Proto-Indo-European people. There is a word for god, and a designation for a priest; words for worship, prayer, praise, prophesy and holy give clear indications of organised religion. There is lexical evidence and evidence from ancient institutions for legal concepts such as religious law, pledge, justice and compensation.

Bibliography

General overviews of the Indo-European languages include Lockwood (1972) and Baldi (1983). Meillet (1937) is a lucid exposition of the principles of Indo-European linguistics, while Szemerényi (1980) is currently the most authoritative handbook.

For recent developments in the conception of Proto-Indo-European phonology, reference may be made to Lehmann (1952) and to the more recent suggestions by Gamkrelidze (1981) and Hopper (1981). Lehmann's often highly controversial statements on Proto-Indo-European syntax may be found in Lehmann (1974).

Pokorny (1951–9) sets the standard in Indo-European etymology and lexicography, while Buck (1951) is a resource of synonyms arranged by semantic class. For particular semantic areas in relation to Proto-Indo-European culture, see Friedrich (1966) and Thieme (1953; 1958). For the relation between the Proto-Indo-Europeans and the Kurgan culture, see Gimbutas (1970).

References

Baldi, P. 1983. *An Introduction to the Indo-European Languages* (Southern Illinois University Press, Carbondale)

Bomhard, A.R. 1984. *Toward Proto-Nostratic* (John Benjamins, Amsterdam)

Brugmann, K. 1903. *Kurze vergleichende Grammatik der indogermanischen Sprachen* (Trübner, Strassburg)

Buck, C.D. 1951. *A Dictionary of Selected Synonyms of the Principal Indo-European Languages* (University of Chicago Press, Chicago)

Friedrich, P. 1966. 'Proto-Indo-European Kinship', *Ethnology*, vol. 5, pp. 1–36

Gamkrelidze, T.V. 1981. 'Language Typology and Language Universals and Their Implications for the Reconstruction of the Indo-European Stop System', in Y.L. Arbeitman and A.R. Bomhard (eds.), *Bono Homini Donum: Essays in Historical Linguistics in Memory of J. Alexander Kerns* (John Benjamins, Amsterdam), pp. 571–609

——— and V.V. Ivanov. 1984. *Indoevropejskij jazyk i indoevropejcy* (Tbilisi State University, Tbilisi)

Gimbutas, M. 1970. 'Proto-Indo-European Culture: The Kurgan Culture During the

Fifth, Fourth, and Third Millennia B.C.', in G. Cardona, H.M. Hoenigswald and A. Senn (eds.), *Indo-European and Indo-Europeans* (University of Pennsylvania Press, Philadelphia), pp. 155–97

Greenberg, J.H. 1963. 'Some Universals of Grammar with Particular Reference to the Order of Meaningful Elements', in J.H. Greenberg (ed.), *Universals of Language* (MIT Press, Cambridge, Mass.), pp. 73–113

Hopper, P. 1981. ' "Decem" and "Taihun" Languages: An Indo-European Isogloss', in Y.L. Arbeitman and A.R. Bomhard (eds.), *Bono Homini Donum: Essays in Historical Linguistics in Memory of J. Alexander Kerns* (John Benjamins, Amsterdam), pp. 133–42

Ivanov, V.V. 1965. *Obščeindoevropejskaja, praslavjanskaja i anatolijskaja jazykovye sistemy* (Nauka, Moscow)

Kuryłowicz, J. 1927. 'ə indo-européen et ḫ hittite', in *Symbolae Grammaticae in Honorem Ioannis Rozwadowski* (Drukarnia Uniwersytetu Jagiellońskiego, Cracow), pp. 95–104.

Lehmann, W.P. 1952. *Proto-Indo-European Phonology* (University of Texas Press, Austin)

—— 1974. *Proto-Indo-European Syntax* (University of Texas Press, Austin)

—— and L. Zgusta. 1979. 'Schleicher's Tale After a Century', in Bela Brogyanyi (ed.), *Festschrift for Oswald Szemerényi on the Occasion of his 65th Birthday* (John Benjamins, Amsterdam), pp 455–66.

Lockwood, W.B. 1972. *A Panorama of Indo-European Languages* (Hutchinson University Library, London)

Mallory, J. 1973. 'A Short History of the Indo-European Problem', *Journal of Indo-European Studies*, vol. 1, pp. 21–65.

Meillet, A. 1937. *Introduction à l'étude comparative des langues indo-européennes*, 8th ed. (reprinted by University of Alabama Press, University, Alabama, 1964)

Pokorny, J. 1951–9. *Indogermanisches etymologisches Wörterbuch* (Francke, Bern and Munich)

Renfrew, C. 1987. *Archaeology and Language* (Jonathan Cape, London)

Schleicher, A. 1876. *Compendium der vergleichenden Grammatik der indogermanischen Sprachen* (Böhlau, Weimar)

Schmalstieg, W.R. 1980. *Indo-European Linguistics: A New Synthesis* (Pennsylvania State University Press, University Park)

Shields, K. 1981. *Indo-European Noun Inflection: A Developmental History* (Pennsylvania State University Press, University Park)

Szemerényi, O. 1980. *Einführung in die vergleichende Sprachwissenschaft*, 2nd ed. (Wissenschaftliche Buchgesellschaft, Darmstadt)

Thieme, P. 1953. 'Die Heimat der indogermanischen Gemeinsprache', in *Abhandlungen der geistes- und sozialwissenschaftlichen Klasse* (Akademie der Wissenschaften und Literatur, Wiesbaden), pp. 535–610

—— 1958. 'The Indo-European Language', *Scientific American*, vol. 199, no. 4, pp. 63–74

2 Germanic Languages

John A. Hawkins

The Germanic languages currently spoken fall into two major groups: North Germanic (or Scandinavian) and West Germanic. The former group comprises: Danish, Norwegian (i.e. both the Dano-Norwegian Bokmål and Nynorsk), Swedish, Icelandic, and Faroese. The latter: English (in all its varieties), German (in all its varieties, including Yiddish), Dutch (including Afrikaans) and Frisian. The varieties of English are particularly extensive and include not just the dialectal and regional variants of the British Isles, North America, Australasia, India and Africa, but also numerous English-based pidgins and creoles of the Atlantic (e.g. Jamaican Creole and Pidgin Krio) and the Pacific (e.g. Hawaiian Pidgin and Tok Pisin). When one adds to this list the regions of the globe in which Scandinavian, German and Dutch are spoken, the geographical distribution of the Germanic languages is more extensive than that of any other group of languages. In every continent there are countries in which a modern Germanic language (primarily English) is extensively used or has some official status (as a national or regional language). Demographically there is an estimated minimum of 440 million speakers of Germanic languages in the world today, divided as follows: North Germanic (including speakers in the USA), 18.55 million (Danish 5.1 million, Norwegian 4.3 million, Swedish 8.9 million, Icelandic and Faroese 250,000); West Germanic apart from English, 128.4 million (German worldwide 103 million, Dutch and Afrikaans 25 million, Frisian 400,000); English worldwide, at least 300 million (comprising at least 250 million native speakers and at least 50 million second language speakers).

There is a third group of languages within the Germanic family that needs to be recognised: East Germanic, all of whose members are now extinct. These were the languages of the Goths, the Burgundians, the Vandals, the Gepids and other tribes originating in Scandinavia that migrated south occupying numerous regions in western and eastern Europe (and even North Africa) in the early centuries of the present era. The only extensive records we have are from a fourth-century Bible translation into Gothic. The Goths had migrated from southern Sweden around the year nought into the area around what is now Gdańsk (originally Gothiscandza). After AD 200 they moved south into what is now Bulgaria, and later split up into two groups, Visigoths and Ostrogoths. The Visigoths established new kingdoms in southern France and Spain (AD 419–711), and the Ostrogoths in Italy (up till AD 555). These tribes were subsequently to become absorbed in the local populations, but in addition to the Bible translation they have left behind numerous linguistic relics in the form of place names (e.g. *Catalonia*, originally 'Gothislandia'), personal names (e.g. *Rodrigo* and *Fernando*, compare Modern German *Roderich* and *Ferdinand*), numerous loanwords (e.g. Italian-Spanish *guerra* 'war'), and also more structural features (such as the Germanic stress system, see below). In addition, a form of Gothic was still spoken on the Crimean peninsula as late as the eighteenth century. Eighty-six words of Crimean Gothic were recorded by a Flemish diplomat in 1562, who recognised the correspondence between these words and his own West Germanic cognates.

The earliest records that we have for all three groups of Germanic languages are illustrated in figure 2.1. These are runic inscriptions dating back to the third century AD and written (or rather carved in stone, bone or wood) in a special runic alphabet referred to as the Futhark. This stage of the language is sometimes called Late Common Germanic since it exhibits

Figure 2.1: The Earliest Written Records in the Germanic Languages (taken from Kufner 1972)

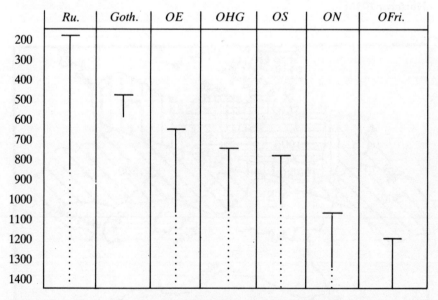

minimal dialect differentiation throughout the Germanic-speaking area. Further evidence of early Germanic comes from words cited by the classical writers such as Tacitus (e.g. *rūna* 'rune') and from some extremely early Germanic loanwords borrowed by the neighbouring Baltic languages and Finnish (e.g. Finnish *kuningas* 'king'). The runic inscriptions, these early citations and loans, the Gothic evidence and the method of comparative reconstruction applied to both Germanic and Indo-European as a whole provide us with such knowledge as we have of the Germanic parent language, Proto-Germanic.

There is much uncertainty surrounding the origin and nature of the speakers of Proto-Germanic, and even more uncertainty about the speakers of Proto-Indo-European. It seems to be agreed, however, that a Germanic-speaking people occupied an area comprising what is now southern Sweden, southern Norway, Denmark and the lower Elbe at some point prior to 1000 BC, and that an expansion then took place both to the north and to the south. Map 2.1 illustrates the southward expansion of the Germanic peoples in the period 1000 to 500 BC. But a reconstruction of the events before 1000 BC is rather speculative and depends on one's theory of the 'Urheimat' (or original homeland) of the Indo-European speakers themselves (see pages 53–5). At least two facts suggest that the pre-Germanic speakers migrated to their southern Scandinavian location sometime before 1000 BC and that they encountered there a non-Indo-European-speaking people from whom linguistic features were borrowed that were to have a substantial impact on

Map 2.1: Expansion of the Germanic People 1000–500 BC (adapted from Hutterer 1975)

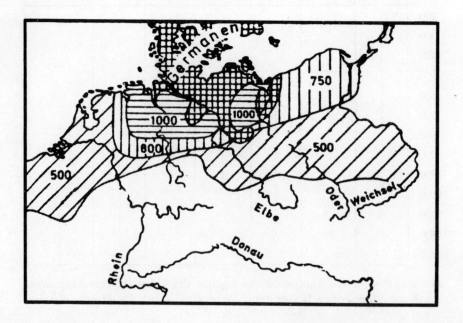

the development of Proto-Germanic from Proto-Indo-European: first fully one third of the vocabulary of the Germanic languages is not of Indo-European origin (see pages 64–5); second, if a substrate language is to have any influence at all on a superimposed language one would expect to see this influence primarily in the lexicon and the phonology (the latter because of the special difficulty inherent in acquiring non-native speech sounds), and indeed the consonantal changes of the First Sound Shift (see below) are unparalleled in their extent elsewhere in Indo-European and suggest that speakers of a fricative-rich language with no voiced stops made systematic conversions of Indo-European sounds into their own nearest equivalents and that these eventually became adopted by the speech community as a whole.

The major changes that set off Proto-Germanic from Proto-Indo-European are generally considered to have been completed by at least 500 BC. In the phonology these were the following: the First (or Germanic) Sound Shift; several vowel shifts; changes in word-level stress patterns; and reductions and losses in unstressed syllables.

The First Sound Shift affected *all* the voiceless and voiced stops of Proto-Indo-European and is illustrated in figure 2.2.

Figure 2.2: The First (Germanic) Sound Shift (adapted from Krahe 1948)

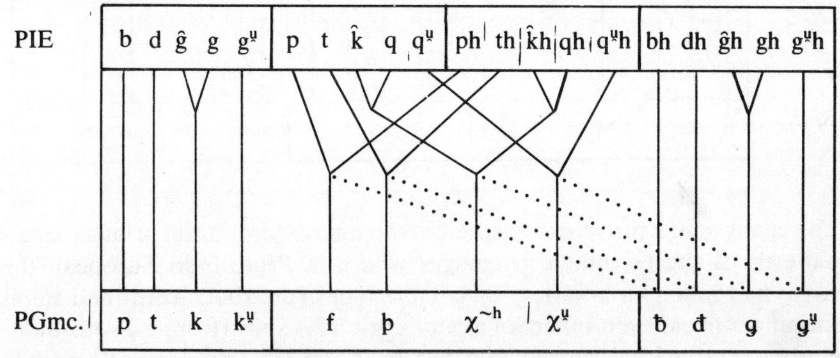

Proto-Indo-European had a voiceless and a voiced series of consonants, each of which could be unaspirated or aspirated, and within each series there was a bilabial, a dental, a palatal, a velar and a labio-velar (labialised velar) stop, as shown. Proto-Germanic abandoned the palatal/velar distinction throughout, and collapsed the unaspirated and aspirated series of voiceless stops. Unaspirated voiced stops shifted to their voiceless counterparts (see, for example, Lat. *decem*, Eng. *ten*), voiceless stops shifted to voiceless fricatives (e.g. Lat. *tres*, Eng. *three*), and aspirated voiced stops shifted to voiced fricatives (most of which subsequently became voiced stops). The dotted line in figure 2.2 indicates the operation of what is called 'Verner's Law'. Depending on the syllable that received primary word stress, the voiceless fricatives of Germanic would either remain voiceless or become voiced. For example, an immediately following stressed syllable would induce voicing, cf. Go. *fadar* 'father' pronounced with [ð] rather than [θ], from PIE *pətér*, cf. Skt. *pitár-*, Gk. *patér*.

The vowel shifts are illustrated in figure 2.3. Short *a*, *o* and *ə* were collapsed into Germanic *a* (compare Lat. *ager*, Go. *akrs* 'field, acre'; Lat. *octo* (PIE *oktō*), Go. *ahtau* 'eight'; PIE *pəter*, Go. *fadar* 'father'). The syllabic liquids and nasals of Proto-Indo-European became *u* plus a liquid or nasal consonant. Long *ā* and *ō* collapsed into *ō* (Lat. *frāter*, Go. *brōþar* 'brother'; Lat. *flōs* (PIE *bhlōmen*), Go. *blōma*, 'flower, bloom'), and the number of diphthongs was reduced as shown.

Figure 2.3: Germanic Vowel Shifts (from Krahe and Meid 1969)

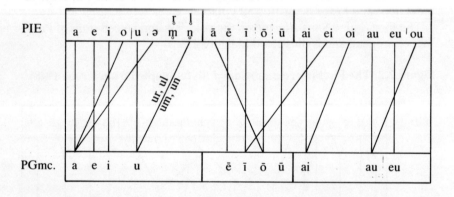

The changes in word stress resulted in the many word-initial primary stress patterns of the Germanic languages where in Proto-Indo-European the stress had fallen on a variety of syllable types (the root, word- and stem-forming affixes, even inflectional endings). This shift (from a Proto-Indo-European accentual system that has been argued to be based on pitch originally, i.e. high versus low tones) is commonly assumed to have occurred after the First Sound Shift, since the operation of Verner's Law presupposes variable accentual patterns of the Indo-European type that were subsequently neutralised by the reassignment of primary stress. Thus, both PIE *bhráter* 'brother' and *pətér* 'father' end up with primary stress on the initial syllable in Go. *brōþar* and *fádar*, and yet the alternation between voiceless [θ] in the former case and voiced [ð] in the latter bears testimony to earlier accentual patterns. Had the stress shifted first, both words should have changed *t* in the same way. A major and lasting consequence of initial stress was the corresponding reduction and loss of unstressed syllables. This process was well underway in predialectal Germanic and was to continue after the separation of the dialects. Indo-European final -*t* was regularly dropped (Lat. *velit*, Go. *wili* 'he will/wants'), and final -*m* was either dropped or reduced to -*n* (OLat. *quom*, Eng. *when*). Final short vowels were dropped (Gk. *oīda* 'I see', Go. *wait* 'I know'), and final long vowels were reduced in length.

The extremely rich morphology of Proto-Indo-European was reduced in Proto-Germanic. The Proto-Indo-European noun distinguished three genders (masculine, feminine, neuter), three numbers (singular, plural, dual) and eight cases (nominative, vocative, accusative, genitive, dative, ablative, instrumental and locative). The three genders were preserved in Germanic, but special dual inflections disappeared (though residual dual forms survive in the pronominal system of the early dialects). The eight cases were reduced to four: the original nominative, accusative, and genitive preserved their forms and functions; the vocative was collapsed with the nominative; the dative, instrumental and locative (and to some extent the ablative) were united in a single case, the Germanic dative, though occasional instrumental forms are attested; and some uses of the ablative were taken over by the genitive.

Proto-Indo-European nouns were also divided into numerous declensional classes depending on the final vowel or consonant of the stem syllable, each with partially different inflectional paradigms. These paradigms survive in Germanic, though some gained, and were to continue to gain, members at the expense of others (particularly the PIE *o*-class (Gmc. *a*-class) for masculine and neuter nouns, and the PIE *ā*-class (Gmc. *ō*-class) for feminine nouns). The inflectional paradigm for masculine *a*-stems in the earliest Germanic languages is illustrated in the chart given here.

The Inflectional Paradigm for Germanic Masculine *a*-Stems. Germanic *a*-stems exemplified by Gothic *dags* 'day' and cognates in the other Germanic dialects derive from Indo-European *o*-stems (cf. Latin *lupus*, earlier *lupos* 'wolf').

	Go.	ON	OE	OS	OHG
Sg. Nom.	dags	dagr	dæg	dag	tag
Gen.	dagis	dags	dæges	dages	tages
Dat.	daga	dege	dæge	dage	tage
Acc.	dag	dag	dæg	dag	tag
Voc.	dag	(=Nom.)	(=Nom.)	(=Nom.)	(=Nom.)
Inst.	–	–	dæge	dagu	tagu
Pl. Nom.	dagōs	dagar	dagas	dagos	taga
Gen.	dagē	daga	daga	dago	tago
Dat.	dagam	dǫgom	dagum	dagum	tagum
Acc.	dagans	daga	dagas	dagos	taga

The syncretism of the case system was accompanied by an expansion in the use of prepositions in order to disambiguate semantic distinctions that had been carried more clearly by the morphology hitherto.

The pronouns of Germanic correspond by and large to those of Indo-European, except for the reduction in the number of dual forms.

As regards the adjective, Germanic innovated a functionally productive distinction between 'strong' and 'weak' inflections, which is still found in Modern German (cf. pages 114–15 for illustration). Proto-Indo-European adjectival morphology was fundamentally similar to that for nouns. The Germanic strong adjective inflections were formed from a fusion of pronominal inflections with the declensional paradigm for nouns and adjectives ending in a stem vowel, while the weak adjective inflections were those of nouns and adjectives with *n*-stems. Strong and weak adjectives in the early dialects carried a meaning difference similar to that of the indefinite versus definite articles of the modern Germanic languages, and it is no accident that adjectives within indefinite versus definite noun phrases are typically strong and weak respectively in German today.

Proto-Indo-European verbal morphology was considerably reduced in Germanic. The Proto-Indo-European medio-passive voice was lost (except for a few relics in Gothic and Old English), and only the active survives. Distinct subjunctive and optative forms were collapsed, and only two of several tense and aspect distinctions were maintained in the Germanic present versus past tenses. Separate verb agreement inflections for dual subjects survive only (partially) in Gothic and Old Norse. A special innovation of Germanic involved the development of a systematic distinction between strong and weak verbs. The former (exemplified by Eng. *sing/sang/sung*) exploit vowel alternations, or 'ablaut' (see pages 39–40), in distinguishing, for example, past from present tense forms, the latter use a suffix containing a dental element without any vowel alternation (e.g. Eng. *love/loved*). The verbal morphology of Proto-Germanic has been maintained in all the modern Germanic languages (though the number of strong verbs has been reduced in favour of weak ones), and in addition new periphrastic forms have evolved for the tenses (e.g. perfect and pluperfect) and voices (the passive) that were lost in the transmission from Proto-Indo-European to Proto-Germanic.

The Germanic lexicon, like the phonology and morphology, reveals clearly the Indo-European origin of Germanic. Yet, as pointed out earlier, a full one third of Germanic lexical items cannot be derived from Proto-Indo-European. These items, far from being peripheral, belong to the very core of the basic vocabulary of Common Germanic. They constitute a particularly high proportion of the following semantic fields: seafaring terms; terms for warfare and weaponry; animal names (particularly fish) and terms for hunting and farming; communal activities and social institutions and titles. Examples (taken from English alone) are: *sea*, *ship*, *strand*, *keel*, *boat*, *rudder*, *mast*, *ebb*, *steer*, *sail*, *north*, *south*, *east*, *west*; *sword*, *shield*, *helmet*, *bow*; *carp*, *eel*, *calf*, *lamb*, *bear*, *stork*; *thing* (originally a communal meeting), *king*, *knight*. Other fundamental terms that belong here are: *drink*, *leap*, *bone*, *wife*, and many others. Common Germanic also took numerous loanwords from neighbouring Indo-European peoples, especially from Latin, though also from Celtic. The Latin loans reveal the strong influence of Roman culture on the early Germanic peoples in areas such as agriculture (cf. Eng. *cherry*/Lat. *ceresia*, *plum*/*pluma*, *plant*/*planta*, *cheese*/*caseus*), building and construction (*street*/*strata*, *wall*/*vallum*, *chamber*/*camera*), trade (*pound*/*pondo*, *fishmonger*/*mango* (= slave-trader), *mint*/*moneta*), warfare (*camp*/*campus*). Most of the days of the week are loan translations from the Latin (e.g. *Sunday*/*solis dies*, etc.).

There is much less certainty about the syntax of Proto-Germanic, though the word order of the earliest inscriptions (Late Common Germanic) has been quite extensively documented by Smith (1971). He establishes that the basic position of the verb was clause-final (62 per cent of the clauses he investigated were verb-final, with 19 per cent verb-second and 16 per cent verb-first). Within the noun phrase, however, the predominant order of adjectival modifiers and of possessive and demonstrative determiners is after the noun, and not before it, as in many OV languages. In the earliest West Germanic dialects, by contrast, the verb is correspondingly less verb-final, and modifiers of the noun are predominantly preposed.

The precise manner in which the proto-language split up into the three groups (North, East and West) is a question of long-standing dispute. With the exception of the earliest runic inscriptions, the tripartite division is already very clearly established in the earliest records of figure 2.1: each of the groups has undergone enough characteristic innovations to justify both the existence of the group itself and the assumption of a period of separate linguistic development for the languages involved following migration from the homeland. But whether these innovations point to the existence of, for instance, a West Germanic parent language which split off from Proto-Germanic and from which all the later West Germanic dialects are descended, or whether the innovations are the result of contact and borrowing between geographically proximate tribes speaking increasingly distinct dialects whose common point of departure was the Germanic parent language itself, is almost impossible to tell. Some scholars argue against the assumption of a West Germanic parent language on the grounds that a threefold dialect grouping within West Germanic (into North Sea Germanic, Rhine-Weser Germanic, and Elbe Germanic — also called respectively Istveonic, Ingveonic and Erminonic) can be reconstructed back as early as the second century AD. The runic inscriptions of this early period do not lend credence to such an early dialect split, however.

Bibliography

For the Indo-European background, reference may be made to Krahe (1948), especially for phonology and morphology. For the phonology and morphology of the early Germanic languages, an excellent summary is Krahe and Meid (1969). Bach (1965), while primarily concerned with German, includes in part I a valuable summary of early Germanic language and history with extensive further references. Hutterer (1975) is an excellent compendium of the history of all the Germanic languages and of the cultures of their speakers.

A useful summary and discussion of word order is Smith (1971), which is discussed by Hawkins (1983) in relation to synchronic word order universals and derivative predictions for language change. Van Coetsem and Kufner (1972) contains many valuable and up-to-date papers in English on the phonology, morphology and syntax of Proto-Germanic, on the position of Germanic within Indo-European as a whole and on the reconstruction of developments within Germanic prior to the first records; it includes Kufner's (1972) summary and synthesis of the divergent theories concerning subgroupings within Germanic.

References

Bach, A. 1965. *Geschichte der deutschen Sprache* (Quelle and Meyer, Heidelberg)

Hawkins, J.A. 1983. *Word Order Universals* (Academic Press, New York)

Hutterer, C.J. 1975. *Die germanischen Sprachen: ihre Geschichte in Grundzügen* (Akadémiai Kiadó, Budapest)

Krahe, H. 1948. *Indogermanische Sprachwissenschaft* (Walter de Gruyter, Berlin)
—— and W. Meid. 1969. *Germanische Sprachwissenschaft*, 2 vols. (Walter de Gruyter, Berlin)

Kufner, H.L. 1972. 'The Grouping and Separation of the Germanic Languages', in Van Coetsem and Kufner (1972)

Smith, J.R. 1971. 'Word Order in the Older Germanic Dialects' (PhD dissertation, University of Illinois, available from University Microfilms, Ann Arbor, Mich.)

Van Coetsem, F. and H.L. Kufner (eds.) 1972. *Toward a Grammar of Proto-Germanic* (Max Niemeyer, Tübingen)

3 English

Edward Finegan

1 Introduction

At least to the extent that ability to read a language presupposes considerable familiarity with its structures, readers may be assumed to have more than a nodding acquaintance with English. English is, moreover, a widely studied language and has received significant attention from linguists in recent decades and from distinguished grammarians since the last century. It thus seems appropriate in this essay to discuss English in terms not altogether parallel to those in which other languages, perhaps less familiar, might best be described. In somewhat more detail than is possible at present for most other languages, this essay will describe the structural variation that characterises English functionally and socially, as well as some of the better-known historical and regional variation.

Section 2 describes the status of English throughout the world, along with its social history and its contact with other languages in the past. Section 3 offers a historical sketch of the lexicon, phonology, morphology and syntax of English, followed by a brief account of orthographic practices. Finally, section 4 treats regional, social and functional variation in present-day English. While this programme for describing English may differ somewhat from the treatment of other languages in this book, it is hoped that this emphasis will be most useful to readers.

2 Status of English

2.1 Current Status of English

Though Chinese is spoken by a greater number of people, English is spoken around the globe and has wider dispersion than any other language. From its earlier home within what is now called the United Kingdom (with 56 million speakers), English has spread to nearby Ireland (three and a half million), across the Atlantic to America (where some 232 million people speak English in the United States, with perhaps as many as 24 million additional speakers in Canada), and across the world to Australia and New Zealand (with about 17 million English speakers between them).

English is the sole official language in more than two dozen other countries: Ghana, Liberia, Nigeria, Uganda and Zimbabwe in Africa; Jamaica, the Bahamas, Dominica and Barbados in the Caribbean; and Vanuatu, Fiji and the Solomon Islands in the Pacific, to name a sample. Elsewhere it shares official status with one or more languages in a score of nations, including Tanzania (with Swahili), Cameroon (French), South Africa (Afrikaans), Singapore (Chinese, Malay and Tamil), the Philippines (Filipino, i.e. Tagalog), Western Samoa (Samoan), Kiribati (Gilbertese), India (where it is an associate official language alongside Hindi) and Pakistan (Urdu). In still other nations, English holds no official status only because its widespread use in government (often alongside an indigenous tongue) and in trade is taken for granted. The two Pacific island nations of Tonga (with 100,000 residents) and Tuvalu (with 9,000) exemplify this situation, as does the United States, where no official language is designated

Substantial portions of the populations of the United States and Canada speak English as a second language, many of them immigrants, but others born within their boundaries and raised in families and neighbourhoods struggling to preserve the language and culture of ancestral lands. One recognised example is that of French speakers in Canada, who constitute a majority only in Quebec province but whose influence is so strong nationally that Canada is officially a bilingual nation. Less well known is the fact that speakers of languages other than English are sufficiently numerous in the United States to warrant using more than a hundred languages of instruction in various primary and secondary schools throughout the land. Los Angeles is a sufficiently bilingual city that balloting materials for all elections are printed in Spanish and English, while the trilingual ballots in San Francisco permit voting in English, Spanish or Chinese. This suggests that a good many residents of the United States speak English as a second language (an estimated 34 million in 1970, including nearly 26 million American born, of whom a third had American-born parents). The same is true, though to a lesser extent, in England. Elsewhere in the world, Nigeria, Ghana and Uganda each have almost two million speakers of English as a second language, while the Philippines has more than 11 million. Likewise, the millions who speak English in Pakistan and India have learned it, for the most part, not in their infancy but as a second language, a lingua franca for governmental and educational functions.

Beyond its uses as a first and second language in ordinary intercourse, English is now established as the lingua franca of much scholarship, particularly of a scientific and technical nature. In addition, throughout the world there are English-speaking universities in which instruction and textbooks use English as the principal medium, though class discussion frequently reflects the greater ease of communication possible in the local vernacular or the national language.

Reflective of the widespread dissemination of English and perhaps of an extraordinary adaptability is the fact that Nobel Prizes in literature have been awarded to more writers using English than any other language, and that these laureates have been citizens of Australia, Ireland and India, as well as the United States and Britain. Finally, it can be pointed out that – along with Arabic, Chinese, French, Russian and Spanish – English is an official language of the United Nations.

2.2   Possible Reasons for Widespread Use of English

The widespread use of English around the globe is often attributed to social prestige and the need for English in technological advancement, as well as to the simplicity of English inflections and the cosmopolitan character of its vocabulary. While these latter grammatical and lexical features do indeed characterise English, they are influential only when coupled with complex social, historical and economic factors, for other languages and other peoples share them, though with different effect.

Among the reasons sometimes suggested for the extension of English (and one or two other widely dispersed languages) is the spread of technology, for the diffusion of American technologies during the twentieth century likewise diffused English words for those technological bits and bytes. So, too, in other arenas, where the artifacts of culture have borne English words with them in their travels, from jeans to discos, not to mention the intangible but ubiquitous *OK*.

Needless to say, English words cropping up in alien lands have not always been welcome. Troubling such watchdog institutions as the *Académie française*, Anglo-Americanisms like *weekend* and *drugstore* have been banned in France, while German guardians balked at the introduction of words like *Telefon* for the native *Fernsprecher*, though the latter compound has now fallen almost completely into disuse. Elsewhere, people are more open to English loanwords. The Japanese, for example, have drafted the words *beesubooru* 'baseball', *booringu* 'bowling' and *futtobooru* 'football', along with the games they name, trading them (so to speak) for *judo*, *jujitsu* and *karate*, which have joined the English team.

Further contributing to the popularity of English may be its inflectional structure, for compared to languages like German and Russian, English exhibits a remarkable inflectional simplicity. Assuming, as many linguists would, that a language simple at one level will be compensatorily complex elsewhere in order to carry out equivalent communicative tasks, it is difficult to assess the impetus of grammatical simplicity of any kind on the spread of a language. To be sure, English inflections are tidy and relatively easy to learn compared with heavily inflected languages and that those that have other complex morphological variations. English nouns, to cite a central example, generally have only two variants in speech, a marked variant for possessive singulars and all plurals, an unmarked one for all other functions. Aside from a few exceptions like *teeth* and *oxen*, plurals are formed by adding /-s/ or /-z/ or /-əz/ to the singular, according to certain straightforward conditions detailed below (page 82). As for possessives, the rules are identical to those for the plural, except that there are no exceptions. Further, English exhibits no variation of adjectives for number, gender, or case, there being but one form each in the positive (*tall*, *beautiful*, *old*), comparative (*-er*) and superlative (*-est*) degrees, the latter two alternating under specified circumstances with the equivalent analytical forms with *more* and *most*. Verbs are only minimally inflected, with suffixes for third person singular concord; for present participle (in *-ing*); for past tense (in /-t/, /-d/, /-əd/); and for past participle (frequently in *-en*). In all, there are but eight productive inflectional suffixes in present-day English: two on nouns, four on verbs and two for adjectives. There are no inflectional prefixes or infixes.

Breadth of vocabulary is the most often cited reason for its acceptance around the globe, and English is indeed lexically rich. *Webster's Third New International Dictionary* (1961) boasts that it contains some 450,000 words; still, an eight-page supplement of new words and meanings was appended to the 1966 printing, and that was expanded to sixteen pages in 1971. When a free-standing supplement appeared in 1976, Merriam-Webster called it *6,000 Words* to reflect the extent of new meanings and new words that had become established in the intervening fifteen years (from *ablator* 'a material that provides thermal protection by ablating' to *zonked* 'being under the influence of alcohol or a drug'). *9,000 Words* appeared in 1983. A supplement to the great *Oxford English Dictionary* (*OED*) is in process of completion, three of four projected volumes already in print (1972, 1976, 1982), the fourth (beginning with the word *sea*) appearing in 1986. This supplement is intended to update the *OED* with words and senses of words that arose during the decades of publication between 1884 and 1928, and since then. When the first volume of the supplement appeared, editor R. W. Burchfield estimated the supplement would contain about 50,000 main word entries. Already, however, in the three existing volumes (up to the word *Scythism*), as many as 49,750 main words have been treated, not a negligible number for a word list intended as a supplement to another dictionary completed only about half a century earlier. Further, the inability of the dictionary makers to predict the number of words to be treated as late as the appearance of the first volume (up to the letter G) is indicative of the current growth rate of the lexicon.

As further evidence of the abundance of the English word stock, we can point to the fact that the number of synonyms (or near synonyms) for many words is quite large, each suggesting some variation on the semantic core. Almost any thesaurus can provide upwards of forty synonyms for the adjective *inebriated* and more than a dozen for the noun *courtesy*, to offer examples from just two parts of speech (without intending to suggest the relative richness of these two notions in the English-speaking world).

English also boasts a distinctively cosmopolitan vocabulary, having borrowed extensively from other Germanic tongues and especially from the Romance languages Latin and French, but absorbing tens of thousands of words from scores of languages over the centuries. From earliest times English has revealed a remarkable magnetism for loanwords, in foods and toponymics of course, but in every other arena of human activity as well. Some indication of the cosmopolitan nature of the English lexicon is suggested by words like *alcove*, *alcohol* and *harem* (from Arabic), *tycoon* and *ikebana* (Japanese), *taboo* (Tongan), some 10,000 words of French origin added during Middle English and an even larger influx from Latin during the Renaissance. (On the French borrowings, Jespersen (1938) and Baugh and Cable (1978) are useful references; on the Latin, Serjeantson (1935).) Recent borrowings reveal an extraordinary range of donor languages, more than seventy-five in number. French provides most items by far, followed by Japanese, Spanish, Italian, Latin, Greek, German, Yiddish, Russian, Chinese, Arabic, more than two dozen African languages and more than three dozen other languages from all parts of the globe.

Maps of the English-speaking parts of the globe are dotted with borrowings from many sources. A map of the City of Los Angeles, to cite the host of the 1984 international Olympiad, exhibits hundreds of street names of Spanish origin (from *La Cienega* to *Los Feliz*) and bears a Spanish name itself. Elsewhere in the USA, place-names like *Mississippi* and *Minnesota* are borrowed from Amerindian languages, while *Kinderhook*, *Schuylerville* and *Watervliet*, all in New York State, are taken from Dutch.

Names for such popular foods as *taco*, *burrito*, *chili* and *guacamole* (from Mexican Spanish), *hamburger*, *frankfurter*, *liverwurst* and *wiener schnitzel* (German), *teriyaki* and *sukiyaki* (Japanese), *chow mein* and *foo yong* (Cantonese), *kimchi* (Korean), *pilaf* (Persian and Turkish), *falafel* (Arabic) and a thousand others indicate the catholic tastes of English speakers both gustatorily and linguistically. Playing a special role, French culinary words have leavened the English lexicon used in kitchens around the world: *hors d'œuvre*, *quiche*, *pâté*, *fondue*, *flambé*, *soufflé*, *sauté*, *carrot*, *mayonnaise*, *bouillon*, *flan*, *casserole*, and the ubiquitous *à la*, as in *à la mode* and *à la carte*, are illustrative. A wide stripe of other languages is represented by the following familiar culinary words: *semolina* (Italian), *chocolate* (Nahuatl, via Spanish and French), *coleslaw* (Dutch), *chutney* (Hindi), *moussaka* (Greek), *bamboo* (Malay), *gazpacho* (Spanish), *yoghurt* (Turkish), *kebob* (Arabic), *caviar* (Persian, via Turkish, Italian and French), *pepper* (Latin), *whiskey* (Irish), *maize* (Taino – an Arawakan language – via Spanish) and *blintz* and *knish* (both Ukrainian, via Yiddish).

Another reason that has been suggested to help explain the spread of English is the fact that its most common words are of such simple structure.

At least in America, 88 of the hundred most frequently written words are monosyllables, from *the* ranking first, to *down* (ranking 100th); among the next most frequent hundred are another 68 monosyllabic words. Of those that are not monosyllables among the first two hundred, all but five are disyllabic, while *American* is the solitary word with more than three syllables. Were similar information available for a wide range of languages, it might be clear that languages generally abbreviate words of frequent use in accordance with Zipf's law. English, however, has had the additional historical impetus that most disyllabic words ending in an unstressed syllable became monosyllabic in early Modern English, as described below.

One final explanation recently offered by some scholars for the diffusion of English lies in the supposed nature of the relationships between grammatical structures and the processing mechanisms for comprehension. Though not universally accepted nor empirically verified, this explanation relies on the fact that English is an SVO language, with subjects preceding verbs preceding objects. The claim is that SVO languages are perceptually simpler than languages whose basic orders are SOV or VSO. It is pointed out that, even granted their sociological and political statuses, it is noteworthy that Chinese, French, Russian and Spanish, all of which are SVO, are languages of wide diffusion, as is the spoken form of Arabic that is spreading. The perceptual advantage of SVO languages is the ready identification of subjects and objects, which are separated (by verbs) in SVO but not SOV or VSO languages. It might also be mentioned that English tends to have topics in sentence-initial position (though to a lesser degree than many other languages); given its preference for SVO word order, subject and topic will often coincide, a coincidence that apparently enhances processibility, especially when the subject is also the semantic agent.

2.3 English and Its Social History

Needless to say, English did not always hold so lofty a position among the world's languages as it holds today. Even in England, to which we trace its beginnings as an independent tongue, English had competitors at times. In America, too, despite its new robustness, it was not always clear that the United States and Canada would be English-speaking countries. Even today, encroachments by Spanish and French on the status of English in North America are vigorous.

English derives from the West Germanic branch of the Indo-European family of languages. It is most closely related to the Low German dialects in northern Germany and to Dutch and Frisian, sharing with them the characteristic absence of the Second, or High, German Sound Shift, occurring around AD 600 and markedly differentiating the phonology of the West Germanic varieties of the highland south from those of the lowland north. (See pages 103–4.) Geographically separated from the Continent since the middle of the fifth century, English would not have been subject to this shift, but its origins in the northernmost part of the Germanic-speaking area would also have spared it.

It was in AD 449, according to Bede's *Ecclesiastical History of the English People* (completed in 731), that bands from the three Germanic tribes of Angles (after whom England and its language were named), Saxons and Jutes began leaving the area known today as northern Holland and Germany and southern Denmark. These Teutons sailed to Britain, which had been deserted by the Romans forty years earlier, to assist the Celtic leader Vortigern, who had called upon them to help repulse the invading Picts and Scots from the north of England. Preferring Britain to their continental homelands, the Teutons settled, driving the hapless Celts into remote corners, where their descendants remain to this day – in Scotland in the north and in Cornwall and Wales in the south-west and west.

Surviving the Roman occupation of the British Isles there remain but few linguistic relics of Latin origin, including the second element of such place names as *Lancaster*, *Manchester* and *Rochester* (from Latin *castra* 'camp'). This influence of Latin through Celtic transmission was the slightest of several Latin influences on the English lexicon. As for direct Celtic influence on the early Germanic settlers, it is slight, noticeable only in place-names like *Dover*, *Kent*, *York*, possibly *London*, and a few other toponymics like the river names *Avon*, *Thames* and *Trent*. The missionary activities of St. Columba, who in 563 established an Irish monastery on the island of Iona off the coast of Scotland, introduced a few Celtic words like *cross* and perhaps *curse* into the English word stock.

It is not until the end of the seventh century that we have written records of the Germanic language spoken in England and not until the reign of King Alfred (871–99) that we have 'Englisc' recorded in quantity. In 597, St. Augustine (not the bishop of Hippo famous for his fifth-century *Confessions* and *City of God*) christianised the English people, giving them scores of Latin words like *abbot*, *altar*, *angel*, *cleric*, *priest* and *psalm* in the religious sphere and *grammatical*, *master*, *meter*, *school* and *verse* in learned arenas.

At the end of the eighth century and during the ninth, a series of invasions from the Scandinavian cousins of the Anglo-Saxons brought a secondary Germanic influence into the English lexicon, though it does not vigorously manifest itself in the written record until after the eleventh century. Sporadic raids started in 787, with monasteries sacked and pillaged at Lindisfarne in 793 and Jarrow (Bede's monastery) in 794. In the year 850, as many as 350 ships carried Danish invaders up the Thames. At length, after King Alfred. defeated these Vikings in 878 and signed the Treaty of Wedmore with Guthrum, who agreed to become Christian, there followed a period of integration during which bilingualism prevailed in the Danelaw, an area governed by Danish practices and including Northumbria, East Anglia, and half of central England.

This intermingling of the two closely allied groups brought an influx of more than 900 everyday words into English from the Scandinavian tongues, including the verbs *take, give* and *get* and such homely nouns as *gift, egg, skirt, skill, skin* and *sky*. In addition, about 1,400 Scandinavian place-names pepper English maps, besides some 600 ending in *-by* (as in *Derby, Rugby*), 600 in *-thorp* or *-thwaite* and another hundred or so in *-toft*, all Scandinavian. Besides this toponymic evidence, the close relationship between the Scandinavians and the English is suggested by the possibility that both pronoun and verb in the phrase *they are* derive not from OE *hīe sindon* but from Scandinavian sources; it is confirmed by the observation that the verbs *take, give, get* are among the ten most frequently occurring lexical verbs in English, to judge by their currency in American writing (see the discussion of the Brown University Corpus of Present-Day Edited American English in sections 3.1, 4.3 and 4.4 below).

In the development of the English language, the most significant historical event is the invasion by the Normans in 1066. In that year, William, Duke of Normandy, crossed the Channel and with his French-speaking retinues established an Anglo-Norman kingdom in England. During the following century and a half, one could not have confidently predicted the reemergence of English and its eventual triumph over French in all domains. Only a series of extraordinary social events contributed definitively to reestablishing a Germanic tongue emblematic of England.

After 1066, the Normans established themselves in the court, in the church and her monasteries, throughout the legal system and the military and in all other arenas of power and wealth. The upper class spoke only French, while English remained chiefly on peasant tongues. Naturally, between such extremes of the social scale a significant number of bilinguals eventually used English and French, but for generations England was ruled by French-speaking monarchs, unable to understand the language of many subjects and unable to be understood. Only when King John lost Normandy to King Philip of France in 1204 did the knot between England and the Anglo-Norman language start to come undone. Following other political and military antagonisms, the linguistic tide turned.

Finally, a plague known as 'The Black Death' struck England in 1348, wiping out perhaps 30 per cent of the population and increasing the value of every peasant life. This shifted the lower (English-speaking) classes to positions of greater appreciation and enhanced value for their work, and along with their own rise in stature came their language. In 1362, the Statute of Pleading was passed by Parliament, mandating that all court proceedings, which had been conducted solely in French since the Norman conquest, should thenceforth be in English. By about 1300 all the inhabitants of England knew English, and French had begun to fall into disuse. During the fourteenth century, English again became the language of England and of her literature. (Details of this story are conveniently found in *A History of the English Language* (Baugh and Cable 1978).)

Literature in English is known since Old English times. *Beowulf*, an heroic poem of some 3,000 lines, is still studied even in secondary schools (though usually in translation). While the surviving *Beowulf* manuscript dates probably from the late tenth century, the poem itself is likely to have been composed in the eighth. In addition, there survive other texts, including poetry (from the end of the seventh century), translations of the Bible, chronicles and religious writings particularly from the time of Alfred. Besides several known translations, including Boethius' *Consolation of Philosophy*, Alfred is thought by some to have translated Bede's *History* from Latin, and he is credited with establishing the practice of maintaining the Anglo-Saxon Chronicles. Alfred reigned from Wessex and his kingdom was thus within the West Saxon dialect area, making it the basis for the study of Old English today even though it is not the ancestor of the London dialect of Chaucer that became the basis of modern standard English.

Less was written in English between 1066 and the thirteenth century, but English language traditions remained vital enough for the fourteenth century to produce Chaucer (1340–1400) and his *Canterbury Tales*, an extraordinary work still enjoyed for its earthy, humorous narrative and its poetic skill. From quite early times English has been robust in its literary manifestation, except for the period of dominance by Anglo-Norman from which it nevertheless emerged a great literary language, lexically enriched and inflectionally simplified in part from that subordination to French.

3   English Structure and its History

English is usually divided into three major historical periods: Old English, dating from either the arrival of the Germanic tribes in 449 or the earliest documents, about 700, to about 1100 (shortly after the Norman conquest); Middle English from about 1100 to 1500; and, from 1500, Modern English, including an early Modern English period between 1500 and 1700. These dates are necessarily arbitrary, for English did not develop at the same rate in all regions nor at all levels of the grammar. These dates are in fact more appropriate to a phonological than a grammatical history, for Modern English morphology and syntax were established essentially in their current form by about 1400, the year of Chaucer's death.

Old English had four principal dialect areas: Northumbrian, Mercian, Kentish and West Saxon; most extant texts are in West Saxon. In Middle English, Mercian is divided into West Midland and East Midland dialects, and East Midland, which incorporated features of other dialects, gave rise to standard Modern English. In the treatment to follow, little attention is given to Middle English for two reasons. First, it represents a transitional period whose general nature can be inferred from knowledge of Old English and Modern English. Second, Middle English is far more diverse in its regional dialects than is susceptible to straightforward, brief exposition. Looked at overall, Middle English is a language in extraordinary flux. The geographical and chronological details of this unusually complex state of affairs can be traced in Mossé (1952).

3.1 Lexicon

Although the English word stock, enriched by compounding of native elements and by influxes of foreign borrowings, has always been abundant, the mechanisms for enriching it have shifted dramatically in the course of history. The Old English lexicon was almost purely Germanic, with traces of Latin and Celtic influence. This lexicon largely shared etymons with the other Germanic languages and like them developed its word stock chiefly by compounding (which is still a vital source of new words in German and English), as well as by prefixing and suffixing. Compounding was especially frequent and imaginative in Old English poetry, and the resulting kennings, illustrated here from *Beowulf*, enhanced poetic resources: *seġlrād* 'sail road' and *hrōnrād* 'whale road' for sea, and *bānhūs* 'bone house' for body. Old English nouns productively suffixed *-dōm*, *-hād*, *-ere*, and *-scipe* (to cite four with reflexes in Modern English), as in *wīsdōm* 'wisdom', *cildhād* 'childhood', *wrītere* 'writer' and *frēondscipe* 'friendship'. Verbs commonly prefixed *ā-*, *be-*, *for-*, *fore-*, *ge-*, *mis-*, *of-*, *ofer-*, *on-*, *tō-*, *un-*, *under-*, and *wiþ-*. As Baugh and Cable (1978) note, Old English could create from *settan* 'to set' all the following: *āsettan* 'place', *besettan* 'appoint', *forsettan* 'obstruct', *foresettan* 'place before', *gesettan* 'people, garrison', *ofsettan* 'afflict', *onsettan* 'oppress', *tōsettan* 'dispose', *unsettan* 'put down', and *wiþsettan* 'resist'. It could prefix *wiþ-* to fifty different verbs, only one of which (*withstand*) survives in Modern English (*withdraw* and *withhold* originating in Middle English).

The Norman invasion gave new impetus to the borrowing practices of English, for when English reemerged in the thirteenth century it did so in a context in which anybody who was anybody spoke French and in which many of the elite did not speak English. From then on, besides smithing with native elements, English imported gleefully from the languages with which it came into contact, and the character of its lexicon became irrevocably international. Baugh and Cable report that 40 per cent of all French words in English were borrowed between 1250 and 1400, the period during which English came again to be used for official and learned purposes. From this flood of more than 10,000 French words inundating Middle English, 75 per cent remain in use.

By no means did the Normans introduce the practice of lexical borrowing. Earlier, English had borrowed from the Celtic tongues and from Latin, and during the ninth and tenth centuries from its Viking cousins, as we saw. Still, the Normans substituted borrowing for the more characteristic English word-smithing practices of affixing and compounding, which had formerly been the most productive springs of new words and have become so again in the twentieth century, as shown by the *OED* Supplement or Merriam-Webster's list of *9,000 Words* added to English since 1961.

A brief look at the lexical character of Modern English texts may be useful here. Until recently, it would have been difficult to describe accurately the size and character of the Modern English lexicon, but the advent of computers and the development of standard corpora have made the beginnings of that task manageable. The data presented in this section are derived from the Standard Corpus of Present-day English, a structured sample of edited American English appearing in print in 1961. Commonly referred to as the Brown Corpus, it comprises slightly more than a million words, representing 500 samples of about 2,000 words each, taken from 15 prose genres, both informational and imaginative. (The composition of the corpus is described in Kučera and Francis (1967) and in Francis and Kučera (1982), from which, along with Kučera (1982), the data here cited are reported. The similarly structured British sample is known as the Lancaster-Oslo/Bergen corpus and is discussed in Johansson (1982).)

The Brown Corpus contains 61,805 different word forms, or types, belonging to 37,851 lemmas. A lemma is a set of word forms, all of which are inflectional variants or spelling variants of the same base word; thus, the lemma *GET* comprises the word forms *get* (and *git*), *gets*, *got* (and *gotta*), *gotten*, *getting* (and *gettin'*). Extrapolating these figures to an infinite sample would yield about 170,000 lemmas in English, excluding proper nouns and highly specialised and technical terms. Remarkably, just 2,124 lemmas (comprising 2,854 word forms) constitute 80 per cent of the corpus tokens. Approximately another 22,000 word forms occur once each; these so-called *hapax phenomena* account for 58 per cent of the lemmas. This fact gives some hint as to the range of the English lexicon, for the most frequently occurring words are grammatical (i.e., function) words, not lexical words (cf. sections 4.3 and 4.4)

The most common lexical lemmas are the verb *say* at rank 33 and the noun *man* at rank 44. The next most common lexical verbs (with their rank) are *go* (47), *take* (58), *come* (60), *see* (61), *get* (62), *know* (63) and *give* (72). The most common nouns after *man* are *time* (46), *year* (54), *state* (64) and *day* (75). The only adjective among the 75 most common lemmas is *new* at rank 56. Kučera (1982) points out that since content words are the least predictable textual elements, knowing the 2,124 lemmas that account for 80 per cent of the corpus would fall far short of leading to comprehension approximating 80 per cent.

The figures presented here are valid, strictly speaking, only for American written English, although it would be surprising if the broad outlines were far different for British writing. To the extent that speech and writing diverge, differences may be anticipated between these figures and those that would characterise speech samples, whether British or American. A corpus of spoken British English is being compiled under the auspices of the Survey of English Usage at University College London and is being computerised at the University of Lund in Sweden. No plan exists at present to develop a standard corpus of American speech, though the American Dialect Society has recently pointed to the need for one. (The distribution of different word classes across genres will be described in sections 4.3 and 4.4.)

3.2 Phonology

Throughout its history, English exhibits striking instability in its system of vowels, while its consonants have remained relatively fixed especially since the fourteenth century. Old English, Middle English and Modern English all exhibit considerable vocalic variation from dialect to dialect, while the consonants show negligible synchronic variation from region to region. Socially significant heterogeneity, on the other hand, affects both consonants and vowels, as described in section 4.2.

Because the evolution of unstressed vowels has played a pivotal role in the development of English morphology and grammar, their history is central to our discussion. The most pregnant phonological feature of the earliest stages of English is the characteristic Germanic stress placement on the first or root syllable. From before the settlement of England, the language of the Angles, Saxons and Jutes suffered certain phonological reductions that differentiate it from High German (e.g. loss of nasals preceding /f/, /θ/, /s/, with compensatory lengthening of the preceding vowel; compare German *Mund* and *Gans* with English *mouth* and *goose*). Such correspondences between High and Low German stressed vowels only begin to suggest the wholesale reductions that were to affect English unstressed vowels and as a consequence the entire inflectional system.

While Gothic (known to us from several centuries earlier than Old English) apparently preserves both long and short vowels in its inflections, Old English exhibits only short vowels, and syncretism among these inflections is apparent starting in late Old English, especially in the Northumbrian dialect. While early Old English had a relatively elaborate inflectional system, the characteristic Germanic stress placement began to effect reductions of such magnitude in unstressed vowels that inflectional suffixes were reduced in late Old English and Middle English essentially to the bare system of Modern English. In particular, unstressed /u/, /a/, /e/ and /o/ fell together into *e* [ə]. Coupled with the merging of final /-m/ and /-n/ in /-n/, the collapse of unstressed vowels and subsequent loss of final inflectional /-n/ and then of final [ə] led to the virtual elimination of all inflectional suffixes except those with final -*s* and -*þ*. This sequence of phonological levellings explains the plural and genitive forms of Modern English nouns, as well as third person singular verbs in orthographic -*s* and past tenses in -*d*.

When we turn to stressed vowels, their history is complicated by the substantial dialectal variation of Old English and the shifting locus of literary standards until the fifteenth century. Still, the extensive diphthongisation and monophthongisation that characterise Old English occur throughout the history of English. When American southerners pronounce *ride* as [raːd], they evidence the same kind of monophthongisation (or smoothing) that took place in late Old English when *sēon* became *seen* 'to see' and *heorte* became *herte* 'heart'.

Today, between fourteen and sixteen phonemic vowels exist in different regional varieties of standard English, including the three diphthongs /ay/, /aw/, and /oy/ (the last of which was borrowed from Anglo-Norman). Similar regional variation exists throughout the English-speaking world. (A detailed treatment of stressed vowels is available by period in Pyles and Algeo (1982) and by sound in Kurath (1964); both cite additional references.) No discussion of English historical phonology can ignore the dramatic shifting of long vowels that occurred in the fifteenth and sixteenth centuries, between Chaucer's death in 1400 and the birth of Shakespeare in 1564. This so-called Great Vowel Shift altered the pronunciation of every long vowel and diphthongised the two high vowels /iː/ and /uː/ to their Modern English reflexes /ay/ and /aw/. Charted in figure 3.1, this shift is responsible for the discrepancy in pronunciation of orthographic vowels between English and the Romance languages. Traditional English spellings were propagated with Caxton's introduction of printing into England in 1476, preceding the completion of the shift.

Figure 3.1: The English Vowel Shift (also called Great Vowel Shift)

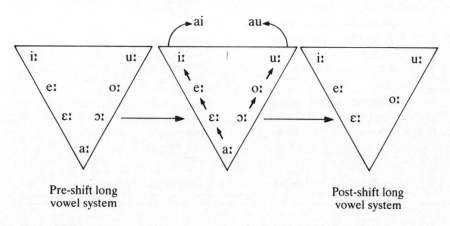

Pre-shift long vowel system

Post-shift long vowel system

Source: Bynon 1977

Subsequent to the Vowel Shift, early ModE /eː/ (< ME /ɛː/) came to be pronounced /i/, thus merging with earlier raised /eː/ and producing two sets of ModE /i/ words, those from OE /eː/ as in *sweet* and *see*, and those from

OE /ɛː/ as in *sheaf*, *beacon*, and *sea*. The raising tendency exhibited in the Vowel Shift continues today, where it is sometimes regionally distinctive and sometimes socially marked.

As to consonants, the English system has remained relatively stable throughout its history, and the inventory of phonemes has changed only slightly since about 1400, although certain allophones have been lost and phonotactic constraints have been altered somewhat. The Modern English spelling of *know* and *knife* is indicative of earlier pronunciations, for Old English allowed initial clusters of /hl-/ as in *hlāf* 'loaf', /hr-/ as in *hring* 'ring' and /kn-/ as in *cniht* 'knight', all of which are now prohibited.

In table 3.1 is a list of Modern English consonant phonemes, followed by words illustrating word-initial, word-medial, and word-final occurrence.

Table 3.1: Modern English Consonants

Phoneme	Initial	Medial	Final
p	pat	caper	tap
b	bat	labour	tab
t	tap	button	bat
d	dad	ladder	pad
k	cad	sicker	talk
g	gab	dagger	gag
f	file	beefy	thief
v	vile	saving	crave
θ	thin	author	breath
ð	then	weather	breathe
s	sin	mason	kiss
z	zebra	posit	pose
š	shame	lashes	push
ž		measure	rouge
č	chin	kitchen	pitch
ǰ	jury	bludgeon	fudge
m	moon	dummy	room
n	noon	sunny	spoon
ŋ		singer	sing
h	hen	ahoy	
y	year	beyond	
r	red	berry	deer
l	lot	silly	mill
w	wind	away	

Several notable differences between the consonant systems of Old English (not illustrated here) and Modern English can be mentioned. The members of the three Modern English voiced and voiceless fricative pairs (/f/–/v/, /θ/–/ð/, /s/–/z/) were allophones of single phonemes in Old English, the voiced phones occurring between other voiced sounds, the voiceless phones occurring initially, finally and in clusters with voiceless obstruents. Relics of the Old English allophonic distribution remain in the morphophonemic alternants *wife/wives*, *breath/breathe* and *house/houses*, where the second word in each pair, disyllabic in Old English, voiced the intervocalic fricative. Significantly, initial /ð/ in Modern English is limited to the function words *the*, *this*, *that*, *these*, *those*, *they* and *them*, *there* and *then*, *thus*, *thence*, *though* and *thither*, with initial voiceless /θ/ in Old English later becoming voiced by assimilation when unstressed, as these words often are. Similarly, /θ/ does not occur medially in any native words, though it can be found in borrowings. During the Middle English period, with the baring of the voiced phones word-finally when the syncreted inflections disappeared, the allophones achieved phonemic status, contrasting in most environments; there may also have been some Anglo-Norman influence, though not so much as is sometimes claimed.

Modern English /n/ and /ŋ/ were also non-distinctive variants in Old English, becoming phonemic during the late Middle English or early Modern English period. Of the Old English allophones of /h/, both [x] and [ç] have disappeared, leaving only [h]. In addition, /g/ had two Old English allophones, ModE [g] and a fricative [g] occurring intervocalically but now lost.

Finally, the gap existing in Old English and Middle English where one might expect a voiced palatal fricative /ž/ to parallel native /š/ was filled about 1600 when /ž/ arose by assimilation of /zy/ from earlier /zi/ (as in *glazier*, *lesion* and *vision*) and /ziu/ (as in *measure* and *usual*). More recently, word-final /ž/ has been borrowed directly from French in words like *mirage*, *prestige* and *rouge* (though /ǰ/ is also often heard). /ž/ is the only Modern English consonant not fully native to the English inventory, for the /zy/ cluster from which it arose entered English mainly in French and Latin loanwords. (This alien sound also developed in American English in words like *Asia(n)*, *emersion* and *version*, where British English has /š/; /ž/ sometimes also occurs in American English in words like *transients* and phrases like *as yet* and *all these years*.) The uneven distribution in the pattern of Modern English consonants apparent in table 3.1 reflects the historical development of these sounds.

3.3 Morphology
Old English morphology was considerably more complex than that of Middle English and Modern English – similar, if such comparisons are useful, to that of Latin or Russian. As a consequence of the extensive phonological reductions and mergers described in section 3.2 above, extensive syncretism of the Old English distinctive inflections occurred, and the inflectional morphology of Modern English is scanty, with a mere eight inflections surviving. Only pronouns preserve anything resembling the complexity of Old English, while adjectives and the definite article preserve the least. We shall describe the Old English and Modern English pronominal

and adjectival systems, with brief discussions of nouns, verbs and the definite article.

3.3.1   Nouns

Old English had several noun declensions, both strong (from Indo-European vowel stems) and weak (from Indo-European consonant, i.e. -*n*, stems). To each noun was assigned a grammatical gender irrespective of its natural gender (although for human nouns there is a notable fit between grammatical and natural gender). Nouns were inflected generally for four cases in the singular, three in the plural (where the nominative and accusative are identical). Given here are paradigms of the nouns *stān* 'stone', *dēor* 'animal', *lār* 'learning' and *fōt* 'foot'.

	a-*stems*		o-*stems*	athematics
	M.	Nt.	F.	M.
Singular				
Nominative	stān	dēor	lār	fōt
Accusative	stan	dēor	lāre	fōt
Genitive	stānes	dēores	lāre	fōtes
Dative	stāne	dēore	lāre	fēt
Plural				
Nom./Acc.	stānas	dēor	lāra	fēt
Genitive	stāna	dēora	lāra	fōta
Dative	stānum	dēorum	lārum	fōtum

From the *stān* declension come the productive Modern English genitive singular in -*s* and all the productive plurals, while the *fōt* declension has yielded the few nouns (like *foot*, *goose* and *tooth*; *louse* and *mouse*; and *man*) whose plurals, generalised from the nominative and accusative, exploit a functional vowel alternation instead of the common suffix in -*s*. This palatal mutation was caused by earlier assimilation of the stem vowels to suffixes. Modern English relic phrases like 'a ten-foot pole' derive from the Old English genitive plural (translated roughly 'a pole of ten feet'), whose form *fōta* has the reflex *foot*. From the *dēor* declension come Modern English uninflected plurals like *deer* and *sheep*.

There were other noun declensions in Old English with variations according to the phonological characteristics of the stems at various periods in their development (and there was considerable dialectal variation over the centuries of Old English). The only productive forms of the genitive singular and of the plural in Modern English are the much reduced reflexes of the masculine *a*-stems, like which many older nouns have been analogically reformed and all new nouns are inflected. Both the plural and the genitive morphemes have the same three phonologically conditioned allomorphs, which by dissimilation have /-əz/ after stems ending in /s, z, š, ž, č, ǰ/, and by assimilation /-s/ after stems ending in other voiceless consonants and /-z/ after voiced segments. The plural and genitive morphemes exhibit syncretism (as in *boys'*), except when the plural noun is marked by a stem change, as in *women's*, *children's*, *geese's*.

3.3.2 Verbs

Like the other Germanic languages, Old English and its reflexes exhibit two types of verbs, called strong and weak by Jakob Grimm. While weak verbs (characteristically Germanic) exhibit a dental suffix ([d] or [t]) in the preterit tense, strong verbs show an internal vowel change (characteristically Indo-European ablaut). Old English had seven classes of strong verbs, with scattered reflexes surviving today, though starting even in Old English many strong verbs have become weak, while others have been reformed analogically. Many Old English strong verbs have developed regular Modern English forms, with past tense and past participle suffixes in /-t/ or /-d/. Listed here are the principal parts (infinitive, past singular, past plural and past participle) for each Old English verb class.

I.	rīdan 'ride'	rād/ridon	geriden
II.	sēoðan 'boil'	sēað/sudon	gesoden
III.	bindan 'bind'	band/bundon	gebunden
IV.	beran 'bear'	bær/bǣron	geboren
V.	giefan 'give'	geaf/gēafon	gegiefen
VI.	standan 'stand'	stōd/stōdon	gestanden
VII.	feallan 'fall'	fēoll/fēollon	gefeallen

From these principal parts can be formed the two tenses (present and preterit) in the indicative and subjunctive moods. A typical weak verb conjugation is provided here, where it will be apparent that while the present indicative exhibits three singular forms and one plural, the subjunctive contrasts only singular and plural forms. The twelve distinct forms of an Old English weak verb have been reduced to four in Modern English.

		Indicative	*Subjunctive*
Pres. Sg.	1	dēme	
	2	dēmst/dēmest	dēme
	3	dēmþ/dēmeþ	
Pl.		dēmaþ	dēmen
Pret. Sg.	1	dēmde	
	2	dēmdest	dēmde
	3	dēmde	
Pl.		dēmdon	dēmden
Gerund		tō dēmenne/dēmanne	
Pres. Part.		dēmende	
Past Part.		dēmed	

The simplicity of the Old English verbal system is striking; inflectionally, it is a mere shadow of its Indo-European predecessors. By way of contrast, recall that Latin is inflected for active and passive voice, for perfective and imperfective aspects and for present, preterit and future tenses, as well as for several moods. On the other hand, the Old English verb is also a far cry from the considerable periphrastic complexity of its modern counterpart in tense and aspect.

3.3.3 Articles

Though its use is complicated and in large measure pragmatically determined, the Modern English definite article is formally simple, having only the single orthographic shape *the* with two standard phonological variants, [ði] before vowels and [ðə] elsewhere. As shown in the chart, the Old English demonstrative (forerunner of today's definite article) was formally complex, inflected for five cases (including the instrumental) and three genders in the singular, and for three cases in the plural without gender distinctions.

	Singular			*Plural*
	M.	F.	Nt.	M./F./Nt.
Nom.	sē	sēo	þæt	þā
Acc.	þone	þā	þæt	þā
Gen.	þæs	þǣre	þæs	þāra
Dat.	þǣm	þǣre	þǣm	þǣm
Inst.	þȳ	þǣre	þȳ	

The initial consonant of the nominative masculine singular *sē* and feminine singular *sēo* differed from all other forms, which begin with [θ], orthographic þ-. Thus, Modern English *the* has no direct Old English etymon, being reformed analogically from the forms with inital [θ] and influenced by parallel Scandinavian forms introduced in the late eighth and the ninth centuries. By Middle English *þe* had become the invariant definite article in the north, and its use soon spread to all dialects. Chaucer uses only *the*. (Voicing of the initial segment occurred because the customary lack of stress on *the* encouraged assimilation to the vocalic nucleus).

Such a history is somewhat surprising for what is by far the most common word in Modern English: *the* occurs twice as often as *of*, its nearest competitor, and about twice as often as all forms of the verb *be* combined; *the* accounts for almost seven per cent of all tokens in the Brown Corpus. Remarkable also is the history of the indefinite article *a/an*, the fifth most common lemma in the Brown Corpus, which also did not exist as such in Old English. Like Modern English indefinite plurals, Old English indefinites were frequently unmarked, except that *sum* 'a certain' and *ān* 'one' appear sometimes for emphasis and are declined like adjectives.

3.3.4 Adjectives

Like the definite article, Old English adjectives were formally much more complex than those of Modern English. They were inflected to agree with their head noun in gender, number and case in 'strong' and 'weak' declensions. With the highly inflected demonstratives or possessive pronouns, the weak declension occurred (ending in *-an* in the genitive, dative and instrumental singular and the nominative and accusative plural for all genders and the masculine and neuter accusative singular; the remaining forms ending in *-a*, *-e*, *-ra* and *-um*). In all other instances, including predicative usage, Old English required the more varied strong declension. Both strong and weak adjectival paradigms are given here.

Strong Declension

	Singular			*Plural*		
	M.	F.	Nt.	M.	F.	Nt.
Nom.	gōd	gōd	gōd	gōde	gōda	gōd
Acc.	gōdne	gōde	gōd	gōde	gōda	gōd
Gen.	gōdes	gōdre	gōdes	gōdra	gōdra	gōdra
Dat.	gōdum	gōdre	gōdum	gōdum	gōdum	gōdum
Inst.	gōde	gōdre	gōde			

Weak Declension

	Singular			*Plural*
	M.	F.	Nt.	M./F./Nt.
Nom.	gōda	gōde	gōde	gōdan
Acc.	gōdan	gōdan	gōde	gōdan
Gen.	gōdan	gōdan	gōdan	gōdra (-ena)
Dat.	gōdan	gōdan	gōdan	gōdum

Nothing remains of the inflectional system of Old English adjectives, which, except for comparative and superlative forms, occur in Modern English in a single shape, as in *tall*, *old* and *beautiful*. The form is invariant regardless of the number and case of the modified noun, and irrespective of attributive or predicative functions.

3.3.5 Pronouns
Personal Pronouns
The Modern English pronominal paradigm maintains more of its earlier complexity than any other form class. It is given in the chart alongside its Old English counterpart, with which it can be readily compared.

	Old English					Modern English				
	1st	*2nd*	*3rd Person*			*1st*	*2nd*	*3rd Person*		
Singular										
			M.	F.	Nt.					
Nom.	ic	þū	hē	hēo	hit	I	you	he	she	it
Acc.	mē	þē	hine	hīe	hit	me	you	him	her	it
Gen.	mīn	þīn	his	hiere	his	mine	yours	his	hers	its
Dat.	mē	þē	him	hiere	him	me	you	him	her	it

Dual

Nom.	wit	git
Acc.	unc	inc
Gen.	uncer	incer
Dat.	unc	inc

Plural

Nom.	wē	gē	hīe	we	you	they
Acc.	ūs	ēow	hīe	us	you	them
Gen.	ūre	ēower	hiera	ours	yours	theirs
Dat.	ūs	ēow	him	us	you	them

As is apparent, the dual number is altogether missing from Modern English, as are distinct singular and plural forms in the second person. Certain varieties of Modern English have evolved second person plural forms but they are either regionally marked (*y'all* in the American South) or socially stigmatised (*yous* [yuz] or [yɪz] in metropolitan New York City and *y'uns* in Western Pennsylvania and the Ohio Valley).

Relative Pronouns

In Old English, an invariant particle *þe* served to mark relative clauses; it was often compounded with a form of the demonstrative *sē, sēo, þæt*, as in *sē þe* masculine and *sēo þe* feminine 'who'. The forms of *sē* also occur alone as relatives, as in *ānne æðeling sē wæs Cyneheard hāten* 'a prince who was called Cyneheard'. Old English relatives are also sometimes marked by *þe* and an appropriate form of the personal pronoun, as with *him* in:

nis	nū	cwicra	nān	þe	ic	him	modsefan	minne	durre	āsecgan
there isn't	now	alive	no one	REL	I	him	mind	my	dare	speak

'There is no one alive now to whom I dare speak my mind.'

Middle English favoured solitary *that* as a relative pronoun, the Old English indeclinable *þe* surviving only into early Middle English. In the fifteenth century, *which* (from Old English interrogative *hwylc* 'which') appears as a relative, alternating with *that*. Modern English relative *that*, which is thus a functionally adapted reflex of the Old English demonstrative, is the relative with broadest pronominal application, anaphoric for noun phrases in nominative and oblique cases other than the possessive, though its use is now limited to restrictive clauses. The Modern English relatives *who/whom/whose* and *which* derive from Old English interrogative pronouns and can be used with restrictive and nonrestrictive clauses. *Whose* (< ME *whōs* by analogy to *whō* < OE *hwā* and to *whōm* < OE *hwām*) ultimately derives from the Old English interrogative pronoun *hwæs*. *Who, whose* and *whom* are late developments; while Chaucer occasionally used relative *whose* and *whom*, relative *who* did not come into widespread use until the sixteenth century.

3.4 Syntax

Old English is considered a synthetic language; it relies chiefly on inflectional morphology to indicate the grammatical relations among sentence constituents and (to a lesser extent) the semantic roles of noun phrases. Noun phrases exhibit concord in gender, number and case among the demonstrative/definite article, adjective and noun, with gender a grammatical rather than semantic category, and with adjectives declined either strong or weak as described above. Verbs are inflected for person, number and tense (present and preterit) in indicative and subjunctive moods, the subjunctive occurring far more frequently than in Modern English. Passive voice is signalled periphrastically with the verbs *wesan* 'to be' or *weorþan* 'to become' and a past participle; infinitives are also sometimes employed passively, and the verb *hātan* 'be called' is generally used with passive force.

As to its word order, late Old English exhibits patterns similar in many respects to those of Modern English. Both are characterised by a strong preference for SVO, which Modern English exploits in both independent and subordinate clauses, whereas Old English, like Modern German, prefers verb-final subordinate clauses. While SOV patterns occur in almost 30 per cent of Old English sentences, the twelfth century witnessed the development of an almost exclusively SVO pattern (according to J. Smith, as reported in Hawkins 1983). Old English negative sentences introduced by the particle *ne* favour verb-second position, producing a VS order as in the first clause of *ne geseah ic næfre þā burg, ne ic þone sēaþ nāt* 'I have never seen that city, nor do I know the well'. The characteristic negative concord of Old English is also apparent in this example (*ne/næfre* in the first clause; *ne/nāt* in the second, where *nāt* is a contraction of *ne wāt* from *witan* 'to know'). Clauses introduced by *þā* 'then' or *hēr* 'here, in this year' also commonly exhibit verb-second order, as in *þā cwæþ sēo hell tō Satane* 'then hell said to Satan'; *þā andswarode Satanas and cwæð ...* 'then Satan answered and said ...'; *þā gegaderode Ælfred cyning his fierd* 'then King Alfred gathered his army'; *hēr gefeaht Ecgbryht cyning wiþ fīf and þritig sciphlæsta æt Carrum* 'in this year King Ecgbryht fought against thirty-five shiploads at Charmouth'.

Within Old English noun phrases, the order of elements is usually determiner–adjective–noun, as in Modern English: *sē gōda mann* 'the good man'. Genitives usually precede nouns (far more frequently than in Modern English), as in *folces weard* 'people's protector', *mæres līfes man* 'a man of splendid life' and *fōtes trym* 'the space of a foot'. It has been calculated that the percentage of postnominal genitives increased from about 13 per cent in the year 1035 to 85 per cent in 1300 (also by J. Smith, as reported in Hawkins 1983). Though prepositions usually precede nominals, with pronouns they often follow, as in *sē hālga Andreas him tō cwæþ...* 'St Andrew said to him ...'. Adjectives too are almost uniformly prenominal (*sē foresprecena here* 'the aforementioned army'), but modifiers can be postnominal, as in these isolated examples cited by Quirk and Wrenn (1955: 88–9): *wadu weallendu* 'surging waters'; *ēþel þysne* 'this country'; *wine mīn Unferð* 'my friend Unferð'. Relative clauses generally follow their head nouns.

To a greater degree than Modern English, Old English exhibits a preference for parataxis over hypotaxis, for much Old English prose and poetry was written as a series of loosely associated independent clauses, often linked solely by a form of *and*, with the relationships among succeeding clauses left unspecified. While certain genres of informal speech exhibit considerable parataxis in Modern English, writing and most spoken genres exploit a high degree of hypotaxis, with logical relationships among the clauses of a discourse explicitly marked by subordinating conjunctions (*that, as, if, than* and *like* being the most common exemplars). While coordinating conjunctions are nearly twice as frequent as subordinators in the running texts of the Brown Corpus, a good portion are presumably phrasal rather than clausal coordinators.

Denied the richness of its earlier inflectional signposts, Modern English has developed into an analytical language, more like Chinese than Latin and the other early reflexes of Indo-European. With nouns inflected only for possessive case, word order is now the chief signal of grammatical relations, displacing the earlier inflectional morphology to such an extent that even the fuller pronominal inflections are subordinate to the grammatical relations signalled by word order; thus, an utterance like *her kicked he* may be understood as *she kicked him*.

Why English should have advanced farther along the path to analyticity than other Germanic languages is uncertain, though a basis for the explanation is likely to be found in the thoroughgoing contact between the Danes and the English after the ninth century, in French ascendance over English for so many secular and religious purposes in early Middle English, and in the preservation of the vernacular chiefly in folk speech for several generations in the eleventh and twelfth centuries. Decades before the Norman conquest (almost a century earlier in Northumbria), those inflectional reductions started that are everywhere apparent when English reemerges, and they were doubtless more advanced in speech than extant texts indicate. The syncretism spread as word-order patterns became fixed. Thus, phonological reductions undermined the inflectional morphology and, as flexion grew less able to signal grammatical relations and semantic roles, word order and the deployment of prepositions (which had somewhat redundantly borne certain aspects of meaning) came to bear those communicative tasks less redundantly; gradually, the freer word order of Old English yielded to the relatively fixed orders of Modern English, whose linear arrangements are the chief carrier of grammatical relations.

Perhaps spurred by the virtual absence of inflectional differentiation in its nouns, Modern English syntax has evolved to permit unusually free interplay among grammatical relations and semantic roles. With nouns marked only for genitive case, and pronouns additionally for objective case, Modern English exercises minimal inflectional constraint on subject noun phrases, which are consequently free to represent an exceptionally wide range of participant roles. Besides being agents (as in sentence (a)), subjects may be patients (b), instruments (c), benefactives (d), experiencers (e), locatives (f), temporals (g) and so on; dummy subjects, empty of any semantic content, also occur as in (h):

(a) The janitor (agent) opened the door.
(b) The door (patient) opened.
(c) His first record (instrument) expanded his audiences from friends and neighbours to thousands of strangers.
(d) The youngest jockey (benefactive) took the prize.
(e) Serge (experiencer) heard his father whispering.
(f) Chicago (locative) is cold in winter.
(g) The next day (temporal) found us on the road to Alice Springs.
(h) It became clear that the government had jailed him there.

In representing pragmatic structure, Modern English exploits neither morphology (as Japanese *wa* indicates topic) nor simple fronting to mark focus. In both morphology and word order, sentences like *Nobody expected revolution* are neutral with respect to focus. Spoken English exploits sentence stress to signal focus on particular constituents. In writing, where intonation is unavailable and the constraints on syntax imposed by real-time processing of speech are greatly reduced, English has available a range of syntactic processes to carry out pragmatic functions; these include passivisation, clefting and pseudo-clefting. In the archetypal focusing of noun phrases that is apparent in questions, English does front, of course, as in *who(m) did he choose?*, *what did she win?* and *what did they do?* Likewise, in relative clauses the relativised noun phrase is fronted irrespective of its grammatical relation within the clause and its participant role in the semantic structure; in other words, noun phrases of any type can be relativised. In example (i) below, the fronted relativised pronoun *that* is semantically a recipient functioning grammatically as an indirect object; in (j), the relative pronoun is a patient functioning as a direct object.

(i) She's the teacher that I gave the book to.
(j) The president vetoed the bill that his party endorsed.

The remarkable flexibility of English syntax in carrying out pragmatic functions permits an unusual degree of discrepancy between surface form and semantic structure. Thus, the syntactic processes known as subject-to-object raising (illustrated in (k)), subject-to-subject raising (l), and object-to-subject raising (m) all reduce the isomorphism between surface syntactic structure and underlying semantic structure.

(k) The coach wanted her to win the race.
(l) The economy seems to be sluggish.
(m) An incumbent is always tough to beat.

In (k), the underlying subject of the subordinate verb *win* appears as a surface object of the verb *wanted*. In (l), the underlying subject of *to be sluggish* becomes the surface subject of *seems*. In (m), the underlying object of *to beat* serves as the surface subject of the predicate *is ... tough*. As a comparison with the treatments of syntax in the chapters on Russian and German will indicate, the syntactic flexibility of English is not universal in the languages of the world. In its syntax, English is an exceptionally versatile language.

3.5 Orthography

Modern English orthographical practice is more out of harmony with the spoken language than that of many other languages, including Spanish, German and Old English. The spelling practices in vogue today reflect scribal practices from earlier than the introduction of printing into England when William Caxton established his press in Westminster in 1476. Since then the language has evolved phonologically, but the almost static spelling practices have not kept pace despite attempts by prominent reformers like Noah Webster (whose dictionaries popularised many of the characteristic spelling differences between American and British orthography) and George Bernard Shaw (who caustically observed that English permitted *ghoti* to be pronounced /fɪš/, the *gh* as in *cough*, the *o* as in *women*, and the *ti* as in *nation*). No wonder that English spelling holds the distinction of being the most chaotic in the world.

Still, there are advantages to the relative distance between orthography and speech in that written English is remarkably uniform throughout the world, and printed material can be distributed internationally without adaptation. Further, because English morphophonemics exhibits considerable variation in the pronunciation of the same morpheme in different environments, a closer correspondence of written to spoken forms would deprive readers of the immediate association apparent between words like *nation* and *nation+al* (with /e/–/æ/ alternation) and *electric* and *electric+ity* (with /k/–/s/), to cite just one vowel and one consonant alternation.

4   Present-day English and its Variation

4.1   Regional Varieties and the Question of Standards

As described earlier, English is widely diffused from its earlier home in England to nearby Scotland and Ireland, across the Atlantic to Canada and the United States, and across the world to Australia and New Zealand; it is vigorous in parts of Asia and Africa as well. In addition, it is spoken in isolated enclaves like the Falkland Islands, Bermuda and Tristan da Cunha. Various pidgins, creoles and creole-based varieties also exist, including Krio, spoken as a lingua franca throughout Sierra Leone in West Africa, and the American variety known as Black English, which is thought by some to be creole-based.

There are several varieties of standard English throughout the world, in addition to many more non-standard varieties. One widely accepted view is that the standard varieties can be divided roughly into two types, British and (North) American. To the latter belong the varieties spoken by educated speakers in Canada and the United States, while British English comprises the standard varieties spoken principally in England, Ireland, Wales, Scotland, Australia, New Zealand and South Africa. The differences that exist among the standard varieties are largely matters of pronunciation and lexicon, though even the latter are not very apparent in public written discourse. Thus, English is not governed by a uniform standard of speaking around the globe. Throughout England and the other English-speaking nations, there is considerable variation, notable in non-standard varieties but plentiful in the standard varieties as well.

Occasional proposals to establish national academies for English have been consistently rebuffed, and any suggestion of an international academy would almost certainly meet with international ridicule. Both regionally within countries and across national boundaries, enormous variation is tolerated especially in the pronunciation of vowels. Excepting principally the pronunciation of /r/ in words like *barn*, *corn* and *hour*, consonants tend to vary socially rather than regionally, as we shall see below. There is also considerable lexical variation especially in folk speech, and in some places it inspires strong local pride. With the advent of televised speech-making and with press conferences broadcast worldwide, such diversity as might be expected to crop up lexically has all but vanished from the public remarks of national leaders, though the same cannot be said of pronunciation. Grammatically, few differences are to be noted in the public speech of political leaders, and these are minor and generally understood across national boundaries (cf. *Cambridge are* (Br.)/*is* (Am.) *ahead by two points*; *she is in hospital* (Br.)/*in the hospital* (Am.)).

While national and regional standards of pronunciation exist, there is broad tolerance of variation. RP (Received Pronunciation), the variety pronounced on the BBC, is spoken only by an estimated three to five per cent of the people of England, according to Trudgill and Hannah (1982: 2). In the United States, considerable latitude exists in standard pronunciation, although a 'network standard' (essentially inland northern) has dominated broadcasting until hints of regional origin (especially southern) appeared recently in the pronunciation of national news broadcasters. And at least to American ears, the 'accents' of several recent presidents have been notably distinct from one another, Carter speaking a marked southern dialect, Kennedy exhibiting a signal Boston accent, and Ford and Reagan the relatively widespread inland northern variety. Yet one could not have distinguished among their written speeches (rhetorical style and political stance aside).

In contrast to speech, standards of writing are very strong and permit surprisingly little variation in grammar, lexicon and orthography. In the major centres of publishing within America, as in England, no regional variation exists except that Canada follows British precedent in certain matters, American increasingly in others. Further, as many publishing houses maintain offices on both sides of the Atlantic, there exists only slight (and diminishing) international variation in a few familiar spellings such as *check*/*cheque* and *color*/*colour* (the first of each pair popularised in America by Noah Webster) and in certain lesser known matters of punctuation that are transparent to readers around the globe.

English writing is relatively remote from the variation and vagaries of its speechways. As *The New York Times* and *Los Angeles Times*, published 3,000 miles apart, exhibit no regional linguistic differences, so only slight variation arises in the 3,000 miles between the language of, say, *The Economist* of London and *Time* magazine of New York (again ignoring politics and style). Established printing conventions and a lengthy multi-national grammatical and lexicographic tradition combine to mute the variation characteristic of English speechways and keep it from impeding written communication across dialect boundaries, whether intra-national or international.

4.2 Social Variation

Recent inquiry into synchronic alternation within particular communities has shown that much of what had previously been judged free variation is in fact significant. In New York City, for example, the occurrence of post-vocalic /r/ in words like *car*, *bear*, *beard*, and *fourth* had been thought non-significant. No difference in meaning was attributed to pronunciations with and without /r/. Labov (1972) demonstrated, however, that meaning does attach to such variation and marks social groups and social circumstances. The notion of linguistic 'significance' was thus broadened beyond semantics to encompass social meaning about language users and the uses to which they put language in their social interactions.

Investigating the usage of /r/ among four groups of New York City residents of ranked socioeconomic status, Labov observed increasing degrees of /r/-pronunciation by successively higher ranked groups. Thus, Upper Middle Class respondents exhibited more /r/ than Lower Middle Class respondents, who in turn exhibited more than Working Class respondents, and these last used more /r/ than Lower Class respondents. In addition, each group pronounced more /r/ as attention paid to speech was increased in various styles. Through several graded speech styles (casual style, interview style, reading of passages and reading of word lists), respondents in all socioeconomic groups increased the percentage of /r/ pronounced.

Similar patterns were recorded for other sounds: the *th* in words like *thirty*, *through*, *fourth*, which varies between [θ] and [t]; the *th* of words like *this*, *those*, *breathe*, which varies between [ð] and [d] (the infamous 'dis', 'dat', 'dem' and 'dose'); and the vowels in the word sets comprising *soft*, *bought*, *law*, etc. and *bad*, *care*, etc. These sounds all showed systematic variation: standard pronunciations occurred more frequently in groups of higher socioeconomic status and in styles with increased attention paid to speech.

Research carried out by Trudgill (1974) in Norwich, England, revealed similar patterns. In Norwich, variation in both syntactic and phonological expression was shown to be related to social structure – the socioeconomic status of speakers and the circumstances of use. Trudgill divided his subjects into five Groups: Middle Middle Class (MMC), Lower Middle Class (LMC), Upper Working Class (UWC), Middle Working Class (MWC), and Lower Working Class (LWC). As in New York, the greatest linguistic boundary in Norwich occurs between the Middle and Working Classes (i.e. between LMC and UWC). In table 3.2 are the figures for alternation between final [n] and [ŋ] in the suffix *-ing* for New York City and Norwich residents. For both socioeconomic status and speaking style, the patterns of distribution are strikingly parallel in the two cities.

Table 3.2: Per cent of Pronunciation of *-ing* Suffix as /in/ for Three Styles and Several Socioeconomic Status Groups in Norwich and New York City

	Norwich			New York City		
	A	B	C	A	B	C
I	28	3	0	5	4	0
II	42	15	10	32	21	1
III	87	74	15	49	31	11
IV	95	88	44	80	53	22
V	100	98	66			

Note: A= Casual Speech; B=Careful or Formal Speech; C=Reading Style. Roman numerals refer to socioeconomic groups: Norwich: I=MMC; II=LMC; III=UWC; IV=MWC; V=LWC; New York City: I=UMC; II=LMC; III=WC; IV=LC. Source: Labov 1972 : 239; Trudgill 1974:92

On the basis of evidence from these and other studies, parallel patterns of distribution may be expected for phonological variables wherever similar social structures are found. It is likely that comparable morphological and syntactic variation also exists, though evidence to date is scanty. Further, what holds true of variation in English may characterise other speech communities as well.

4.3   Variation across Modes: Writing and Speaking

Considerable attention has been focused recently on identifying similarities and differences between written and spoken English. In efforts to uncover what influence mode itself may exercise in the deployment of linguistic features, researchers have investigated, for example, whether speech or writing is more complex in sentence structure. Exploring other possible dimensions of comparison, attempts have been made to determine which mode is more nominal, which more verbal; how reliance on context differs and how pragmatic focus is signalled differently; in what ways the syntactic constraints imposed by the exigencies of real-time speech processing are altered in writing, creating degrees of integration of expression; how coherence is established in each mode; and so on. Findings based on a single dimension differ depending on choice of measures and selection of texts. Perplexingly, conclusions have been contradictory.

The use of computerised corpora and certain statistical techniques has demonstrated that the differences between speech and writing cannot be adequately characterised using any single dimension such as 'complexity' or 'reliance on context' or 'integration vs. fragmentation'. Biber (1988) shows that a multi-dimensional construct is needed to account for the distribution of textual features that have been explored as markers of mode. He characterises three of the needed textual dimensions as 'Interactive vs. Edited Text', 'Abstract vs. Situated Content' and 'Reported vs. Immediate Style'. Each dimension is defined by a set of empirically identified cooccurring lexical and syntactic features that function to characterise similarities among texts in a fashion suggested by the name of the dimension.

Along the dimension called 'Abstract vs. Situated Content', for example, a text is placed relative to other texts by the degree to which it exploits the features defining this dimension: nominalisations, prepositions, passives and *it*-clefts, as opposed to place and time adverbs, relative pronoun deletion and subordinator *that* deletion. The same text is independently situated along the 'Interactive vs. Edited' dimension by the degree to which it exploits a different set of defining features: *wh*- and other questions, *that* and *if*-clauses, final prepositions, contractions, the pronouns *I*, *you* and *it*, general emphatics (*just*, *really*, *so* + adjective), a low type/token ratio and shorter words. A third dimension representing 'Reported vs. Immediate Style' characterises measures of past tense markers, third person pronouns, perfect aspect and an absence of adjectives.

The resulting model can be perceived as a multi-dimensional space throughout which texts are distributed according to their exploitation of the feature sets characterising each dimension. From the above, it may be apparent that texts cannot be differentiated along a single dimension of 'complexity' (to take one commonly discussed construct) because the cluster of linguistic features representing complexity do not in fact cooccur significantly in the same texts. Nominalisations and passives, for example, differentiate texts according to their content (as abstract vs. situated), while *that*-clauses, *if*-clauses, relative clauses and other subordinate clauses differentiate texts by degrees of interaction and planning (or 'editing') – irrespective of differentiation with respect to content. Thus, 'complexity' does not comprise a set of textual features with a unified function and hence cannot serve as a linear gauge for comparing texts.

4.4   Register Variation

The computerised corpora used in the analysis of spoken and written English have also proved fruitful in the analysis of register, or situational, variation. Characteristics of various genres in the Standard Corpus of Present-Day Edited American English will be discussed here, although these findings are indicative of other possibilities for analysing styles of individual authors, historical periods and so on. Counts of textual features and inferences about structure that can be drawn from them promise enhanced understanding of textual variation of every kind.

The fifteen genres of the Brown Corpus can be grouped into informational (INFO) and imaginative (IMAG) prose. From an analysis of the distribution of form classes across these subdivisions, Francis and Kučera (1982) document that function words are the least contextualised word classes; that is, articles, coordinating conjunctions, infinitival *to*, determiners (*this*, *some*) and prepositions are the most evenly distributed classes across all genres of prose. Least evenly distributed, on the other hand, are nominative

Table 3.3: Normalised Ratio Values for Some Word Classes

Numerals	2.23
Adjectives	1.43
Common nouns	1.36
Prepositions	1.29
Subordinating conjunctions	1.06
The verb *BE*	1.03
Coordinating conjunctions	0.99
Modal verbs	0.88
All verbs	0.78
Main verbs	0.75
Adverbs	0.64
The verb *HAVE*	0.60
The word *not*	0.52
The verb *DO*	0.43
Pronouns	0.40
Interjections	0.11

and objective personal pronouns, adverbs/particles and past tense in main verbs.

To compare relative distributions, Francis and Kučera (1982) developed a normalised ratio value (NR). An NR of 1.00 for a particular word class would indicate a proportionate distribution of exemplars in INFO and IMAG genres. Values higher than 1.00 indicate proportionately greater representation in INFO, values less than 1.00 a higher proportion in IMAG prose. NR values for several word classes are presented in table 3.3. From these figures it is apparent that certain word classes are about evenly distributed across INFO and IMAG genres; witness coordinating and subordinating conjunctions, with scores close to 1.00. At the extremes of distribution, not surprisingly, are interjections (NR = 0.11), which occur almost exclusively in IMAG, while numerals (NR = 2.23) occur lopsidedly in INFO.

With nouns, prepositions and adjectives all exceeding the norm of 1.00 by more than 20 per cent, INFO is markedly more nominal than IMAG, while IMAG prose, with verbs and adverbs falling more than 20 per cent below the norm, is markedly more verbal in its character. The distribution of pronouns represented by a score of 0.40 suggests that pronominal anaphora provides a major signal of textual cohesion in imaginative prose, as Francis and Kučera (1982) point out.

Over the past several decades, sentence length has been a frequent object of study not least because of the assumption that it indexes structural complexity and therefore comprehensibility. All the INFO genres in the Brown Corpus exhibit mean sentence-lengths greater than the corpus mean of 18.4 words, while all the IMAG genres exhibit sentence-lengths less than the corpus mean. This pattern was initially interpreted as demonstrating that INFO genres were characterised by sentences of greater complexity than IMAG genres. Since those initial calculations were made, however, every token in the corpus has been given an identifying grammatical tag. This enables more valid estimates of complexity based on the number of predications per sentence and of words per predication. As it happens, the corpus averages 2.64 predications per sentence. The nine INFO genres range from 2.59 to 2.93, with the three genres of Press-Reportage, Press-Reviews and Skills/Hobbies falling slightly below the corpus mean. The IMAG genres, on the other hand, range from 2.23 predications per sentence for Science Fiction to 2.82 for Humour, which thus ranks well above the corpus mean. Thus, informational prose genres are not structurally more

Table 3.4

	INFO	IMAG	CORPUS
Words per sentence	21.06	13.38	18.40
Predications per sentence	2.78	2.38	2.64
Words per predication	7.57	5.62	6.96

complex than imaginative prose but deploy more words per predication. In fact, all INFO genres exhibit more words per predication than the corpus mean of 6.96, while all genres of IMAG prose rank below the corpus mean. The data in table 3.4 from Francis and Kučera (1982) summarise these findings.

Francis and Kučera present frequency figures for all 87 tags and an additional 92 combinations of tags for all 15 genres. Exploration of other patterns of variation is possible with large-scale corpora and with tagging procedures and other algorithms for identifying membership in grammatical and lexical categories. The possibilities that such approaches suggest for studying stylistic variation of many kinds are only beginning to be recognised. The findings that are emerging from corpora-based studies also present challenges to theorists – for example, to explain the relationship between the psychological, or processing, functions of textual features on the one hand and the social value that attaches to such functionally conditioned distributions on the other. As the notion of 'significance' was earlier broadened beyond semantics to encompass social meaning, a still further extension may be useful in understanding the regularity of distributions emerging from corpora-based studies of English.

Bibliography

The standard grammar for the modern language is Quirk et al. (1985); Huddleston (1984) is another excellent source, more directed towards problems of linguistic analysis.

Jespersen (1938) is a classic history of English. Pyles and Algeo (1982) is a well balanced treatment of both internal and external history, accompanied by a superb workbook, while Baugh and Cable (1978) is excellent for the external history of the language. For vocabulary, Serjeantson (1935) may be consulted in addition. Grammars of Old English include Quirk and Wrenn (1955), strong on phonology and morphology, and Mitchell and Robinson (1986), strong on syntax, while Mossé (1952) is the standard work for Middle English.

Detailed sociolinguistic studies of English are available in Labov (1972) and Trudgill (1974). Greenbaum (1985) is a collection of essays by more than thirty scholars on the 'state' of the language. Mencken (1963) deals with the development of American English, while Ferguson and Heath (1981) is a collection of 23 essays with an essentially ethnographic and sociolinguistic approach to the former and current languages in the USA (not only English); Trudgill (1984) is a companion volume, similar in scope, for the British Isles. Changing attitudes towards standard English are discussed by Finegan (1980), and Trudgill and Hannah (1982) deal with cross-national variation within standard English, especially British versus American.

Among works concerned with computerised corpora and their use in stylistic research, important references are Kučera and Francis (1967), Francis and Kučera (1982), Johansson (1982) and Biber (1988).

Acknowledgement

I am indebted to John Algeo, Niko Besnier and Douglas Biber for useful comments on an earlier draft of this chapter.

References

Baugh, A. C. and T. Cable. 1978. *A History of the English Language*, 3rd ed. (Prentice-Hall, Englewood Cliffs, N.J.)

Biber, D. 1988. *Variation across Speech and Writing* (Cambridge University Press, Cambridge)

Bynon, T. 1977. *Historical Linguistics* (Cambridge University Press, Cambridge)

Ferguson, C. A. and S. B. Heath. 1981. *Language in the USA* (Cambridge University Press, Cambridge)

Finegan, E. 1980. *Attitudes Toward English Usage: The History of a War of Words* (Teachers College Press, Columbia University, New York)

Francis, W. N. and H. Kučera. 1982. *Frequency Analysis of English Usage: Lexicon and Grammar* (Houghton Mifflin, Boston)

Greenbaum, S. (ed.) 1985. *The English Language Today* (Pergamon Institute of English, Oxford)

Hawkins, J. A. 1983. *Word Order Universals* (Academic Press, New York)

Huddleston, R. 1984. *Introduction to the Grammar of English* (Cambridge University Press, Cambridge)

Jespersen, O. 1938. *Growth and Structure of the English Language*, 9th ed. (Basil Blackwell, Oxford)

Johansson, S. (ed.) 1982. *Computer Corpora in English Language Research* (Norwegian Computing Centre for the Humanities, Bergen)

Kučera, H. 1982. 'The Mathematics of Language', in *The American Heritage Dictionary*, 2nd college ed. (Houghton Mifflin, Boston), pp. 37-41

—— and W. N. Francis. 1967. *Computational Analysis of Present-Day American English* (Brown University Press, Providence, R.I.)

Kurath, H. 1964. *A Phonology and Prosody of Modern English* (University of Michigan Press, Ann Arbor)

Labov, W. 1972. *Sociolinguistic Patterns* (University of Pennsylvania Press, Philadelphia)

Mencken, H. L. 1963. *The American Language: An Inquiry into the Development of English in the United States*, 4th ed. and two supplements, abridged, with annotations and new material by Raven I. McDavid, Jr. (Alfred A. Knopf, New York)

Mitchell, B. and F.C. Robinson. 1986. *A Guide to Old English*, 4th ed. (Basil Blackwell, Oxford)

Mossé, F. 1952. *A Handbook of Middle English*, translated by J. A. Walker (The Johns Hopkins Press, Baltimore)

—— 1959. *Manuel de l'anglais du moyen âge des origines au XIVe siècle* (Aubier Montaigne, Paris)

Pyles, T. and J. Algeo. 1982. *The Origins and Development of the English Language*, 3rd ed. (Harcourt Brace Jovanovich, New York)

Quirk, R. and C. L. Wrenn. 1955. *An Old English Grammar* (Methuen, London and Holt, Rinehart and Winston, New York)

—— S. Greenbaum, G. Leech and J. Svartvik. 1985. *A Comprehensive Grammar of the English Language* (Longman, London)

Serjeantson, M. S. 1935. *A History of Foreign Words in English* (reprinted Routledge and Kegan Paul, London, 1961)

Trudgill, P. 1974. *The Social Differentiation of English in Norwich* (Cambridge University Press, Cambridge)

—— (ed.) 1984. *Language in the British Isles* (Cambridge University Press, Cambridge)

—— and J. Hannah. 1982. *International English: A Guide to Varieties of Standard English* (Edward Arnold, London)

Wrenn, C. L. 1959. *The English Language* (Methuen, London)

4 German

John A. Hawkins

1 Historical Background

German, together with English, Dutch and Frisian, is a member of the West Germanic group within the Germanic branch of Indo-European. It is currently used by over 94 million speakers within Europe, and has official national language status (either alone or in conjunction with other languages) in the following countries: the Federal Republic of Germany (61.3 million users); the German Democratic Republic (16.8 million); Austria (7.5 million); Switzerland (4.2 million); Luxembourg (330,000 users of the Letzebuergesch dialect); Liechtenstein (15,000); and also Namibia (formerly German South West Africa; at least 25,000). Bordering on the official German-language areas there are some sizable German-speaking minorities in Western Europe: Alsace-Lorraine (1.5 million users); South Tirol (200,000); and Belgium (150,000). There are also an estimated two million people in Eastern Europe with German as their mother tongue: the Soviet Union (1.2 million); Rumania (400,000); Hungary (250,000); Czechoslovakia (100,000); Poland (20,000); and Yugoslavia (20,000).

Outside Europe, German is an ethnic minority language in numerous countries to which Germans have emigrated. The extent to which German is still used by these groups varies, and in all cases there is gradual assimilation to the host language from one generation to the next. Nonetheless, an estimated minimum of nine million people currently consider German their mother tongue in countries such as the following: USA (6.1 million according to the 1970 census); Brazil (1.5 million); Canada (561,000); Argentina (400,000); Australia (135,000); South Africa (50,000); Chile (35,000); and Mexico (17,000). As many as four million of the German speakers outside the official German-speaking countries speak Yiddish, or Judaeo-German, which has undergone strong lexical influence from Hebrew and Slavonic.

The current political borders of the German-speaking countries of Europe are shown in map 4.1. Map 4.2 gives an indication of the major regional dialects. There are three main groupings of these dialects: Low

German in the north (comprising North Lower Saxon, Westphalian etc.);
Central German (comprising Middle Franconian, Rhine Franconian,
Thuringian etc.); and Upper German in the south (comprising Swabian,
Alemannic etc.). The major basis for the threefold division involves the

Map 4.1: The German-speaking Countries

Map 4.2: Dialects and Dialect Groups (adapted from Clyne 1984)

– – –	Border between the Federal Republic of Germany and the German Democratic Republic
–·–·–	Boundary between Low German and Central German dialects
········	Boundary between Central German and Upper German dialects

extent to which the Second Sound Shift of the Old High German period was carried out (cf. below for discussion of the historical periods of German). It changed voiceless stops p, t, k to voiceless fricatives f, s, x ([ç] or [x]) and affricates pf, ts, kx; and voiced stops b, d, g to voiceless stops p, t, k. The Low German dialects (as well as Dutch, Frisian and English) were unaffected by these changes. The Central German dialects carried them out in varying degrees, and Upper German carried them out (almost) completely. The following pairs of words provide examples:

Low German *p*ad, Upper German *Pf*ad (English *p*ath)
Low German ski*p*, Upper German Schi*ff* (English shi*p*)
Low German hei*t*, Upper German heis*s* (English ho*t*)
Low German i*k*, Upper German i*ch* (English I)
Low German bö*k*, Upper German Bu*ch* (English boo*k*)
Low German, Central German *K*uh, Swiss German *Ch*ue (English *c*ow)
Low German *b*äk, Upper German (Bavarian) *P*ach (English *b*rook)
Low German *d*ör, Upper German *T*ür (English *d*oor)
Low German *g*enuch, Upper German (Bavarian) *k*enug (English enough)

The increasing realisation of these changes within the Central German dialects is illustrated for some representative words involving the p, t, k shifts in map 4.3. The gradual conversion of these voiceless stops to the corresponding fricatives or affricates follows the progression shown below, and hence there are dialects of German whose pronunciation of these words corresponds to each of the lines, with Low German shifting at most *ik* to *ich* and Upper German completing all the shifts:

'I'	'make'	'village'	'that'	'apple'	'pound'	
ik	maken	dorp	dat	appel	pund	Low German
ich	maken	dorp	dat	appel	pund	
ich	machen	dorp	dat	appel	pund	
ich	machen	dorf	dat	appel	pund	Central German
ich	machen	dorf	das	appel	pund	
ich	machen	dorf	das	apfel	pund	
ich	machen	dorf	das	apfel	pfund	Upper German

The term High German is used to subsume Central and Upper German (both of which underwent the Second Sound Shift to some extent at least) as opposed to Low German.

There are also numerous other linguistic features which now distinguish the dialects of map 4.2 (see the references listed in the bibliography for discussion of these). In addition to these regional dialects many scholars now

Map 4.3: Isoglosses Resulting from the Second Sound Shift (Map adapted from T. Bynon. *Historical Linguistics*, Cambridge University Press, Cambridge (1977))

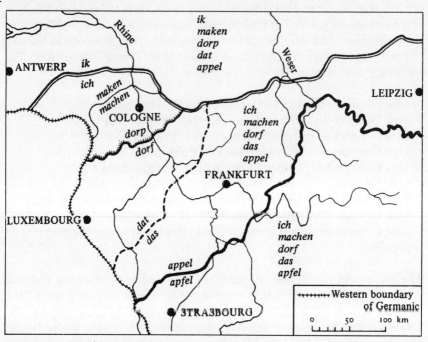

distinguish four national varieties of German, corresponding to the four major political areas in which German is spoken (the Federal Republic, the German Democratic Republic, Austria and Switzerland) on account of various supra-regional and supra-dialectal norms that are accepted as standard in each. The standard languages of the two Germanies, however, differ but little from one another and are both founded on a pre-1945 standard.

This standard emerged much later than the corresponding standard languages of England and France, on account of the political and cultural fragmentation of the German-speaking regions of Europe. There was no centre comparable to London or Paris that could impose its variety as the dominant one, so each region employed its own form of German at least until the sixteenth century. Prior to this point there had been a supra-regional 'compromise language' in the south (*das gemeyne Deutsch*), while in the north Low German enjoyed a privileged status until the seventeenth century as the commercial language of the Hanseatic League and was even used as a lingua franca throughout northern Europe. The basis for the emerging standard language in the fifteenth and early sixteenth centuries, however, was East Central German (see map 4.2). This variety of German was itself a compromise that had arisen as a result of the contact between speakers of numerous dialects following the extensive migration of Germans in the Middle Ages, as they occupied hitherto Slavonic-speaking areas. East Central German was therefore intrinsically well suited to becoming a standard language, and its subsequent acceptance by the remainder of the German-speaking population can be attributed to numerous external factors: the invention of the printing press (1450), which made possible publication on a large scale, the most influential printed work being Luther's translation of the Bible written in East Central German (1522–34) and deliberately intended to be accessible to all German speakers; the use of German instead of Latin for legal records (c. 1400), and the influential and normative role of East Central German legal writing in particular; and the rise of the cities, which attracted people from various regions and increased trade and commerce, making the need for a common language all the more urgent.

The emerging standard gradually permeated both the northern Low German-speaking regions and the south, and during the seventeenth and eighteenth centuries slowly penetrated into Austria and Switzerland as well. However, it was only in the nineteenth century that the phonological norms were finally set. By this time Prussia had become the dominant political force in all the German-speaking areas of Europe except for Switzerland and the Austro-Hungarian Empire, first through a customs union (the *Zollverein*), and then in 1871 through political unification. But prior to its expansion Prussia was originally a northern Low German-speaking state, whose speakers had learnt High German as a second language. With the spread of the emerging High German standard to the north, northern speakers tended to accentuate a close relationship between phonemes and graphemes. And with minor modifications this North German pronunciation of the originally High German standard became the norm for standard German pronunciation or *Bühnendeutsch* (stage German), both in Germany proper, and later in Austria and Switzerland as a result of an agreement concluded between the three countries in 1899. Today, television and radio announcers in Munich, Stuttgart and Baden-Baden sound much the same as their North German counterparts. Despite the 1899 agreement, however, the same does not hold true for Austrian and Swiss announcers. But as far as the written language is concerned, there is now a widespread consensus among the German-speaking countries.

The historical evolution of High German is divided into the following stages: Old High German (OHG), covering the runic inscriptions from the sixth century AD and written texts from the eighth century to 1050; Middle High German (MHG) from 1050 to 1350; Early New High German (ENHG) from 1350 to 1650; and thereafter New High German (NHG) proper.

The Old High German texts are primarily religious writings and translations (from Latin) produced in the monasteries of Central and Upper Germany. Some of the main linguistic changes that separate Old High German from Proto-Germanic are: the Second Sound Shift; numerous vocalic sound changes, including the monophthongisation (in certain environments) of Gmc. *ai* > *ē* and *au* > *ō*, the diphthongisation of Gmc. closed *ē* > *ea* or *ia* and *ō* > *oa*, *ua* or *uo* (depending on the dialect) and the beginnings of *i*-umlaut revealed orthographically in the conversion of *a* > *e* before *i*, *ī*, *j*; the development of a definite article out of a demonstrative determiner; and the emergence of new periphrastic verbal constructions for the passive, future, perfect and pluperfect. In late Old High German some morphological syncretism sets in, anticipating Middle High German, but otherwise Old High German contains a very richly differentiated morphology for nouns, adjectives, determiners, pronouns and verbs.

Middle High German is the language of the great German poets of the late Middle Ages (Walther von der Vogelweide, Wolfram von Eschenbach, Gottfried von Strasburg etc.). The two most characteristic phonological differences between Old High German and Middle High German are: the weakening and partial loss of vowels in unstressed syllables; and the spread of *i*-umlaut (or at least of its graphic representation). Both short vowels *a*, *e*, *i*, *o*, *u* and long vowels *ā*, *ē*, *ī*, *ō*, *ū* could be reduced to schwa [ə] (orthographic *e*) or lost altogether: compare OHG *wola* 'well' (adv.), *aro* 'eagle', *beran* 'to bear', *salida* 'bliss' with the corresponding MHG *wol(e)*, *ar(e)*, *hërn*, *sælde*. The *i*-umlauting is responsible for the front rounded vowels of Modern German (see section 2) which became phonemic with the reduction of the *i*-umlaut environment that had triggered their presumably allophonic variation hitherto (e.g. OHG *mūsi* > *MHG miuse* [müːsə]). The reduction of unstressed syllables is also responsible for widespread syncretism in morphological paradigms as hitherto distinct vowels became reduced to [ə]. Otherwise the morphological paradigms of Middle High German remain much as they were in Old High German, and retain the lexical members and forms characteristic of the latter. Increasingly, however, the phonologically induced syncretism led to uncertainty as more and more words adopted morphological forms that originally belonged to other paradigms. These analogical formations eventually led to widespread restructuring in the morphology, but only in the Early New High German period. Among syntactic changes in Middle High German the replacement of the Old High German negative morpheme *ne* 'not' by *nicht* (etymologically 'no thing') is one of the more striking, as is the further expansion in the uses of the definite article. And in the area of the lexicon, the strong influence of French courtly society is reflected in numerous loanwords. Some of these were not to survive (e.g. *garzūn* 'page' and *tjost* 'joust') but many have, e.g. *Abenteuer* 'adventure', *fein* 'fine', *Lanze* 'lance', *Melodie* 'melody', *Tanz* 'dance', *Tournier* 'tournament'.

The Early New High German period saw numerous important changes throughout the grammar. In the phonology, short open syllables, for example, underwent either vowel or consonant lengthening (e.g. MHG [ligən] > NHG [liːgən], [hamər] > [hammər]); MHG [ə] was lost altogether in numerous environments (in some dialects much more than others) e.g. *legete* > *legte* 'laid'; the Middle High German diphthongs *ie*, *üe*, *uo* became long monophthongs *i:*, *ü:*, *u:* (in Central but not Upper German, which retains the diphthongs), MHG *biegen* > [biːgən] 'bend', *küene* > *kühn* 'bold', *ruofen* > *rufen* 'call'; the Middle High German long closed vowels *i:*, *ü:*, *u:* were correspondingly diphthongised to *ei*, *öu* (*eu*), *ou* (again subject to dialectal differentiation), MHG *zīt* > *Zeit*, [lütə] > *Leute*, *hūs* > *Haus*. There were profound restructurings in the morphology. For example, new plural paradigms for nouns evolved and expanded to compensate for the vowel reductions in unstressed syllables, particularly umlauted plurals: compare MHG *vogel/vogele* 'bird/birds' with NHG *Vogel/Vögel*. This process went even further in certain dialects with the result that one still hears today *Täg*, *Ärm*, *Hünd* in lieu of the standard *Tage* 'days', *Arme* 'arms' and *Hunde* 'dogs', while certain earlier distinct dialectal variants such as *Worte/Wörter* 'words' have both become standard German, though with slightly different meanings (words within a continuous text as opposed to individual words). Another plural suffix that was greatly expanded is *-er*, as in *Kind/Kinder* 'child/children', and also the *-en* suffix. The verb morphology also underwent some reductions, including a certain levelling of alternations in strong verbs (see section 3) and also a levelling of the Middle High German consonantal alternation between *ich was* 'I was' and *wir wāren* 'we were'. In the syntax, Early New High German was the period in which the characteristic verb position of Modern German was fixed: final position in subordinate clauses, second and first position in main clauses (see section 4). This had been the basic tendency in earlier periods as well, but there had been much more variation, especially in Middle High German, during which there were numerous postposings of constituents to the right of the verb in hitherto verb-final structures. Prenominal participial relative clause constructions are first attested in this period: *die von dem Bauer geschlachtete Kuh* 'the by the farmer killed cow', i.e. 'the cow which was killed by the farmer'. Certain postposed adjectives and possessive determiners (*den vater almechtigen* 'the father almighty') were replaced by prenominal orders. And there were widespread changes involving subordinate conjunctions: certain conjunctions died out (*wande*, *wan* 'because'); new ones emerged (e.g. *während* 'while', *falls* 'in the event that'); and the use of *daß* 'that' alone was frequently replaced by more semantically specific and precise forms such as *so daß* 'with the result that', *damit* 'in order that', *weil* 'because', etc.

With the completion of the Early New High German period (1650) we reach what is essentially Modern German. The precise phonological norms of the standard were still to be set (see above), but morphology and syntax

Table 4.1: The Lord's Prayer

Old High German	Modern German	English
East Franconian, Tatian, c. 830		Authorised Version, 1611
Fater unser thu thar bist in himile, si giheilagot thin namo, queme thin rihhi, si thin uuillo, so her in himile ist so si her in erdu; unsar brot tagalihhaz gib uns hiutu, inti furlaz uns unsara sculdi, so uuir furlazemes unsaren sculdigon; inti ni gileitest unsih in costunga, uzouh arlosi unsih fon ubile.	Vater unser, du bist da im Himmel. Geheiligt werde Dein Name. Dein Reich komme. Dein Wille geschehe, wie er im Himmel geschieht, so geschehe er auf Erden. Unser tägliches Brot gib uns heute. Und vergib uns unsere Sünden, wie wir unseren Schuldigern vergeben. Und du mögest uns nicht in Versuchung führen, sondern erlöse uns von Bösem.	Our father which art in heauen hallowed be thy name. Thy kyngdome come. Thy will be done in earth, as it is in heauen, Giue vs this day our daily bread. And forgiue vs our debts, As we forgiue our debtors. And lead vs not into temptation, but deliuer vs from euill.

now undergo only minor modifications compared with the changes that have been outlined. It is instructive to get a sense of the extent of some of these changes by comparing a short text in Old High German with its Modern German translation. The text is the Lord's Prayer, see table 4.1, as it appeared in the East Franconian Tatian of c. 830. Alongside it is a New High German translation and also the English of the Authorised Version of 1611.

2 Phonology

The segmental phonemes of Modern Standard German (consonants and vowels) are set out in table 4.4. Twenty-one consonant phonemes are normally distinguished. Each of these is illustrated in the minimal pairs of table 4.2, in word-initial, word-medial and word-final position. The blanks in the table indicate that the consonant in question does not occur in the relevant position in a word.

Table 4.2: Minimal Pairs for German Consonant Phonemes

/p/	/pasə/	passe	/raupən/	Raupen	/riːp/	rieb
/b/	/bas/	Baß	/raubən/	rauben		
/t/	/tasə/	Tasse	/baːtən/	baten	/riːt/	riet
/d/	/das/	das	/baːdən/	baden		
/k/	/kasə/	Kasse	/haːkən/	Haken	/ziːk/	Sieg
/g/	/gasə/	Gasse	/haːgən/	Hagen		
/f/	/fasə/	fasse	/höːfə/	Höfe	/raif/	reif
/v/	/vas/	was	/löːvə/	Löwe		
/s/	/sateŋ/	Satin	/raisən/	reißen	/rais/	Reis
/z/	/zats/	Satz	/raizən/	reisen		
/š/	/šats/	Schatz	/raušən/	rauschen	/rauš/	Rausch
/ž/	/žeːniː/	Genie	/raːžə/	Rage		
/ç/	/çiːna/	China	/raiçən/	reichen	/raiç/	reich
/x/			/rauxən/	rauchen	/raux/	Rauch
/h/	/hasə/	hasse				
/m/	/masə/	Masse	/hemən/	hemmen	/ram/	Ramm
/n/	/nasə/	nasse	/henən/	Hennen	/ran/	rann
/ŋ/			/heŋən/	hängen	/raŋ/	rang
/l/	/lasə/	lasse	/koːlə/	Kohle	/vil/	will
/r/	/rasə/	Rasse	/boːrə/	bohre	/vir/	wirr
/j/	/jakə/	Jacke	/koːjə/	Koje		

One of the most striking things about the minimal pairs in table 4.2 is the absence of any voiced obstruents (stops and fricatives) in word-final position, i.e. /b d g v z ž/. This is no accident. Voiced obstruents are regularly converted to their voiceless counterparts in syllable-final position, i.e. before a syllable break. Such syllable breaks occur in three types of positions: at the end of a word, e.g. /liːp/ *lieb* 'dear'; at the end of part of a compound word, e.g. /liːp+oigəln/ *liebäugeln* 'to make eyes at'; and before suffixes beginning with a consonant, e.g. /liːp+liŋ/ *Liebling* 'darling'. By contrast, the voiced /b/ occurs in syllable-initial position in forms such as /liː+bən/ *lieben* 'to love' and /liː+bər/ *lieber* 'rather', and so does not get devoiced. Devoicing also takes place in consonant clusters before /t/ and /s/: /liːpt/ *liebt* 'loves', /liːpst/ *liebst* 'lovest'. Notice that the orthography retains the voiced stop in these examples, thereby representing the morphological relatedness between the different forms of the same stem.

The status of /ç/ and /x/ in German is a matter of some dispute. The velar fricative /x/ occurs only after central and back vowels, and never in initial position. The palatal /ç/ occurs after front vowels, after the consonants /n l r/, and in word-initial position. This looks like a classic case of complementary distribution which should lead us to analyse these fricatives as allophones of the same phoneme. But there is an exception. The German diminutive suffix spelled -*chen* occurs as /çən/ in all positions, even after central and back vowels, and hence /ç/ sometimes stands in contrast with /x/: /tauçən/ *Tauchen* ('little rope') versus /tauxən/ *tauchen* ('to dive'); /kuːçən/ *Kuhchen* ('little cow') versus /kuːxən/ *Kuchen* ('cake').

Another problem involves the status of the affricates [pf] and [ts], created by the Second Sound Shift. Are these unit phonemes or clusters of two phonemes? They are historically derived from unit phonemes and minimal pairs are readily found which suggest that they retain this status. Nonetheless, German (like English) has numerous other clusters of stop plus fricative, and there seems to be no clear basis for distinguishing [pf] and [ts] from these: e.g. /ps/ in /gips/ *Gips* 'plaster', /pš/ in /hüpš/ *hübsch* 'pretty', /tš/ in /doitš/ *deutsch* 'German' and /ks/ in /zeks/ *sechs* 'six'.

The phoneme /r/ has a complicated set of allophones and is subject to a certain variation in pronunciation among speakers. When /r/ is followed by a vowel, as in /roːt leːrə besərə/ *rot* 'red', *leere* '(I) empty', *bessere* 'better (pl.)' (i.e. whether or not it is also preceded by a vowel), most speakers pronounce it as a uvular trill or fricative (phonetic symbol [ʀ]), although some use an apico-alveolar trill or flap (phonetic symbol [ř]). When /r/ is not followed by a vowel, its pronunciation varies depending on whether the vowel which does precede it is long, short or /ə/. After a long vowel, /r/ is always a non-syllabic [ᴧ], much like the /ʌ/ of English *but*. The word *leer* /leːr/ 'empty' is phonetically [leᴧ]. After unstressed /ə/, the /r/ and /ə/ combine to give syllabic [ʌ]. The word *besser* /besər/ 'better' is phonetically [besʌ]. After a short vowel, /r/ may either be a non-syllabic [ᴧ] again or else it may be pronounced as a uvular trill or fricative or as an apico-alveolar trill or fricative, like an /r/ which precedes a vowel. There are therefore three possible pronunciations for a word like *irrt* /irt/ 'errs': [iᴧt] [iʀt] and [iřt].

There are 19 separate vowel phonemes of German (including three diphthongs), exemplified in the minimal pairs of table 4.3. The vowels written with umlauts /ü: ü ö: ö/ are front rounded vowels resulting from *i*-

Table 4.3: Minimal Pairs for German Vowel Phonemes

/iː/	bieten	Stiele	ihn	ihre
/i/	bitten	Stille	in	irre
/üː/	Güte	fühle	kühn	führe
/ü/	Mütter	fülle	dünn	Dürre
/uː/	Rute	Buhle	Ruhm	Fuhre
/u/	Kutte	Bulle	Rum	murre
/eː/	beten	stehle	wen	zehre
/e/	Betten	Stelle	wenn	zerre
/öː/	Goethe	Höhle	tönt	höre
/ö/	Götter	Hölle	könnt	dörre
/oː/	rote	Sohle	Sohn	bohre
/o/	Rotte	solle	Bonn	Lorre
/ɛː/	bäte	stähle	wähne	währe
/ə/	gesagt	bitte	wartete	bessere
/aː/	rate	fahle	Bahn	Haare
/a/	Ratte	falle	Bann	harre
/ai/	leite	Feile	Bein	
/oi/	Leute	heule	neun	eure
/au/	Laute	faule	Zaun	

mutation in Old and Middle High German. The colon is a length symbol used for distinguishing the long versus short pairs /iː/ versus /i/, etc. (though see below). There are also articulatory phonetic differences associated with these length distinctions, which are indicated approximately in table 4.4. The short /i ü u/ are lower and more central than /iː üː uː/, the short /e ö o/ are also lower and more central than /eː öː oː/, and /a/ is higher and more central than /aː/. The three diphthongs involve glides from one tongue position to another: in /ai/ the tongue begins in low central position and glides towards a position which is higher and further front; in /oi/ the tongue begins in lower mid back rounded position gliding also towards a position higher and further front; and with /au/ the tongue begins in low central position and glides towards a position higher and further back.

The important difference between long and short vowels in German is more accurately described as a difference of tense versus lax articulation. Tense vowels are produced with greater muscular energy than lax vowels, and it is this that causes them to be articulated in more extreme positions in the vocal tract. The reason for considering the tense/lax opposition more fundamental is that the additional feature of length is found only in stressed syllables: all the examples in table 4.3 involve stressed syllables in which the tense vowels are long (those with a colon), and the lax vowels are short (those without). But in unstressed syllables, it is often possible to perceive a tense/lax distinction, and yet both sets of vowels are now short. There are perceptible differences between tense /iː/ in /diːneː/ *Diner* and lax /i/ in /difuːs/ *diffus*, in both of which the stress falls on the second syllable, and yet both *i* vowels are technically short. Similarly, the unstressed initial syllables of /koːlumbus/ *Kolumbus* and /koleːgə/ *Kollege* differ in tense versus lax articulation of the *o*, but both vowels are again short. In more informal and faster speech, even this tense/lax distinction disappears in unstressed syllables. Nonetheless, the distinctiveness of tense versus lax vowels is not restricted to stressed syllables, whereas the long versus short distinction is. Notice finally that the /ə/ of German occurs only in unstressed syllables.

Table 4.4: Segmental Phonemes of German

Consonants

	Bilabial	Labio-dental	Dental-alveolar	Palato-alveolar	Palatal	Velar	Glottal
Stops	p b		t d			k g	
Fricatives		f v	s z	š ž	ç	x	h
Nasals	m		n			ŋ	
Laterals			l r				
Semi-vowels					j		

Vowels

	Front			Central	Back	
High	iː (üː)				(uː)	
	i (ü)				(u)	
Mid	eː (öː)				(oː)	
	e (ö)	ɛː	ə	(o)		
Low				a		
				aː		

Plus: diphthongs ai, oi, au

Note: ( ) designates lip-rounding

3   Morphology

Despite the morphological syncretism of the Early New High German period (see section 1), the inflectional morphology of Modern German is very rich and preserves major features of the Old High German system. Few among the other modern Germanic languages have a morphology of comparable richness. The biggest changes involved the inflectional paradigms for nouns. The Proto-Indo-European and Proto-Germanic system of classification according to the phonology of the stem (which is still evident in, for example, Russian, see the chapter in this volume) was destroyed and new paradigms evolved. Nouns are now classified according to their inherent gender (masculine, feminine or neuter) and according to their plural forms. The major plural allomorphs are: suffixed *-e* (*Tier/Tiere* 'animal'), *-er* (*Kind/Kinder* 'child'), *-Ø* (*Fenster/Fenster* 'window'), *-en* (*Frau/Frauen* 'woman'), *-s* (*Kino/Kinos* 'cinema'), stem vowel mutation plus *-e* (*Stadt/Städte* 'city'), stem vowel mutation plus *-er* (*Mann/Männer* 'man') and stem vowel mutation alone (*Mutter/Mütter* 'mother'). The noun phrase as a whole distinguishes separate case inflections for nominative, accusative, genitive and dative in both singular and plural, but these are now only residually marked on the noun itself (because of the reduction of unstressed syllables) and are primarily carried by preceding determiners and adjectives. However, the dative plural of all nouns still exhibits an *-(e)n* suffix, the genitive singular of most masculine and neuter nouns an *-(e)s* suffix, and the dative singular of many masculine and neuter nouns an optional *-e* suffix.

The full set of morphological distinctions carried by the German noun phrase (i.e. gender, number and case) can be illustrated by considering the sequence of definite article + noun in the chart given here.

Definite Article and Noun Inflections

	Singular			Plural
	M.	F.	Nt.	All genders
Nom.	d*er* Mann	d*ie* Frau	d*as* Haus	d*ie* Männer
	'the man'	'the woman'	'the house'	'the men'
Acc.	d*en* Mann	d*ie* Frau	d*as* Haus	d*ie* Männer
Gen.	d*es* Mann*es*	d*er* Frau	d*es* Haus*es*	d*er* Männer
Dat.	d*em* Mann(*e*)	d*er* Frau	d*em* Haus(*e*)	d*en* Männer*n*

The definite article assumes just six forms: *der*, *den*, *des*, *dem*, *das* and *die* (morphologically analysable as two bound morphemes *d+er*, *d+en* etc.). Since gender distinctions are inherent in the noun, and since plurality is richly marked on the noun itself, the most important function of the determiner is to mark case. Individual definite article forms can be used in more than one case function without risk of intolerable ambiguity: *der* followed by a masculine singular noun is a nominative; followed by a feminine singular noun a genitive or dative; and followed by a noun with plural marking a genitive; etc. The expressive power of these definite article case distinctions is identical to that of all other sequences of determiner + noun, and also to determiner + adjective + noun and Ø + adjective + noun sequences as well. The weakest distinction is between nominative and accusative, which is marked only by the *der/den* alternation in the masculine singular. However, the nominative is fully distinguishable in all genders and numbers from the genitive, and is also fully distinguishable from the dative.

The accusative is also fully distinguishable from both genitive and dative. The genitive is in turn distinct from the dative, except for feminine singular nouns.

An adjective following the definite article receives case inflections according to the weak paradigm, with -e or -en endings, as shown in the chart of adjective inflections.

Adjective Inflections

Weak Adjective Inflections

	Singular			Plural
	M.	F.	Nt.	All genders
Nom.	der gute Mann	die gute Frau	das gute Haus	die guten Männer
	'the good man'	'the good woman'	'the good house'	'the good men'
Acc.	den guten Mann	die gute Frau	das gute Haus	die guten Männer
Gen.	des guten Mannes	der guten Frau	des guten Hauses	der guten Männer
Dat.	dem guten Mann(e)	der guten Frau	dem guten Haus(e)	den guten Männern

Strong Adjective Inflections

	Singular			Plural
	M.	F.	Nt.	All genders
Nom.	guter Wein	gute Milch	gutes Obst	gute Äpfel
	'good wine'	'good milk'	'good fruit'	'good apples'
Acc.	guten Wein	gute Milch	gutes Obst	gute Äpfel
Gen.	guten Weines	guter Milch	guten Obstes	guter Äpfel
Dat.	gutem Wein	guter Milch	gutem Obst	guten Äpfeln

Mixed Weak and Strong Adjective Inflections

	Singular			Plural
	M.	F.	Nt.	All genders
Nom.	kein guter Mann	keine gute Frau	kein gutes Haus	keine guten Häuser
	'no good man'	'no good woman'	'no good house'	'no good houses'
Acc.	keinen guten Mann	keine gute Frau	kein gutes Haus	keine guten Häuser
Gen.	keines guten Mannes	keiner guten Frau	keines guten Hauses	keiner guten Häuser
Dat.	keinem guten Mann	keiner guten Frau	keinem guten Haus	keinen guten Häusern

Other determiners requiring weak adjective endings are: dieser 'this', jener 'that', welcher 'which', jeder 'each', alle 'all'. It will be apparent that these adjective inflections do not increase the expressive power of the German case system, compared with the definite article + noun inflections. When an adjective + noun sequence has no preceding determiner (with indefinite mass nouns and plurals), the same case distinctions can be carried by adjective inflections of the strong paradigm, also shown in the chart of adjective inflections. These strong adjective inflections (-er, -en, -es, -em,

-e) are practically identical in form and distribution to the bound morphemes of the definite article, and the expressive power of the whole paradigm is again identical to the definite article + noun inflections. Indefinite count nouns in the singular require the indefinite article *ein* 'a'. This determiner, together with *kein* 'no' and the possessives *mein* 'my', *dein* 'your', *sein* 'his', etc., is itself inflected more or less like the definite article, but requires accompanying adjective inflections which are a mixture of weak (*-en*, *-e*) and strong (*-er*, *-e*, *-es*). The chart of adjective inflections illustrates this mixed adjective paradigm following *kein*.

Personal Pronouns

Singular

	1st	*2nd* (*familiar*)	*3rd* M.	F.	Nt.
Nom.	ich	du	er	sie	es
Acc.	mich	dich	ihn	sie	es
Gen	meiner	deiner	seiner	ihrer	seiner
Dat.	mir	dir	ihm	ihr	ihm

Plural

	1st	*2nd* familiar	*polite: s. & pl.*	*3rd*
Nom.	wir	ihr	Sie	sie
Acc.	uns	euch	Sie	sie
Gen.	unser	euer	Ihrer	ihrer
Dat.	uns	euch	Ihnen	ihnen

German personal pronouns exhibit a rich set of case distinctions, as shown in the chart of personal pronouns. All four cases are fully distinct in the singular for first, second (familiar) and masculine third persons, while feminine and neuter third person forms are identical only in the nominative and accusative. In the plural the four cases are on each occasion represented by three separate forms. In the first and second (familiar) persons accusative and dative fall together, and in the second (polite) and third persons nominative and accusative fall together. Relative and interrogative pronouns are also case-marked. The relative pronoun, for example, is identical in form to the definite article, except for all the genitives and the dative plural (the relative pronoun having *dessen* instead of *des*, *deren* instead of *der*, and *denen* instead of *den*).

The existence of a productive case system sets German off from the other Germanic languages except for Icelandic and Faroese. As regards the use of the cases, the most important factor which determines the assignment of case to a noun phrase is the nature of the 'governing category', loosely, the category which forms an immediate constituent with this noun phrase and which determines the syntactic type of the resulting phrase. Thus, a preposition combines with a noun phrase to make a prepositional phrase and it assigns a case to this noun phrase; a verb combines with a noun phrase to make a verb phrase and assigns case to this noun phrase; and so on. Different prepositions assign accusative case, dative case or genitive case, as illustrated below:

(a) durch das Zimmer; für mich. (acc.)
     'through the room; for me'
(b) aus dem Hause; mit mir. (dat.)
     'out of the house; with me'
(c) an die/der Wand; auf den/dem Stuhl. (acc./dat.)
     'on the wall; on the chair'
(d) trotz des Wetters; während des Jahres. (gen.)
     'despite the weather; during the year'

The case alternation in (c) carries a difference in meaning: *auf den Stuhl* with an accusative noun phrase signals motion towards the place in question, as in 'the cat jumped on(to) the chair'; *auf dem Stuhl* with a dative designates a location without a change in state, e.g. 'the cat was lying on the chair'.

An adjective within an adjective phrase may also assign case to a noun phrase. Different adjectives assign accusative, dative or genitive case, as in:

(a) Ich bin ihn los. (acc.)
     'I am him rid', i.e. 'I am rid of him.'
(b) Sie ist ihrem Vater ähnlich. (dat.)
     'She is her father similar', i.e. 'similar to her father.'
(c) Er ist dieser Taten schuldig. (gen.)
     'He is these deeds guilty', i.e. 'guilty of these deeds.'

A head noun within a noun phrase assigns genitive case to a modifying possessor noun phrase:

der Hut der Anna; Annas Hut.
'the hat of the Anna; Anna's hat'

The most complex governing category is the verb. The single argument of a one-place predicate (verb or predicate adjective) is most typically in the nominative case, as below, though both accusative and dative are found in so-called 'impersonal constructions':

(a) Ich schlafe. Ich friere. (nom.)
     'I am sleeping. I am freezing.'
(b) Mich hungert. Mich friert. (acc.)
     'Me hungers. Me freezes', i.e. 'I am hungry; I am freezing.'
(c) Mir ist warm. (dat.)
     'Me is warm', i.e. 'I am warm.'

These impersonal constructions were more frequent in earlier stages of

German, but they still exist in the modern language. With two-place predicates, one argument is in the nominative case (the subject), but the second argument may be accusative, dative or genitive, depending on the choice of verb. Most verbs take the accusative (and these noun phrases then behave syntactically as direct objects), a not inconsiderable number take the dative and just a handful take the genitive (only one or two of which are really productive in modern usage):

(a) Ich liebe dich. Er sieht meinen Vater. (nom.-acc.)
     'I love you. He sees my father'.
(b) Er hilft mir. Sie antwortete ihrem Vater. (nom.-dat.)
     'He is helping me. She answered her father.'
(c) Sie bedarf des Trostes. Er ermangelt der nötigen Kraft. (nom.-gen.)
     'She needs consolation. He lacks the requisite strength.'

In three-place predicate constructions consisting of a verb and three (prepositionless) noun phrases the most common case assignments are nominative–accusative–dative, followed by nominative–accusative–genitive, with just a handful of nominative–accusative–accusative:

(a) Ich schrieb meinem Vater einen Brief. Das rate ich dir. (nom.-acc.-dat.)
     'I wrote my father a letter.   That advise I you (to do).'
(b) Man enthob ihn seines Amtes. Er schämt sich seines Sohnes. (nom.-acc.-gen.)
     'One relieved him (of) his office. He shames himself (of) his son.'
(c) Er lehrt mich eine Sprache. Er hieß mich einen Toren. (nom.-acc.-acc.)
     'He is teaching me a language. He called me a fool.'

As in the other Germanic languages, many verbs also take prepositional phrases with characteristic prepositions when expanding on their minimally present argument noun phrases, e.g.:

(a) Ich denke oft *an* dich.
     'I think often *of* you.'
(b) Ich danke dir *für* deinen Brief.
     'I thank you *for* your letter.'

Not all case assignment in German is determined by a governing category in this way. For example, there are productive case contrasts in sentence time adverbials such as those shown below, in which the accusative refers to a specified (definite) time, and the genitive to an unspecified (indefinite) time:

(a) Er kam *letzten Freitag*. (acc.)
     'He came last Friday.'
(b) *Eines Tages* kam er. (gen.)
     'One day came he.'

Finally, the major morphological distinctions carried by the verb are illustrated in the chart of verb inflections.

Verb Inflections

	WEAK		STRONG	
Infinitive				
	sag+*en* 'to say'		trag+*en* 'to bear'	
Participles				
Present	sag+*end*		trag+*end*	
Past	*ge*+sag+*t*		*ge*+trag+*en*	
Imperative				
2nd Sg.				
(familiar)	sag+*(e)*		trag+*(e)*	
2nd Pl.				
(familiar)	sag+*t*		trag+*t*	
Polite form	sag+*en* Sie		trag+*en* Sie	

Present

	Indicative	*Subjunctive*	*Indicative*	*Subjunctive*
ich (1st)	sag+*e*	sag+*e*	trag+*e*	trag+*e*
du (2nd)	sag+*st*	sag+*st*	träg+*st*	trag+*st*
er, sie, es (3rd)	sag+*t*	sag+*e*	träg+*t*	trag+*e*
wir (1st)	sag+*en*	sag+*en*	trag+*en*	trag+*en*
ihr (2nd)	sag+*t*	sag+*t*	trag+*t*	trag+*t*
sie (3rd),				
Sie (2nd)	sag+*en*	sag+*en*	trag+*en*	trag+*en*

Past

	Indicative	*Subjunctive*	*Indicative*	*Subjunctive*
ich (1st)	sag+*te*	sag+*te*	trug	trüg+*e*
du (2nd)	sag+*test*	sag+*test*	trug+*st*	trüg+*st*
er, sie, es (3rd)	sag+*te*	sag+*te*	trug	trüg+*e*
wir (1st)	sag+*ten*	sag+*ten*	trug+*en*	trüg+*en*
ihr (2nd)	sag+*tet*	sag+*tet*	trug+*t*	trüg+*t*
sie (3rd),				
Sie (2nd)·	sag+*ten*	sag+*ten*	trug+*en*	trüg+*en*

As in all the other Germanic languages, two basic classes of verb need to be distinguished: weak (exemplified by *sagen* 'to say') and strong (exemplified by *tragen* 'to bear'). The strong class undergoes vowel alternations in the stem (so-called 'ablaut') in addition to taking inflectional affixes for person and number agreement, etc. The number of strong verbs has been historically on the decline and there has been a certain levelling and redistribution of vowel alternants among the different tense and person categories that these alternants distinguish (especially in Early New High German), but Modern German still has a large class of strong verbs which includes some of the most common verbs in the language (*geben* 'to give', *essen* 'to eat', *liegen* 'to lie', *sehen* 'to see', *riechen* 'to smell', *gießen* 'to pour', *fliegen* 'to fly', *schreiben* 'to write', *sprechen* 'to speak', *fallen* 'to fall', *fahren* 'to travel', and many others). The weak class does not undergo such vowel alternations and takes (partially different) inflectional affixes for person and number agreement.

Proceeding down the chart of verb inflections, the German infinitive marker is an *-en* suffix attached to the stem. The present participle is formed by adding the suffix *-end*. The past participle consists of a *-t* suffix for weak verbs and an *-en* suffix for strong verbs, with a *ge-* prefix for both in cases where the first syllable of the stem is stressed. If the first syllable is not stressed (e.g. *bemérken* 'to notice'), this initial *ge-* is omitted (*bemérkt* 'noticed' not **gebemérkt*). There are three imperative forms with identical morphologies for weak and strong verbs, as shown. German has only two simple tenses, present and past, both inherited from Proto-Germanic and shared with other Germanic languages. Numerous compound tenses are formed from combinations of *haben* 'to have', *sein* 'to be' and *werden* 'to be/ become' plus past participle or infinitive, e.g. the perfect (*ich habe gesagt* 'I have said'), pluperfect (*ich hatte gesagt* 'I had said'), future (*ich werde sagen* 'I will say'), future perfect (*ich werde gesagt haben* 'I will have said') and so on. These compounds were fixed in the Old High German period. The person and number agreement suffixes of the present tense are identical for weak and strong verbs: four suffixes (*-e, -st, -t, -en*) are divided among the six grammatically distinguishable types of subjects that the verb agrees with (first, second and third persons singular, first, second and third persons plural). For stems ending in various (primarily dental) consonants, e.g. *-t* in *wart+en* 'to wait', an epenthetic *e* appears before the *-st* and *-t* suffixes (compare *sag+st/wart+est* and *sag+t/wart+et*). A special form for the subjunctive exists only in the third person singular (*er sage* as opposed to *er sagt*); otherwise subjunctive and indicative are identical (though productive paradigms for a distinct present subjunctive do exist for *sein* 'to be', the modal auxiliaries and one or two other verbs). The past tense indicative inflections for weak verbs all contain an initial *t-*, and differ in several respects from the corresponding strong verb indicative inflections, as shown. The past subjunctive of weak verbs is identical to the indicative, but the past subjunctive of strong verbs exhibits numerous contrasts with the indicative: first and third persons singular show *-e* rather than *-Ø* and the stem vowel is umlauted wherever possible.

4   Syntax

One of the most interesting features of Modern German syntax, in comparison with other languages, is its word order (particularly the position of the verb). Within the Germanic language family, German is striking for the extent to which it has remained conservative, preserving structural properties of both Old High German and the Germanic parent language itself. The Scandinavian languages and English, by contrast, have undergone more extensive syntactic changes in the same time period, with Dutch being intermediate between German and English. The present summary will accordingly illustrate some of the basic features of German verb position, and will outline some of the major syntactic differences which now distinguish German from one of the more radical Germanic languages, namely English.

There are three major positions of the verb in German clauses: final position, second position (i.e. the verb is the second clause-level constituent) and first position. The basic rule is: final position in subordinate clauses; second and first position in main clauses. A more precise statement, however, must first distinguish between finite and non-finite (i.e. infinitival and participial) verb forms. In subordinate clauses containing a finite verb (and, optionally, any additional non-finite verbs), all verb forms are final (in the order non-finite before finite), e.g.:

(a) Ich weiß, daß Heinrich die Frau *liebt*.
    'I know that Henry the woman *loves*', i.e. 'loves the woman.'
(b) Ich glaube, daß mein Vater vor einigen Tagen nach London *gefahren ist*.
    'I believe that my father several days ago to London *travelled has*.'

In non-finite subordinate clauses, non-finite verbs are again final:

Ich freue mich darauf, abends in der Wirtschaft Bier *zu trinken*.
'I am looking forward to-it, evenings in the pub beer *to drink*', i.e.
'I am looking forward to drinking beer in the pub in the evenings.'

And so they are even in main clauses, although the finite verb now stands in second position (a-b) or first position (c-d):

(a) Heinrich *liebt* die Frau.
    'Henry *loves* the woman.'
(b) Mein Vater *ist* vor einigen Tagen nach London *gefahren*.
    'My father *has* several days ago to London *travelled*.'
(c) *Liebt* Heinrich die Frau?
    'Loves Henry the woman?' i.e. 'Does Henry love the woman?'
(d) *Ist* mein Vater vor einigen Tagen nach London *gefahren*?
    '*Has* my father several days ago to London *travelled*?'

German verb compounds consisting of a separable element (e.g. an adjective, particle, even a prepositional phrase or a noun phrase) in conjunction with a verb provide further examples of verb-final structures. The separable element assumes the same position as a non-finite verb form, and hence German main clauses frequently end in a verbal satellite constituent, such as *tot* 'dead' from the compound *totschlagen* 'to beat dead':

Der König *schlug* den Feigling *tot*.
'The king *beat* the coward *dead*.'

In subordinate clauses, satellite and verb stand together, and the verb alone, not the whole verbal complex, provides the domain for the attachment of infinitival *zu* 'to':

(a) Ich weiß, daß der König den Feigling *totschlug*.
     'I know that the king the coward *dead-beat*', i.e. 'beat the coward dead.'
(b) Ich freue mich darauf, den Feigling *totzuschlagen*.
     'I look forward to-it, the coward *dead-to-beat*.'

The final position of verbal forms in the above structures is not rigidly adhered to, however. Various constituents can stand to the right of the verb, and the frequency with which they do so is a matter of style: postposings are more frequent in informal, conversational German; and less frequent in formal, written German. There are strict rules governing which constituents can be postposed and which cannot. Direct objects, for example, cannot be postposed over the verbal satellite *über* 'across' (from *übersetzen* 'set across') in the following example, regardless of style:

(a) Man *setzte* die Urlauber in einem Boot *über*.
     'One set the holidaymakers in a boat across'
(b) * Man *setzte* in einem Boot *über* die Urlauber.
     'One set in a boat across the holidaymakers'

Nor can obligatory adjuncts (or strictly subcategorised constituents) move to rightmost position, as exemplified in the ungrammatical (b) in which the obligatorily present prepositional phrase has been postposed behind the infinitive *verleiten* 'to lead (astray)':

(a) Die Gelegenheit *wird* ihn bestimmt zu einem voreiligen Schritt *verleiten*.
     'The opportunity will him certainly to a rash move lead', i.e. 'will certainly encourage him to make a rash move.'
(b) * Die Gelegenheit *wird* ihn bestimmt *verleiten* zu einem voreiligen Schritt.
     'The opportunity will him certainly lead to a rash move.'

The constituents which can move are in general: (1) those which are heavy, i.e. which are long in terms of number of words, and complex in their internal structure; and (2) those which are more loosely integrated into the interpretation of the sentence, e.g. optional adverbial constituents which can serve as 'afterthoughts'. With regard to (1), notice that non-subject embedded finite clauses in German *must* be postposed behind a 'final' verb form:

(a) * Er *hatte* daß er nicht lange leben würde *gewußt*.
     'He had that he not long live would known.'

(b) Er *hatte gewußt*, daß er nicht lange leben würde.
     'He had known, that he not long live would.'

With infinitival embeddings (which are typically shorter than finite clauses), the postposing is regularly optional rather than obligatory:

(a) Er *hatte* die Frau zu gewinnen *gehofft*.
     'He had the woman to win hoped', i.e. 'He had hoped to win the woman.'
(b) Er *hatte gehofft*, die Frau zu gewinnen.
     'He had hoped, the woman to win.'

As an example of (2), consider:

(a) Ich erzähle dir gleich, was ich bei Müllers *gehört habe*.
     'I tell you right-away, what I at the Müllers (place) heard have.'
(b) Ich erzähle dir gleich, was ich *gehört habe* bei Müllers
     'I tell you right-away, what I heard have at the Müllers (place).'

The verb-second structures of the main clauses allow a wide variety of constituents to occupy first position, not just a subject. Some typical examples are given below, involving various fronted adverbials (a-d), non-subject noun phrases (e-f), a verb phrase (g), non-finite verb forms (h-i), an adjective (j) and an embedded clause (k):

(a) Möglicherweise *hat* Heinrich uns *vergessen*.
     'Possibly has Henry us forgotten', i.e. 'Possibly Henry has forgotten us.'
(b) Gestern *sind* wir ins Theater *gegangen*.
     'Yesterday have we to-the theatre gone.'
(c) In München *wohnt* der Mann.
     'In Munich resides the man.'
(d) Schön singt die Opernsängerin.
     'Beautifully sings the opera singer.'
(e) Den Hund *sieht* die Katze.
     'The dog (acc.) sees the cat (nom.)', i.e. 'The cat sees the dog.'
(f) Dem Mann *habe* ich das Buch *gegeben*.
     'The man (dat.) have I the book (acc.) given.'
(g) Das Auto zu reparieren *hat* der Junge *versucht*.
     'The car to repair has the boy tried', i.e. 'The boy has tried to repair the car.'
(h) *Gewinnen müssen* wir.
     'Win must we', i.e. 'Win we must.'
(i) *Bestraft muß* er werden.
     'Punished must he be.'
(j) Dumm *bin* ich nicht.
     'Stupid am I not.'
(k) Daß er oft lügt *wissen* wir alle.
     'That he often lies know we all.'

Only one constituent can typically precede the verb in these constructions. A slight exception is provided by structures such as *gestern abend auf der*

Party fehlte Heinrich 'yesterday evening at the party was-missing Henry', in which two thematically related constituents precede, *gestern abend* and *auf der Party*. But normally this is not possible. The most normal position for the subject in the above verb-second structures is immediately after the verb, though it can sometimes stand further to the right as well.

All of the structures just given are semantically declarative statements. Verb-first structures, by contrast, occur in a variety of primarily non-declarative sentence types, including yes-no questions (see above). Other verb-first structures are: imperatives (a), exclamations (b), and counterfactual and conditional clauses (c-d):

(a) *Bringen* Sie das Buch herein!
     'Bring you the book in-here.'
(b) *Bist* du aber schmutzig!
     'Are you ever dirty.'
(c) *Hätte* ich nur Zeit, ich würde Ihnen helfen.
     'Had I only time, I would you help.'
(d) *Kommt* er, so sehe ich ihn.
     'Comes he, then see I him', i.e. If he comes, then I will see him.'

Modern colloquial German also exhibits a verb-first pattern in 'dramatic' narrative style :

Kommt da plötzlich jemand hereingeschneit.
'Comes then suddenly someone bursting-in', i.e. 'Then suddenly someone comes bursting in.'

This pattern was more productive in earlier stages of the language.

The verb-second and verb-first structures of German main clauses have close parallels in all the modern Germanic languages. Even English, which has gone furthest in the direction of fixing SVO, employs a verb-first rule in an almost identical set of environments to German, and it has numerous subject-verb inversion rules creating verb-second structures in a significant number of the environments that we have seen for German (see Hawkins 1986: chs. 11 and 12 for a summary).

Before leaving the topic of word order, notice that the positioning of other sentence-level constituents in German apart from the verb is relatively free. Within the other major phrasal categories, however (the noun phrase, the adjective phrase, the prepositional phrase), the ordering of daughter constituents is just as fixed as in English.

With its rich inflectional morphology, verb-final structures and word order freedom, Modern German preserves syntactic features that were common to all the older West Germanic languages. Modern English, by contrast, has essentially lost its case morphology on nouns (as well as other inflectional morphology), has fixed basic SVO word order, and permits less sentence-level word order freedom. Modern English syntax also differs from that of

Modern German in other significant ways. Most of these are the result of English having effected changes which were either not carried out, or carried out to a much lesser extent, in German. We shall conclude with a very brief enumeration of some more of these contrasts.

English has larger and semantically broader classes of subject and direct object noun phrases than German, i.e. the quantity and semantic type of noun phrases that undergo rules sensitive to these grammatical relations is greater in English than in German. For example, many direct objects of English correspond to dative-marked noun phrases in German, which are arguably not direct objects since they cannot be converted to passive subjects. Compare the English sentences below with their German translations and with the corresponding passive sentences:

(a) She loves the man/him.
(b) Sie liebt *den Mann/ihn*. (acc.)

(a) She helped the man/him.
(b) Sie half *dem Mann/ihm*. (dat.)

(a) The man/He is loved.
(b) Der Mann/Er wird geliebt.

(a) The man/He was helped.
(b) *Der Mann/Er wurde geholfen.

The accusative-marked (and semantically prototypically patient) noun phrases of German in these constructions correspond to English direct objects and are also direct objects in German. But the dative (and semantically recipient) argument of *helfen* 'to help' also corresponds to a direct object in English, though it is not itself a direct object in German. The case syncretism of English has collapsed the distinct classes of noun phrases in German into a larger class of direct objects, with consequences for both the productivity of various syntactic operations, and for the semantic breadth or diversity of the direct object relation.

Grammatical subjects in English also constitute a larger and semantically more diverse class. English frequently has subjects with non-agentive semantic roles where these are impossible in German, as the following selection shows:

(a) *The king* visited his people. (Su. = agent)
(b) *Der König* besuchte sein Volk.

(a) *My guitar* broke a string. (Su. = locative; cf. *on my guitar...*)
(b) *Meine Gitarre* (zer)riß eine Saite.

(a) *This hotel* forbids dogs. (Su. = locative; cf. *in this hotel...*)
(b) *Dieses Hotel* verbietet Hunde.

(a) *A penny* once bought 2 to 3 pins. (Su = instrumental; cf. *with a penny...*)
(b) **Ein Pfennig* kaufte früher 2 bis 3 Stecknadeln.

(a) *This advertisement* will sell us a lot. (Su. = instrumental; cf. *with this ad...*)
(b) **Diese Anzeige* verkauft uns viel.

Related to this contrast is the existence of a productive set of raising rules in English, creating derived subjects and objects. These operations are either non-existent or extremely limited in German, as the following literal German translations of the English structures show. The English sentences (a-c) exemplify subject-to-subject raising, i.e. *John* is the original subject of *to be ill* and is raised to become subject of *seems*, etc.; (d-e) involve subject-to-object raising, whereby *John* has been raised to become direct object of *believe*, etc.; and (f-h) give examples of object-to-subject raising (or tough movement), in which the original object of *to study* has been raised to become subject of *is easy*, etc.:

(a) John seems to be ill.
(b) John happens to be ill.
(c) John ceased to be ill.

(a) Johann scheint krank zu sein.
(b) *Johann geschieht krank zu sein.
(c) *Johann hörte auf krank zu sein.

(d) I believe John to be ill.
(e) I understand him to be stupid.

(d) *Ich glaube Johann krank zu sein.
(e) *Ich verstehe ihn dumm zu sein.

(f) Linguistics is easy to study.
(g) Literature is pleasant to study.
(h) History is boring to study.

(f) Die Linguistik ist leicht zu studieren.
(g) *Die Literatur ist angenehm zu studieren.
(h) *Die Geschichte ist langweilig zu studieren.

Related to these more productive clause-external raising rules in English is the fact that the extraction of *wh* elements out of subordinate clauses is also more productive in English than in German. For example, German can typically not extract out of finite subordinate clauses:

That is the prize which I hope (that you will win △).

*Das ist der Preis, den ich hoffe (daß du △ gewinnen wirst).

Nor can German extract out of a prepositional phrase, thereby stranding a preposition, whereas such extraction and stranding is typically optional in English:

(a) The woman who I went to the movies pp(with △).
(b) The woman pp(with whom) I went to the movies.

(a) *Die Frau, der ich ins Kino pp(mit △) ging.
(b) Die Frau, pp(mit der) ich ins Kino ging.

The (b) versions of these sentences involve a fronting (or 'pied piping') of the whole prepositional phrase, rather than extraction out of it. German also has a productive verb phrase pied piping rule which is without parallel in English:

(a) *The man vp(to kill whom) I have often tried
(b) The man who I have often tried vp(to kill △).

(a) Der Mann vp(den zu töten) ich öfters versucht habe
(b) Der Mann, den ich vp(△ zu töten) öfters versucht habe; OR
Der Mann, den ich öfters versucht habe vp(△ zu töten)

Finally, numerous deletions which are possible in English are blocked in German, in part because the case system of German renders non-identical deletion targets which are identical in English. An example is given below, in which the leftmost occurrence of *the king* can delete in English, whereas the accusative-marked *den König* in German is not identical to the dative *dem König* and cannot be deleted by this latter:

(a) Fred saw *the king* and thanked *the king*.
(b) Fred saw   and thanked *the king*.

(a) Fritz sah *den König* und dankte *dem König*.
(b) *Fritz sah   und dankte *dem König*.

Deletions are also more restricted in German for other reasons as well. For example, deletions, like the extractions discussed above, cannot strand a preposition, even when the relevant noun phrases have identical cases:

(a) He is the father of *the boy* and the friend of *the boy*.
(b) He is the father of   and the friend of *the boy*.

(a) Er ist der Vater von *dem Jungen* und der Freund von *dem Jungen*.
(b) *Er ist der Vater von   und der Freund von *dem Jungen*.

Deletion of a relative pronoun is also impossible in German, but possible in English:

(a) The woman who(m) I love is coming tonight.
(b) The woman   I love is coming tonight.

(a)   Die Frau, die ich liebe, kommt heute abend.
(b) *Die Frau   ich liebe kommt heute abend.

Summarising, we have the following overall typological contrasts between English and German:

German	English
More grammatical morphology	Less grammatical morphology
More word order freedom	Less word order freedom
Less semantic diversity of grammatical relations	More semantic diversity of grammatical relations
Less raising	More raising
Less extraction	More extraction
More pied piping	Less pied piping
Less deletion	More deletion

Bibliography

Among numerous grammars of German written in English, Russon (1967) is the best concise traditional statement. For phonology, reference may be made to Moulton (1962), while Hawkins (1986) contains a survey of the major areas of syntactic and morphological contrast between German and English. In German, Althaus et al. (1973a) includes a valuable summary of major areas of German grammar, with extensive further references; Bierwisch (1963) is the first detailed generative treatment of the syntax of the German verb and of numerous related rules, and is still considered a classic.

Althaus et al. (1973b) includes an excellent summary of dialect differences among German regions, the major historical changes in the different periods of both High and Low German and the current status of German in countries where German is not a national language, with extensive further references throughout. Bach (1965) is a standard reference work on the history of the German language, with extensive further references, while Lockwood (1968) is an excellent summary of the major syntactic changes from Old High German to New High German. Keller (1961) is a useful summary of numerous dialects. Clyne (1984) is a most useful discussion of the sociolinguistic situation in those countries in which German is the national language or one of the national languages.

References

Althaus, H.P., H. Henne and H.E. Wiegand. 1973a. *Lexicon der germanistischen Linguistik. Studienausgabe I* (Max Niemeyer Verlag, Tübingen)
———— 1973b. *Lexicon der germanistischen Linguistik. Studienausgabe II* (Max Niemeyer Verlag, Tübingen)

Bach, A. 1965. *Geschichte der deutschen Sprache* (Quelle and Meyer, Heidelberg)

Bierwisch, M. 1963. *Grammatik des deutschen Verbs* (=Studia Grammatica 2) (Akademieverlag, Berlin)

Clyne, M. 1984. *Language and Society in the German-speaking Countries* (Cambridge University Press, Cambridge)

Hawkins, J.A. 1986. *A Comparative Typology of English and German: Unifying the Contrasts* (University of Texas Press, Austin, and Croom Helm, London)

Keller, R.E. 1961. *German Dialects. Phonology and Morphology with Selected Texts* (Manchester University Press, Manchester)

Lockwood, W.B. 1968. *Historical German Syntax* (Clarendon Press, Oxford)

Moulton, W.G. 1962. *The Sounds of English and German* (University of Chicago Press, Chicago)

Russon, L.J. 1967. *Complete German Course for First Examinations* (Longman, London)

5 Dutch

Jan G. Kooij

1 Introduction

Modern Standard Dutch is the official language of the Netherlands and one of the official languages of Belgium. In the two countries together, the number of speakers is approximately 20 million. The official Dutch name of the language is *Nederlands*. It is sometimes called *Hollands*, after the most influential province, and the variety of Dutch that is spoken in Belgium is often, incorrectly, referred to as Flemish (*Vlaams*). Frisian (Dutch *Fries*) is a separate language spoken in the north-east of the Netherlands and is in some respects closer to English than to Dutch. *Afrikaans*, the language of part of the white and mixed-race population of the Republic of South Africa, is derived from Dutch dialects but is now regarded as a separate language. Dutch is also the official language of administration in Surinam (formerly Dutch Guyana) and in the Dutch Antilles but it is not widely spoken there. Some Dutch is still spoken in Indonesia. Dutch-based creole languages have never had many speakers, and the language known as *Negerhollands* ('Negro Dutch') on the Virgin Islands has become virtually extinct. Both Sranan, the English-based creole spoken by a large number of inhabitants of Surinam, and Papiamentu, a Spanish-based creole spoken in the Antilles, have been influenced by Dutch, and Sranan increasingly so. Afrikaans also shows definite features of creolisation.

The word *Dutch* derives from Middle Dutch *Diets* or *Duuts*, the name for the (Low) German vernacular; somewhat confusingly for speakers of English, *Duits* is now the Dutch name for (High) German.

Dialect variation in the Dutch language area is considerable, and a number of geographical dialects are not mutually intelligible. Ever since compulsory education was introduced uniformity in speaking and writing has increased, though less so in the Belgian area than in the Netherlands. The process of standardisation still continues. The large majority of inhabitants have a fair command of the standard language, but in some areas in the north, the east and the south a number of people are virtually bilingual. Language variation is politically insignificant in the Netherlands, but the situation in Belgium is more complex. After the establishment of the

129

boundaries of the Dutch Republic in the seventeenth century, the prestige of Dutch in the southern provinces that are now part of Belgium rapidly declined. Its official recognition next to French has been the subject of bitter controversies, and the language situation is still an important factor in political and cultural life. The boundary between the Dutch-speaking area and the French-speaking area runs from west to east just south of Brussels. In the south-east of the country lives a small German-speaking minority. Minority languages in the Netherlands include Chinese (mostly the Cantonese dialect), Bahasa Indonesia and other forms of Malay, Sranan and, more recently, Turkish and North African dialects of Arabic.

2 History and Typology

Dutch belongs to the West Germanic branch of the Germanic languages and is based on Low Franconian dialects spoken in the south of the present language area. Compared to the two other major West Germanic languages, English and German, Dutch is in fundamental respects closer to German. Like English, however, it has lost most of the original Germanic noun morphology, and the proximity of the Romance language area is apparent from the presence of a sizable Romance vocabulary in the Dutch lexicon. Some characteristic differences and similarities among Dutch, English and German are the following.

(a) Germanic [g] went to [x]: Dutch *goed* [xut] vs. English *good*, German *gut*,

(b) Short back vowel before [l] plus consonant went to [ɑu]: Dutch *oud* vs. English *old*, German *alt*,

(c) Initial [sk] went to [sx]: Dutch *schip* vs. English *ship*, German *Schiff*, and in other positions [sk] went to [s]: Dutch *vis* vs. English *fish*, German *Fisch* with [š],

(d) Final devoicing of obstruents: Dutch *pond*, German *Pfund* with final [t] vs. English *pound*,

(e) Initial voicing of fricatives: Dutch *zien*, German *sehen* with initial [z] vs. English *see*,

(f) Predominance of older plural endings over the more recent ending -*s*: Dutch *boeken*, German *Bücher* vs. English *books*,

(g) No grammatical umlaut: Dutch *dag–dagelijks*, English *day–daily* vs. German *Tag–täglich*,

(h) No initial [š] in consonant clusters: Dutch *steen*, English *stone* vs. German *Stein* [štain],

(i) No affricates and fricatives from original plosives [p], [t], [k]: Dutch *pond*, English *pound* vs. German *Pfund*; Dutch *tien*, English *ten* vs. German *zehn*; Dutch *maken*, English *make* vs. German *machen*.

The latter feature Dutch shares with Low German, which was once a major literary language in the German-speaking area (see page 104).

From the period of Old Dutch or Old Low Franconian (*Oud Nederlands*) only a few texts have survived, mainly fragments of psalms translated into the vernacular. From the period of Middle Dutch (*Middelnederlands*, 1100–1500) a considerable number of literary and non-literary texts have been preserved and edited; most of these are written in the dialects of the leading southern provinces, Flanders and Brabant. By the time that Modern Dutch (*Nieuw Nederlands*) developed, the language had already lost most of its case distinctions and flectional morphology, though some of it was still represented in the orthography. The modern standard language is based on the dialects spoken in and around Amsterdam, since by that time political and cultural leadership had gravitated to the northern provinces; pronunciation was influenced considerably by the speech of immigrants from the Brabant area after the fall of Antwerp in 1585. Typical features of the developing standard pronunciation were the fixation of the diphthongised long [i] as [ɛɪ] rather than [ɑɪ], Dutch *rijden* vs. English *ride* and German *reiten*, and the diphthongisation of original Germanic [u] to [ʌü], Dutch *huis* vs. English *house*, German *Haus*. Diphthongisation also affected French loans: compare English *brewery* and Dutch *brouwerij* with final [ɛɪ], English *flute* and Dutch *fluit* with [ʌü]. Another recent feature in the phonology is the weakening of intervocalic [d] to [j] in inflected forms: *goed*, 'good', inflected form *goede* or *goeie*; many of these forms coexist as formal vs. informal variants.

As elsewhere in Europe, the writing of grammars in the native language began in the period of the Renaissance; the main focus of the older grammarians was proper usage, standardisation and orthography. The most important early contribution to the scholarly study of Dutch and its relationships with the surrounding languages was made by the Amsterdam linguist Lambert ten Kate (1723). Not until the nineteenth century did Dutch universities introduce chairs for the study of the Dutch language and for Dutch philology and lexicography. There is no Language Academy, but the foundation of a Council for the Dutch Language (Raad voor de Nederlandse Taal) in which the Netherlands and Belgium participate has now been agreed upon.

The uniformisation of the orthography was accomplished in the nineteenth century on the initiative of the central government. The basic rules for the present orthography were laid out in 1863 by De Vries and Te Winkel. They are mildly etymological, for instance the diphthong [ɛɪ] is spelled either *ij* or *ei* according to its history. The spelling of inflected forms of nouns and verbs follows the morphology rather than the phonology. So, the stem *vind* 'find', pronounced [ɣɪnt] is spelled with final -*d* because of the infinitive *vinden*, and the form *hij vindt* 'he finds', also pronounced [ɣɪnt] is spelled with final -*dt* because of *loop* 'walk', *hij loopt* 'he walks'. This aspect of the system has been challenged but it has never been changed. Otherwise, Dutch orthography follows the principle that distinct sounds are represented by different letters of the Roman alphabet, with the additional convention that a long vowel in closed syllables is represented by two letters and a short vowel by one: *aap* 'monkey' and *stap* 'step'; in open syllables, the difference between long vowels and short vowels is indicated by single and double consonants, respectively: *apen* 'monkeys' vs. *stappen* 'steps'. The spelling of vowels is less conservative than in English because the major developments in the standardisation of the pronunciation were taken into account. Peculiar features of Dutch orthography are the use of the letter *ij*, which is considered a single letter, for diphthongised [i] as in *rijden* 'ride', and the use of *oe* for the monophthong [u] as in *boek*, *Oeganda* vs. German *Buch*, *Uganda*. The spelling of the Romance vocabulary has been rationalised to some extent, as appears from Dutch *fotografie* vs. English *photography*, but proposals for further adaptation, e.g. *k* instead of *c* in *collectie* 'collection' have met with resistance, especially in Belgium.

3 Phonology

Tables 5.1 and 5.2 show the distinctive segmental phonemes of standard Dutch. Dutch has a comparatively simple consonant system. The main distinctive features are place of articulation, manner of articulation and

Table 5.1: Vowel Phonemes of Dutch, Schematised

	Front		Centralised	Back
High	i	ü		u
Mid	e, ɪ	ö	œ, ə	ɔ, o
	ɛ			ɑ
Low			a	
Diphthongs	ɛɪ		ʌü	ɑu

Table 5.2: Consonant Phonemes of Dutch

	Obstruents Plosive	Fricative	Nasals	Liquids	Glides
Labial	p, b	f, v	m		ʋ
Alveolar	t, d	s, z	n	l	
Palatal					j
Velar	k, -	x, ɣ	ŋ		
Uvular				R	
Glottal					h

presence vs. absence of voicing. The language has no affricates, and no palatal obstruents. Labial fricatives and [ʋ] are labio-dental and all fricatives are strident. Nasals and liquids are never syllabic. [ʀ] is mostly uvular and not often rolled with the tip of the tongue; in most positions, it is distinctly audible: *water* [ʋatəʀ] 'water', *hard* [hɑʀt] 'hard'. The [l] is more velarised than it is in German. In some dialects in the south-west, initial [h] is dropped: *oek* [uk] instead of *hoek* [huk], 'corner'. Palatalisation is mostly restricted to alveolars before [j] or non-syllabic [i̯]: [t] in *kat+je* 'cat (diminutive)' and [š] in *sociaal* 'social'. Nasalisation of vowels before nasal consonants is absent: *hond* 'dog' is [hɔnt], not [hɔ̃nt] and *hond+je* 'dog (diminutive)' is [hɔɲtjə] not [hɔ̃ɲtjə]. It is also avoided in French loans: *plafond* 'ceiling' is [plafɔ́n] rather than [plafɔ́].

The voiced-voiceless opposition is phonetically quite distinct in plosives, but not in fricatives. For many speakers, the difference between *s/z* and *f/v* is one of tenseness rather than one of voicing. The difference between the voiceless and voiced velar fricatives has become almost allophonic: voiced (or lax) after long vowels word-medially, and voiceless elsewhere. A few exceptions to this regularity are historical and are indicated by the orthography: *lachen* 'laugh' [lɑxən] vs. *vlaggen* 'flags' [ɣlɑɣən]. The realisation of the velar fricative as [ç] as in German *ich* 'I', or as voiced [ɣ] in word-initial position is regarded as dialectal, more particularly as 'southern'. In the non-native vocabulary, the word-medial alveolar fricative is predictably voiced after long vowels: *televisie*, 'television', *Indonesië* 'Indonesia', *NASA* 'id'. Voiced word-initial fricatives are only minimally distinct from the voiceless fricatives that were reintroduced into the language in loanwords: *fier* 'proud' (from French *fière*) [fiːʀ] vs. *vier* 'four' [ʋiːʀ]. Voiced [g] is lacking because it changed to [x], also in French loans: *galant* 'gallant' [xalɑ́nt].

The vowel system of Dutch is somewhat more complex. The opposition long-short is important in the lexicon and in the morphology: *maan* 'moon' vs. *man* 'man'; *boos* 'angry' vs. *bos* 'woods'; *veel* 'much' vs. *vel* 'skin'; *vies* 'dirty' vs. *vis* 'fish'. High vowels are tense rather than long, but pair with long vowels in the phonological system. Dutch has a full set of rounded front vowels.

Non-low back vowels are rounded. Long [a] is central and very open, but its pronunciation differs considerably across the language area. Long [e] is closed, and diphthongal: [eʲ], but long [o] is markedly less diphthongal than its counterpart in English. Short vowels, except schwa, cannot occur in word-final position. Long variants of the short vowels occur before [ʀ], as in *deur* [døːʀ] 'door' vs. *deuk* [dök] 'dent', and also in loanwords, e.g. *militair* 'military (adj.)', [militέːʀ] vs. *ver* [vɛʀ] 'far'. The unstressed vowel and epenthetic vowel [ə] is not always phonetically distinguishable from short [œ] but is clearly a separate phoneme in the system. The pronunciation of the three rising diphthongs varies, but the very open varieties, e.g. [ɑɪ] for [εɪ] are socially stigmatised, and so are the non-diphthongised varieties that occur in the larger cities in the western part of the country, e.g. Amsterdam [ε:] for [εɪ] in [fε:n] *fijn*, 'fine', and The Hague [œ:] for [ʌü] in [dœ:n] *duin* 'dune'.

One of the most typical features of Dutch pronunciation, which it shares with German, is the devoicing of all obstruents in word-final and syllable-final position. This led to morphological contrasts such as *kruis–kruisen* 'cross–crosses' vs. *huis–huizen* 'house–houses', *hees–hese* 'husky–id., inflected form' vs. *vies–vieze* 'dirty–id., inflected form' and *eis–eisen* 'to demand' vs. *reis–reizen* 'to travel'. That the rule is still operative can be seen from the pronunciation of foreign words like *Sidney* [sɪtni], *Rizla* [ʀɪsla]. Its effects can be undone through regressive voicing assimilation at morpheme boundaries and in sandhi position: *huisdeur* 'front door' is pronounced [hʌüzdœ:ʀ] and *Mazda* is pronounced [mɑzda]. But when the second of two adjacent obstruents is a fricative, voicing assimilation is progressive: *huisvuil* 'garbage' is [hʌüsfʌül], and *badzout* 'bathing salts' is [bɑtsɑut].

Another typical feature is the insertion of [ə] in non-homorganic consonant clusters in word-final position and at morpheme boundaries: *melk* 'milk' [mɛlək], *arm* 'arm' [ɑʀəm], *hopeloos* 'hopeless' [hopəlos]. A 'linking phoneme' [ə] also occurs in some compounds: *geitemelk* 'goat milk'. This is a characteristic difference between the pronunciation and the lexicons of Dutch and German: Dutch *mogelijk* 'possible', German *möglich*; Dutch *adelaar* 'eagle', German *Adler*. Glottalisation of initial vowels hardly occurs in Dutch and glides are inserted automatically between vowels except after [a]: *douane* 'customs' [duwánə], *theater* 'theatre' [tejátər], compare German [teʔá:tɐ] 'id'. (Re)syllabification is pervasive, and V(C)C-V sequences will preferably be restructured to V(C)-CV, so that the word *gást+àrbeid+er* 'immigrant worker' will be pronounced [χás-tɑʀ-bɛɪ-dər]. Geminates disappeared from the language, but can occur at morpheme boundaries and in sandhi position: *uit+trekken* 'to pull out' [ʌüt:ʀɛkən] vs. *uit+rekken* 'stretch' [ʌütʀɛkən]. Word-final *-n* after schwa is dropped in almost all contexts, so that for most speakers the difference between singular and plural has been reduced to a difference between Ø ending and *-e* ending: *straat–straten* 'street–streets', [stʀat]–[stʀatə]. This situation has been reinforced by a historical rule that deleted word-final schwa in nouns: Dutch *zon* 'sun', German *Sonne*; as a result of this rule, a large majority of native nouns end in a consonant. That this rule is no longer operative can be seen from the pronunciation of loans like English *score* [skó:ʀə] and French *elite* [elítə]. Deletion of final [t] in consonant clusters is determined by complex morphological, phonological, and stylistic factors, but it is standard in the formation of diminutives: *lucht+je* 'smell (diminutive)' is pronounced [lœxjə].

Word stress in Dutch is lexical, which means that the location of main stress is unpredictable to a high degree. In words without internal morphological structure main stress tends to be on the (pre)final syllable, and there is a complex interaction between the distribution of stresses, vowel length and syllable weight. Compare *kóning* 'king' [kónɪŋ] and *koníjn* 'rabbit' [konέɪn]. All vowels can be stressed except schwa, unstressed vowels are often reduced but not in word-final position: *banáan* 'banana' [banán], [bənán] but *Amérika* 'America' [amέʀika]. In the Romance vocabulary, Dutch has preserved (pre)final stress; as a consequence, there are systematic differences between the pronunciation of these words in Dutch and the pronunciation of their English cognates: *relátion–relátie* [ʀelátsi] but: *rélative–relatiéf* [ʀèlatíf], *sócial–sociáal* [sošjál]. Most suffixes of Romance origin have kept their stress in Dutch, including the verbal suffix *-eer* that was formed from the original French infinitive ending: *organiseer* 'organise' [ɔʀxaniʓέ·ʀ]. Secondary stress on these words is predictably on the initial syllable when main stress is final. In contrast with the pattern of derived Romance words, most native suffixes and early Latin loans have lost their stress. Main stress in complex native words is usually on the stem: *lángzaam* 'slow' – *lángzaamheid* 'slowness', *árbeid* 'work' – *árbeider* 'worker', *vriend* 'friend' – *vríendelijk* 'friendly'. Nominal and verbal compounds normally have primary stress on the first element and secondary stress on the second element: *húisdeùr* 'front door', *uítvoèr* 'export', *ínleìd* 'introduce'. In some classes of derived forms, especially adjectives, main stress shifts to the last syllable preceding the suffix: *ínleìd–ìnleídend* 'introductory'.

Sentence intonation in Dutch is more 'flat' than the sentence intonation of (British) English. The typical intonation pattern for the Dutch declarative sentence involves two basic contours: a Low declining contour at the beginning and at the end, and a High declining contour in the middle. What is perceived as 'accent' is the result of either a rise towards the High contour or a fall from the High contour: *die **jongen** schrijft een **brief*** 'that boy is writing a letter'.

4 Morphology

Since Dutch lost most of its inflectional endings and case endings in the course of its history, its morphology, in that respect, is closer to English than it is to German. Compare the nominal paradigms for the phrase 'the day' in the chart given here. Case distinctions have been preserved to some extent

Nominal Paradigms

	Middle Dutch	Modern Dutch	Modern German
Singular			
Nom.	die dach	de dag	der Tag
Acc.	dien dach	de dag	den Tag
Gen.	des daghes	(van) de dag	des Tages
Dat.	dien daghe	(aan) de dag	dem Tag(e)

Plural

Nom.	die daghe		de dagen	die Tage
Acc.	die daghe		de dagen	die Tage
Gen.	der daghe	(van)	de dagen	der Tage
Dat.	dien daghen	(aan)	de dagen	den Tagen

in the forms of pronouns and in some relic forms such as *'s nachts* 'at night'. The basic distinction in both the nominal and the verbal paradigms, however, is the distinction between singular and plural. In the regular (or 'weak') verbal paradigm, singular forms are differentiated for person in the following way: first person stem + Ø, second and third person stem + *t*. As in the nominal paradigms, the contrast between stem-final voiced consonants and stem-final voiceless consonants is neutralised in the singular forms and not consistently represented in the orthography.

Verbal Paradigms

	'travel'	'demand'	'find'	'put'
Stem	reiz-	eis-	vind-	zet-
1st	reis	eis	vind	zet
Sg. 2nd	reist	eist	vindt	zet
3rd	reist	eist	vindt	zet
Pl.	reizen	eisen	vinden	zetten
Infinitive	reizen	eisen	vinden	zetten
Past part.	gereisd	geëist	gevonden	gezet

The basic tense opposition in verbs is between past and non-past. Past forms in regular verbs are made by adding *-de/-te* to the stem, and *-den/-ten* for the plural. Like English and German, Dutch has retained a number of 'strong' verbs where the past is formed by vowel change: *ik vond–I found–ich fand*. Regular past participles are formed by adding the prefix *ge-* and the suffix *-d/ -t*; strong verbs and a few others have the suffix *-en*. The auxiliaries of the perfect tense are *hebben* 'have' or *zijn* 'be'. Transitive verbs take *hebben*, but intransitives are split into two classes: *ik lach–ik heb gelachen* 'I laugh, I have laughed' and *ik val–ik ben gevallen* 'I have fallen'. The perfect tense is largely aspectual, and the future tense with the auxiliary *zullen* expresses modality rather than tense. The auxiliary of the passive voice is *worden*, but the perfect of the passive takes *zijn* 'be'. The phrase *de deur is gesloten* can be interpreted either as 'the door has been closed (by somebody)' or as 'the door is shut'.

The personal pronouns have subject forms and object forms, and full forms and reduced forms in both categories; see the chart of personal pronouns. In the spoken language, full forms have become almost emphatic and the reduced forms are commonly used. The neuter pronoun *het* is pronounced [ət]; *het* [hɛt] is used in the orthography. After prepositions, it is obligatorily replaced by the adverbial pronoun *er*: **ik denk aan het / ik denk*

Personal Pronouns

		Subject forms		Object forms	
		Full forms	Reduced forms	Full forms	Reduced forms
	1st	ik	'k	mij	me
Sg.	2nd	jij, u	je, -	jou, u	je, -
	3rd	hij, zij	-ie, ze	hem, haar	'm, 'r
		(het)	't	(het)	't
	1st	wij	we	ons	-
Pl.	2nd	jullie, u	-	jullie, u	-
	3rd	zij	ze	(hen), hun	ze

er aan 'I think of it'. The clitic pronoun *-ie* and reduced object pronouns cannot be preposed in the sentence: *ik heb 'm niet gezien* 'I haven't seen him', but not *'m heb ik niet gezien*. In the third person, there is strong interaction between personal pronouns and demonstratives, as can be seen from the following sequence of sentences:

Waar is *Jan*? *Die* komt vandaag niet. *Hij* is ziek; ik geloof dat-*ie* griep heeft.
'Where is John? He is not coming today. He is sick; I think he has the flu.'

The third person plural object pronoun *hen* was artificially introduced into the language and is hardly used; the pronoun *hun* occurs mostly after prepositions: *aan hun* 'to them'. In some dialects it is also used as a subject pronoun: *hun hebben 't gedaan* 'they did it'. A third person reflexive pronoun, *zich*, was introduced under the influence of German. Its syntactic distribution is notoriously complex, and many geographical and social dialects of Dutch still use *hem* instead of *zich*: *Jan heeft geen jas bij zich/bij'm* 'John doesn't have a coat with him'.

The difference between the polite form of address *u* (pronounced [ü]) and the informal forms *jij/jullie* is comparable to the difference between German *Sie* and *du* and French *vous* and *tu*. As everywhere, the sociology of their usage is complicated. Southern forms of Dutch have different forms of address which include the older pronouns *gij/ge*.

In spite of the strong simplification of the nominal and pronominal paradigms, or, maybe, because of these developments, the gender system of Dutch is actually quite complex. Its major features may be summarised as follows:

(1) Nouns are divided into two classes: nouns with common gender, which take the definite determiner *de*, and nouns with neuter gender, which take the definite determiner *het*. In the plural, the determiner is *de* for both classes. In noun phrases with the indefinite determiner *een*, adjectives that modify a *de* word have the inflected form, and adjectives that modify a *het* word have the uninflected form. Compare the chart of gender distinctions in nouns.

Gender Distinctions in Nouns

	'the big city'	'the big house'
Sg. def.	de grote stad	het grote huis
Sg. indef.	een grote stad	een groot huis
Pl. def.	de grote steden	de grote huizen

(2) Nouns belonging to the *de* class are distinguished as masculine and feminine. For instance, words with the ending *-ing* are feminine and require the anaphoric pronoun *zij/ze*. For many speakers in the western area, however, the masculine/feminine distinction is no longer alive, or is felt to be a distinction of natural gender. Anaphoric reference to words denoting a non-human object by the pronouns *hij/hem* or *zij/haar* is sometimes avoided, as in the example: *wat vond je van die lezing? ik vond het vervelend* 'what did you think of that lecture? I found it boring'. In the Belgian area, the masculine/feminine gender distinction is very much alive.

(3) Normally, grammatical gender overrides natural gender, as appears from the usage of the relative pronouns *die* and *dat: de stad, die* 'the town which' vs. *het huis, dat* 'the house which' but also *de jongen, die* 'the boy who' vs. *het jongetje dat* 'the boy (diminutive) that'. However, when relative pronouns are combined with prepositions, the form of the relative pronoun is determined by the distinction human/non-human and not by the distinction between *de* words and *het* words. Compare: *de man, met* **wie** *ik gesproken heb* 'the man with whom I have been speaking' vs. *de stad* **waar** *ik geen kaart van had* 'the city of which I did not have a map'. In the spoken language, sentences like *de man waar ik mee gesproken heb* are not at all uncommon, and they are another indication that the gender system and the system of pronominal reference are unstable. The adverbial pronouns *er*, *daar*, *waar*, which replace the pronouns *het*, *dat*, *wat* in combination with prepositions are the only elements that allow prepositions to be stranded, as appears from the examples above. A sentence like *de man wie ik mee gesproken heb* is incorrect.

Both flection and derivation are predominantly suffixal. With respect to derivation (word formation), many native suffixes were originally elements with independent meanings that they lost in the course of history, and it would seem that, in the present-day language, some elements are going the same way: *rijk* 'rich', *arm* 'poor'; *zuurstofrijk* 'having much oxygen', *zuurstofarm* 'having little oxygen'. Most native suffixes also lost their stress, but some retained their stress and occur in compound-like derivations such as *vriendelijk+heid* 'friendliness' (German *-heit*), *verklaar+baar* 'explainable' (German *-bar*) and *werk+loos* 'unemployed' (German *-los*). Romance suffixes are often fully stressed, as shown in the section on phonology, but the morphological structure of the Romance vocabulary is by and large opaque. The main reason for this is that Dutch formed its own verbal stems on the basis of the original French infinitive: *demonstreer* 'demonstrate'.

Consequently, the common element in related nominal and verbal forms is a 'root' that cannot occur as an independent element: *demonstr+eer* 'demonstrate', *demonstr+atie* 'demonstration'. This is atypical for native word formation.

The Romance vocabulary also has a highly involved morphophonology, whereᶜˢ native word formation in Dutch typically has not. With few exceptions, non-native affixes cannot be attached to native stems, but native affixes can be attached to non-native stems. For instance, a number of Romance verbs ending in *-eer* have both a Romance and a native nominalisation: *realis + atie* as well as *realis + eer + ing* 'realisation'. But a formation like English *reopen* would be totally impossible (the correct form is *heropen*, with the native prefix *her-*) though the prefix *re-* does occur, e.g. in *constructie* 'construction', *reconstructie* 'reconstruction'. All in all, it appears that the Romance vocabulary has been much less integrated into Dutch than it has been into English, and that both phonologically and morphologically it is still very much [-native], in spite of the fact that a number of Romance words are actually quite common, also in the spoken language.

A much discussed feature of Dutch morphology is the system of diminutives. The diminutive suffix is, actually, one of the few really productive derivational suffixes of the modern language. The basic form of the suffix is *-tje*, the variants are *-je* (after obstruents), *-etje* (in some cases after liquids and nasals); *-pje* and *-kje* are assimilated variants of *-tje*. So we have: *ei–eitje* 'egg', *aap–aapje* 'monkey', *man–mannetje* 'man', *maan–maantje* 'moon', *koning–koninkje* 'king' and *raam–raampje* 'window'. Diminutives are very frequent, and semantically they express a whole range of negative as well as positive attitudes and feelings besides the basic meaning of 'small'. A much used variant of the *-je* forms in the spoken language (after consonants except [t]) is *-ie*: *meisje–meissie* 'girl'. The same paradigm, with the additional ending *-s* is used to form adverbs from certain adjectives: *zacht* 'soft', *zachtjes* 'softly'; *bleek* 'pale', *bleekjes* 'somewhat pale'.

Prefixation is, generally speaking, more transparent and more productive than suffixation and the phonological boundary between prefix and stem is more distinct as well. The prefix *be-* is used to form transitive verbs from intransitives, as in *spreken* 'speak', *bespreken* 'discuss', and can also be used to form verbs from nouns: *dijk* 'dike', *bedijken* 'to put a dike around—'. The prefix *ver-* has a causative meaning in some verbs: *hitte* 'heat (noun)' – *verhitten* 'heat (transitive)', *breed* 'large, broad' – *verbreden* 'enlarge, broaden', but a more complex meaning in other verbs: *draaien* 'turn' – *verdraaien* 'turn into another direction; twist'.

Dutch is like German in that it still exploits a large number of the Indo-European compounding devices. Some of the more familiar types are compounds with nouns as heads: *huisdeur* (noun noun) 'house door; front door', *breekpunt* (noun noun) 'breaking point', *hoogspanning* (adjective noun) 'high voltage' and compounds with verbs as heads: *pianospelen* (noun verb) 'play the piano', *losmaken* (adjective verb) 'make loose, loosen, untie' and *uitvoeren* (particle verb) 'export'. The second group represents the so-called separable compounds. In independent clauses, the complements are separated from the verb as in: *dit land voert bananen uit* 'this country exports bananas'. This type of incorporation, which is actually on the boundary of morphology and syntax, is extremely common and a number of these formations have acquired specialised meanings: *afmaken* 'finish, kill', *zwartmaken* 'blacken, spoil somebody's reputation'. Another special class of compounds are the so-called derivational compounds. On the surface, these formations have the shape of a compound plus derivational suffix, but there is no corresponding non-derived compound, and for some formations, there is no corresponding non-composite derivation either. Some examples: *langslaper* 'somebody who sleeps long' (**langslaap*, but, possibly, *lang* + *slaper*); *werknemer* 'employee' (**werkneem*, and hardly *werk* + ?*nemer*); *loslippig* 'talkative' (**loslip*, nor *los* + **lippig*); *driewieler* 'vehicle on three wheels' (**driewiel*, nor *drie* + **wieler*). Here too, it would seem, morphology borders on syntax: one way to account for these words is to assume that they are phrasal at an underlying level: *langslaper* 'somebody who sleeps long'; *loslippig* 'the property of having loose lips', and that they arise through incorporation rather than through simple concatenation of independent elements.

Though some rules of word formation lead to complex forms, it would be wrong to conclude that Dutch is the type of language that allows for fairly unlimited combination of stems and affixes. On the contrary, there are severe, and as yet ill-understood restrictions on affixation and on compounding. Repeated application of compounding rules also has its limitations: compounds of the type *zitkamertafeltje* 'sitting-room-table-diminutive' or *autoverkoopcijfers* 'car-sales-figures' are not very common, and often avoided in favour of more analytical constructions like *cijfers van de autoverkoop*.

5   Syntax

The syntax of Dutch is of the familiar nominative-accusative type. Subject and object are the major grammatical relations. Since the case distinctions have been lost, objects are bare noun phrases and other grammatical relations are expressed by prepositional phrases. Grammatical subjects, including the subjects of passives, agree with the finite verb in person and number and the subject also plays a dominant role in various anaphoric processes, e.g. reflexive pronouns often can only refer to the subject of the sentence. The prominent role of the subject in Dutch is particularly clear from the use of the dummy subject *het* and the use of the dummy subject *er* in impersonal passives, as well as from the fact that subjects in declarative sentences cannot easily be omitted. Compare:

Het is vervelend dat Wim niet komt. 'It is annoying that Bill is not coming'.
Er wordt gedanst. 'There is dancing.'
*(Er) komt niemand. '(There) comes no one.'

In declarative sentences, the subject precedes the finite verb; in questions, requests and certain types of conditionals the finite verb is sentence-initial: *komt Wim vanavond?* 'Is Bill coming tonight?' Question words are sentence-initial, and when a non-subject is preposed, the subject moves to the position after the finite verb: *wat doe je?* 'what are you doing?'.

All this is, indeed, familiar from many other European languages. Nevertheless, Dutch as well as German, Afrikaans and Frisian differ in their surface syntax from both English and, to a lesser extent, the Scandinavian languages in a number of ways, and some of these differences are more than superficial. The prominent features of the Dutch declarative clause can be summarised as follows:

(a) In independent clauses, the finite verb is in second position.

(b) In clauses where the finite verb is an auxiliary, the main verb (whether infinitive or participle) is placed at the end of the clause. The nominal object and any other nominal complement of the verb precede the main verb.

(c) In independent clauses with more than one auxiliary, all verbs except the finite verb are placed at the end of the clause.

(d) In dependent clauses, the finite verb is placed at the end of the clause as well.

(e) In independent clauses, almost any type of constituent can be preposed to sentence-initial position without special emphasis or so-called comma intonation. Compare:

Wim   heeft het boek aan Marietje gegeven.
Het boek   heeft Wim aan Marietje gegeven.
(Aan) Marietje heeft Wim het boek gegeven.
'Bill has given the book to Mary.'

And, with some emphasis:

Mòoi is het níet.
'Beautiful is it not' i.e. 'It is not exactly beautiful.'
Gelàchen hebben we wél.
'Laughed have we modal' i.e. 'We certainly laughed!'

So, it appears that the Dutch independent clause is both verb-second and verb-final. Most grammarians assume that, at a somewhat more abstract level of representation, the Dutch clause is verb-final, and that the second position of the finite verb in the independent clause is 'derived'. It can actually be shown that in the unmarked case, the ordering of constituents proceeds from right to left with the final position of the main verb as the focal point:

Wim heeft	gisteren met een schroevedraaier	het slot opengemaakt.
Bill has	yesterday with a screwdriver	the lock open made

'Bill (has) opened the lock with a screwdriver yesterday'.

Another conclusion is that the Dutch independent clause is not subject-initial but verb-second. The ordering of constituents in those sentences where the subject is not in sentence-initial position is more adequately and more easily accounted for, not by assuming the traditional rule of subject-verb inversion, but by assuming that one constituent has to be preposed to the position before the finite verb. If no other constituent appears in that position, the grammatical subject fills it 'by default'. Preposing is blocked in the dependent clause, but peripheral adverbials can precede the subject in such clauses: *omdat morgen gelukkig de winkels open zijn* 'because tomorrow fortunately the shops open are'.

These constraints on the position of the verb and of its nominal complement developed relatively late in the history of the language and they seem to have been fixed not before the beginning of the period of Modern Dutch. Sentences with a more random word order, including dependent clauses with verb-object order can easily be attested in medieval texts. In the course of the process, Dutch developed another construction that shows a complement ordered to the left of its head, namely, preposed participial modifiers in the noun phrase: *de door de regering genomen beslissing*, 'the by the government taken decision'. The rise of this pattern was probably facilitated by the existence of noun phrases with prenominal adjectives, which is still the basic pattern in all Germanic languages. It should be added that the construction is more typical of the written language than of the spoken language where it can hardly compete with the regular, postnominal relative clause: *de beslissing die de regering genomen heeft* 'the decision that the government has taken'.

As a result of these developments and their codification into the standard language, Dutch, like German, is more of a hybrid in terms of word order typologies than most other Germanic languages are. The noun phrase bears witness to this as well. As we already saw, both prenominal and postnominal modifiers do occur. The genitive construction is predominantly postnominal: *het boek van die man* 'the book of that man', but there is a residue of the prenominal genitive when the 'possessor' is a proper name: *Wim's boek* 'Bill's book', but not *die man's boek*. Interestingly, Dutch developed another genitive construction that is similar to the prenominal genitive, and quite common in the spoken language though not always accepted in the formal style: *die man z'n boek (ligt op tafel)* 'that man his book (is on the table)'. Also adpositions have a somewhat ambiguous position in Dutch syntax. Prepositions are clearly the unmarked case: *in de tuin* 'in the garden'. But postpositions are common, though not always required, when the phrase expresses direction rather than location:

> Wim liep de tuin in. 'Bill walked into the garden.'

Here, too, positing a verb-final position at a more remote level of description is of some explanatory value. Compare:

> Het regende toen Wim de tuin in liep
> it rained   as   Bill the garden into walked
> 'It rained as Bill walked into the garden.'

It is plausible that these postpositions are, at least in origin, complements to the verb. In not a few cases, they can be interpreted both ways. The sentence *Wim zwom de rivier over* 'Bill swam the river across' can be paraphrased both as: 'Bill swam across the river' and as 'Bill crossed the river swimming'. The high frequency of so-called separable verbal compounds, or verb particle constructions, that was noted in the section on morphology may thus be explained through the syntax.

The modal verbs of Dutch are main verbs rather than auxiliaries. They have regular inflection, and they take clausal complements just like other verbs do. In sentences that combine several predicates, all verbs are strung together at the end of the clause. This phenomenon, known as clause union or verb raising manifests itself in different ways in different West Germanic languages (and is absent in English). Dutch sides with German in the curious fact that the expected past participle of non-finite auxiliaries is replaced with the infinitive. This does not occur in (West) Frisian:

> Dutch   dat hij het boek heeft *kunnen* lezen
>   that he the book has   can   read
>   'that he has been able to read the book'
> German   daß er das Buch hat lesen *koñnen*
> Frisian   dat er it boek lêze *kent* hat

But Dutch differs from German in that the usual ordering of the modals with respect to the main verb in verbal clusters is the exact mirror image, which is more clear from a comparison of the following sentences:

> Dutch   dat hij het boek moet kunnen lezen
>   that he the book must can read
>   'that he must be able to read the book'
> German   daß er das Buch lesen können muß

And the verbal cluster in Dutch can separate the main verb from its complement, something which does not occur in standard German and is also avoided in many varieties of Dutch in Belgium:

dat hij het boek *uit* moet kunnen *lezen*
that he the book out must can   read
'that he should be able to finish reading the book'

The order main verb–auxiliary is to be expected in a language where the verb phrase is basically OV; the reverse ordering in the verbal cluster of Dutch has, consequently, been interpreted as a tendency to move away from OV ordering. In sequences of a single auxiliary and a main verb, Dutch has an option: *omdat hij het boek heeft gelezen* / *omdat hij het boek gelezen heeft* 'because he has read the book'. It is a subject of debate among Dutch grammarians and dialectologists whether the main verb–auxiliary order is a Germanism or whether it is the more natural one.

Apart from the fixed positions of the finite verb and the main verb, the Dutch clause shows considerable freedom of constituent ordering. That freedom is exploited for the foregrounding or backgrounding of information and for embedding the sentence in its context. Preposing is one way to achieve this. Calculations on a fair sample of the written language have shown that less than fifty per cent of declarative clauses are subject-initial. Also, definite nominal objects can easily be moved to a position right after the finite verb, and prepositional phrases can be moved to a position after the main verb:

Wim heeft *dat slot* gisteren met een schroevedraaier opengemaakt.
Wim heeft gisteren dat slot opengemaakt *met een schroevedraaier.*

The latter rule also applies to prepositional phrases that are complements of noun phrases:

Ik heb gisteren *een vogel* gezien *met een hele lange staart.*
I have yesterday a bird seen with a very long tail
'I saw a bird with a very long tail yesterday.'

In the German grammatical tradition this phenomenon is known as *Ausklammerung* ('Exbraciation') and it has sometimes been interpreted as a way to avoid difficulties that might be caused by the long distance between the finite verb and its complement in independent clauses. However, the rule applies equally well in dependent clauses where the finite verb and its complement are adjacent. Postposing a nominal complement remains fully ungrammatical and can be achieved only by dislocation and the use of a resumptive pronoun:

Wim heeft *'t* gisteren met een schroevedraaier opengemaakt, *dat slot*.
'Bill has it yesterday with a screwdriver open made, that lock.'

The sentence-initial position is also available for topicalisation of elements from the dependent clause, with more restrictions than in some of the Scandinavian languages but, it would seem, with fewer restrictions than in standard German.

Die man die jij zei dat je niet — kende is de minister-president.
'That man that you said you didn't know — is the prime minister.'

That topicalisation by preposing is a pervasive feature of Dutch syntax also appears from the occurrence, in the spoken language, of an incorrect construction that can be regarded as a form of 'repeated topicalisation':

Toen hebben ze *die man* hebben ze gearresteerd.
then have they that man have they arrested

Sentence-initial anaphoric elements are commonly omitted, as in *waar is Wim? (Dat) weet ik niet*, 'where is Bill? (That) I don't know'. This phenomenon is easiest described as deletion of a topic, which would reinforce the view that the Dutch independent clause is topic-first rather than subject-first.

Summarising, Dutch has an absolute constraint on the order of the verb and its nominal complement, and a strong tendency towards ordering complements to the left of their heads in general, but other features of its syntax indicate that it is, nevertheless, far from being a consistent OV language. It is, therefore, not surprising that the concept of the verb phrase is essential for an adequate description of its syntax, whereas the usefulness of such a concept has been seriously doubted for classical OV languages like Japanese.

Bibliography

There are no good comprehensive grammars of Dutch published in English, but some practical grammars for foreign students are available. Den Hertog (1903–4) is by far the best grammar of the Dutch language, in spite of the fact that it is now more than 75 years old, and is modern in its treatment of syntax. Geerts et al. (1984) is a practical and descriptive grammar of the present-day language written by a team of Dutch and Belgian linguists; it is meant for the general public, and is important for its wide coverage of facts. Zonneveld et al. (1980) is a collection of recent articles on various aspects of Dutch phonology, and contains a useful bibliography compiled by Zonneveld.

Franck (1910) is the best available grammar of the older stages of the language. Van Loey (1970) is the standard reference work for the development of Dutch in the context of Germanic, but some sections have been enlarged so often that it would be better if the whole book were rewritten. Van Haeringen (1960) is a critical and comprehensive survey of the study of Dutch in the Netherlands and abroad, by one of the outstanding scholars in the field.

References

Den Hertog, C.H. 1903–4. *Nederlandse Spraakkunst*, 3 vols., 2nd ed. (Amsterdam, reprinted with an introduction by H. Hulshof, Versluys Amsterdam, 1972–3)

Franck, J. 1910. *Mittelniederländische Grammatik mit Lesestücken und Glossar* (Tauchnitz, Leipzig, reprinted Gysbers and van Loon, Arnhem, 1967).

Geerts, G., W. Haeseryn, J. de Rooij and M.C. van den Toorn (eds.) 1984. *Algemene Nederlandse Spraakkunst* (Groningen and Leuven, Wolters)

Van Haeringen, C.B.1960. *Netherlandic Language Research: Men and Works in the Study of Dutch*, 2nd ed. (E. J. Brill, Leiden)

Van Loey, A. 1970. *Schönfeld's Historische Grammatica van het Nederlands*, 8th ed. (Thieme and Co., Zutphen)

Zonneveld, W., F. Van Coetsem and O.W. Robinson (eds.) 1980. *Studies in Dutch Phonology* (Martinus Nijhoff, The Hague)

6 Danish, Norwegian and Swedish

Einar Haugen

1 Introduction

Non-Scandinavians are occasionally astonished to hear Danes, Norwegians and Swedes conversing, each in their own language, without interpreters. The fact that some degree of mutual intelligibility exists between these languages, which we shall refer to as the mainland Scandinavian languages, has led some to suggest that together they should really be regarded as only one language. While for some purposes it is convenient to bracket them together, it is hardly correct to speak of only one Scandinavian or Nordic tongue. Such a practice would require a rather restricted definition of the term 'language'. It would neglect those aspects that are not purely linguistic, but are also social and political. To call them 'dialects' is only historically true, i.e. in that they have branched off from a once common Nordic.

In speaking of them as 'languages', we take into account the facts as Scandinavians themselves also see them: that they constitute separately developed norms of writing and speaking. Each language has an officially accepted form, taught in schools, used by journalists and authors, required for government officials, enshrined in grammars and dictionaries and spoken at least by educated members of the nation. They are, in short, what linguists refer to as 'standardised', making them standard languages. This is indisputably true of Danish and Swedish. The fact that Norwegian is spoken and written in two somewhat deviating forms only means that we must distinguish two standard Norwegian languages. These will here be referred to as B-Norwegian (BN), for Norwegian *bokmål* 'book language', formerly *riksmål* 'national language', and as N-Norwegian (NN), for Norwegian *nynorsk* 'New Norwegian', formerly *landsmål* 'country language'. The names used in Norway are misnomers resulting from political conflict and compromise.

In reckoning here with only four mainland languages, we are setting aside what we may call the *insular* Scandinavian languages *Faroese* (in the Faroe Islands) and *Icelandic* (in Iceland). Danish is still one of the two official languages in the Faroes and in Greenland. Swedish is official not only in Sweden, but also alongside Finnish in Finland, although today only 5 or 6 per cent of the population speak it natively. We exclude Finnish from this account, since it is wholly unrelated to the Indo-European languages that surround it. It belongs to the Finno-Ugric family, as does Samic, formerly called Lappish, the dialectally divided speech of the Sami (Lapps), who inhabit the far north of Scandinavia and nearby Russia. Greenlandic, a variety of Eskimo (Inuit), is also spoken within Scandinavia, as are Romany (Gypsy) and along the south Danish border some German. The following account is thus limited to the central, mainland Scandinavian of Indo-European descent, the standard languages of the Scandinavian heartland.

2 Historical Background

The earliest written evidence of language in this area is epigraphic, i.e. consisting of inscriptions from about AD 200, mostly quite short. They were written in an alphabet known as a futhark from the sounds of its first six letters. The letters are called runes and the type of writing is runic. The earliest centres of its use are in the Danish peninsula of Jutland, which may also be its place of origin. The 24 runes of the futhark (also known as the 'older' futhark) are clearly based on a classical alphabet, most likely the Latin, but differently ordered and named. Designed for carving in wood, it is mostly preserved on more permanent objects of stone and metal. It was never used for writing on parchment, although it was in use down to c. AD 800, when it was replaced by a shorter 16-rune 'younger' futhark. Although the latter appeared in several regional variations, it steadfastly maintained the number sixteen well into the modern period.

The Older Futhark

ᚠᚢᚦᚨᚱᚲᚷᚹ:ᚺᚾ ᛁ ᛃᛇᛈᛉᛊ:ᛏᛒᛖᛗᛚ ᛜᛞᛟ

f u þ a r k g w : h n i j ė p z s : t b e m l ng d o

The Younger Futhark

ᚠᚢᚦᚨᚱᚴ:ᚼᚾᛁᛆᛋ : ᛏᛒᛘᛚ ᛦ

f u þ a̧ r k : h n i a s : t b m l R

The earliest runic material, though scanty, is sufficient to assure us that at this time the inhabitants of Scandinavia were of Germanic speech. These inscriptions are in fact the earliest written evidences of any Germanic language, earlier than the extinct East Germanic Gothic or the West Germanic Old English, Old Saxon, Old High German, Old Low Franconian or Old Frisian. The Proto-Scandinavian of the earliest inscriptions constitutes the North Germanic ancestor of the present-day Scandinavian languages.

The line of descent is best (if somewhat roughly) visualised as a branching tree, starting from a hypothetical Common Scandinavian and ending on the bottom line with the present-day languages properly called 'Scandinavian'.

Figure 6.1: The Scandinavian Languages

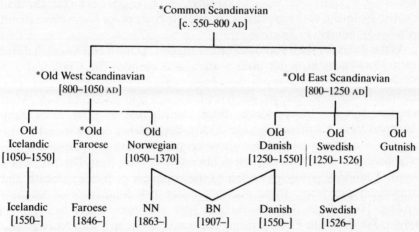

The dates are only approximations. We shall here be dealing with the last four, Danish (Da.), B-Norwegian (BN), N-Norwegian (NN), and Swedish (Sw.). Occasionally it will be convenient to group both Norwegian languages together as 'Norwegian' (Nw.). 'Old Norse' is a commonly used term for a normalised form of Old Icelandic and Old Norwegian, used in the publication of reading texts.

In its medieval, handwritten form there is a large body of Scandinavian writing on parchment or paper. This skill was brought to Scandinavia by Christian missionaries and monks at the end of the Viking Age (AD 750–1050), when the Scandinavians were weaned from their worship of Odin and Thor. The missionaries also taught them the Latin alphabet, significantly adapted to suit the language forms then in use. Traditions of writing gradually grew up, reflecting the practices of Latin orthography, but also innovative.

The most extensive, as well as the most notable of this writing, intellectually, historically and as literature, was that part of it produced by Icelanders in the language which Norway and Iceland then still shared. Among its monuments are the collection of pagan mythical and heroic poems called *The Elder Edda*, the handbook of poetics by Snorri Sturluson (1178–1241) known as *The Younger Edda*, and a multitude of so-called *Sagas*, more or less historical tales from Norwegian and Icelandic life in the pagan and post-pagan period. The Icelanders functioned as recorders of tradition for all Scandinavia, and their work is today claimed as part of the heritage of all the Nordic nations. Symbolic is the use of words like 'Viking' and 'Saga', which enter into everyone's stereotyped conceptions of the Scandinavian countries. Today there is a deep cleft between the language of Iceland (and the Faroes) and those of the mainland. Whereas Icelandic and Faroese have retained nearly all the morphological categories of Proto-Germanic, the mainland languages have retained only the genitive as a distinct case (apart from some archaisms), and have gone even further than English by losing verb agreement completely (except for some obsolescent number agreement in Swedish).

As the dates for their standardisation suggest, Danish and Swedish differ from Norwegian in being both unitary and earlier. Their political and cultural development assured their languages of independent status from the time of the Reformation, when the Bible was translated into each. After Sweden won her independence from Danish rule in 1526 under King Gustavus Vasa, a written language in close dependence on the speech of the court in Stockholm and of the whole central Swedish area around it was established, even to some extent deliberately deviant from Danish. When Swedish military power extended to the conquest of former Danish and Norwegian provinces, these also fell under the dominance of Swedish writing. Henceforth Scandinavia was split into two clearly demarcated halves, Sweden with Finland facing the Baltic, Denmark with Norway and the islands facing the Atlantic.

Denmark, with a language taking shape around Copenhagen (and neighbouring Lund), also got its own Lutheran church and its own Bible, which it succeeded in imposing on Norway as well. Four centuries of Danish dominion (c. 1380–1814) taught Norwegians to write Danish, but not to follow all the newer developments in speech. After an independence gradually won through rupture of the Danish union in 1814 and the Swedish in 1905, the Norwegians found themselves with a cultivated spoken language which, though written like Danish, was spoken with Norwegian sounds and shot through with elements from the folk language. It was a 'Dano-Norwegian' that is still the dominant language, but now written according to its Norwegian pronunciation and known as *bokmål*. The major break with Danish orthography took place in 1907 and was followed by further radical changes in 1917 and 1938. Hence B-Norwegian is shown above as being descended both from Old Norwegian (via speech) and Old Danish (via writing). The father of its spelling reforms was Knud Knudsen (1812–95), schoolmaster and language reformer.

N-Norwegian (known today as *nynorsk*) also goes back to the efforts of a single man, the self-taught linguist and language reformer Ivar Aasen (1813–96). His work was done from 1836 to 1873, including a definitive grammar (1864) and a dictionary (1873). His N-Norwegian was a reconstructed form, a standard based on the spoken dialects, which he was the first to investigate. He was guided also by the Danish and Swedish standards and by Old Norse, which led him to build on the more conservative dialects of western Norway. His norm has been considerably modernised by later users and grammarians, but has won only about one sixth of the school districts of the country. Even so, it must be taken seriously as the standard of a not inconsiderable section of the Norwegian people, including many authors, scholars and institutions.

The consequence of these historical and social developments has been that the old division of Scandinavia into a western and eastern half has been replaced by a much more complex overlapping. Norwegian has had its form returned to a closer relation to Swedish, geographically natural; while at least B-Norwegian has retained a great deal of its cultivated lexicon from Danish. The present-day relation may be seen as a right triangle, with the hypotenuse between Danish and Swedish. Speaking very generally, B-Norwegian (and to some extent even N-Norwegian) has its lexicon common with Danish, but phonology common with Swedish. When Norwegians and Swedes communicate orally, they can tell what word is being spoken, though they may be uncertain of its meaning. When Norwegians and Danes communicate, they have to listen hard to be sure which word the other is using, but once they get that, they usually know what it means. Or as one wit has put it: Norwegian is Danish spoken in Swedish.

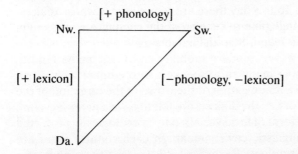

Even though the present-day norms of writing were established with the help of the printing press, at the time of the Reformation, they were not spread to the common people until the nineteenth century, with the establishment of universal public school systems.

3   The Common Heritage

The degree of intelligibility that does exist in Scandinavia today, as well as the obstacles that have led to what I have called 'semi-communication' within the area, have their origin in two major factors: (1) a basic common ancestry in the Old Scandinavian languages; and (2) common influences from outside the area. We do not know how unified Proto-Scandinavian really was; its unity may be an artifact of linguistic reconstruction. There are striking basic similarities that immediately identify the Scandinavian languages, some of them unique, others shared with other Germanic languages. On the other hand, we can follow, at least since the beginning of the manuscript tradition, many of the differential choices made in the course of time. We can also see how the influence of such foreign languages as Greek, Latin, Low German, High German, French, and today English has been incorporated into Scandinavian often giving the same results in each language, but at times also quite different results. Since there has always been some communication within the area, influences of all kinds have spread from one country to the other. It will be noted that the languages listed as providing most of the outside influence are all of the West European type. It is striking that in spite of a certain contact with Celtic languages in the west and with Slavonic languages in the east, very few influences are detectable from these.

The loss of unity in this area is reflected in the growth of dialectal differences both within the countries and between them. Before the standard had been popularised, the mostly rural population split into local and regional dialects. Local communities functioned as closed societies, whether as in Denmark and southern Sweden they were villages, or as in Norway and northern Sweden they were parishes with individual farms. The area turned into a mosaic of dialects, crisscrossed by geographical differences that can be mapped as isoglosses. To this day there are remote areas whose dialects are partly or wholly unintelligible to citizens of the capital, e.g. Jutland in Denmark, Dalecarlia in Sweden, Setesdal in Norway.

For the most part, however, modern mobility and mass media tend to reduce the gap by bringing many rural speakers into contact with urban dialects, often leading to a modification of their own in the direction of the standard. Especially in Norway the dialects are felt to have a national value, a charming and diverting form of local variation to be ecologically protected as part of a vanishing linguistic environment. In each country there are institutes devoted to dialectology. Recent years have seen the growth of a sociolinguistic awareness of speech variation, including the full spectrum from rural dialects and working-class speech to elite and formal varieties.

4 Accent: Stress and Tone

Dynamic stress is distributed over words and sentences in patterns similar to those of other Germanic languages, in degrees varying from primary to weak (also called 'unstressed'). The basic rule of dynamic stress on the first syllable, inherited from Germanic, is still the major rule, but it is now preserved in full only in Icelandic. On the mainland, as in German and English, the rule has been broken to permit a large number of loanwords with stress on the last or penultimate syllable. Post-initial stress may be taken as a marker of 'foreignness' in such words: Da. Nw. Sw. *natu´r* 'nature', *natu´rlig* 'natural'; Nw. *gemytt´* 'temper', *gemytt´lig* 'good natured' (Da. Sw. *gemy´t*, *gemy´tlig*) (note that stress is marked with an accent at the end of the stressed syllable). Differences between the languages may require one to check on one's neighbours with the help of a dictionary: e.g. *egentlig* 'really' is Sw. [ejen´tli], but Nw. [e´gentli], from German *eigentlich*. Verb-particle phrases also have definite, language-specific rules: Danish and Swedish usually stress the particle, Norwegian often the verb, as in Da. *stå opp´/* Sw. *stå upp´/* vs. Nw. *stå`-opp* 'get up'.

Compounds usually have primary stress on the first member, secondary or reduced stress on the second, e.g. Da. *kal´veste͵g* [-stai͵]/BN. *kal`veste͵k/* Sw. *kal`vste͵k* 'veal roast'. Again there are exceptions, as in Da./BN *hushold´ning/* Sw. *hu`shållning* 'housekeeping'. Especially confusing are occasional place-names, like Da. *København´n* [-hau´n], Nw. *Kristiansan´d*, Sw. *Drottninghol´m*.

Parallel to similar developments in English and German, the mainland Nordic languages have over the centuries undergone an extensive process of *stress reduction* in the less conspicuous syllables, reflected especially in the quality of vowels and in the inflectional system. While Old Scandinavian regularly had unstressed syllables containing the vowels *-i/-e*, *-u/-o* and *-a*, the modern languages have mostly levelled the three to one, *-e* (pronounced [ə]) in Danish and B-Norwegian, to *-e* and *-a* (and an occasional *-o*) in Swedish and N-Norwegian. It is unclear whether the phonological or the morphological development is primary here, but the result is part of a general trend from a more to a less inflected language, i.e. from a synthetic to an analytic language.

The most striking feature of the Scandinavian accentual system is its preservation of a distinction that probably arose in Common Scandinavian, namely its two contrasting prosodemes, which we shall here designate as 'Accent 1' and 'Accent 2'. In most forms of Norwegian and Swedish and in some Danish dialects, these are realised as tonemes, i.e. musical differences that are regularly associated with the primary dynamic stress and are heard as rising or falling word melodies. The difference is significant in poly-syllables, where minimal pairs are common (Accent 1 is marked by an acute, Accent 2 by a grave marker): Nw. *huset* 'the house' [hʉ´sə] vs. *huse* 'to house' [hʉ`sə], *fin´ner* 'finds' vs. *fin`ner* 'finder'; Sw. *bu´ren* 'the cages' vs. *bu`ren* 'borne', *nub´ben* 'the tack' vs. *nub`ben* 'the drink'. The distinction goes back to a difference in Common or Old Scandinavian between monosyllables (with Accent 1) and polysyllables (with Accent 2). Every stressed syllable gets one of the two accents.

In standard Danish the distinction of accent is similar in distribution, but very different in phonetic realisation. Here Accent 1 is realised as a glottal catch or glottalisation, known in Danish as *stød* 'thrust'. It occurs in words that in Old Norse were monosyllables, e.g. *finder* 'finds' [fin?ɔ] from ON *finnr*, not in old polysyllables, e.g. *finder* 'finder' from ON *finnari*. There are some special factors in the Danish case, e.g. in the effect of certain consonants in preventing *stød* in monosyllables. While the rules in each case are complex, their similarity to the Norwegian-Swedish situation is so great that scholars agree they are connected. It is not certain which is primary, but most scholars have assumed that the tonemes are primary and the glottalisation secondary.

5   Vowels

Each language has nine basic vowels, the five Latin vowels *a, e, i, o, u* plus four additional ones: *y* (high front round), Da. Nw. *ø*/Sw. *ö* (mid front round), Da. Nw. *æ*/Sw. *ä* (low front unround) and *å* (mid to low back round; in Da. Nw. formerly written *aa*). The last three are placed at the end of the alphabet: Da. Nw. *æ, ø, å*, Sw. *å, ä, ö*.

All the vowels can be either *long* (tense) or *short* (lax). In Norwegian and Swedish length depends on the following consonant: in stressed syllables vowels are long before short (single) consonants and finally; elsewhere they are short, cf. Nw. Sw. *tak* [taːk] 'roof, ceiling' vs. Nw. *takk*, Sw. *tack* [takː] 'thanks'. This inverse syllabic relationship does not apply in Danish, which lacks long consonants. Hence Nw./Sw. *takk/tack* 'thanks' is written *tak* in Danish, but still with a short vowel. Before a vowel the consonant may be written double to mark the preceding vowel as short, but the consonant is pronounced short: *takke* 'to thank' [tag′ə]. In Danish the symbol *ø* has two values, not distinguished in spelling, its usual mid round front value of [ø] and a lower variety, especially before *r*: [œ].

The vowel qualities are less distorted from the old Latin values of the letters than in English, but even so they have done some shifting. If we visualise the relationship in terms of a traditional vowel diagram, we can say that in Danish they have moved clockwise, in Norwegian and Swedish counterclockwise: see figure 6.2.

Figure 6.2: Vowel Shifts in Danish, Norwegian and Swedish

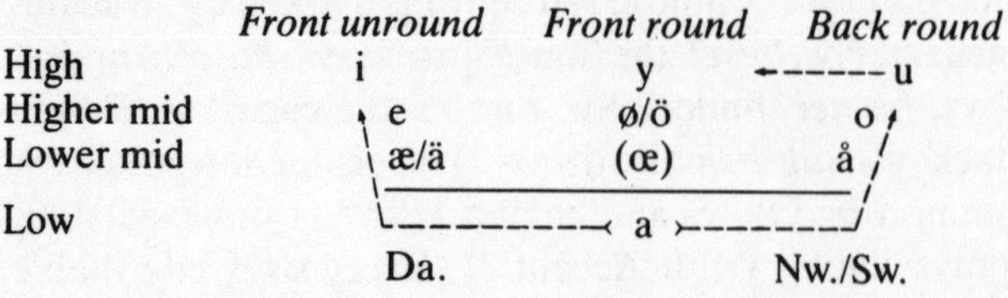

	Front unround	*Front round*	*Back round*
High	i	y	←------ u
Higher mid	↖ e	ø/ö	o ↗
Lower mid	↖ æ/ä	(œ)	å ↗
Low	↖_____	↤ a ↦	_____↗
	Da.		Nw./Sw.

In Danish the *a* has been fronted, bringing it closer to *æ*, *æ* has moved towards *e* and *e* towards *i*. But in Norwegian and Swedish *a* has moved closer to *å*, being backed and rounded, while *å* has moved toward *o* and *o* to *u*, and *u* has been fronted and rounded to become almost an *y*. To a Norwegian and a Swede the Da. *ja* sounds like *jæ/jä*, while to a Dane the Nw./Sw. *ja* sounds like *jå*.

Only N-Norwegian has retained the Old Norse diphthongs in full, now written *au* [æʉ], *ei* [æi], *øy* [œy]: *laus* 'loose', *bein* 'leg, bone', *løysa* 'loosen'. In Danish and Swedish (and conservative B-Norwegian) these are monophthongs: *løs/lös*, *ben*, *løse/lösa*. B-Norwegian has acquired some diphthongs in recent reforms, e.g. *bein*, *øy* 'island'. Some are found in loanwords, e.g. BN *feide* 'feud', *mausoleum* 'mausoleum', *føye* 'yield; join'. Others are BN *oi* in *boie* 'buoy', *ai* in *kai* 'quay', *ui* in *hui* 'whee'. In Danish and Swedish these are considered vowel plus consonant, e.g. Da. *fejde*/Sw. *fejd*, Da. *føje*, Da. *bøje*/Sw. *boj*, Da./Sw. *kaj*, Da./Sw. *huj*. Further examples are:

Da.	BN	NN	Sw.
sten 'stone'	sten/stein	stein	sten
høre 'hear'	høre	høyra	höra
rød 'red'	rød	raud	röd

6 Consonants

The symbols of the Latin alphabet are taught in full, but the following are largely limited to proper names, foreign words and place-names: *c q w x z*. In 1801 Sweden adopted a policy of nativising many of these by replacing *c* with *k* (*kapital* 'capital') or *s* (*siffra* 'cipher'), *qu* with *kv* (*kvantum* 'quantity'), *w* with *v* (*valross* 'walrus'), *z* with *s* (*sebra* 'zebra'). Only *x* was regularly retained (*lax* 'salmon'). In 1917 Norway followed suit, going a step further, e.g. adopting *s* for *c* in *sirkus* 'circus' and *sigar* 'cigar' as well as *ks* for *x*: *laks* 'salmon'. Denmark has been more conservative, except for adopting *ks* for *x* (but keeping *x*, e.g. in *sex*, if only to distinguish it from *seks* 'six').

Certain phonemes are written as clusters (like English *sh*, *th*, *ng* etc.). Thus Nw./Sw. [š] may be *sj* (Nw. *sjel*/Sw. *själ* 'soul'), *skj* (Nw. *skjorte*/Sw. *skjorta* 'shirt') or just *sk* before front vowels (Nw./Sw. *ski* [šiː] 'ski', Sw. *sköld* 'shield' but Nw. *skjold*). Similarly [ç] may be spelled *tj* or *kj* (Nw. *tjue*/Sw. *tjugo* 'twenty', Nw. *kjole* 'dress'/Sw. *kjol* 'skirt') or just *k* before front vowels (BN *kirke*/NN *kyrkje*/Sw. *kyrka* 'church'). These fricatives (or affricates) of Norwegian and Swedish are results of the palatalisation of velar stops, a process not shared by standard Danish, although many Danish dialects have them. Further examples are:

Da.	BN	NN	Sw.
skære 'cut'	skjære	skjera	skära
kysse 'kiss'	kysse	kyssa	kyssa

A feature of modern Scandinavian is the absence of voiced sibilants [z ž dž], lost in Common Scandinavian. But they retain traces of an ancient 'hardening' of the medial sequences -*jj*- and -*ww*-, giving forms like Da. *æg*/Nw. *egg*/Sw. *ägg* for German *Ei* (English *egg* is a Viking-age borrowing from Norse). A much later development was the trend in Danish and adjacent areas of Norwegian and Swedish to voice short fortis stops *p t k* to *b d g* after vowels. In Danish proper this development went even farther, turning *d* and *g* into spirants or even vocalic glides, a development not reflected in the spelling. The result of this and a general Danish devoicing of the lenis consonants is to make Danish word endings extremely difficult for other Scandinavians to hear correctly:

Da.	*BN*	*NN*	*Sw.*
ta*be* [taːb̥ə] 'lose'	ta*pe*	ta*pa*	ta*pp*a
bi*de* [biːð̥ə] 'bite'	bi*te*	bi*ta*	bi*ta*
le*ge* [lajə] 'play'	le*ke*	lei*ka*	le*ka*

While most of Norwegian and Swedish has retained the Germanic (and Indo-European) *r* as a tongue-tip trill (or tap), Danish has adopted the French and German uvular *r* [ʀ], weakening it usually to a vocalic glide. This insidious sound has spread also into many areas of southern and western Norway and Sweden, still not including either Oslo or Stockholm. But both countries show a widespread weakening of the trills before dentals, resulting in a set of retroflex consonants of Indic type: *rt* [ʈ], *rs* [ʂ], *rl* [ɭ], *rn* [ɳ], *rd* [ɖ]. The same dialects have a so-called 'thick' (cacuminal) flap derived from *rð* and *l* [ɫ] that is virtually unique among the world's languages; though it is universal in the dialects of eastern Norway and north-central Sweden, it is not accepted in elite circles.

7 Morphology

The mainland languages show a parallel and remarkably similar development from the highly synthetic language of Germanic and Old Scandinavian to an analytic, i.e. greatly reduced, formal grammar. Its movement has been in the same direction as Low German and English. The only remaining case is a possessive -*s* that is really a generalised group genitive (see below). Most plural nouns now end in -*r*, and verbs lack markers for person or number of the subject. Definite and indefinite articles, unknown in Proto-Germanic, have developed. Various ways of marking formality of address have arisen, mostly in imitation of German practices.

7.1 Nouns

These still have gender distinction, in which neuter (nt.) is the most stable. In Danish and Swedish and traditional B-Norwegian, masculine (m.) and feminine (f.) have merged into a common (c.) gender having the markers of the masculine. Only in N-Norwegian and folk-oriented B-Norwegian is the feminine retained, in the latter only for certain words or styles. The genders are marked only by accompanying articles, adjectives and referential (anaphoric) pronouns, but are in part also reflected in the forms of the plural.

Plural classes

Eng.		Da.		BN	NN		Sw.		
m.	'day'	dag	dage	dag	dager	dag	dagar	dag	dagar
	'park'	park	parker	park	parker	park	parker	park	parker
m.f.	'sun'	sol	sole	sol	soler	sol	soler	sol	solar
m.	'shoe'	sko	sko	sko	sko	sko	skor	sko	skor
m.f.	'goose'	gås	gæs	gås	gjess	gås	gjæs	gås	gäss
m.	'brother'	broder	brødre	bror	brødre	bror	brør	bror	bröder
m.	'cock'	hane	haner	hane	haner	hane	hanar	hane	hanar
m.f.	'song'	vise	viser	vise	viser	vise	viser	vise	visor
nt.	'house'	hus	huse	hus	hus	hus	hus	hus	hus
nt.	'kingdom'	rige	riger	rike	riker	rike	rike	rike	riken
nt.	'ear'	øre	ører (obs. øren)	øre	ører	øre	øyra	øyro	öra	öron

N-Norwegian and Swedish show rudimentary remains of older declensions; all four retain old umlaut classes (like English *geese*, *feet*, *men* etc.). Possessive *-s* is regularly suffixed (without an apostrophe unless the word ends in *s*): Da. *dags*, *dagens*, *dages*, *dagenes*, but *gås'*. It is often avoided in favour of compounds or prepositional phrases: Da. *dagsverk* 'day's work', *ord for dagen* 'a word for the day, the day's word'. As in English it can be added to any noun phrase (the so-called group genitive), e.g. Da. *kongen af Danmarks brystsukker* 'the King of Denmark's cough drops.' Formal Swedish rejects this genitive, preferring *kungens av Danmark bröstsocker*, but general usage is the same as in Danish and Norwegian.

7.2 Articles

As in English, nouns can appear either with or without articles, depending on context and meaning. The definite articles are historically earlier, and the indefinite articles are a development of the late Middle Ages (that never reached Iceland). Usage is similar to that of English, though for instance abstracts like 'love' and 'hate' usually are definite (Da. *kærligheden*/ BN *kjærligheten*/NN *kjærleiken*/Sw. *kärleken* 'love').

The definite article is an interesting and characteristic feature of all Scandinavian languages (aside from some dialects in west Jutland). There are actually two, one suffixed to the noun and one preceding adjectives (which we will discuss below under adjectives). Originally a separate word *inn* m. (*in* f., *it* nt.) 'that, yon', it was already in Old Norse attached to the noun and became a morphological suffix. To illustrate its uses we take some of the same words as in the previous table and include the indefinite article, which is an unstressed form of the word for 'one'; it is used only in the singular, except for an occasional Swedish form *ena* 'some'.

Articles: Indef. sg., def. sg., and def. pl.

	Da.		BN		NN		Sw.	
m.	en dag	en park	en dag	en park	ein dag	ein park	en dag	en park
	dag*en*	park*en*	dag*en*	park*en*	dag*en*	park*en*	dag*en*	park*en*
	dag*ene*	park*ene*	dag*ene*	park*ene*	dag*ane*	park*ene*	dag*arna*	park*erna*
m.f.	en gås	en vis*e*	en gås	en vis*e*	ei gås	ei vis*e*	en gås	en vis*a*
	gås*en*	vis*en*	gås*a*/-*en*	vis*a*/-*en*	gås*a*	vis*a*	gås*en*	vis*an*
	gæss*ene*	vis*erne*	gjess*ene*	vis*ene*	gjæs*ene*	vis*ene*	gäss*ena*	vis*orna*
nt.	et hus	et rig*e*	et hus	et rik*e*	eit hus	eit rik*e*	ett hus	ett rik*e*
	hus*et*	rig*et*	hus*et*	rik*et*	hus*et*	rik*et*	hus*et*	rik*et*
	hus*ene*	rig*erne*	hus*ene*	rik*ene*	hus*a*	rik*a*	hus*en*	rik*ena*

In Norwegian the suffixed -*t* of the neuter singular is silent.

7.3 Adjectives

There are no case endings, but unlike English, there are still gender, definiteness and plurality markers. Gender appears only by the addition of -*t* in the neuter indefinite singular. Definiteness is shown by adding -*e* (Sw. -*a*/-*e*), plurality by adding -*e* (Sw. -*a*/-*e*). Definiteness is expressed by the article *den* m.f., *det* nt., *de* (NN *dei*) pl. It may also be dictated by such determiners as the demonstratives *denne* m. f., *dette* nt., *disse* (NN *desse*) pl. 'this, these' and the possessive adjectives (*min* 'my' etc.). The general pattern is displayed in the following chart:

Eng.	Da.	BN	NN	Sw.
'a big goose'	en stor gås	en stor gås	ei stor gås	en stor gås
'big geese'	stor*e* gæs	stor*e* gjess	stor*e* gjæser	stor*a* gäss
'a big house'	e*t* stor*t* hus	e*t* stor*t* hus	ei*t* stor*t* hus	et*t* stor*t* hus
'big houses'	stor*e* hus	stor*e* hus	stor*e* hus	stor*a* hus
'the big goose'	den stor*e* gås	den stor*e* gås*en*	den stor*e* gås*a*	den stor*a* gås*en*
'the big geese'	de stor*e* gæs	de stor*e* gjess*ene*	dei stor*e* gjæs*ene*	de stor*a* gäss*ena*
'the big house'	det stor*e* hus	det stor*e* hus*et*	det stor*e* hus*et*	det stor*a* hus*et*
'the big houses'	de stor*e* hus	de stor*e* hus*ene*	dei stor*e* hus*a*	de stor*a* hus*en*

In Swedish *de* is often replaced in speech by *dom*. The suffix -*a* may be replaced by -*e* with masculine nouns, e.g. *min gamle far* (but *min gamla mor*).

In all the languages the definite form (known as 'weak') may be used without a preceding article (a) in set phrases and in place and personal names, e.g. BN *siste natten* 'the last night', Sw. *Stora Torget* 'The Big Market Place', Da./Nw. *lille Harald* 'little Harold'; and (b) as a vocative in phrases of address: Da. *kære ven*/Nw. *kjære venn*/Sw. *kära vän* 'dear friend'.

There is a marked internal difference in the use of what is usually known as the 'double definite', i.e. the use of both definite articles in the same phrase. As shown in the chart above, this usage is avoided in Danish, but is common in Norwegian and Swedish, in N-Norwegian even required.

The definite article with an adjective is used in noun functions: common gender a. .ut animates, neuter gender about inanimates: Nw. *den unge* 'the young one (person)', *de unge* 'the young (people)', *det nye* 'the new (idea, thing etc.)'.

Comparison occurs in three degrees: positive, comparative and superlative. It is formed in one of four ways: (a) regular, by adding Da./BN *-ere*, NN/Sw. *-are* to the positive to form the comparative, and Da./BN *-est(e)*, NN/Sw. *-ast(e)* to form the superlative; (b) umlauting, by vowel change and adding *-re* and *-st(e)*; (c) analytic, by using the words for 'more' and 'most' as modifiers (Da./BN *mer*, NN *meir*, Sw. *mer(a)*, and *mest* for all the languages); (d) suppletion, e.g. *mange*/Sw. *många* 'many' – *fler*, NN *fleir* 'more' (in number). Further examples of (a) and (b):

	Da.		BN		NN		Sw.	
Positive	klar	ung	klar	ung	klår	ung	klar	ung
Comp.	klar*ere*	*yngre*	klar*ere*	*yngre*	klår*are*	*yngre*	klar*are*	*yngre*
Sup.	klar*est*	*yngst*	klar*est*	*yngst*	klår*ast*	*yngst*	klar*ast*	*yngst*

7.4 Adverbs

Most of these are morphologically unmarked and may be classed as particles. But two groups are visibly marked: (1) adverbs derived from adjectives; these are always identical with the neuter indefinite singular of the latter, i.e. they (mostly) add *-t*: e.g., *godt*, Sw. *gott* from *god* 'good' means 'well'; *stort* from *stor* 'big' means 'greatly' etc.; (2) adverbs derived from simple adverbs of motion by adding *-e* (Sw. also *-a*), making them adverbs of place (often with a change of stem); the most important are:

Eng.	Da.		BN		NN		Sw.	
'up'	op	opp*e*	opp	opp*e*	opp	opp*e*	upp	upp*e*
'down'	ned	ned*e*	ned	ned*e*	ned	ned*e*	ned	nere
'out'	ud	ud*e*	ut	ut*e*	ut	ut*e*	ut	ute
'in'	ind	ind*e*	inn	inn*e*	inn	inn*e*	in	inne
'home'	hjem	hjemm*e*	hjem	hjemm*e*	heim	heim*e*	hem	hemm*a*
'away'	bort	bort*e*	bort	bort*e*	bort	bort*e*	bort	bort*a*

In their locative sense these can be compared, e.g. Da. *indre* 'inner', *inderst* 'innermost' etc.

7.5 Pronouns

The structure is much the same as in English, aside from the second person and the reflexives. In the following chart only the informal second person is listed; the honorific will be discussed below.

Personal pronouns: synopsis of 1–3 person sg. and pl., subject and object

	Da.		BN		NN		Sw.	
1p.	jeg mig	vi os	jeg meg	vi oss	eg meg	vi oss	jag mig	vi oss
2p.	du dig	I jer	du deg	dere	du deg	de dykk	du dig	ni er
3p.m.	han ham	⎱ de dem	han ham	⎱ de dem	han honom	⎱ dei	han honom	⎱ de dem
3p.f.	hun hende	⎰	hun henne	⎰	ho henne	⎰	hon henne	⎰

The inanimate pronoun is *den* common gender and *det* neuter gender 'it' in all languages; but in N-Norwegian it is replaced in anaphoric use by the appropriate masculine and feminine pronouns (i.e. *han/ho*).

The possessives in the first and second persons are declined like strong adjectives (e.g. for Da. *min* c., *mit* nt., *mine* pl.). Possessive pronouns:

	Da.		BN		NN		Sw.	
1p.	min	vor(es)	min	vår	min	vår	min	vår
2p.	din	jeres	din	deres	din	dykkar	din	er
3p.m.	hans	⎱ deres	hans	⎱ deres	hans	⎱ deira	hans	⎱ deras
3p.f.	hendes	⎰	hennes	⎰	hennar	⎰	hennes	⎰
Refl.	sin		sin		sin		sin	

The reflexive pronoun is Da./Sw. *sig*, Nw. *seg* in the third person but identical with the objective form of the pronouns in the first and second persons. Danish restricts the reflexive to the third person singular. It is a pecu"liarity of Scandinavian that the third person reflexive is in syntactic complementation with the personal. The reflexive is restricted to possessors that are also the subject of the clause in which they occur: *han tok sin hatt* 'he took his (own) hat' vs. *han tok hans hatt* 'he took his (somebody else's) hat'.

English 'you' corresponds to *du* in informal conversations, e.g. in families, among friends and close colleagues and among rural people. But in urban settings and between strangers more formal modes of address have been common. In Danish and B-Norwegian the formal pronouns are identical with the third person plural, capitalised when written: *De, Dem, Deres*. In N-Norwegian and Swedish they are identical with the second person plural: NN *Dykk, Dykk, Dykkar*; Sw. *Ni, Er, Er*. However, in Swedish the *ni* has acquired a touch of condescension, and politeness requires the use of the third person, often including the title: *Vad önskar professoren?* 'What does the professor (i.e., you) want?' The awkwardness of this mode of address became obvious after World War II, and the solution has been a general adoption of *du*, followed in part in Norway (less in Denmark).

7.6 Verbs

The mainland languages have developed a common morphology, eliminating person and number while retaining the distinctions of tense, including complex tense forms. A verb is adequately described if we know its 'principal parts', i.e. the infinitive (also used as citation form), the preterit and the perfect participle (used in complex tenses).

Strong verbs are characterised by vowel changes in the stem and the absence of a suffix in the preterit. We list the seven main classes: 1 'bite'; 2 'enjoy'; 3 'find'; 4 'bear'; 5 'give'; 6 'go'; 7 'cry'.

	Da.			*BN*			*NN*			*Sw.*		
1	bide	bed	bidt	bite	bet	bitt	bita	beit	bite	bita	bet	bitit
2	nyde	nød	nydt	nyte	nøt	nytt	nyta	naut	note	njuta	njöt	njutit
3	finde	fandt	fundet	finne	fant	funnet	finna	fann	funne	finna	fann	funnit
4	bære	bar	båret	bære	bar	båret	bera	bar	bore	bära	bar	burit
5	give	gav	givet	gi	gav	gitt	gje	gav	gjeve	giva	gav	givit
6	fare	for	faret	fare	for	faret	fara	for	fare	fara	for	farit
7	græde	græd	grædt	gråte	gråt	grått	gråta	gret	grete	gråta	gråt	gråtit

These are only examples; there is great variation in the verbs of each class. In the infinitive N-Norwegian can have *-e* for *-a*. N-Norwegian forms its present by dropping the final vowel and when possible changing the stem to its umlaut form, e.g. *fer* from *fara*, *kjem* from *koma*. The others add *-(e)r* and change to Accent 1 (*fa'rer*, *kom'mer*), except that Swedish drops all suffixes after *r* or *l* (*far* 'go(es)', *stjäl* 'steal(s)'). In the perfect participle N-Norwegian may have *-i* for *-e*; Swedish has *-e-* for *-i-* when the perfect participle is used adjectivally.

Weak verbs form preterits by adding a dental (*-d-*, *-t-*, *-dd-*, lost in N-Norwegian class 1) with a following vowel that is not in the perfect participle. Class 3 is special for Norwegian/Swedish; the Danish verbs of the same type belong to class 1. We list the main classes below: 1 'throw'; 2a 'choose'; 2b 'judge'; 3 'believe'. In Swedish the perfect participle may end in *-d* for *-t* when used adjectivally: *kastad* for *kastat*.

	Da.			*BN*			*NN*			*Sw.*		
1	kaste	kastede	kastet	kaste	kastet	kastet	kasta	kasta	kasta	kasta	kastade	kastat
2a	vælge	valgte	valgt	velge	valgte	valgt	velja	valde	valt	välja	valde	valt
2b	dømme	dømte	dømt	dømme	dømte	dømt	døma	dømde	dømd	döma	dömde	dömt
3	(tro	troede	troet)	tro	trodde	trodd	tru	trudde	trudd	tro	trodde	trott

Modal verbs are a special group by means of which certain nuances of meaning may be signalled when they are used as auxiliaries (usually with an infinitive verb). As elsewhere in Germanic, most of them are preterit-present verbs, i.e. their present forms are old preterits, and their preterits are newly modelled after the weak verbs. We list only 'can', 'must', 'shall' and 'will' in the present and preterit:

Da.		*BN*		*NN*		*Sw.*	
kan	kunne	kan	kunne	kan	kunne	kan	kunde
må	måtte	må	måtte	må	måtte	måste	måste
skal	skulle	skal	skulle	skal	skulle	skall	skulle
vil	ville	vil	ville	vil	ville	vill	ville

The middle voice is a specially Scandinavian form, now signalled by -s (NN -st) added to many verb forms. Originally a reflexive, it is now used also to form passives, reciprocals and deponents (i.e. active verbs with passive form). An example of each type (here taken from B-Norwegian) follows:

- (a) passive: *sangen synges* 'the song is being sung' or 'the song gets sung'
- (b) reciprocal: *vi møtes i morgen* 'we will meet tomorrow'
- (c) reflexive: *jeg trivs her* 'I enjoy myself here'
- (d) deponent: *han synes godt om stedet* 'he thinks well of the place'

These are all in competition with differently structured phrases:

- (a) *sangen blir sunget*
- (b) *vi møter kl. 10* 'we meet at 10 o'clock'
- (c) *jeg liker meg her*
- (d) *han tror godt om stedet*

Similar contrasts can be shown for all the languages: the middle voice is highly restricted ('marked'), while the more analytic phrases are relatively unrestricted.

The passive is, as shown above, normally analytic, consisting of an auxiliary (Da. *blive*/BN *bli*/Sw. *bliva*/NN *verta*) plus the perfect participle.

The perfect and the pluperfect are formed by 'have' in the present and preterit tense plus the perfect participle. Except in Swedish (and to some extent in Norwegian) verbs of motion (going, becoming) require the auxiliary 'be'.

Da.	BN	NN	Sw.
har set 'have seen'	har sett	har sett	har sett
havde set 'had seen'	hadde sett	hadde sett	hade sett
er kommet 'have come'	er kommet	er kome	har kommit
var kommet 'had come'	var kommet	var kome	hade kommit

Other verb forms are:

(a) the imperative, formed by dropping the unstressed vowel of the infinitive (except Swedish and N-Norwegian weak class 1: Sw. *kasta!* 'throw!', NN *vakne!* 'awake!');

(b) the present participle, used only adjectivally, formed by adding -ende to the verb stem in Danish/B-Norwegian, -ande in N-Norwegian/Swedish, except in Swedish after long vowels: *kommande* 'coming', *boende* 'living';

(c) the subjunctive (optative), formed by adding -e to the stem of the present, which is used chiefly in set phrases of greeting or cursing: BN *kongen leve* '(long) live the king', *fanden steike* 'may the devil roast (him, me)'. A preterit is found in contrary-to-fact conditional sentences, usually identical in form to the regular preterit: BN *om jeg var...* 'if I were'. However, Swedish (and N-Norwegian) have certain relic forms of the old subjunctive: *om jag vore...* 'if I were' (NN *um eg vøre...*). These are also in competition with analytic forms using auxiliaries: *om jag skulle vara...*

8   Syntax

Only a few of the more significant features will be listed here.

8.1   Basic Word Order

An independent declarative sentence has the same subject-verb-object (SVO) order as English. But the absence of 'do' and 'is' as auxiliaries means that in the present and preterit there are no divided verb forms: Da. *hun kører bilen* 'she drives/does drive/is driving the car'.

8.2   Inversion

In questions the order of subject and verb is simply reversed: Da. *kører hun bilen?* 'does she drive/is she driving the car?'. The same inversion occurs after an initial adverb: Da. *i dag kører hun bilen* 'today she is driving the car'. If the adverb is in its usual position, after the object, sentence order is basic: *hun kører bilen i dag* 'she is driving the car today'.

8.3   Sentence Adverbs

An important subgroup of adverbs, which function as modifiers of the whole sentence, follow the verb immediately, usually in the order modals–negatives: Da. *hun kører jo bilen i dag* 'she is, you know, driving the car today'; *hun kører ikke bilen i dag* 'she is not driving the car today'; *hun kører jo ikke bilen i dag* 'she is not driving the car today, you know'. When the sentence is inverted, the negative follows a pronoun subject, but precedes a noun subject: *kører hun ikke bilen i dag?* vs. *kører ikke min søster bilen i dag?* 'isn't she driving the car today?' vs. 'isn't my sister driving the car today?'

8.4   Subordination

Subordinate clauses have (contrary to German) the same SVO order as independent clauses, except that sentence adverbs then normally precede the verb: *hvis hun ikke kører bilen i dag...* 'if she isn't driving the car today...' In some cases the same word may be either an adverb or a conjunction, e.g. *da* 'then' or 'when'. In such a case the following word order signals the difference: *da kørte hun bilen* 'then she drove the car' vs. *da hun kørte bilen...* 'when she drove the car...'

8.5   Relative Clauses

Relative clauses have subordinate order and are usually introduced by *som* (or in Danish also by *der* when it is the subject). This is not a pronoun but a particle, which cannot be preceded by a preposition. Hence prepositions come at the end of the clause, contrary to an English practice consecrated by some English grammarians: *det var bilen (som) hun kørte i* 'that was the car (which) she rode in'. When the relative particle is the object of the subordinate verb, it may be omitted (as in English).

8.6 Imperatives
Imperatives mostly appear without a subject, since this is understood to be 'you'. But the subject may be expressed, as a vocative: *kør bilen ind, Jørgen!* 'drive the car in, Jørgen!' There are of course more polite ways of formulating requests, e.g. with modal auxiliaries or with subjunctives.

8.7 Impersonal Sentences
Impersonal sentences are rather more common than in English, especially in so-called 'cleft' sentences. These have *det* as formal subject, whoever may be the real ('underlying') subject: *det er hun/hende som kører bilen i dag* 'it is she/her who is driving the car today'. 'Cleaving' is used to give emphasis.

8.8 Indefinite Subject
Basically subjectless sentences fill the subject slot with *det* 'it', as in *det regner* 'it's raining', *det sner/snør/snöar* 'it's snowing'. Norwegian and Swedish use *det* also as an equivalent of English 'there', e.g. *det kommer en bil* 'there's a car coming; a car is coming'. Here Danish (and older B-Norwegian) prefers *der*.

8.9 Conditional Clauses
These may be explicitly introduced by *om* 'if' in all languages, Da./BN *dersom*, *hvis*, Sw. *därest*, *ifall* 'in case'. But the conjunction may be dropped if the clause inverts subject and verb: *kommer bilen i dag...* 'if the car comes today...' One cannot tell if this is a question or a conditional until one hears the conclusion.

8.10 Prepositions
Prepositions can govern clauses and infinitives: Da. *efter at ha kørt bilen...* 'after having driven the car...'; *efter at hun hadde kørt bilen...* 'after she had driven the car...'

8.11
Norwegian has the option of letting possessives either precede or follow the noun, the latter requiring the definite form of the noun: *min bil* 'my car' (more emphatic) vs. *bilen min*.

8.12
Swedish (and some Norwegian dialects) keep the verb together with a

conjoined adverbial particle, while Danish and B-Norwegian separate them: Sw. *vill du köra in´ bilen* vs. Da. *vil du køre bilen ind´* 'will you drive the car in?'.

8.13
Only Swedish can omit the perfect auxiliary in a subordinate clause: *jag vet inte om han (har) lämnat staden* 'I don't know if he has left the city'.

8.14
The inferential perfect is a characteristic Scandinavian construction. Normally the perfect is used as in English, not as in German, to mark past events without specified time, but with ongoing effects. If time is specified, it is implied that the statement is an inference rather than an observed fact: *hun har kørt bilen i går* 'she has driven the car yesterday', i.e. '(I suppose that) she must have etc.'.

8.15   The exclamatory preterit
This is a common use of that tense to express a taste or opinion: *det var da en køn bil!* 'that was a lovely car!' i.e. 'that is a lovely car!'. This may be said as one is looking at it, but the experience is made more emphatic by placing it in the past.

8.16   Durative expressions
In the absence of a special 'progressive' verb form like English 'is going', the Scandinavian languages often make use of a verb of motion or position, followed by 'and' and the corresponding tense of the main verb: Da. *jeg sidder og spiser* 'I sit and eat', i.e. 'I am eating'; BN *han stod og spekulerte* 'he stood and speculated', i.e. 'he was speculating (about something)'; Sw. *hon låg och drömde* 'she lay and dreamt', i.e. 'she lay dreaming'. Verbs available for this usage are those that indicate coming, going, sitting, standing and lying.

8.17   Modal adverbs
Certain adverbs, which have regular meanings when stressed, become vague sentence modifiers when unstressed. The chief examples are Da./BN *da* 'then', *dog* 'yet', *jo* 'yes', *nok* 'enough', *vel* 'well', Da. *nu*/BN *nå*/NN *no*; corresponding to Sw. *då*, *dock*, *ju*, *nog*, *väl*, *nu*. They suggest the speaker's degree of assurance or doubt, roughly 'you see', 'after all', 'of course', 'I suppose', 'no doubt' etc.

9   Lexicon
The word stock of any language reflects the needs over time of its speakers and writers and the state of their culture. As suggested above, the similarity

and the divergence of the Scandinavian languages mirror their common as well as their separate historical experiences. The lexicon is enshrined in the dictionaries of each language, including massive historical dictionaries. Bilingual dictionaries are also numerous, especially for such familiar languages as English, French and German, and even some intra-Scandinavian.

The origin of the lexicon is multifarious, but overwhelmingly West European, as one can see by consulting the etymological dictionaries. The 'native' stock, i.e. the original Germanic with later native creations, is the bread-and-butter part of the lexicon. The Nordic languages were well equipped to deal with their natural environment of sea, land and mountains in all its variations from the plains of Denmark to the highlands of Norway and the forests of Sweden. Their location as the population closest to the North Pole has left its mark.

The earliest outside influence that is still perceptible was that of the Roman traders who taught them such words as 'buy' (*købe/kjøpe/køypa/ köpa*) and 'wine' (*vin*) from Latin *caupo* and *vinum*. They were followed in due course by Roman-trained missionaries who brought them such originally Greek words as 'church' (*kirke/kirke/kjørkja/kyrka*) and 'priest' (*prest*, Sw. *präst*) from *kuriakon* and *presbuteros* and Latin words like 'dean, provost' (*prost*) and 'mass' (*messe*, Sw. *mässa*) from *prōpositus* and *missa*. Actually, there were various intermediaries, such as Old English and Old High (and Low) German, often hard to distinguish. Scandinavia was at the end of a West European chain of transmission of Catholic Christian vocabulary, most of which was common European property.

But the chief source of Scandinavian loans in the later Middle Ages was northern Germany, where the dominant language was Low German. The distance between Low German and the Nordic languages was small, since both were Germanic and had not undergone the High German Sound Shift. One may even suspect that with a little effort they could converse, at least on everyday topics. In any event, thousands of Low German loanwords flooded the North during the period from 1250 to 1500. Low German was the language not only of the powerful Hanseatic League, the trading towns of northern Germany, but also of the North German princes, who often sat on Scandinavian thrones. Cities like Bergen in Norway, Kalmar and Stockholm in Sweden and of course Copenhagen in Denmark were heavily settled by German merchants and craftsmen.

Some Old Norse words were even displaced by Low German loans, e.g. *vindauga* 'window' in Swedish by LG *fenster* > *fönster*, *vōna* 'hope' by LG *hopen* > Da. *håbe*/BN *håpe*/Sw. *hoppas* (but NN *vona*). Prefixes and suffixes attached to Low German words were also adopted, e.g. *be-*, *ent-*, *vor-* and *-heit*, *-ness*, *-ske*. Old Scandinavian had a very restricted set of affixes, which were greatly expanded by Low German influence.

At the time of the Reformation (in the sixteenth century) the source of influence changed to High German, the language of Luther's Bible, which became normative for the now converted Scandinavians. Translations of the Bible were modelled on Luther's, giving a heavy freight of German loans. As late as the seventeenth century the Swedish grammarian Samuel Columbus could still write that German and Swedish were sister languages, so that Swedes were justified in taking over words from German. The eighteenth century saw a shift in the direction of French influence, but also a clarification of the independence of the northern languages. A Nordic purism arose, leading to the replacement of French words like *passion* with *lidenskab*, though the latter was ultimately modelled on German *Leidenschaft*. The rediscovery of Old Scandinavian, specifically of Old Icelandic literature, led to a Nordic renaissance.

The nineteenth and even more the twentieth century brought on the Industrial Revolution and with it the rise of English to the status of a world language. Its proximity to Scandinavia and involvement in Nordic affairs made it the source of a new era of influence. Rejection of German led to an adulation of English that changed the attitudes of a whole generation in Scandinavia. An influence already apparent in the 1930s, often transmitted by sailors, merchants and tourists, now led to a flood of military, scientific and literary, as well as generally popular culture, terms. English, once a remote and inaccessible language to most Scandinavians, quickly became a medium not only of information and insight, but a possibly insidious influence on popular thinking and speech.

Only Sweden had a traditional language academy, the Swedish Academy (founded 1786), which still publishes under its ægis a guide to the spelling (and in part the pronunciation) of 'correct' Swedish. But in modern times each country has established special committees or commissions charged with the care of its language. In 1978 a cooperative Nordic Language Secretariat was established under the auspices of the Nordic Council of Ministers. Like its member organisations, the secretariat has only advisory powers. But it is hoped that it will prove to be a useful forum for the discussion of language problems in the area. Aside from issues of correctness, a major concern is for the development and coordination of technical terminology.

Since each language has developed its own lexicon, often along different principles, there are many discrepancies both in words and meanings. These add spice to intra-Scandinavian contacts, but rarely lead to basic misunderstandings.

Differences are either semantic or lexical.

(a) Semantic differences in historically identical words, often called false friends, reflect preferences for one nuance over another. Thus *rar* from Latin *raris*, cognate with English 'rare', means 'good, fine, sweet' in Danish and Swedish, but 'queer, strange' in Norwegian: the 'rare' may be regarded either positively or negatively. *Rolig*, a native word cognate with German *ruhig*, means 'quiet' in Danish and Norwegian, but 'funny, amusing' in Swedish. *Affär*, from French *affaire*, means 'store, place of business' in Swedish, while Danish and Norwegian *affære* means 'affair', as in English. *Anledning*, from German *Anleitung* 'guidance', means 'cause, reason' in Swedish, but 'opportunity, occasion' in Danish/Norwegian. *Blöt* is a native word meaning 'wet' in Swedish (as *blaut* in N-Norwegian), but Da. *blød*/BN *bløt* means 'soft, weak' (with a more recent meaning of 'soft-headed').

(b) Lexical differences may be due to the extinction of a word in one language or to borrowing from a different source. In Swedish a common word for 'poet' is *skald*, an Old Norse word revived in modern times; in Danish and Norwegian it is used only about Old Norse times, the usual word being *digter/dikter* from German *Dichter* (which Swedish also has as *diktare*). While the words for 'man' and 'woman' are much the same, 'boy' and 'girl' are markedly deviant: Da. *dreng*/BN *gutt*/NN *gut*/Sw. *pojke* 'boy' and Da. *pige*/BN *pike*/NN *jente*/Sw. *flicka* 'girl'. Slang is a part of language that reflects innovation most readily and that is often local; in Swedish it has given rise to terms little known in the other languages, e.g. *kille* 'boy', *kul* 'fun' etc. There are also areas of clothing or vegetation that may surprise neighbours: a '(man's) suitcoat' is Sw. *kavaj*, Da./Nw. *jakke*; an 'overcoat' is Sw. *rock*, Da. *frakke* (Nw. *frakk*). Berries are differently named, e.g. what Swedish calls *hallon* 'raspberry', *smultron* 'strawberry', *hjortron* 'cloudberry', *krusbär* 'gooseberry' and *vinbär* 'currant' will be known in Danish and Norwegian as *bringebær*, *jordbær*, *multe(r)*, *stikkelsbær*, and *ribs/rips*. And so forth.

Bibliography

For more detailed surveys of Scandinavian, with comprehensive bibliographies, the reader is referred to Haugen (1976), a survey of the successive periods of the languages' history with extensive background and illustrative material — an updated German translation by Magnús Pétursson, under the title *Die skandinavischen Sprachen*, has been published by Helmut Buske, Hamburg — and Haugen (1982), a more concentrated survey of the history, organised by linguistic levels and emphasising linguistic rules of historical change.

For descriptive grammars, the best sources are in the original languages: Diderichsen (1957) for Danish; Næs (1972) for B-Norwegian; Beito (1970) for N-Norwegian; Thorell (1973) and Collinder (1974) for Swedish. An outline Norwegian grammar (both B-Norwegian and N-Norwegian) in English is contained in Haugen (1964), while Haugen and Chapman (1982) is a pedagogical grammar of Norwegian in English.

Haugen (1966) is a detailed account of language planning in relation to Norwegian.

References

Beito, O. 1970. *Nynorsk grammatikk* (Det Norske Samlaget, Oslo)

Collinder, B. 1974. *Svensk språklära* (C.W.K. Gleerup, Stockholm)

Diderichsen, P. 1957. *Elementær dansk grammatik* (Gyldendal, Copenhagen)

Haugen, E. 1964. *Norsk-engelsk ordbok/Norwegian-English Dictionary: With a Historical and Grammatical Introduction* (University of Wisconsin Press, Madison; 3rd ed., Universitetsforlaget, Oslo, 1984)

—— 1966. *Language Conflict and Language Planning: The Case of Modern Norwegian* (Harvard University Press, Cambridge, Mass.)

—— 1976. *The Scandinavian Languages: An Introduction to Their History* (Faber and Faber, London)

—— 1982. *Scandinavian Language Structures: A Comparative Historical Survey* (Max Niemeyer, Tübingen and University of Minnesota Press, Minneapolis)

—— and K.G. Chapman. 1982. *Spoken Norwegian*, 3rd ed. (Holt, Rinehart and Winston, New York)

Næs, O. 1972. *Norsk grammatikk*, 3rd ed. (Fabritius, Oslo)

Thorell, O. 1973. *Svensk grammatikk* (Esselte Studium, Stockholm)

7 Latin and the Italic Languages

R.G.G. Coleman

1 Introduction

Latin is the chief representative of the Italic group of Indo-European languages. The most important of the others were Oscan, which was spoken over most of Southern Italy in the last four centuries BC and is attested in substantial inscriptions from Avella and Banzi, and Umbrian, which was spoken further north and survives almost exclusively in a series of liturgical inscriptions from Gubbio dating from 350 to 50 BC. A large number of the Oscan and Umbrian texts are in native alphabets, ultimately derived like those of Latin and Etruscan from the Greek alphabet. Some are in the Latin alphabet, and collation of the two graphic systems provides valuable insights into the phonology of the two languages. In this chapter words attested in the native alphabets appear in capitals, those in the Latin alphabet in lower case.

Neither Oscan nor Umbrian is as closely related to Latin as Faliscan, a language attested in a small number of inscriptions from near Cività Castellana. Of the non-Italic languages spoken in Italy after 500 BC Venetic in the far north-east was closely related to Italic; Etruscan, which is attested, again epigraphically, over a large area of central and northern Italy, was totally unrelated. Although Oscan was still in use at Pompeii until AD 79, Latin had long since become the written language of all Italy. Some dialects of Latin were partly shaped by the native languages, but it is doubtful whether the latter survived long into the Christian era. In this chapter Oscan and Umbrian phenomena will be treated only in relation to Latin as providing evidence for the Italic complex within which Latin must historically be placed.

For Latin phonology the most valuable source is the spellings, both standard and deviant, and the diachronic changes in spelling that are discernible in the numerous inscriptions recorded from about 500 BC onwards and the manuscripts of contemporary texts written on papyrus and subsequently on other soft materials. The manuscripts of literary texts from antiquity, usually written centuries after their composition, provide fuller testimony for morphology, syntax and lexicon. Among these texts are

170

treatises on the language itself and on rhetoric. These are especially important as revealing the criteria, derived mostly from Greek theory, by which the norms of classical usage were formulated and applied in the period 150 BC–AD 150.

At all periods alongside the formal registers of the written documents there was the Latin spoken by the illiterate majority. Vulgar Latin had of course its own diachrony and, as it spread with the expansion of Roman power, must have acquired the dialectal variations from which the Romance languages emerged. It is partially recoverable from the written documents whose spelling, grammar and lexicon deviate in the direction of Romance from the standard Latin that can be established for the period concerned. Many of these deviations are identifiable with or can be directly linked to the asterisked reconstructions of Proto-Romance. The conservative traditions of the schools of grammar and rhetoric did not entirely immunise classical usage against vulgar infiltration. However, they did ensure that by the ninth century AD written Latin and the diverse spoken forms of Latin had ceased to be registers of one language, coexisting in a state of diglossia like Greek *katharévusa* and *dēmotikḗ*, but were now quite separate, if closely related, languages. Caesar and Livy would have recognised the Latin of Nithard's *Historiae* as a form of their own language; they would have found his citations of the Strassburg oaths as baffling in the *romana lingua* as in the *teudisca*. Latin was to survive for another thousand years after that as a vehicle for liturgy and learned discourse, but in a state of suspended animation dependent upon transfusions from the ancient models. These guaranteed it a homogeneity in time and space, in marked contrast to the independently live and divergent Romance languages.

2 Phonology

The Italic word accent was fixed and not phonemic. In Proto-Italic it is generally thought to have been a stress accent falling on the initial syllable. That this situation continued into the independent history of the languages is confirmed by the fact that both vowel raising ('weakening') in early Latin and syncope in Oscan and Umbrian affected only non-initial syllables. By about 250 BC the rule of the penultimate was established in Latin: in words of more than two syllables the accent was on the penultimate unless it contained a short unchecked vowel (i.e. in an open syllable), in which case the accent retreated to the antepenult. The range of possibilities is illustrated by:

fác 'make!'	fácis 'you make'	fácilēs 'easy' (nom. pl.)
	fécit 'he made'	fēcístis 'you made' (pl.)
	fáctō 'made' (abl.)	factū́rō 'about to make' (abl.)

The Latin grammarians borrowed from the Greeks the terminology of tonic accentuation, but although some educated native speakers may have affected Greek practice, the frequency of syncope in spoken Latin of all periods and the shortening of the unaccented vowels in *uólō*, *míhī* and later *dícō*, etc. show that the accent remained one of stress.

Table 7.1: The Segmental Phonemes of Latin in the Classical Period (c. 150 BC–AD 150)

Vowels

	i		u	
	e		o	
		a		

all ± length

Diphthongs: ae au oe eu ui

Consonants:

	Stop tense	lax	Fricative	Nasal	Lateral	Semi-vowels
Labial	p	b		m		w
Labio-dental			f			
Dental	t	d		n	l r	
Alveolar			s			j
Velar	k	g				
Labio-velar	kʷ					
Glottal			h			

The relative frequency and distribution of Latin short vowels had been affected by the raising that took place in non-initial syllables before 250 BC. The raising was higher in unchecked than in checked vowels; e.g. **dēfacites > dēficitis* 'you fail' vs. **dēfactos > dēfectus* 'feeble', **homones > hominis* 'of the man' vs. **fācondom > fācundum* (acc.) 'eloquent'. /i/ and /u/ became more frequent as a result. Syncope, the terminal point in raising, occurred in all periods of spoken Latin: prehistorically in *reppulī* 'I drove back' (< **repepolai*, cf. *pepulī* 'I drove') and in *mēns* 'mind' (< *mentis*); later in *postus* for *positus* 'placed', *caldus* for *calidus* 'hot', *oclus* for *oculus* 'eye'.

Vowel length was phonemic in Latin, e.g. *leuis* 'light', *lēuis* 'smooth'; *rosa* (nom.), *rosā* (abl.) 'rose'. It was never marked systematically in writing, though sporadic devices are found, in Latin (mostly diacritics) as in Oscan (gemination) and Umbrian (addition of *h*). (The long vowels of classical Latin words cited in this chapter are marked diacritically.) /e·/ and /o·/ came to be raised: hence from the first century AD onwards deviant spellings like *filix*, *flus* for *fēlīx*, *flōs*. Eventually the ten vowels were reduced in many areas of Vulgar Latin to seven:

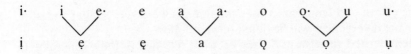

with length merely a concomitant of stress.

There was a general tendency to monophthongise diphthongs: early Latin *deicō* 'I say', *oino(m)* 'one', *ious* 'law' > *dīcō*, *ūnum*, *iūs* by 150 BC. Only /ae/ (< early Latin /ai/), /au/ and the rare /oe eu ui/ survived in the classical period. In some dialects of central Italy /ae/ and /au/ were monophthongised by the second century BC, e.g. *cedre*, *plostrum*, for standard *caedere* 'to cut', *plaustrum* 'cart', and the [ɛ] pronunciation of *ae* was standard by the fourth century AD. The monophthongisation in *cecīdit* (< *cecaidet*) and *accūsō* 'I accuse' (< *adcausō*) implies a form of raising, /ai/ > /ei/, /au/ > /ou/. The result was again to increase the frequency of high vowels, specifically /i·/ and /u·/.

The Oscan vowel system differs in two principal respects from the Latin one. Firstly it was asymmetrical, with three front vowels /i̭ i̭ e/ and only two back /ṷ o̭/ in addition to /a/. The raising of /e·/ and /o·/, which came relatively late in Latin, had occurred prehistorically in both Oscan and Umbrian. But in Oscan, whereas the resultant /i̭·/ was distinguished from existing /i·/, as in *LÍGATÚÍS* 'to the ambassadors' (< *lēgatois*) vs. *SLAAGID* 'from the place' (< *stlāgīd*), the corresponding raised back vowel merged with /u·/ as in *FRUKTATIUF* 'profit' (< *frūktātiōns*). The raising of /o/ to [o̭] as in *PÚD* 'which' (< *kʷod*, cf. the allograph *pod*) merely increased the asymmetry of the system.

Secondly all but one of the Proto-Italic diphthongs were retained until the latest records of Oscan. Thus *DEÍVAÍ* 'to the goddess', *AVT* 'but', *ÚÍTTIUF* (nom.) 'use', but *LÚVKEÍ* 'in the grove' with /ou/ < */eu/; cf. Lat. *dīuae, aut, ūsiō, *lūcī*.

The Umbrian vowel system was more symmetrical. Somewhat like Attic Greek it included two pairs of middle-to-high long vowels, recoverable from the Latin allographs, e.g. *TUTE*, *tote* 'to the people' with /o̭·/ and /ẹ·/ (< *toutai*) and *HABETU*, *habitu* 'let him have' with /ẹ·/ and o̭·/ (< *habētōd*). In monophthongisation Umbrian was further advanced even than Latin, as the following correspondences illustrate: O. *PRAÍ* = Lat. *prae* = U. *PRE* 'before'; O. *DIÚVEÍ* = Lat. *Iouī* = U. *IUVE* 'to Jupiter'; O. *AVT* = Lat. *aut* = U. *UTE* 'but'; u-stem gen. sg. O. *[castr]ous* = Lat. *[trib]ūs* = U. *[trif]or*.

Although neither Oscan nor Umbrian orthography reveals evidence of short vowel raising, the frequency of syncope in non-initial syllables implies its presence; e.g. O. *actud*, U. *AITU* < *agtōd* < *agetōd* 'let him act'; cf. Lat. *agitō*; O. *MEDDÍSS* < *medodikes* (nom. pl.) 'magistrates'. U. *ANTAKRES* < *antagreis* (abl.) 'intact' (cf. Lat. *integrīs*) and similar spellings must be presumed archaisms.

The Oscan and Umbrian consonant systems were very similar to Latin. The chief divergences will be noted in what follows.

The inherited velar stops /k/ and /g/ were retained in Italic generally. In Oscan and Latin palatalisation of [g] before [j] occurred prehistorically; e.g. O. *mais* 'more', Lat. *maiius* 'bigger' < **magjos* (adj. nt.) beside *magis* 'more' < **magios*. Umbrian shows palatalisation before front vowels, e.g. *šesna* 'dinner' (the native alphabet has a separate letter, transliterated as Ç, representing [tʃ] or [ʃ]), cf. O. *KERSNÚ*, Lat. *cēna*; *muieto*, cf. Lat. *mūgītus* 'a roar'.

The Oscan dialect of Banzi shows palatalisation of [tj] and [dj] (< [ti di]) before vowels: *bansae* 'at Bantia', *zicolom* 'day' < **diēklom*, and it was in this context that the Latin shift began. Lat. *peiius* 'worse' (< **pedjos*) certainly, *Iouī* 'to Jupiter' like O. *IUVEÍ*, U. *IUVE*, (< **djowei*) possibly, provides evidence for a prehistoric tendency. Instances exactly parallel to Oscan are attested in the second century AD: *terciae* for *tertiae* 'third' (Rome), *oze* for *hodiē* 'today' (Algeria). By the fifth century AD the grammarians report the pronunciation of *iustitia* with [tsɪa] as normal. Secure Latin examples comparable to U. *šesna* do not occur before the fifth and sixth centuries AD: *intcitamento* 'encouragement' for *incitāmentō* (Italy), *dissesit* 'left' for *discessit* (Algeria), *septuazinta* 'seventy' for *septuāgintā* (Spain). They are abundant in Lombard and Merovingian documents of the seventh and eighth centuries.

The inherited labio-velars **/kʷ/ and **/gʷ/ were replaced by /p/ and /b/ in Oscan and Umbrian. In Latin they merged with /kw/ and /gw/. Thus *equus* 'horse' <PIt. **ekwos*, *quid* 'what?' < **kʷid*, cf. O. *PÍD*, U. *PEŘE* < **pid-i* with the distinctive Umbrian affricate reflex of intervocalic /d/. It is probable that Lat. *qu* represents /kʷ/ rather than /kw/, almost certain that *gu* represents [gw]. Inherited **/gʷ/ > Lat. /w/ except after a nasal: PIt. **gʷīwos* > *uīuus* 'alive', cf. O. *BIVUS* (nom. pl.), **snigʷm* > *niuem* (acc. sg.) 'snow' but **ongʷen* > *unguen* 'ointment', cf. U. *UMEN* (< **omben*).

The labial glide /w/, which was distinguished graphically from *u* in Oscan and Umbrian, was represented by *u* in Latin. Its phonemic status is guaranteed by rare pairs like *uoluī* with /wi·/ 'I rolled' and *uoluī* with /ui·/ 'I wished'. In some areas /w/ > [β] as early as the first century AD, e.g. *baliat* for *ualeat* 'farewell!' at Pompeii. By the third century AD consonantal *u*, formerly transliterated as ου in Greek, was frequently rendered by β. Whereas the earliest Germanic borrowings from Latin show [w], later ones prefer a labio-dental fricative: e.g. OE *wīn*, *weall* < *uīnum* 'wine', *uallum* 'fence', but *fers* < *uersus* 'verse'. The invention of *double u* in the eighth century AD to represent Germanic [w] indicates that the value of Latin consonantal *u* was now [v]. Hence Latin borrowings from Germanic have *w* or *gu* for Germanic [w], e.g. Go. *wadi* 'pledge' > *wadium* (seventh century AD), OHG *werra* 'strife' > *werra/guerra* (ninth century AD).

The palatal glide /j/ was not distinguished graphically in any Italic language. Its phonemic status is guaranteed not by any minimal opposition with /i/ but by pattern congruity in *iam*, *tam* etc. Invervocalic /j/ was regularly [jj]. Secure evidence of an affricate pronunciation [dz] or [dʒ] for /j/ occurs in *Zanuario* (Pozzuoli, fourth century AD) and *Genoarias* (Arles, sixth century AD) for *Ianuar-*.

/f/ and /h/ were more frequent in Oscan and Umbrian than in Latin, often occurring non-initially in uncompounded words. Thus O. *MEFIAÍ* (loc. sg.), cf. Lat. *medius* 'middle' (< *medhio-*); U. *rufru*, cf. Lat. *rubrōs* (acc. pl.) 'red' (< *ə₁rudhro-*); U. *VITLAF*, cf. Lat. *uitulās* 'calves' (< *-āns*); O. *FEÍHÚSS* (acc.) 'walls', cf. Lat. *figulus* 'potter' (< *dh(e)igh-*); U. *REHTE*, cf. Lat. *rēctē* 'rightly'. (The diachronic complex that produces the idiosyncratic pattern of reflexes of the Proto-Indo-European voiced aspirates */bh dh gh gʷh/, partially exemplified in some of these forms, is a notable witness to the existence of a unified Proto-Italic.) /h/ was unstable in both Latin and Umbrian. Initially it is ignored in classical versification and there was learned debate about the correct forms of *ūmor* 'moisture' and *harēna* 'sand'; cf. U. *heritu ERETU* 'let him choose'. Medially /h/ is often lost in Latin, e.g. *praehibeō* > *praebeō* 'I provide', *nihil* > *nīl* 'nothing' and, when it remains, it merely marks hiatus, e.g. *ahēnus/aēnus* 'brazen', U. *AHESNES* (abl. pl.); cf. O. *STAHÍNT* 'they stand' (< *stāint*). In Vulgar Latin /h/ disappeared almost completely.

Final /m/ was often omitted in Umbrian and early Latin, e.g. U. *PUPLU* for *PUPLUM* 'people' (acc.), Lat. *oino* for *oinom* 'one' (acc.); rarely in Oscan, except at Pompeii, e.g. *VÍA* for *VÍAM* 'road'. In classical versification it fails to prevent the elision of vowels: *făcĭlem ēssĕ* with [em] > [e]; cf. *făcĭle ēssĕ*. However, *făcĭlēm dărĕ* contrasts with *făcĭlĕ dărĕ*, which implies either [em] > [e·] or an assimilation [emd] > [end]. In Vulgar Latin final /m/ was almost totally lost. Hence the homophony of *facilem* and *facile*, *bonum* (acc. sg.) and *bonō* (dat., abl. sg.), with [um] > [ŭ] > [ǫ].

The frequency of /s/ was much reduced by rhotacism in Latin and Umbrian. In the latter both intervocalic and final /s/ were affected. Thus *FURENT* < *bhusenti* 'they will be', Lat. *foret* but O. *FUSÍD*, both < *bhusēt* (3 sg. subj.); *dequrier* (earlier *TEKURIES* dat. pl.) cf. Lat. *decuria* 'ten-man group'. In Latin final /r/ for /s/ occurs only by paradigmatic analogy; e.g. *honor*, *honōrem* replacing *honōs*, *honōrem* (acc.).

In early Latin final /s/ preceded by a short vowel was apparently lost before consonants but retained before vowels. Together with the normal treatment of final /m/ this would have given the following variants for 'the master's son':

nom. (filius): fīlius erī, fīliu dominī
acc. (fīlium): fīliu erī, fīlium dominī

This pattern underlies the graphic and metrical data of the period 250–180 BC. Both -*s* and -*m* were restored in standard orthography by the early second century BC, but final -*s*, unlike -*m*, always counts as a consonant in classical versification: *fīlĭŭs ĕrī*, *fīlĭūs dŏmĭnī*. Vulgar Latin, like Umbrian earlier, shows frequent loss of final consonants, e.g. of /t/ in VL *ama* 'he loves', U. *HABE* 'he has', but in contrast to e.g. U. *SESTE* for *sestes* 'you set up' it seems to have kept final /s/ in all regions until at least the sixth century AD and only in eighth-century documents from Italy does -*s* begin to disappear on a large scale.

There was a tendency in most periods of Latin to reduce all but a small range of consonant clusters by the assimilation or omission of one or more components or by anaptyxis. Thus */sn/ in *nix* 'snow' < **snigʷs* and *cēna* 'dinner', cf. U. *ṡesna*, O. *KERSNU*; */ns/ in *uiās* 'roads' < **-āns*, cf. O. *VÍASS*, U. *VITLAF* 'calves' with /f/ < */ns/, and in *mēnsis* 'month', *sedēns* 'sitting', where early Latin usually has *s*, cf. U. *MENZNE* (< **mensenei* loc.) with [ents], *ZEŘEF* (< **sedens*). Paradigmatic analogy restored /n/ in *sedens*: *sedentem* (acc.), and a spelling pronunciation [e·ns] was standard in classical speech; but /n/ was never restored in Vulgar usage and spellings like *mesis* were widespread in late Latin. Initial and final clusters were the more vulnerable, e.g. /gn/ in *nātus*, early Lat. *gnātus* 'son' but *cognātus* 'relative'; */tl/ simplified in *lātus* 'raised', but in *piāculum* 'sacrifice' (cf. U. *pihaclu* (abl.) < **piātlo-*) /t/ has been assimilated to the velar allophone of /l/ and resultant /kl/ has undergone anaptyxis; /kt/ simplified in *lac* 'milk' but retained in *lactis* (gen.). As the preceding examples show, Oscan and Umbrian, though they have the same general tendency, often diverge in detail: thus O. *ARAGETU* (abl.) beside Lat. *argentō* 'silver', *ÚPSANNAM* 'which is to be done' beside Lat. *operandam*, *MEDDÍSS* 'magistrate' beside Lat. *iūdex* 'judge', U. *acnu* (acc.) beside O. *AKENEÍ* (loc.), Lat. *annus* 'year'.

3 Morphology and Syntax

The case system of Italic was typologically close to Proto-Indo-European. The cases were fusional, encoding the categories of case, number and partly gender. The noun morphology was organised in six paradigms, exemplified from Latin in the chart given opposite. All save (4) and (5) are shared with adjectives, and all reflect Proto-Indo-European paradigms except (5), which seems to have developed in Proto-Italic; cf. U. *RI* (dat.-abl.) with Lat. *reī*, *rē*.

The diachrony of these paradigms as a whole is notable in two respects. Firstly the *i*-stems (3b) became progressively more unlike the *u*-stems (4), to which in Proto-Indo-European they were structurally parallel. This process had not gone so far in Oscan and Umbrian as in Latin, where the cases exhibited for *turris* represent the most conservative form of the paradigm attested, and the distinctive (3b) cases were gradually replaced by those of (3a). Prehistorically assimilation had been in the opposite direction; cf.

Classical Latin Nominal Paradigms

	1	2	3(a)	3(b)	4	5
Sg. Nom.	ui-a	popul-us	lēx	turr-is	trib-us	r-ēs
	'road'	'people'	'law'	'tower'	'tribe'	'thing'
Voc.	-a	-e	lēx	-is	-us	-ēs
Acc.	-am	-um	lēg-em	-im	-um	-em
Gen.	-ae	-ī	-is	-is	-ūs	-ēī
Dat.	-ae	-ō	-ī	-ī	-uī	-ēī
Abl.	-ā	-ō	-e	-ī	-ū	-ē
Loc.	[Rōm-ae 'at Rome']	[hum-ī 'on the ground']	[rūr-e 'in the country']	[Septembr-ī 'in September']	–	[di-ē 'on the day']
Pl. Nom.⎫ Voc. ⎬	ui-ae	popul-ī	lēg-ēs	turr-ēs	trib-ūs	r-ēs
Acc.	-ās	-ōs	-ēs	-īs	-ūs	-ēs
Gen.	-ārum	-orum	-um	-ium	-uum	-ērum
Dat.⎫ Abl. ⎬ Loc.⎭	-īs	-īs	-ibus	-ibus	-ibus	-ēbus

nom. pl. *hominēs* 'men' for -*ĕs*, reflected in O. *HUMUNS*; abl. pl. *legibus*, O. *ligis* as if < *lēg-ifs* < *-ibhos*; cf. U. *homonus* < *-ufs*, with anaptyctic *u*, < *-bhos*.

Secondly there were in Latin from an early date doublets belonging to (1) and (5), e.g. *māteria*/-*ēs* 'timber' and to (2) and (4), e.g. *senātus* 'senate' and *pīnus* 'pine tree'. This led to the wholesale transfer of nouns in Vulgar Latin from (4) and (5) to (2) and (1) respectively and thus to the elimination of the former pair.

The dual number has not survived in Italic noun or verb morphology. The distinction between singular and plural remained systematic.

There are three genders in Italic: masculine, feminine and neuter. The category is systematically encoded in adjectives and partly in pronouns. Hence, while most nouns in (1) and (5) are feminine, (2) and (4) masculine, there are exceptions, and these are recoverable only from concordant pronouns and adjectives. predicative or attributive; e.g. *nauta est ualidus* 'the sailor is strong', *ille diēs* 'that day' (m.); *humus dūra* 'the hard ground', *haec tribus est* 'this is the tribe' (f.). The neuter gender is usually marked in nouns as well as adjectives but only in the nominative and accusative: *bellum* 'war' (sg.), *maria* 'seas' (pl.). Sex is signalled systematically by the gender of adjectives: *rēx bonus* 'the good king', *honestae mulierēs* 'virtuous women'; but the masculine acts as common gender: *hominēs sunt ualidī* 'humans are strong'. Inanimate nouns are assigned to all three genders; e.g. *flūmen lātum* (nt.) but *fluuius lātus* (m.) 'broad river', *silua dēnsa* (f.) but *nemus dēnsum* (nt.) 'thick forest'. The neuter is the unmarked form of adjectives and pronouns: *facile est dēscendere* 'to go down is easy', cf. *facilis est dēscēnsus* 'the descent is easy' (m.).

Many of the specific case forms are cognate in the different languages even when sound changes have obscured their identity, as in O. *HÚRZ* 'grove' with /ts/ < *-tos* beside Lat. *hortus* (2 nom. sg.) 'garden' and U. *TRIF* 'three' < *trins* (3b acc. pl.), beside Lat. *trīs*. Divergences occur of course; e.g. in paradigm (2) nom. pl. Lat. *Nōlāni, Iguuīnī* with *-ī* < PIE pronominal *-oi* contrast with O. *NÚVLANÚS* 'Nolans', U. *iiouinur* 'Iguvines' < PIE nominal *-ōs*. In addition to the interaction between (3a) and (3b) already noted, (3a) abl. sg. shows Lat. *lēge*, U. *KAPIŘE* 'bowl' with *-e* < PIE loc. *-i* against O. *ligud* < *lēgōd* with the ablative form of (2).

The most remarkable divergence occurs in what is otherwise a very homogeneous paradigm throughout Italic, namely in the genitive singular of (2). PIE *-osio*, reconstructed from Ancient Greek and Indo-Iranian, is directly attested in Faliscan *Kaisiosio* 'Caesius', and in *Valesiosio* 'Valerius' on an inscription, possibly Volscian, from Southern Lazio. Oscan and Umbrian have *-eis*: *SAKARAKLEÍS* 'temple', *popler* 'people'. This was originally the (3b) form, which has also spread to (3a), as in *MEDÍKEÍS* 'magistrate'. Latin *-ī* has cognates in the Venetic and Celtic genitive singular forms, e.g. OIr. *maqi* 'son's'. It reflects either *-iə₂*, for which cf. Vedic *devī́* 'goddess' (< 'belonging to a god, *deváḥ*') or *-ie*, the suffix which was inflected to form adjectives like Latin *patrius* 'belonging to a father, *pater*' and Vedic *divyáḥ* 'belonging to the sky, *dyáuḥ*'.

It will be observed in the chart of nominal paradigms that, although there are fourteen possible cases, no paradigm has more than eight (*populus, lēx*) or fewer than six (*rēs*) distinctive forms. The pattern of syncretism, however, varies from one paradigm to another and the only general syncretism is in the dative-locative-ablative plural. This is also one of the maximally differentiated cases, along with the accusative singular and genitive plural, which have distinctive forms in every paradigm. Least marked are the vocative, the case of second person address, and the locative, which signals position in space or time. The vocative is distinguished only in (2) singular, the declension to which most male personal and family names belong. The locative is more distinct morphologically and more active functionally in both Oscan and Umbrian, e.g. O. *AKENEÍ* but Lat. *annō* (abl.) 'in the year'; U. *MANUVE* but Lat. *in manū* (abl.) 'in the hand'; O. *eizeic uincter* 'he is convicted in this', cf. *in hāc rē conuincitur*. In Latin it is reserved for physical location and subject to severe lexical constraints, e.g. *Rōmae* but *in urbe, in Italiā, humī* 'on the ground' but *in solō*.

The syncretism of the Proto-Indo-European case system had already begun in Proto-Italic with the merging of comitative and ablative cases. Thus early Lat. *dedit meretōd* 'he gave with justification', O. *com preiuatud actud* 'let him plead together with the defendant' (Lat. *cum reō agitō*), where the case forms reflect the Proto-Indo-European ablative. In the plural, as we have remarked, this syncretism also absorbed locative and dative functions; e.g. O. *FIÍSÍAÍS* 'at the festival', Lat. *fēriīs*, *LÍGATÚÍS* 'to the ambassadors', Lat. *lēgātīs*.

A number of Indo-European languages show the apparently independent development of phrases composed of nominal + participle in an appropriate case to signal the temporal location or attendant circumstances of a verbal action or state; e.g. the 'absolute' use of the locative (and genitive) in Sanskrit, and the genitive (and accusative) in Ancient Greek. The corresponding Italic construction has the comitative ablative: O. *lamatir toutad praesentid* 'the penalty is to be exacted with the people being present', Lat. *populō praesente*; U. *ESTE PERSKLUM AVES ANZERIATES ENETU* 'this sacrifice, with the birds having been examined, he is to begin', Lat. *auibus obseruātīs initō*. Frequent in Latin is the parallel nominal + (predicative) adjective or noun: *auibus secundīs* 'with the birds (being) auspicious', *auibus magistrīs* 'with the birds (being) instructors'. The detachment of the construction from its original comitative meaning is reflected by several developments in the classical period, notably the extension to future participles and to active participles of transitive verbs along with their complements; e.g. *sortītīs cōnsulibus prōuinciās* 'the consuls having been allotted their provinces', *oppugnātūrīs hostibus castra* 'the enemy being about to attack the camp'. The incorporation of prepositional phrases within the ablative phrase itself, as in *rēbus ad profectiōnem comparātīs* 'things being prepared for the departure', and the replacement of the head noun by a clause or phrase, as in *quor praetereātur dēmōnstrātō* 'why it is omitted having been demonstrated' and *cognitō uīuere Ptolemaeum* 'that Ptolemy was alive having been discovered', also added to the internal complexity of the construction. The term 'ablative absolute' is appropriate once it has become the equivalent of a full adverbial clause, *quom cognōuisset uīuere Ptolemaeum* 'when he discovered that Ptolemy...', etc. Not surprisingly, once the case orientation was lost, the ablative came to be replaced in Vulgar Latin by the nominative or accusative; cf. *reliquias recollectas tumulum tibi constitui* 'having gathered up your remains, I set up a grave for you' (fourth century AD, Africa), *coiux moriens non fuit alter amor* 'your husband dying, there was no second love' (sixth century AD, Rome).

There are several distinctively Latin idioms in which a case usage is transferred from verbal to nominal dependency. For instance, the purposive use of the dative in *trīs uirōs ēlēgēre lītibus iūdicandīs* 'three men they chose for deciding law suits' → *trēs uirī lītibus iūdicandīs*; *sēmen sātui parāuī* 'I prepared the seed for sowing' → *sātui sēmen* 'seed for sowing'. A half-way stage is the so-called predicative dative, e.g. *auxiliō tibi est* 'he is of assistance (dat.) to you' ← *adest auxiliō tibi* 'he is here for assistance to you'. Similarly the comitative use of the ablative in *singulārī industriā labōrāuit* 'she worked with exceptional industry' → *mulier singulārī industriā* 'a woman of exceptional industry', the so-called ablative of description.

Prepositions originally defined the case meanings more precisely and hence could accompany more than one case, but they came to usurp more and more of the meaning of the phrase and so to be restricted to a single case. Thus the use of the simple accusative with directional verbs survived as an archaism in a few nouns, e.g. Lat. *Rōmam uēnit* 'he came to Rome', *domum rediī* 'I returned home'; but it was generally replaced by prepositional phrases: O. *ANT PÚNTTRAM* 'up to the bridge', cf. Lat. *ante pontem* 'in front of the bridge'; U. *SPINAM-AŘ* 'to the column', cf. *ad spīnam* 'to the spine'.

The encroachment of prepositional phrases on the simple case is well exemplified in the Latin ablative. The ablative functions of the case and those derived from them, e.g. agency, normally have prepositions except with certain words. Thus *parentibus caret* 'of his parents he is deprived' but *ab eīs sēparātus* 'from them separated', *ab eīs dēsertus* 'by them deserted'. Regularly without prepositions are for instance *cōnsule nātus* 'of a consul begotten', *melle dulcius* 'than honey sweeter'. The comitative function normally has prepositions where the accompaniment is physical: *cum agricolīs labōrābat* 'with farmers he was working' vs. *magnā (cum) cūrā* 'with great care'. The instrumental function acquires prepositions only in post-classical documents; e.g. *dē gladiō percussus* 'by a sword struck'.

Prepositional phrases also encroached upon the functions of other cases. In Oscan and Umbrian the preposition (or rather postposition) *en* 'in' was sometimes attached to the locative, as in O. *HÚRTÍN* 'in the grove', Lat. *in hortō* 'in the garden', *exaisc-en ligis* 'in these laws', Lat. *in hīs lēgibus*.

By analogy with the plural forms the ablative singular also came to be used in locative functions with prepositions, which were, however, generally omitted when the noun was temporal. Thus O. *ÚP SAKARAKLÚD* 'at the temple' beside *SAKARAKLEÍ* (loc.), *meddixud* beside *MEDIKKIAÍ* 'in the magistracy'. In Latin, apart from the lexical group referred to above — *Rōmae, domī* etc. — the locative case had been entirely replaced by the ablative: *in templō, in magistrātū* and *eō tempore* 'at that time'. In Vulgar Latin even the temporal nouns acquired prepositions.

Prepositional ablative phrases in Latin also encroached upon the genitive case: e.g. *iūdicātus dē capite* for *capitis* 'judged on a capital charge' (cf. O. *dat castrid* for *castrous zicolum deicum* 'for a capital charge the day to name') and especially *maior pars ex hostibus* 'the greater part of the enemy', *dīmidium dē praedā* 'half of the loot' beside the genitives *hostium* and *praedae*. Similarly *ad* + accusative phrases encroached upon the dative. The original distinctions between *ad haec respondit* 'in the face of these (arguments) he replied' and *hīs respondit* 'to these persons he replied' and between *ad rēgem id mīsī* 'to (in the direction of) the king it I sent' and *rēgī id dedī* 'to the king it I gave' became blurred, and in post-classical Latin the

Vulgar generalisation of prepositional phrases leads to occasional uses like *ad hōs respondit, ad rēgem id dedī.*

Some of the phonetic changes remarked in section 2 eroded important distinctions in the Latin case paradigms. Thus the disappearance of final /m/, the loss of distinction between /a/ and /a·/ and the merging of /u/ and /o·/ produced homophony between *lēgem* (acc.) and *lēge* (abl.) in paradigm (3a), between *populum* (acc.) and *populō* (dat., abl.) in (2) and between *uia* (nom.), *uiam* (acc.) and *uiā* (abl.) in (1). The plural inflections, being more distinctively marked, were less vulnerable. However, the combined effect of grammatical and phonetic changes was a steady reduction of the cases in Vulgar Latin, until of the four surviving paradigms three had three cases, the fourth, (3b), only two:

Sg.	Nom.	*vi̯a	*pǫpolǫs	*lęss	*torręs
	Obl.	-a	-ǫ	*lęgę	-ę
Pl.	Nom.	-ę	-i̯	-ǵęs	-ęs
	Obl.	-as	-ǫs	-ǵęs	-ęs

(ǵ = a palatalised reflex of /g/)

Pronominal morphology was idiosyncratic to particular languages in both its lexical forms and its inflections, though many of the cases are identical with nouns of (1) and (2). Vulgar Latin developed articles from the deictic pronoun *ille* 'that one' and the cardinal number *ūnus* 'one', the former perhaps partly under Greek influence. This was an innovation in Italic.

The comparison of adjectives was signalled morphologically. Comparatives were formed with inherited *-ios-*; e.g. Lat. *maiior* < *magjōs* (: *magnus* 'big'), O. *mais* < *magjos* (nt.), and its allomorph *-is- + *-tero-* in Oscan and Umbrian, e.g. U. *MESTRU* < *magisterā* (f. nom.), cf. Lat. *magister* 'master'. Superlative forms were more varied. Inherited were *-mo-* in *supmo-* > Lat. *summum*, U. *somo* (acc.) 'highest', *-t(m̥)mo-* in Lat. *ultimam*, O. *ÚLTIUMAM* (f. acc.), *-is(m̥)mo-* in *magism̥mo-* > Lat. *maximās*, O. *maimas* (f. acc. pl.). Unique to Latin is *-is-sm̥mo-* as in *strēnuissimus* 'most vigorous'. The analytic exponents *magis/plūs strēnuus, maximē strēnuus*, etc. encroached, especially in Vulgar Latin.

The Italic verbal inflections too were fusional, encoding the categories of tense, (past, present, future), aspect (imperfective, perfective), mood (indicative, subjunctive, imperative), number (singular, plural), person (first, second, third) and voice (active and medio-passive). Typologically this system was close to Proto-Indo-European. The specific innovations were the creation of a future tense, the merging of perfect and unmarked (aorist) aspectual distinctions in a new perfective, the absorption of optative into subjunctive and of dual into plural, and the decline of the middle functions of the medio-passive.

Minimal oppositions can be illustrated from Latin:

	imperfect:	dīcēbat	'he was saying'
dīcit 'he says' present	perfect:	dīxit	'he said'
indicative singular third	subjunctive:	dīcat	'let him say'
person active	plural:	dīcunt	'they say'
	second person:	dīcis	'you say'
	passive:	dīcitur	'he is said'

all of which are exactly paralleled in Oscan and Umbrian.

There are three Italic participles: (a) the inherited -nt- acts as imperfective active; e.g. U. ZEŘEF = Lat. sedēns 'sitting' (nom. sg.); (b) the inherited -to- verbal adjective signalling state, which was originally neutral as to voice, as in U. TAÇEZ 'silent' = Lat. tacitus beside tacēre 'to be silent', ÇERSNATUR 'having dined' (nom. pl.), cf. Lat. cēnāti beside cēnāre 'to dine', became the medio-passive perfect participle; e.g. O. scriftas 'written' (nom. pl.), Lat. scrīptae beside scrībere 'to write', and indūtus 'having put on' beside induere 'to clothe'; (c) a prospective passive in -ndo-, the gerundive, peculiar to Italic; e.g. O. ÚPSANNAM 'to be done' (acc. sg.), U. anferener 'to be carried about' (gen. sg.), cf. Lat. operundum, ferendī. Latin also has a prospective active participle, e.g. dictūrus 'about to say'.

There are infinitives, reflecting verbal noun case forms, e.g. dīcere < *deikesi (s-stem loc. sg.); dīcī < *deikei (loc. of *deikom or dat. of *deiks) and O. DEÍKÚM (the corresponding accusative). Latin developed a systematic marking of tense and voice in the infinitives, starting with the arbitrary assignment of *deikesi to present active, *deikei to present passive and the extension of *-si from the present active to form a perfect active *deix-is-si (> dīxisse). The system was completed by an assortment of makeshift analytic formations.

Apart from the verb 'to be' (Lat. esse, O. ezum U. erom) and, at least in Latin, 'to go' (īre) and 'to wish' (uelle, with its compounds), the Italic verb was organised into four conjugations, classified according to the present infinitive and first person singular present indicative, as in the chart of Latin verb conjugations.

Conjugation (3a) reflects inherited thematic-stem verbs, e.g. agere, O. acum, cf. Gk. ágein 'to lead', together with a few verbs from the Proto-Indo-European athematic class, e.g. iungō 'I join', cf. Ved. yunájmi, sistō 'I set up', U. SESTU, cf. Gk. hístāmi. The transfer of the latter probably began in the plural, with the remodelling of *iungmos, *sistamos (cf. Ved. yunjmāḥ, Gk. hístamen) etc. (1) also contains some athematic reflexes, e.g. fārī 'to speak', cf. Gk. phāmí 'I say', and stāre 'to stand', which was formed from the aorist, cf. Gk. éstān 'I stood'. But its largest constituency is denominative formations, originally from declension (1), e.g. cūrāre, O. KURAIA (3 sg. subj.), North O. coisatens (3 pl. perf.) all from *koisā (> Lat. cūra), but extended to other declensions, e.g. Lat. termināre from the (2)-noun terminus, O. TEREMNATTENS (3 pl. perf.) from a (3a)-neuter attested in TEREMENNIÚ (nom. pl.). In fact it was to this conjugation that all new

Latin Verb Conjugations

		1	2	3a	3b	4
Infin.		cūrāre	monēre	dīcere	facere	uenīre
		'to care'	'to warn'	'to say'	'to make'	'to come'
Sg.	1	cūr-ō	mon-eō	dīc-ō	fac-iō	uen-iō
	2	-ās	-ēs	-is	-is	-īs
	3	-at	-et	-it	-it	-it
Pl.	1	-āmus	-ēmus	-imus	-imus	-īmus
	2	-ātis	-ētis	-itis	-itis	-ītis
	3	-ant	-ent	-unt	-iunt	-iunt

denominatives and loan-verbs were assigned; e.g. *iūdicāre* from *iūdex* 'judge', cf. O. *medicatud* (abl. part.) 'having been judged', *aedificāre* 'to build' from **aedifex*, *baptizāre* from Gk. *baptízein*, *guardāre/wardāre* from Go. *wardōn* 'to keep watch'.

Conjugation (2) absorbed the Proto-Indo-European stative formant in **-ē-*, e.g. *uidēre* 'to see', the causative **-ejo-*, e.g. *moneō* 'I warn' (cf. *meminī* 'I recall'), and some denominatives from declension (2), e.g. *fatērī* 'to confess', O. *FATÍUM* from **fato-* 'spoken'. (4) has a few denominatives from (3b)-nouns, e.g. *fīnīre* from *fīnis* 'finish'. Together with (3b) it also reflects **-jo-* verbs, as in *ueniō* (4) < **gʷṇjō*, *faciō* (3b, cf. O. *FAKIIAD* 3 sg. subj) < **dhə₁jō*. The distribution between the two conjugations, at first phonologically determined, had long since become more casual. A number of verbs show doublet forms in (3b) and (4), e.g. Lat. *cupiō* 'I desire', U. *HERTER* 'it is required' (<**heri-*) but *HERI* 'he wishes' (< **herī-*).

Some verbs with long-vowel presents show a different formation in the perfect, e.g. *moneō* : *monu-ī*, *ueniō* : *uēn-ī*, also *iuuō* (1) 'I help' : *iūuī*. Others generalised the long vowel, e.g. *cūrō* : *cūrāuī*, *audiō* 'I hear' : *audīuī*. This is typical of a general Latin tendency: cf. the spread of the infixed nasal from *iungō* 'I join' to *iunxī* beside the more conservative *rumpō* : *rūpī*.

The most important opposition in the Latin verb was originally between (I) imperfective and (II) perfective aspect. Within each of these two divisions there was a further opposition between (A) the unmarked base form and a pair marked for (B1) prospective and (B2) retrospective tense. The unmarked imperfective form was located in the present tense, the unmarked perfective form was temporally ambivalent between present and past. The following second singular forms of *monēre* illustrate the original distribution of the forms that they reflect:

I	A	monē-s				
		B1	monē-b-is	B2	monē-b-ās	
II	A	monu-istī				
		B1	monu-er-is	B2	monu-er-ās	

This system was not inherited, and the conjugation that is closest to a Proto-Indo-European type, (3), shows a different pattern in IA and B:

I   A   dīc-is   B1   dīc-ēs

                                    B2   dīcē-bās

where *dīcēs* was originally the subjunctive to *dīcis*. This pattern in fact spread via (3b) to (4): *audīs, audiēs*. It has a parallel in the relation between U. **PURTUVIS* 'you offer' and *PURTUVIES* 'you will offer'.

The Oscan and Umbrian material is very incomplete; there are no reflexes of II B2, for instance, and only one of I B2. But the following Oscan forms reveal a system, and it is different both from Proto-Indo-European and from Latin:

I   A   FAAMA-T (3 sg.)
          B1   deiua-s-t (3 sg.)
                      B2   FU-F-ANS (3 pl.)
II   A   PRÚFATT-ENS (3 pl.)
          B1   TRÍBARAKATT-U-S-ET (3 pl.)
                      B2   —

Here the I B1 form is from **-se-*, also attested in early Lat. *faxit*, an infrequent synonym of *faciet* 'he will do', while the unique I B2 form is from **-bhwā-*, attested in Lat. **bā-*.

Also exemplified in these examples is the diversity of perfective formants: Lat. /w/ in *curā-uī, mon-ŭ-ī*, O. /tt/ in *PRÚFATTENS*. There are others too; e.g. U. /l/ in *apelus* 'you will have weighed (< **anpend-luses*), O. /f/ in *SAKRAFIR* (pass. subj.) 'let there be a consecration'. Some are shared with Latin, e.g. reduplication in U. *DEDE* 'he gave', Lat. *dedit*; long root vowel in O. *hipid* 'he had' (< **hēb-* beside Lat. *habuit*), cf. Lat. *cēpi* 'I took'. The sigmatic formation, productive in Latin, e.g. *dīxī* (cf. Gk. aor. *édeixa*), has no other Italic attestation.

The six tenses had by historical times been reorganised thus:

Future (< I B1): monēbis 'you will warn', deiuast 'he will swear'.
Past-in-the-Future/Future Perfect (< II B1): monueris 'you will have warned', TRÍBARAKATTUSET 'they will have built'.
Present (< I A): monēs 'you warn', FAAMAT 'he orders'.
[Past] Imperfect (< I B2): monēbās 'you were warning', FUFANS 'they were'.
[Pres.] Perfect/Past Definite (< II A): monuistī 'you warned', PRÚFATTENS 'they approved'.
Past-in-the-Past/Past Perfect (< II B2): monuerās 'you had warned'

The original aspectual oppositions survive only in the imperfect and perfect, having become neutralised in the future and present. The temporal relationship between imperfect and past-in-the-past, *monē-b-ās*: *monu-er-ās*, has been replicated in *monē-b-is* : *monu-er-is*, with the transfer of the latter from perfective-future to future-perfect function.

The syncretic character of the Italic perfect is reflected in Latin both in its stem classes, which contain inherited perfect (reduplication) and aorist (sigmatic) formants, and in its personal inflections: sg. *uēn-ī, uēn-istī, uēn-it*; pl. *uēn-imus, uēn-istis, uēn-ēre* and *uēnĕrunt*. This contrasts sharply with the inflections of all the other five tenses, which, apart from first person singular forms in vowel + *m* in the imperfect, past perfect and all subjunctives, are very homogeneous. (In Oscan and Umbrian what can be discerned of the perfect inflections is less idiosyncratic).

The present-perfect functions of the Latin perfect are well attested, e.g. *nōuī* 'I know', perfect of *nōscō* 'I come to know', *periī* 'I am ruined', perfect of *pereo* 'I perish'. They were especially prominent in the passive, where a stative meaning is predictably more frequent anyway and the analytic exponents had a present orientation: *epistulae scrīptae sunt* like O. *scriftae set* was originally a present-perfect 'the letters are in a written state', even though it is the regular passive also to the past-definite meaning of *scrīpsī* 'I wrote'.

The ambiguities resulting from the syncretism in the perfect were resolved in the classical period of Latin by the development of two new tenses: an active present-perfect corresponding to *scrīptae sunt* 'they are written' and a passive past-definite for *scrīpsī (epistulās)*:

	Act.		Pass.
Perf.	scrīptās habeō (new)	←	scrīptae sunt
			↓
Past Def.	scrīpsī		scrīptae fuērunt (new)

The innovations never established themselves fully in the written language but became current in Post-Classical Vulgar Latin.

The Italic exponents of medio-passive voice are partly reflexes of middle forms in *-r*, which are attested in Hittite and Old Irish, partly the ph ses with the *-to-* participle cited above. Thus U. *EMANTUR* 'they are to be taken', Lat. *emantur* 'they are to be bought', U. *screhto est*, Lat. *scriptum est* 'it has been written'. The relation between the medio-passive and active paradigms can be seen in:

	1		*3a*	
	Sg.	*Pl.*	*Sg.*	*Pl.*
1	cūr-o-r	cūr-ā-mu-r	dīc-o-r	dīc-i-mu-r
2	-ā-ris	-ā-minī	-e-ris	-i-minī
3	-ā-t-ur	-a-nt-ur	-i-t-ur	-u-nt-ur

Most transitive verbs show the live opposition of passive to active. Sometimes the verb is intransitive and the passive therefore subjectless, an impersonal equivalent to an active form, e.g. *pugnātur* 'there is fighting' = *pugnant* 'they (unspecified) are fighting'.

The old middle voice is discernible in occasional uses of these forms, e.g. *mouētur* 'it moves (itself)', *uertitur* 'he turns (himself) around' and more rarely accompanied by a direct object *indūtus tunicam* 'having put on a tunic', cf. *induit tunicam* 'he puts a tunic on (somebody else)'. Sometimes the active and middle forms are synonymous, e.g. *adsentiō/or* 'I agree', *mereō/or* 'I earn'. In a number of verbs, the so-called deponents, only the medio-passive form occurs, either with a middle meaning, e.g. *moror* 'I delay (myself)', O. *KARANTER* 'they enjoy', cf. Lat. *uescuntur*, or more often with a meaning indistinguishable from the active, e.g. *opīnor* 'I believe' beside *crēdō*, *prōgredior* 'I advance' beside *prōcēdō*.

Of the three moods the imperative has only second and third person forms; Lat. *ī* 'go!', *ītō* 'go!' or 'let him go!' < *ei+tōd*, cf. U. *ETU*: Lat. *agitō*, O. *actud*, U. *AITU* 'let him act/move' < *age+tōd*. Italic subjunctives reflect in form and function both the subjunctive and optative moods of Proto-Indo-European. Thus O. *FUSÍD* = Lat. *foret* 'it was to be' with Proto-Indo-European thematic subjunctive *-ē-*; U. *EMANTUR* 'they are to be taken', cf. Lat. *emantur*, with *-ā-*, a subjunctive formant also found in Celtic, U. *sir* = Lat. *sīs* 'may you be' with *-ī-*, originally the plural allomorph of *-iē-*, the athematic optative formant. The meanings of will (subjunctive) and wish (optative) are illustrated by these examples and by O. *NEP PÚTÍAD* 'nor may he be able', Lat. *nēue possit*, O. *ni hipid* 'let him not hold', with perfect subjunctive as in Lat. *nē habuerit*. Prospective (subjunctive) and hypothetical (optative) meanings are found in Lat. *sī id dīcās, ueniat* 'if you were to say it [in future], she would come' (pres. subj.), *sī id dīcerēs uenīret* 'if you were saying it [now], she would be coming' (imperf. subj.). The introduction into the subjunctive of temporal distinctions modelled on the indicative (*dīcat : dīceret : dīxerit* ← *dīcit : dīcēbat : dīxit*) and the decline of the purely aspectual ones (as in *nē dīxerit* 'he is not to say' vs. *nē dīcat* 'he is not to be saying') are notable innovations in Italic.

Sometimes in Latin subordinate clauses the distinction between indicative and subjunctive is neutralised; cf. *currit nē cōnspiciātur* 'he runs in order not to be seen' (volitive: purpose) with *tam celeriter currit ut nōn cōnspiciātur* 'he runs so fast that he is not seen' (for *cōnspicitur*, declarative); *haec quom dīxisset* (subj.), *ēuāsimus* with *ubi haec dīxit* (indic.), *ēuāsimus* 'when she had said this (declarative), we left'.

In indirect discourse declarative utterances were normally represented by the accusative plus infinitive. It was precisely in order to encode the necessary tense and voice distinctions that Latin developed its heterogeneous collection of infinitives, possibly under the influence of

Greek, the only other Indo-European language to employ elaborate forms of accusative plus infinitive. The tense of the direct-discourse verb was reproduced in the infinitive: *uenīs* 'you are coming', *dīcō/dīxī tē uenīre* 'I say you are/said you were coming'. The construction was very inefficient: the temporal distinctions between *ueniēbās* 'you were coming', *uēnistī* 'you came' and *uēnerās* 'you had come' were lost in *dīcō/dīxī tē uēnisse* 'I say you have/said you had come'; similarly the modal distinction between *ueniās* 'you would come' and *ueniēs* 'you will come' disappears in *tē uentūrum esse*. Eventually the accusative plus infinitive was replaced by *quod* or *quia* + finite verb constructions, perhaps partly under Greek influence, though in contrast to Greek there is a tense shift (see below). The replacement was almost total in Vulgar Latin but only partial in the written language.

In indirect commands, questions, etc. and in all subordinate clauses within indirect discourse finite verbs were used, but with transpositions of mood and tense, the indicative being replaced by subjunctive and the tense being determined not by the tense in direct discourse but by the tense of the governing verb: *imperāuī ut uenīrēs* 'I gave orders for you to come' (← imper. *uenī!*), *rogāuī quor uēnissēs* 'I asked why you had come' (← indic. *quor uēnistī?*). This was almost certainly a native Italic development within the register of laws and edicts: cf. O. *KÚMBENED THESAVRÚM PÚN PATENSÍNS MÚÍNÍKAD TANGINÚD PATENSÍNS* 'it was agreed that the treasury, when they opened it, by a joint decision they should open' with Lat. *conuēnit ut thēsaurum cum aperīrent commūnī sententiā aperīrent*; U. *EHVELKLU FEIA SVE REHTE KURATU SIT* 'a vote he is to hold (as to) whether the matter rightly has been taken care of' with Lat. *sententiam roget num rēctē cūrātum sit*.

The Italic languages had a free word order in the sense that variations from normal patterns did not affect syntactic relationships or make nonsense, but were motivated by pragmatic considerations — topicalisation, emphatic juxtaposition — or by the aesthetics of prose or verse rhythm, etc. However, the unmarked, viz. most frequent, order was SOV. Thus in Latin *informīs hiemēs redūcit Iuppiter*, from a lyric poem by Horace, contrasts with the unmarked classical prose order *Iuppiter hiemēs informīs redūcit* 'Jupiter winters ugly brings back'. The cooccurrence of SOV with noun-adjective patterns generally in Italic characterises the languages as typologically mixed or 'transitional'. Consistent with SOV are: (i) the order genitive-noun attested in O. *SENATEÍS TANGINÚD*, cf. Lat. *senatūs cōnsultō* 'by decision of the senate'; (ii) the anastrophe of prepositions, common in Umbrian but rare in Oscan and Latin, e.g. U. *ASAMAŘ* = Lat. *ad āram* 'to the altar', U. *FRATRUSPER* = *prō frātribus* 'for the brothers' (cf. O. *censtom-en* = *in cēnsum* 'for the census', Lat. *mēcum* 'with me'); (iii) the early Latin placing of relative clauses before their antecedents. However, none of these was an unmarked order in Latin of the classical period, a fact that confirms its mixed character. The order SOV is overwhelmingly the most frequent in the prose of Cicero and Caesar, and in the post-classical written registers was especially tenacious in subordinate clauses, where it provided a 'punctuating' signal, often combined with rhythmic cadences (*clausulae*). Nevertheless there are signs in the dialogue of Plautus' comedies (early second century BC) that SVO was becoming established in Vulgar Latin. The reduction of morphological distinctions between nominative and accusative in Vulgar Latin drastically limited the choice of the marked options OSV and OVS. Furthermore the replacement of certain cases by prepositional phrases favoured the fronting of head nouns: *dīmidium praedae* seems to have been replaced by *dīmidium dē praedā* more easily than the marked *praedae dīmidium* by *dē praedā dīmidium*.

A notable feature of the literary register in Classical and Post-Classical Latin was the elaboration of complex and in particular periodic sentence structure. Heavily influenced by Greek rhetoric doctrine and oratorical practice, it became a feature of both formal prose and verse. In a highly inflected language the grammatical concords facilitate the detachment of participial phrases from the nominals on which they depend and enable clausal exponents of subordinate constituents to be embedded without any loss of semantic coherence. The following is typical:

(1) posterō diē,
(2)   quom per explōrātōres cognōuisset
(3)   quō in locō hostēs
(4)   quī Brundisiō profectī erant
(3)   castra posuissent,
(1) flūmen trānsgressus est,
(5)   ut hostīs,
(6)   extrā moenia uagantēs
(7)   et
(8)   nūllis custōdibus positīs
(7)   incautōs,
(5)   ante sōlis occāsum aggrederētur.

(lit. 'on the next day, | when by reconnaissance patrols he had discovered | in what place the enemy | who from Brindisi had set out | camp had pitched, | the river he crossed | in order that the enemy, | outside the camp wandering | and [being] | with no guards posted | unwary, | before the sun's setting he should attack').

This is not strictly a period since a well-formed sentence can be concluded before the final clause, in fact at *trānsgressus est*; but it illustrates the technique very well. (4) is embedded in (3) and the group (2)–(4) in (1); similarly (8) in (7) and (6)–(8) in (5). All the modes of subordination are exemplified: adverbial and relative clauses in (2) and (4), participial and absolute phrases in (6) and (8). The deployment of information in participial exponents ((6)–(8)) dependent on the object of the volitional verb in (5) has both pragmatic significance and the aesthetic effect of contributing variety and balance to the sentence. Latin complex and periodic structure provided the model for similar developments in the formal discourse of later European vernaculars, though none of these possessed the morphological resources to emulate it fully.

4   Lexicon

With so small and specialised a body of data from Oscan and Umbrian it is hazardous to generalise, and we can do no more than note a few specific items in their basic vocabulary. For instance, U. *pir* (cf. O. *PURASÍAÍ* (adj.)) and *UTUR* have widespread Indo-European cognates outside Italic, e.g. *fire*, *water*, but not in Latin (*ignis*, *aqua*); O. *touto*, U. *totam* (acc.) 'community' have specifically West Indo-European cognates, again excluding Latin. On the other hand, some words are peculiar to Italic; e.g. Lat. *cēna*, O. *KERSNU* 'dinner' (the root is Indo-European, meaning 'cut'); *habēre* 'to have', cf. U. *HABIA* (3 sg. subj.); *ūtī* 'to use', cf. O. *ÚÍTTIUF* 'use' (nom. sg.), of no certain etymology; and *familia*, O. *famelo* 'household', probably from Etruscan. Many words attested in Italic generally have of course Indo-European cognates; e.g. *māter* 'mother', O. *MAATREÍS* (gen.); *pēs* 'foot', U. *PEŘI* (abl.); *duodecim*, U. *desenduf* (acc.) 'twelve (two + ten)'; *ferre* 'to bear', U. *FEREST* (3 sg. fut.); *sedēre* 'to sit', U. *ZEŘEF* (pres. part.). A few of these show a semantic specialisation peculiar to Italic; e.g. *dīcere*, O. *DEÍKUM* 'to say' (< 'to point, show'); *diēs*, O. *zicolom* 'day' (< 'sky'); *agere*, O. *acum* 'to do' (< 'to move along').

In addition to the items just mentioned there are a number of Latin words for which neither cognates nor synonyms happen to be recorded in Italic but which have well established Indo-European etymologies; e.g. *ego* 'I', *canis* 'dog', *nix*, 'snow', *pectus* 'breast', *rēx* 'king', *dūcere* 'to lead', *loquī* 'to speak'. Among the older Indo-European languages Latin's basic vocabulary has closest affinities with Gothic, with which it shares some 38 per cent of items, and Vedic (35 per cent); it has least in common with Old Irish (27 per cent) and Old Armenian (26 per cent). The relatively low percentages and the narrow band within which they cluster indicate a long period of separation between Latin (presumably with Italic) and the rest.

Some frequent Latin words have no etymology even in Italic; e.g. *bonus* 'good', *hīc* 'this', *mulier* 'woman', *omnis* 'all'. Loanwords can be identified at all periods, often by their phonology; e.g. *rosa* 'rose' from an unknown Mediterranean source, *bōs* 'cow' from Sabine, *taberna* 'shop' from Etruscan, *carrus* 'cart' from Celtic, *wadium* 'pledge, wage' from Gothic. By far the largest group is from Greek: not only cultural terms — *balneum* 'bath', *epistula* 'letter', *māchina* 'device', *nummus* 'coin' (all early), *architectus*, *poēta* and Christian terms like *ecclēsia* 'church' and *baptizāre* 'to baptize' — but also more basic items like *āēr* 'air', *bracchium* 'arm', *camera* 'room', *hōra* 'hour' and in Vulgar Latin *colpus* 'blow', *gamba* 'leg', *petra* 'stone', replacing the native words *ictus*, *crūs* and *lapis*. A number of Latin words, especially in the technical registers of philosophy, philology and the arts and crafts, were either created on Greek models, e.g. *quālitās* 'quality' (Gk. *poiótēs*), *indīuiduum* 'the indivisible thing' (Gk. *átomos*), *accentus* 'accent' (Gk. *prosōdía* lit. 'a singing in addition'), or semantically adjusted to them e.g. *cāsus* 'a falling' > 'noun case' (Gk. *ptōsis*) and *conclūsiō* 'an enclosing' > 'syllogism' (Gk. *sullogismós*).

The lexical stock was extended by the usual morphological processes. Complex words were created by suffixation. For instance, the diminutive *-lo-* used both literally, e.g. *puella* '(little) girl' : **puera* (cf. *puer* 'boy'), *ōsculum* 'kiss' (cf. *ōs* 'mouth'), *articulus* '(small) joint' (cf. *artus* 'joint, limb'), and affectively, e.g. *misellus* 'poor little' (cf. *miser* 'wretched'), *ocellus* 'dear little eye' (cf. *oculus*). In Vulgar Latin some words were displaced by their diminutives, e.g. *culter* 'knife' by *cultellus*, *uetus* 'old' by *uetulus*.

Among the most frequent verbal noun formants in Italic were **-ion-* and **-tion-*, which originally signalled action but were often extended by metonymy to the concrete result of action; e.g. O. *TRÍBARAKKIUF* ('act of building' >) 'a building', *legio* ('act of choosing' >) 'a legion', O. *medicatinom* (acc.) 'judgement' from **medicaum* 'to judge', U. *NATINE* (abl. 'act of birth' >) 'tribe', cf. Lat. *nātiō*. In fact *-tiōn-* was productive at all periods of Latin, e.g. *mentiō* 'an act of reminding' > 'mention' (cf. OIr. *air-mitiu* 'respect, honour') beside *mēns* (< *mentis*) 'mind'; *ōrātiō* 'act of pleading' > 'a speech, a prayer' from *ōrāre*; Medieval Lat. *wadiātiō* 'the act of *wadiāre* (to pledge, give security)'. Often associated with *-tiōn-* in Latin is the agent suffix *-tōr-*, e.g. *ōrātor*, *wadiātor*. By contrast *imperātor* (O. *EMBRATUR*) 'commander' is from *imperāre* but the action noun is *imperium*; *auctor* (U. *UHTUR*) 'initiator' from *aug-* 'to enlarge' but *auctoritās*, U. *UHTRETIE* (loc.) 'the status of initiator' with the denominative suffixes in *-tāt-* and *-tiā-* (cf. Lat. *amīc-itia* 'friendship').

Among the productive verb suffixes is *-tā-*, with intensive, in particular frequentative, meanings: *itāre* 'to go often' beside *īre* 'to go', cf. U. *ETAIANS* (3 pl. subj.) < **eitā-*; *habitāre* 'to live' beside *habēre* 'to have'; *tractāre* 'to handle' beside *trahere* 'to drag'. There was a tendency especially in Vulgar Latin for these to replace the simple verbs; e.g. *spectāre* 'to look at', *cantāre* 'to sing', *iactāre* 'to throw' for *specere* (archaic), *canere*, *iacere*. This led to greater morphological uniformity; cf. *cantō*, *cantāuī* and *iactō*, *iactāuī* with *canō*, *cecinī* and *iaciō*, *iēcī*. The intensive meanings themselves came to be hypercharacterised, as *dict-itāre* for *dic-tāre* from *dīcere* 'to say'.

Italic compound words, formed from the stems of two or more distinct

lexemes, mostly conform to the OV type. Thus O. *MEDDÍSS* 'magistrate' <
medo-dik- 'rule-declaring', cf. Lat. *iū-dex* 'judge' < 'law-setting/giving', O.
KÚM-BENN-IEIS (gen.) 'assembly' < 'a together-coming', cf. Lat. *con-
uen-tūs*, O. *TRÍB-ARAK-AVÚM* (infin.) 'to build' < 'to house-strengthen',
cf. Lat. *aedi-fic-āre*, U. *petur-purs-us* (dat.) 'animals' < 'four-footed', cf.
Lat. *quadru-ped-ibus*. Some prefixes acquired intensive force; cf. *cōnficere*
'to complete' with *cōnferre* 'to bring together', *efficere* 'to effect' with
effluere 'to flow out'. In the literary register compounding was usually a
mark of Greek influence. It was associated particularly with high epic, e.g.
caelicola 'sky-dweller', *suāuiloquēns* 'pleasant-speaking', and parodies
thereof, e.g. *dentifrangibulus* 'teeth-breaking'; also with philosophical and
philological terminology, where, as we have seen, the precise models were
Greek. Latin was never a heavily compounding language like Ancient
Greek, Vedic or modern German, and the chief morphological expansions
of the lexicon were through the formation of compound-complex words,
e.g. **prīmo-cap-* 'first taking' in *prīnceps* 'chief', whence *prīncipium* 'a
beginning' (< *-iom*, as in O. *KÚMBENNIEÍS*), *principālis* 'primary'
(< *-āli-*, as in O. *FERTALIS* 'with sacrificial cakes, *ferta*'), *prīncipātus*
'leadership' (< *-ātu-* (4); cf. *-āto-* (2) reflected in U. *FRATRECATE* <
*fratr-ik-ātei (loc.) 'in the office of the master of the brothers, **frātrik(o)s*').
These processes and many of the actual formants continued in use for as long
as Latin survived.

Bibliography

Brief but reliable accounts of the history of Latin are Stolz et al. (1966) and Collart
(1967). More detailed, especially on the literary registers, is Palmer (1954). The most
comprehensive description of the language is Leumann et al. (1963-72); it is,
however, inadequate for Vulgar Latin, for which see Väänänen (1963), and for the
written registers of post-classical periods, for which see Löfstedt (1959) and Norberg
(1968). On particular topics, Kent (1945) on phonology and Kent (1946) on
morphology are both predominantly historical, while Woodcock (1958) on syntax is
predominantly descriptive; for word order, Adams (1976) is important.

For the other Italic languages, Buck (1928) is still the standard work on Oscan and
Umbrian, while Poultney (1959) is comprehensive on Umbrian. Pisani (1964)
includes all the Italic languages and also Venetic, Messapic and Etruscan.

References

Adams, J.N. 1976. 'A Typological Approach to Latin Word Order', *Indogermanische
Forschungen*, vol. 81, pp. 70-99
Allen, W.S. 1975. *Vox Latina: A Guide to the Pronunciation of Classical Latin*
(Cambridge University Press, Cambridge)
Bonioli, M. 1962. *La pronuncia del latino nelle scuole dall'antichità al rinascimento*,
vol. 1 (Università di Torino Pubblicazioni, Facoltà di Lettere e Filologia, Turin)
Buck, C.D. 1928. *A Grammar of Oscan and Umbrian* (Ginn, Boston)

Collart, J. 1967. *Histoire de la langue latine* (Presses Universitaires de France, Paris)

Cooper, F.C. 1895. *Word Formation in the Roman Sermo Plebeius* (Trow Directory, New York)

Grandgent, C.H. 1907. *An Introduction to Vulgar Latin* (D.C. Heath, Boston)

Kent, R.G. 1945. *The Sounds of Latin* (Linguistic Society of America, Balitmore)

—— 1946. *The Forms of Latin* (Linguistic Society of America, Baltimore)

Leumann, M., J.B. Hoffmann and A. Szantyr. 1963-72. *Lateinische Grammatik*, 2 vols. (C.H. Beck, Munich)

Löfstedt, E. 1959. *Late Latin* (Aschehoug, Oslo)

Norberg, D. 1968. *Manuel pratique de latin médiéval* (Picard, Paris)

Palmer, L.R. 1954. *The Latin Language* (Faber and Faber, London)

Pisani, V. 1964. *Le lingue dell' Italia antica oltre il latino*, 2nd ed. (Rosenberg and Fellier, Torino)

Poultney, J.W. 1959. *The Bronze Tablets of Iguvium* (American Philological Association, Baltimore)

Stolz, F., A. Debrunner and W.P. Schmid (eds.) 1966. *Geschichte der lateinischen Sprache* (Walter de Gruyter, Berlin)

Vaananen, V. 1963. *Introduction au latin vulgaire* (Klincksieck, Paris)

Woodcock, E.C. 1958. *A New Latin Syntax* (Methuen, London)

8 Romance Languages

John N. Green

The Romance languages derive, via Latin, from the Italic branch of Indo-European. Their modern distribution is the product of two major phases of conquest and colonisation. The first, between c. 240 BC and c. AD 100, brought the whole Mediterranean basin under Roman control; the second, beginning in the sixteenth century, annexed the greater part of the Americas and sub-Saharan Africa to Romance-speaking European powers. Today, some 580 million people speak, as their first or only language, one that is genetically related to Latin. Although for historical and cultural reasons preeminence is usually accorded to European Romance, it must not be forgotten that European speakers are now outnumbered by non-Europeans by a factor of more than two to one.

The principal modern varieties of European Romance are indicated on the map. No uniformly acceptable nomenclature has been devised for Romance and the choice of term to designate a particular variety can often be politically charged. The Romance area is not exceptional in according or withholding the status of 'language' (in contradistinction to 'dialect' or 'patois') on sociopolitical rather than linguistic criteria, but additional relevant factors in Romance may be cultural allegiance and length of literary tradition. Five national standard languages are recognised: Portuguese, Spanish, French, Italian and Rumanian (each treated in an individual chapter below). 'Language' status is usually also accorded on cultural/ literary grounds to Catalan and Occitan, though most of their speakers are bilingual in Spanish and French respectively, and the 'literary tradition' of Occitan refers primarily to medieval Provençal, whose modern manifestation is properly considered a constituent dialect of Occitan. On linguistic grounds, Sardinian too is often described as a language, despite its internal heterogeneity. Purely linguistic criteria are difficult to apply systematically: Sicilian, which shares many features with southern Italian dialects, is not usually classed as an independent language, though its linguistic distance from standard Italian is no less than that separating Spanish from Portuguese. 'Rhaeto-Romance' is nowadays used as a cover term for a number of varieties spoken in southern Switzerland (principally Engadinish, Romansh and Surselvan) and in the Dolomites, but it is no longer taken to subsume Friulian. Romansh (local form *romontsch*) enjoys an official status for cantonal administration and so perhaps fulfils the requirements of a language. Another special case is Galician, located in Spain but genetically and typologically very close to Portuguese; in the wake of political autonomy, *galego* is now generally referred to in Spain as a language, although elsewhere it continues to be thought of (erroneously) as a regional dialect of Spanish. Corsican, which clearly belongs to the Italo-Romance group, would be in a similar position if the separatist movement gained autonomy or independence from France.

Map 8.1

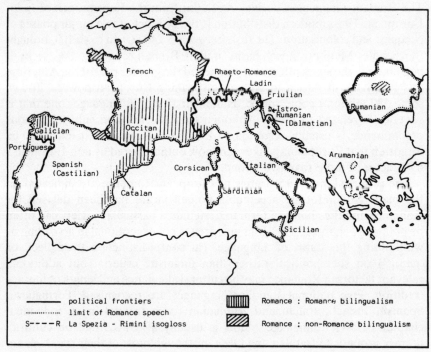

Outside Europe, Spanish, Portuguese and French, in descending order of native speakers, have achieved widest currency, though many other varieties are represented in localised immigrant communities, such as Sicilian in New York, Rumanian in Melbourne, Sephardic Spanish in Seattle and Buenos Aires. In addition, the colonial era gave rise to a number of creoles, of which those with lexical affinities to French are now the most vigorous, claiming upward of eight million speakers.

In general, European variants are designated by their geographical location; 'Latin', as a term for the vernacular, has survived only for some subvarieties of Rhaeto-Romance (*ladin*) and for Biblical translations into

Judaeo-Spanish (*ladino*). 'Romance' derives, through Spanish and French, from *ROMĀNICĒ* 'in the Roman fashion' but also 'candidly, straightforwardly', a sense well attested in early Spanish. The terminological distinction may reflect early awareness of register differentiation within the language, with 'Latin' reserved at first for formal styles and later for written language and Christian liturgy. The idea, once widely accepted, that Latin and Romance coexisted for centuries as *spoken* languages, is now considered implausible.

Among the chief concerns of Romance linguists have always been: the unity or otherwise of the proto-language, the causes and date of dialect differentiation and the classification of the modern variants. Plainly, Romance does not derive from the polished literary models of Classical Latin. Alternative attestations are quite plentiful, but difficult to interpret. Attempts to echo popular speech in literary works may be suspected of stylistic artifice; inscriptional evidence is formulaic; the abundant Pompeian graffiti may be dialectal, and so on. Little is known of Roman linguistic policy or of the rate of assimilation of new conquests. We may however surmise that a vast territory, populated by widely differing ethnic groups, annexed over a period exceeding three centuries, conquered by legionaries and first colonised by settlers who were probably not native speakers of Latin, and never enjoying easy or mass communications, could scarcely have possessed a single homogeneous language.

The social conditions which must have accompanied latinisation — including slavery and enforced population movements — have led some linguists to postulate a stage of creolisation, from which Latin slowly decreolised towards a spoken norm in the regions most exposed to metropolitan influences. Subsequent differentiation would then be due to the loss of administrative cohesion at the break-up of the Empire and the slow emergence of local centres of prestige whose innovations, whether internal or induced by adstrate languages, were largely resisted by neighbouring territories. Awareness of the extent of differentiation seems to have come very slowly, probably stimulated in the west by Carolingian reforms of the liturgical language, which sought to achieve a uniform pronunciation of Church Latin at the cost of rendering it incomprehensible to uneducated churchgoers. Sporadic attestations of Romance, mainly glosses and interlinear translations in religious and legal documents, begin in the eighth century. The earliest continuous texts which are indisputably Romance are dated: for French, ninth century; for Spanish and Italian, tenth; for Sardinian, eleventh; for Occitan (Provençal), Portuguese and Rhaeto-Romance, twelfth; for Catalan, thirteenth; for Dalmatian (now extinct), fourteenth; and for Rumanian, well into the sixteenth century.

Most classifications of Romance give precedence, explicitly or implicitly, to historical and areal factors. The traditional 'first split' is between East and West, located on a line running across northern Italy between La Spezia and

Rimini. Varieties to the north-west are often portrayed as innovating, versus the conservative south-east. For instance, West Romance voices and weakens intervocalic plosives: *SAPŌNE* 'soap' > Ptg. *sabão*, Sp. *jabón*, Fr. *savon*, but It./Sard. *sapone*, Rum. *săpun*; *RŌTA* 'wheel' > Ptg. *roda*, Sp. *rueda*, Cat. *roda*, Fr. *roue*, but It./Sard. *rota*, Rum. *roată*; *URTĪCA* 'nettle' > Ptg./Sp./Cat. *ortiga*, Fr. *ortie*, but Sard. *urtica*, It. *ortica*, Rum. *urzică*. The West also generalises /-s/ as a plural marker, while the East uses vocalic alternations: Ptg. *as cabras* 'the goats', Cat. *les cabres*, Romansh *las chavras*, contrast with It. *le capre* and Rum. *caprele*. In vocabulary, we could cite the verb 'to weep', where the older Latin word *PLANGĔRE* survives in the East (Sard. *pranghere*, It. *piangere*, Rum. *a plînge*) but is completely replaced in the West by reflexes of *PLORĀRE* (Ptg. *chorar*, Sp. *llorar*, Cat. *plorar*, Oc. *plourà*, Fr. *pleurer*). In this classification, each major group splits into two subgroups: 'East' into Balkan-Romance and Italo-Romance, 'West' into Gallo-Romance and Ibero-Romance. The result is not entirely satisfactory. While, for example, Arumanian dialects and Istro-Rumanian group quite well with Balkan-Romance, our scant evidence of Dalmatian suggests it shared as many features with Italo-Romance as with the Balkan group. Catalan is a notorious difficulty, having been subject for centuries to alternating Occitan and Spanish influences. The unity of 'Rhaeto-Romance' also fails to survive close scrutiny: Ladin groups fairly well with Friulian as part of Italo-Romance, but southern Swiss varieties share many features with eastern French dialects.

'Family-tree' classifications, in which variants are each assigned to a single node, give only a crude indication of relationships in Romance and tend to obscure the convergence brought about by centuries of borrowing from Latin and criss-crossing patterns of contact. This is readily illustrated from the lexicon. The *PLANGĔRE/PLORĀRE* example, though supportive of the East-West split, is in fact rather atypical. More common are innovations spreading from central areas but failing to reach the periphery. 'To boil' is Ptg. *ferver*, Sp. *hervir*, Rum. *a fierbe* (< *FERVĒRE/FERVĔRE*), but Cat. *bullir*, Oc. *boulí*, Fr. *bouillir*, It. *bollire* (< *BULLĪRE*, originally 'to bubble'); 'to request' is Ptg./Sp. *rogar*, Rum. *a ruga* (< *ROGĀRE*), but Cat. *pregar*, Oc. *pregá*, Fr. *prier*, It. *pregare* (< *PRECĀRE*, originally 'to pray'); 'to find' is Ptg. *achar*, Sp. *hallar*, Rum. *a afla*, but Cat. *trobar*, Oc. *trobà*, Fr. *trouver*, It. *trovare* (both forms are metaphorical — classical *INVENĪRE* and *REPERĪRE* do not survive). Among nouns, we may cite 'bird': Ptg. *pássaro*, Sp. *pájaro*, Rum. *pasăre* (< **PASSARE*), versus Oc. *aucèu*, Fr. *oiseau*, Romansh *utschè*, It. *uccello* (< *AUCELLU*); and 'cheese': Ptg. *queijo*, Sp. *queso*, Rum. *caş* (< *CĀSEU*), versus Cat. *formatge*, Oc. *froumage*, Fr. *fromage*, It. *formaggio* (< *[CĀSEU] FORMATICU* 'moulded [cheese]'). Almost the same distribution is found in a morphosyntactic innovation: the Latin synthetic comparative in *-IŌRE* nowhere survives as a productive form, but peripheral areas have *MAGIS* as the analytic replacement ('higher' is Ptg. *mais alto*, Rum. *mai înalt*) whereas the centre prefers *PLŪS* (Fr. *plus haut*, It. *più alto*).

Despite this differential diffusion and the divergences created by localised borrowing from adstrate languages (notably from Arabic into Portuguese and Spanish, from Germanic into northern French, from Slavonic into Rumanian), the modern Romance languages have a high degree of lexical overlap. Cognacy is about 40 per cent for all major variants using the standard lexicostatistical 100-word list. For some language pairs it is much higher: 65 per cent for French-Spanish (slightly higher if suffixal derivation is disregarded), 90 per cent for Spanish-Portuguese. This is not, of course, a guarantee of mutual comprehensibility (untrained observers are unlikely to recognise the historical relationship of Sp./oxa/ 'leaf' to Fr./fœj/), but a high rate of cognacy does increase the chances of correct identification of phonological correspondences. Intercomprehensibility is also good in technical and formal registers, owing to extensive borrowing from Latin, whether of ready-made lexemes (abstract nouns are a favoured category) or of roots recombined in the naming of a new concept, like Fr. *constitutionnel*, *émetteur*, *exportation*, *ventilateur*, etc. Indirectly, coinings like these have fed the existing propensity of all Romance languages for enriching their word stock by suffixal derivation.

Turning to morphosyntax, we find that all modern Romance is VO in its basic word order, though southern varieties generally admit some flexibility of subject position. A much reduced suffixal case system survives in Rumanian, but has been eliminated everywhere else, with internominal relations now expressed exclusively by prepositions. All variants have developed articles, the definite ones deriving overwhelmingly from the demonstrative *ILLE/ILLA* (though Sardinian uses *IPSE/IPSA*), the indefinite from the numeral *ŪNU/ŪNA*. Articles, which precede their head noun everywhere except in Rumanian where they are enclitic, are often obligatory in subject position. Concord continues to operate throughout noun phrases and between subject and verb, though its range of exponents has diminished with the loss of nominal case. French is eccentric in virtually confining plural marking to the determiner, though substantives still show number in the written language. Parallel to the definite articles, most varieties have developed deictic object pronouns from demonstratives. These, like the personal pronouns, often occur in two sets, one free and capable of taking stress, the other cliticised to the verb. There is some evidence of the grammaticalisation of an animate/inanimate distinction, both in the clitic pronouns and in the prepositional marking of specific animate objects. This latter is widespread (using *a* in West Romance and *pe* in Rumanian) but not found in standard French or Italian.

Suffixal inflection remains vigorous in the common verb paradigms everywhere but in French. Compound tense forms everywhere supplement the basic set, though the auxiliaries vary: for perfectives, *HABĒRE* is most common: 'I have sung' is Fr. *j'ai chanté*, It. *ho cantato*, but Ptg. *tenho cantado* (< *TENĒRE* originally 'to hold') and Cat. *vaig cantar* (< *VĀDO CANTĀRE* 'I am going to sing'), a combination which would elsewhere be interpreted as a periphrastic future. Most Romance varieties have a basic imperfective/perfective aspectual opposition, supplemented by one or more of punctual, progressive and stative. The synthetic passive has given way to a historically-reflexive medio-passive which coexists uneasily with a reconstituted analytic passive based on the copula and past participle. The replacement of the future indicative by a periphrasis expressing volition or mild obligation (*HABĒRE* is again the most widespread auxiliary, but *deppo* 'I ought' is found in Sardinian and *voi* 'I wish' in Rumanian) provided the model for a new paradigm, the conditional, which has taken over a number of functions from the subjunctive. The subjunctive has also been affected by changes in complementation patterns, but a few new uses have evolved during the documented period of Romance, and its morphological structure, though drastically reduced in spoken French, remains largely intact.

In phonology, it is more difficult to make generalisations (see the individual language sections below and, for the development from Latin to Proto-Romance, pages 172–3). We can, however, detect some shared tendencies. The rhythmic structure is predominantly syllable-timed. Stress is on the whole rather weak — certainly more so than in Germanic — and is dynamic rather than tonal, some variants, notably Italian, use higher tones as a concomitant of intensity, but none rely on melody alone. The loss of many intertonic and post-tonic syllables suggests that stress may previously have been stronger, witness *IŪDĬCE* ['iu-di-ke] 'judge' > Ptg. *juiz*, Sp. *juez*, Cat. *jutge*, Fr. *juge*; *CUBĬTU* ['ku-bi-tu] 'elbow' > Sp. *codo*, Fr. *coude*, Rum. *cot*. The elimination of phonemic length from the Latin vowel system has been maintained with only minor exceptions. A strong tendency in early Romance towards diphthongisation of stressed mid vowels has given very varied results, depending on whether both higher and lower mid vowels were affected, in both open and closed syllables, and on whether the diphthong was later levelled. Romance now exhibits a wide range of vowel systems, but those of the south-central group are noticeably simpler than those of the periphery: phonemic nasals are found only in French and Portuguese, high central vowels only in Rumanian, and phonemic front rounded vowels only in French, some Rhaeto-Romance and north Italian varieties and São Miguel Portuguese. Among consonantal developments, we have already mentioned lenition, which led to wholesale reduction and syllable loss in northern French dialects. Latin geminates generally survive only in Italo-Romance, and many other medial clusters are simplified (though new ones are created by various vocalic changes). Although Latin is in Indo-European terms a centum language (with *k* for PIE *k̂*), one of the earliest and most far-reaching Romance changes is the palatalisation, and later affrication, of velar and dental consonants before front vowels. Only the most conservative dialect of Sardinian fails to palatalise (witness *kenapura* 'Holy supper = Friday'), and the process itself has elsewhere often proved cyclic.

Developments in phonology illustrate a more general characteristic of Romance: the tendency for a small number of identical *processes* to affect all varieties, though at slightly different rates and with slightly different exponents as the outcome. Whether this is due to directly inherited tendencies, or to analogical development of shared stock, remains a matter of debate — neither standpoint would question the fundamental unity of Romance.

Bibliography

Harris and Vincent (1988) provides detailed typological descriptions of Latin and all principal varieties of modern Romance including creoles. Agard (1984) is a compendious introduction to synchronic description and internal history; it usefully complements Elcock (1975), an excellent external history concentrating on philological aspects. Wright (1982) deals with early history and the reconceptualisation of Romance as independent of Latin. Manoliu-Manea (1985) is an authoritative discussion of comparative syntax, while Hope (1971) is a copiously illustrated study of vocabulary enrichment, with particular reference to French–Italian exchanges. Rohlfs (1971) is an approachable introduction to dialectology, with some 100 maps showing the diffusion of individual words and expressions; Rohlfs (1986) is a sequel, with a further 275 maps.

Anderson and Creore (1972) is a collection of 27 articles dealing with phonology, morphology and syntax, some pan-Romance in scope. A state-of-the-art survey of the discipline, with detailed bibliographic appraisals, is given by Posner and Green (1980–2): vol. 1 concentrates on historical linguistics, vol. 2 on synchronic perspectives, vol. 3 on philology and 'minor' languages, and vol. 4 on national and regional approaches to the subject.

References

Agard, F.B. 1984. *A Course in Romance Linguistics*, 2 vols. (Georgetown University Press, Washington D.C.)
Anderson, J.M. and J.A. Creore (eds.) 1972. *Readings in Romance Linguistics* (Mouton, The Hague)
Elcock, W.D. 1975. *The Romance Languages*, 2nd ed. (Faber and Faber, London)
Harris, M. and N. Vincent (eds.) 1988. *The Romance Languages* (Routledge, London and Oxford University Press, New York)
Hope, T.E. 1971. *Lexical Borrowing in the Romance Languages*, 2 vols. (Basil Blackwell, Oxford)
Manoliu-Manea, M. 1985. *Tipología e historia* (Gredos, Madrid)
Posner, R. and J.N. Green (eds.) 1980–2. *Trends in Romance Linguistics and Philology*, 4 vols. (Mouton, The Hague)
Rohlfs, G. 1971. *Romanische Sprachgeographie* (C.H. Beck, Munich)
—— 1986. *Panorama delle lingue neolatine* (G. Narr, Tübingen)
Wright, R. 1982. *Late Latin and Early Romance* (Francis Cairns, Liverpool)

9 French

Martin Harris

1 Introduction

French, currently by any standards one of the major languages of the world, is a Romance language, descended directly from the Latin which came to be spoken in what was then Gaul during the period of the Roman Empire. As that Empire crumbled, a number of major dialectal divisions developed, which do not necessarily correspond to present-day political or linguistic frontiers. Such a major division was to be found within medieval France (see map 9.1), with the dialects of the north and centre (and part of modern

Map 9.1: The Dialect Divisions of Medieval France

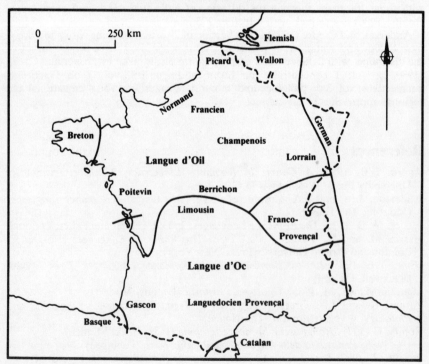

Belgium), known collectively as *langue d'oil*, being sharply distinguished from those of the south, *langue d'oc* (*oil* and *oc* being characteristic markers of affirmation in the relevant areas), with a third smaller area in the south-east, known as Franco-Provençal, generally taken to include the French dialects of Switzerland and the Val d'Aosta in Italy. The division between north and south is so marked that it has frequently been argued that, on purely linguistic grounds, the dialects of the south, now generally known collectively as *occitan*, are best not regarded as Gallo-Romance at all, but rather as closely linked with Catalan, the resultant grouping being distinct from Hispano-Romance also.

Within these major dialectal areas, further linguistic fragmentation took place, divergence being strongly favoured by the lack of social cohesion during the so-called Dark Ages. One of the dialects of the *langue d'oil* which emerged in this way was *francien*, the dialect of the Ile de France, and it is from this dialect that, once circumstances arose which favoured the growth of a national language, modern standard French has developed. (Another northern dialect was Norman, which had such a profound influence on the development of English.) The establishment of a fixed royal court in Paris, the recrudescence of an educational and of a legal system in that same city, and the fact that the abbey at St.-Denis, close by, was in effect the spiritual centre of the kingdom, all of these factors tended to favour the dialect of Paris and the surrounding area for the status of national language. Since the twelfth and thirteenth centuries, when *francien* (a modern name) gradually came to be accepted as a norm to aim towards, at least in writing and in cultivated speech in northern and central France, progress has been slow but steady. It is worth pointing out, however, that although the literary form of *occitan*, Provençal, never recovered from the devastation caused by the Albigensian crusade, and although French came to be virtually ubiquitous as the written language after the *Ordonnances de Villers Cotterets* (1539), it was not until the nineteenth and even the twentieth centuries, particularly in the south, that French came to be so wholly dominant within the boundaries of France, at first among the bourgeoisie and in the cities, and later also in the remoter rural areas. Indeed, French's long period of predominance as the major international language of culture and diplomacy long antedates its general use as a spoken language within France: by the end of the seventeenth century, French had in effec' replaced Latin in the former role, to the point that the Berlin Academy was able to ask in 1782, as a matter of fact, 'Qu'est-ce qui a rendu la langue françoise universelle?' ('What has made the French language universal?'). This situation persisted until the First World War and even beyond.

Within Europe, French is now spoken by some 51 million people within France (and Monaco), and by some 4 million Walloons in Belgium, principally in the four francophone districts of the south, Hainaut, Namur, Liège and Luxembourg, and in the bilingual district of Brussels the capital.

The rivalry between French and Dutch within Belgium, which extends far beyond the linguistic plane, is well known. Around half a million people live in the Grand-Duchy of Luxembourg, where the native language of most speakers is a German dialect but where French is the language of education and administration, while in Switzerland, the most recent figures suggest that approaching 20 per cent of a total population of some 6.3 million are French speakers. In northern Italy, the Val d'Aosta has a French-speaking population of around 100,000.

Outside Europe, indigenous French speakers are to be found in almost every continent. In Canada, there are some six million francophone descendants of the original colonists, three quarters of these living in the province of Quebec (where they form some 80 per cent of the total population). Strenuous efforts are made to preserve and strengthen French, particularly in Quebec, within what has been since 1867 officially a bilingual country. Descendants of another group of French colonists in Acadia (the easternmost provinces of Canada), driven out in the mid-eighteenth century, carried their language southwards down the eastern seaboard of the United States and into Louisiana. As a result, although there are relatively few French speakers in Acadia today except in New Brunswick (some 200,000), there are significant numbers — approaching one million — in New England (where there is a major admixture also directly from Quebec) and in Louisiana, French until 1803, where the immigrants were primarily from Acadia, and are indeed called 'Cajuns': their form of speech, *français acadien*, is in regular use by perhaps a further one million people, alongside a small elite speaking more or less standard French and also a French-based creole.

Elsewhere, French is generally in competition not with another European language but with indigenous non-European languages and/or with French-based creoles in former French (or Belgian) colonies. In the West Indies, French is found for instance in Haiti (where it is the official language of some five million people but where the great majority actually use creole) and in islands such as Martinique and Guadeloupe. By far the most important areas, however, are the countries of the Maghreb (Algeria, Morocco and Tunisia), where French appears to be holding its own since independence: in Algeria, for example, it is estimated that some 20 per cent of the population can read and write French, with a much higher proportion able to speak it, above all in the cities. In black Africa, there are sixteen independent francophone states comprising a great swathe across the west and the centre of the continent from Senegal to Zaire, together with Madagascar, and there is a further group of French-creole-speaking islands (e.g. Mauritius, Seychelles, Réunion) in the Indian Ocean. In most of these countries, the future of French as a second language, used for a variety of official, technical or international purposes in place of one or more indigenous languages, seems secure.

Like all languages with any significant degree of diffusion, French is of course not a single homogeneous entity. Just as in France itself there is within most regions a spectrum of variation from 'pure' patois (the original local dialect, now often moribund) through *français régional* (largely the standard grammar, with a more or less regionally-marked phonology and a greater or lesser number of non-standard lexical items) to the standard language (which itself has a wide range of styles and registers), so too one finds a similar spectrum in most if not all of the areas discussed above, often with the added dimension of a French-based creole. In Quebec, for example, one finds 'educated Quebec French' shading imperceptibly through to the fully popular variant known as *joual* (from the local pronunciation of *cheval* 'horse') associated primarily with Montreal. French-based creoles are spoken not only in Louisiana (alongside Cajun, discussed above), Haiti and various islands mentioned earlier, but arguably also in parts of black Africa, in the form of such variants as *petit-nègre* or *petit français*. As in the case of *français régional*, there is very frequently a standard-creole continuum, with more educated speakers tending perhaps increasingly towards the metropolitan norms. It is these which are described in what follows, although some attempt will be made to indicate major divergences between popular and more educated varieties of the language.

Before the internal structure of the language itself is examined, however, one should look briefly at French orthography. When the first vernacular texts came to be written down, it was natural that the scribes should turn to the Latin alphabet, despite the obvious fact that it was less than ideal to represent a language whose phonological system had, as we shall see, already evolved considerably from Latin and which was to continue to develop rapidly. Nevertheless, despite the difficulties, a relatively standardised and quasi-phonemic orthography was widely used during the eleventh, twelfth and thirteenth centuries, 'quasi-phonemic' in the sense that it relied in part on 'distributional rules' (e.g. 'c' represents [k] in certain environments but [ts] (later [s]) in others) and in part on the use of one letter to indicate that an adjacent letter had a special value ('g' before 'n' marks the palatal nasal: thus 'gn' = [ɲ]). The shortcomings of the vowel system, however, especially the need to use one symbol (e.g. 'e') with various values (e.g. [e], [ɛ], [ə]), could only be somewhat alleviated by the use of certain conventional digraphs (e.g. 'ez' for [e]).

During the following three centuries, two major developments occurred to overturn the relative stability just described. Firstly, there was a further period of very rapid and radical phonetic change (one particular consequence of which was the emergence of many monosyllabic homophones), and secondly, not unconnected, there was a marked increase in the use of quasi-etymological spellings, in which one or more letters appropriately present in a Latin etymon were reinserted in the corresponding French derivative, even though the sound they represented

had been modified or lost in the interim, thus *doi(g)t* < *DIGITUM* 'finger'
although the [g] had long been effaced and similarly *pie(d)* < *PEDEM*
'foot', *se(p)t* < *SEPTEM* 'seven'. (The label 'quasi-etymological' is used
because recourse was not infrequently had to incorrect etyma: thus *poi(d)s*
'weight' does *not* come from *PONDUS* but from **PENSUM*.) The sixteenth
and seventeenth centuries saw various attempts at reform, and in particular
the acceptance of distinction between 'i' and 'j' and between 'u' and 'v' and
the use of the cedilla; the other three principal accents were not finally
accepted by the Academy until 1740. Some of the more extraordinary
'gothic' spellings (e.g. *sçapvoir* for *savoir* 'know') have also been
resimplified. The nineteenth and twentieth centuries have seen repeated
attempts at reform, both unofficial and official, the best known of the latter
being the reports of the two Beslais commissions, in 1952 and 1965. The
second of these proposed a small number of sensible and limited reforms,
such as the use of 's' as a standard plural marker (thus *bijous* for *bijoux*
'jewels'), the simplification of many unnecessary double consonants, and the
rationalisation of the use of accents (e.g. *è* for *é* as the second vowel in
événement 'event'). However, nothing has in fact happened, and the
situation remains more or less as it has been since the 1740 edition of the
Academy dictionary.

2   Phonology

One of the most immediately striking facts about French in comparison with
its sister languages is the radical nature of the phonological changes which
the language has undergone, changes which differentiate not just French
from, say, Spanish or Italian but indeed the *langue d'oil*, and *francien* in
particular, from the dialects of the south of the country. Four processes in
particular have contributed to this global effect: the evolution of the tonic
vowel system and the very significant reduction of atonic vowels; a period of
nasalisation and subsequent partial denasalisation of vowels preceding nasal
consonants; the widespread palatalisation of many consonants in
appropriate environments (which in turn affected the vowel system); and,
more recently, the effacement of most final consonants and, for most
speakers, of final /ə/ also.

Consider first the effects of stress on the overall shape of French words. In
the Latin of Gaul, the intensity of the stress accent grew, to the point where
most tonic vowels lengthened and broke (i.e. diphthongised) and even more
significantly, virtually all post-tonic vowels except /ə/ were eventually lost.
The effect of this was to create a fixed-stress language, with the stress either
on the final syllable or the penultimate syllable if the vowel of the final
syllable was /ə/; subsequent effacement of final /ə/ in (standard) spoken
French has further simplified the position, and the tendency for both verbal
and nominal groups to function as ever more tightly bound units, discussed

later, has meant that such units have increasingly borne only one stress. Essentially, therefore, we may say that modern French is a final-stress, phrase-stress language, with a very strong tendency, in non-learned words, towards monosyllabism. A clear example of the process can be seen by comparing the development of the trisyllabic Latin word *PÓPULUM* 'people' to a monosyllable *peuple* /pœpl/ (via /pœ-plə/) in French, compared with It. *popolo* and Sp. *pueblo*.

Of the seven tonic vowels inherited by Gallo-Romance, no fewer than five diphthongised in free syllables; only /i/ remained essentially unchanged, while /u/ fronted to /y/. The most interesting development is the passage of Latin /a/, via a diphthong, to a front mid vowel very early, a marked characteristic of *langue d'oil* (*MATREM* > *mère* /mɛʁ/ 'mother'). Of the four remaining diphthongs, two ([we] < GR /ɔ/ and [eu] < GR /o/) monophthongised and merged as /ø~œ/ (see below), i.e. as a second front rounded vowel, another distinguishing mark of northern French. A third diphthong, OFr. /oi/, passed to [wɛ] and then split in a most unusual way, passing either to ModFr. /wa/ or to /ɛ/, on no discernible phonetic or lexical basis: compare, for example, the nationality adjectives *français* 'French' and *anglais* 'English', with /ɛ/, and *danois* 'Danish' and *suédois* 'Swedish', with /wa/. The fourth diphthong /jɛ~je/ remains largely unchanged.

Various other developments of tonic vowels in specific environments ensured that both half-open and half-close back and front vowels and a back close vowel were once again present in the system by the Middle French period, and we end up with an oral vowel system in the modern language as shown in table 9.1.

Table 9.1: Oral Vowel Phonemes in Contemporary French

i	y		u
e	ø		o
ɛ	(œ) (ə)	ɔ	
a	(ɑ)		

Note: There is in addition a wide range of diphthongs and triphthongs incorporating the semi-consonants /j/ /w/ and /ɥ/. In this connection, one should note in particular the passage of /ʎ/ to [j], a process which began in the seventeenth century and was fully accepted by the nineteenth, and which contributed to such forms as /vjej/ (*vieille* 'old' (f.)) in the modern language from earlier /viɛʎ/.

Two main points need to be noted about this system. Firstly, of the pairs of half-open and half-close vowels, only the opposition between /o/ and /ɔ/ is clear and stable (*saute* /sot/ 'jumps': *sotte* /sɔt/ 'foolish' (f.)); /o/ has generalised in free final position. In the case of /œ~ø/, again the close variant has generalised in free final position, but the position is less clear elsewhere, with analogical forces noticeably at work. In terms of classical minimal pairs, however, there are very few indeed (e.g. *jeune* /ʒœn/ 'young' vs. *jeûne* /ʒøn/ 'fasts'), and the distinction is certainly not made by all native speakers. It is for this reason that /œ/ as a phoneme is bracketed in the table above. In the case of /e/:/ɛ/, neutralisation would almost certainly have occurred (with [e] in free final syllables and [ɛ] elsewhere), but for a concerted attempt, dating back to the seventeenth century, to retain [ɛ] also in free final position, and thus minimal pairs of the type *piqué* 'stung':*piquait* 'was stinging' (/pike/: /pikɛ/). Again, this distinction is not by any means consistently made: however, it seems that both /e/ and /ɛ/ should be retained within the inventory of phonemes for the time being. Finally in this section we should note that the phonological opposition between /ɑ/ and /a/ has already been lost in much of France (to the profit of /a/), and is retained only by older speakers in the Parisian area: hence /ɑ/ is firmly bracketed in the table above.

The last topic we should mention briefly in this sketch of the French vowel system is the existence of a set of four nasal vowel phonemes. During the period from the tenth to the thirteenth centuries, all vowels and diphthongs occurring before any nasal consonant nasalised, the low vowels first, then the mid and finally the close vowels. This development took place regardless of whether the syllable concerned was blocked or free and in many instances the resulting nasalised vowel was lowered; diphthongs tended to monophthongise. To give just one example, *FINEM* gave [fin] then [fĩn] then /fẽn/. During the latter part of the Middle French period, syllable structure became crucial, in that where the nasal consonant was in a different syllable from the preceding vowel, nasalisation was reversed, and the vowel became once again oral, sometimes before lowering (*FINAM* > *fine* 'fine' (f.) /fi-nə/), sometimes afterwards (*FEMINAM* > *femme* 'woman' /fa-mə/, not */fɛ-mə/). This left nasalised vowels only in blocked syllables, where the nasal consonants ceased to be pronounced: contrast *inconfortable* (initial vowel /ẽ/) and *inévitable* (initial vowel /i/). The net result of these changes was that nasalised vowels ceased to be conditioned allophones of oral vowels before a nasal consonant, and became phonemes in their own right, the number of minimal pairs being greatly increased by the effacement of final [ə] (see above) after denasalisation. (Thus /fi-nə/ and /fa-mə/ in our examples passed to /fin/ and /fam/.) Compare the development of the masculine and feminine forms of the adjective *SANUM* 'healthy': both nasalise, but only the latter denasalises, thus: (m.) *SANUM* > sãin > sẽn > sẽ; (f.) *SANAM* > sãinə > sẽnə > sɛn.

The outcome was the addition of the following nasal phonemes to the vowel inventory of French: /ɛ̃/, (/œ̃/), /ɔ̃/, /ɑ̃/. Of these four nasal monophthongs, one, /œ̃/, has a very low functional yield, and is in the process of being absorbed by /ɛ̃/, the few distinctions such as that between *brin* 'sprig' /bʀɛ̃/ and *brun* 'brown' /bʀœ̃/ thus being lost. It is therefore bracketed. There is also a full range of nasal diphthongs, e.g. /bjɛ̃/ *bien* 'well' ([bjɛ̃]).

Various attempts to view nasal vowels as conditioned allophones of oral vowels in specifiable contexts do not appear convincing, and their status as phonemes seems secure.

The French consonant system will be dealt with even more summarily. The inventory of phonemes is given in table 9.2.

Table 9.2: French Consonant Phonemes

	Labial	Dental	Palatal	Velar	Uvular
Plosive	p b	t d		k g	
Fricative	f v	s z	ʃ ʒ		ʀ
Nasal	m	n	ɲ		
Lateral		l			

Several points are worth noting. In Old French, there were four affricates, /ts, dz, tʃ, dʒ/, all of which had resulted from palatalisation under many and varied circumstances. One particular source of /tʃ/ was from /k/ before /a/, tonic or atonic, a development highly characteristic of *francien* vis-à-vis almost every other Romance dialect, thus *CARUM* > *cher* 'dear' OFr. [tʃier], *CABALLUM cheval* 'horse' OFr. [tʃəval]. /ts, dz/, originally palatal, early dentalised and later simplified, to merge with /s, z/. /tʃ, dʒ/ simplified to the palatal fricatives shown in the table above. The palatal lateral was progressively lost, as we have seen, from the seventeenth century onwards, whereas the palatal nasal still flourishes. /h/ survived in initial position, mostly though not exclusively in words of Germanic origin, until the Middle French period, but its loss was acknowledged as irreversible by the seventeenth century: one residual effect is the absence of liaison in cases such as /la aʃ/ *la hache* 'axe'. Finally, we should note that /ʀ/ is included in the table, as a uvular fricative is the normal urban pronunciation of the 'r' phoneme, at least in northern French, although a uvular trill is not infrequent and a dental trill is still found, particularly in the south.

One aspect of the French consonant system is worthy of special note. Consonants already final in Latin were widely effaced in earliest French, only the dentals /s, n, l, r/ in general surviving. A whole range of secondary final consonants were created in Old French, however, by the loss of post-tonic syllables, already discussed: *PONT(EM)* > *pont* 'bridge' (OFr. [pɔnt]) is a case in point, as is *CAP(UT)* > *chef* 'chief' (OFr. [tʃief]). In fact, the Old

French final consonant system, which subsumed the four earlier survivors mentioned above, consisted of twelve phonemes, involving all the modes and points of articulation. Of these twelve, the fate of nasals and of /ʎ/ has already been considered, while /l/ and to some extent /ʁ/ have been maintained. The fate of final voiceless plosives and fricatives, however, has been more complex. The general tendency was for two or even three distinct pronunciations to develop, one before a pause, one before a subsequent initial consonant and one before a subsequent initial vowel, a situation which has survived in some cases to the present day: an obvious example is that of *dix* 'ten', pronounced as /dis/ in isolation, /di/ before a consonant (*dix femmes* 'ten women'), and /diz/ before a vowel (*dix élèves* 'ten pupils'). It will be noted that the final consonant has been lost completely before a following initial consonant, and it is in this environment that the effacement of many final consonants appears to have begun. By the middle of the seventeenth century, most final plosives and fricatives — including /s/, the plural marker, a point discussed later — had fallen silent, except in a number of monosyllables (where the danger of homonymic clash is greatest), and except before a word beginning with a vowel within the same sense group.

The modern phenomenon of liaison has its roots in this development. According to the traditional rules, final consonants are pronounced if the following word within the immediate sense unit begins with a vowel, a voiceless fricative (though not a plosive) being voiced. Thus we find *il faut y aller* /ifotialo/ or *les enfants* /lezãfã/. It has to be said, however, that the principle of invariability exerts a strong pressure, and that even in careful speech, let alone more casual registers, liaison is often not made: in other words, the last vestiges of the secondary final plosives and fricatives are tending to be lost, thus *pas encore* 'not yet', often /paãkɔʁ/.

It might be thought that that would be the end of the story of final consonants. Not so, however. With the effacement of final /ə/, already alluded to on several occasions, a range of tertiary final consonants has come into being, a range which includes in fact every one of the consonantal phonemes of the modern language, thus *vache* 'cow' /vaʃ/, *vigne* 'vine' /viɲ/ etc. These consonants show no sign whatever of weakening or loss: that particular stage in the language's history is over. Indeed, as will be noted in the discussion of English loanwords (page 224), blocked monosyllables are currently very much a favoured word type in French.

Finally a last word about /ə/. Its loss in word-final position is in fact part of a much more general tendency for it to be effaced in speech whenever its loss would not lead to unacceptable initial or medial consonant clusters. Given that words within a sense group function, as we have seen, very much like a single word, these rules apply across the phrase rather than to words in isolation. Thus *elle est petite* 'she is small' may well be pronounced /ɛ-lɛp-tit/, whereas *une petite femme* 'a small woman' is more likely to be /yn-pə-tit fam/ to avoid the sequence /npt/. Compare also *petite amie* 'small friend' /p(ə)-ti-ta-mi/ (initial /pt/ being acceptable only in fairly rapid speech) with *ma petite amie* 'my small friend' /map-ti-ta-mi/ where the problem does not arise. Interestingly, in speech, /ə/ may actually be introduced, for instance to avoid a three consonant cluster, thus *Arc de Triomphe* /aʁ-kə-də-tʁi-ɔ̃f/, *des contacts pénibles* '(some) uncomfortable contacts' /dekɔ̃taktəpenibl/. The question of the phonemic status of [ə] is left open here. It may well be acceptable to view schwa in contemporary French as a positional variant of /ø/, its realisation in those rare instances when it is stressed (e.g. *fais-le* do it /fɛlø/); at times, however, it is simply introduced in speech in the way just described.

3   Morphology

The verbal morphology of contemporary French is not particularly complex. Superficially at least, the four conjugation types of Latin have been retained, as *-er* (*donner* 'give'), *-oir* (*voir* 'see'), *-re* (*rompre* 'break') and *-ir* (*venir* 'come') verbs respectively. In practice, however, the *-oir* and *-re* classes are closed in contemporary French, membership of the former group in particular being heavily restricted. Almost all new verbs in French enter the *-er* class, though the *-ir* class will admit new members if there is a strong analogical reason to do so (e.g. *alunir* 'to land on the moon': cf. *atterrir* 'to land', i.e. on earth). The *-ir* class in fact comprises three subtypes, those (the vast majority) which have incorporated an infix *-iss* (originally inceptive in value, but now an empty morph) into verbal paradigms based on the present stem ((*nous*) *fin-iss-ons* 'we finish' < *fin-ir*), a much smaller group which do not ((*nous*) *ven-ons* 'we come' < *ven-ir*), and an even smaller group (essentially *ouvrir* 'open', *couvrir* 'cover' and derivatives) which form their present tense like *-er* verbs.

French inherited a set of suffixed person markers which varied according to conjugation type and paradigm. The history of the language shows a marked tendency for the generalisation of a lesser number of variants, the clearest cases being in the plural where (with the sole exception of the past simple, discussed below) the appropriate suffixes are now orthographed 1 pl.: *-ons*; 2 pl.: *-ez*; 3 pl.: *-nt*. In the singular, there are in effect three patterns in the written language, namely (i) 1 sg.: *-e*; 2 sg.: *-es*; 3 sg.: *-e*, (ii) 1 sg.: *-s*; 2 sg.: *-s*; 3 sg.: *-t* and (iii) 1 sg.: *-ai*; 2 sg.: *-as*; 3 sg.: *-a*, i.e. the present tense of *avoir* 'have' which, in the singular at least, has resisted analogical levelling. The first of these sets is associated primarily with the present indicative of *-er* verbs, and with the present (and imperfect) subjunctive of all verbs; the second set is associated with the present indicative of non-*er* verbs, and with the imperfect and conditional paradigms of all verbs (and compounds thereof), the third set with the present perfect and future paradigms of all verbs, for reasons to be discussed hereafter. A heavily simplified tabulation of French verbs as they appear in the written language is thus as shown in the chart of indicative verbal paradigms and participles.

Indicative Verbal Paradigms and Participles

(a) Conjugation type and present indicative

donner	*rompre*	*voir*	*finir*	*venir*	*ouvrir*
donn-e	romp-s	voi-s	fini-s	vien-s	ouvr-e
donn-es	romp-s	voi-s	fini-s	vien-s	ouvr-es
donn-e	romp-t	voi-t	fini-t	vien-t	ouvr-e
donn-ons	romp-ons	voy-ons	fin-iss-ons	ven-ons	ouvr-ons
donn-ez	romp-ez	voy-ez	fin-iss-ez	ven-ez	ouvr-ez
donn-ent	romp-ent	voi-ent	fin-iss-ent	vienn-ent	ouvr-ent

(b) Imperfect of all verbs
   donn-ais (cf. fin-iss-ais)
   donn-ais
   donn-ait
   donn-ions
   donn-iez
   donn-aient

(c) Present subjunctive of all verbs
   romp-e
   romp-es
   romp-e
   romp-ions
   romp-iez
   romp-ent

(d) Future of all verbs
   fini-r-ai
   fini-r-as
   fini-r-a
   fini-r-ons
   fini-r-ez
   fini-r-ont

(e) Conditional of all verbs
   fini-r-ais
   fini-r-ais
   fini-r-ait
   fini-r-ions
   fini-r-iez
   fini-r-aient

(f) Past participle
   donn-é, romp-u, v-u, fin-i, ven-u, ouv-ert

Several things need to be noted about this tabulation. Firstly, the stress pattern inherited from Latin varied through the paradigm of the present indicative, thus *DÓN-AT* 'he gives' (a 'strong' form stressed on the root) but *DON-ÁMUS* 'we give' (a 'weak' form stressed on the desinence). Given what we have already seen about the divergent development of tonic and atonic vowels in French, it is not surprising that paradigms with two stems frequently emerged, thus OFr. *aim-e* < *ÁMAT* 'he loves' but *am-ons* < *AMÁMUS* 'we love'. In general, the 'weak' form prevailed, thus for example the stem *treuv-e* 'finds' (strong) ceded to *trouv-ons* (weak) during the sixteenth century: persistence of the strong stem *aim-* is accordingly exceptional. In a small number of cases, both stems have survived: *venir* in the chart (*vient* : *venons*) is an instance of this.

The chart of verbal paradigms omits the past simple. This paradigm, and the related imperfect subjunctive paradigm, unlike those considered so far, is not morphologically based on the 'present' stem inherited from Latin, but on the so-called 'historic' stem, which in the case of irregular verbs may be significantly different. It has also resisted the analogical levelling of its personal suffixes. Both these paradigms have been ousted from normal spoken French (see below). Specimen paradigms are given in the chart of past simple paradigms.

Past Simple Paradigms

(a) Regular
   donn-ai, donn-as, donn-a, donn-âmes, donn-âtes, donn-èrent (*donner*)
   fin-is, fin-is, fin-it, fin-îmes, fin-îtes, fin-irent (*finir*)
(b) Irregular
   vins, vins, vînt, vînmes, vîntes, vinrent (*venir*)

The future tense of modern French derives from the infinitive followed by (a reduced form of) the present tense of *avoir* 'have' which has now been fully assimilated, thus *fini-r-ai* '(I) shall finish' in the chart of verbal paradigms. The conditional is formed in the same way with an even more reduced form of the imperfect of *avoir*. There is a full range of compound tenses formed with the various paradigms of *avoir* (or *être* in the case of certain intransitive verbs) and the past participle, thus *ai donné* 'have given' (cf. *suis venu* 'have come', lit. 'am come'). The uses of certain of these paradigms are discussed later, as is that of the so-called *temps surcomposés*, the 'double compound' tenses. The combination of forms of *être* with the past participle of transitive verbs as a marker of the passive should also be noted.

Two verbs only in contemporary French may be said to have a truly idiosyncratic morphology: *être* 'be' (combining forms of both Vulgar Latin *ESSERE* and *STARE* 'stand') and *aller* 'go' (combining forms of *VADERE* 'go', 'walk' (e.g. *va* '(he) goes'), *IRE* 'go' (e.g. *ira* '(he) will go') and *ALLARE*, generally thought to be a reduced form of *AMBULARE* 'to walk').

Finally, we should note that in respect of most paradigms in actual usage four of the six personal endings whose orthographic representations we have discussed are in fact silent (and hence of course homophonous) in modern French, only -*ons* ([ɔ̃]) and -*ez* ([e]) being pronounced. How the identity of the subject is in fact marked in the contemporary language is discussed below.

As far as noun morphology is concerned, French has dramatically simplified the five-declension, five-case, three-gender system it inherited.

The case system in fact survived longer in French than anywhere else except Rumanian, to the extent that, for many nouns at least (mainly those of masculine gender), a nominative:oblique distinction was maintained in Old French, being progressively lost only during the thirteenth and fourteenth centuries to the profit in all but a few cases of the oblique form, which thus underlies almost all French nouns. Thus, to take a typical case, Lat. *ÍNFANS* (nom.) gave OFr. *enfes* while *INFÁNTEM* (acc.) gave *enfant*. (Recall the earlier discussion of strong and weak verb forms.) It is *enfant* which has prevailed as the modern French form. In a handful of instances only, the nominative form prevailed, either alone (*prêtre* < *PRESBYTER* 'priest') or as well (*sire* < *SENIOR* (nom.), *seigneur* < *SENIOREM* (acc.), lit. 'elder'). One interesting such doublet is *on* 'one' < *HOMO* (nom.) and *homme* 'man' from *HOMINEM* (acc.). In synchronic terms, however, such nouns are no longer in any way distinctive.

The only survivor of Latin inflectional noun morphology lies in the almost universal use of *-s* (of which *x* is an orthographic variant) as the marker of plurality; this derives directly from the *-s* of the Latin accusative plurals *-AS*, *-OS* and *-ES*, and thus generalised as oblique forms ousted nominatives. This final *-s*, however, is now purely orthographic in all but liaison contexts: plurality, like gender, which survives in the form of a binary masculine: feminine opposition, is actually dependent for overt marking in almost all instances on the form of the associated determiner (see section 4) thus *le père* 'father' : *la mère* 'mother' : *les pères* 'fathers' : *les mères* 'mothers' (/lə pɛʁ/:/la mɛʁ/:/le pɛʁ/:/le mɛʁ/). Oppositions such as *le cheval* : *les chevaux* (/lə ʃəval/ : /le ʃəvo/), due to earlier phonetic changes (in this case the vocalisation of /l/ preconsonantally ([ls] > [us]) but not finally, i.e. in the plural but not the singular), are very much the exception in the modern language.

Adjective morphology is extremely simple. Adjectives vary according to the number and gender of the noun with which they are collocated. In respect of number, the point just made applies: the distinction is orthographic rather than phonetic in most cases. Many feminine adjectives, however, are quite distinct from their masculine counterparts, in that the presence of [ə] at the time final consonants were effaced prevented their loss in feminine adjectives. Numerous pairs of adjectives are therefore distinguished orthographically by the presence or absence of a final *-e*, but phonetically by the presence or absence of a final consonant, thus m. *grand*: f. *grande* 'big' (/gʁã/ : /gʁãd/). Current thinking is that these consonants should not be viewed as underlyingly present but deleted from the masculine forms, but that the feminine forms, seen (traditionally) as derived, should be considered to undergo rules of consonant insertion. In other cases, that same [ə] prevented devoicing at an earlier stage in the language's history (m. *vif* : f. *vive* 'lively') or provoked denasalisation (see above), thus m. *plein* /plɛ̃/ : f. *pleine* /plɛn/ 'full'. In many instances, however, there is no phonetic distinction between masculine and feminine adjectives in contemporary French (e.g. m.-f. *rapide*). Adjectives derived from the Latin third declension frequently did not distinguish between masculine and feminine forms in Old French for etymological reasons: gradually, however, these came to be assimilated to the normal pattern, with the result that forms such as *Rochefort* and *grand-mère* 'grandmother' (for *Rocheforte and *grande-mère) are isolated relics.

Among the various sets of pronouns, we shall note just two. Personal pronouns in French fall into two sets, conjunctive (i.e. those which can occur only immediately preceding a verb form) and disjunctive (i.e. those which can occur independently of a verb). (Special rules apply in relation to pronouns cooccurring with imperatives.) Conjunctive pronouns retain a nominative:oblique distinction in the first and second persons singular (*je* 'I', *me* 'me'/'to me') and a unique threefold distinction in the third person (e.g. masculine *il* 'he', *le* 'him', *lui* 'to him'): there is also a third person reflexive form *se* serving for both genders and both numbers. In the first and second persons plural, the nominative:oblique distinction is neutralised, as is indeed the conjunctive:disjunctive opposition, *nous* and *vous* serving with all values: elsewhere, the disjunctive pronoun is formally distinct, *moi* for instance in the case of the first person singular (cf. *je/me* above). We may therefore contrast singular *tu te lèves, toi?* (with three distinct forms) with plural *vous vous levez, vous?* ('are you getting up, you?').

The position in the third person is rather complex. A system in which the basic distinctions were gender and case is rivalled, at least in part, by one in which sex rather than gender is a crucially relevant parameter. Thus the conjunctive subject pronouns *il* and *elle* (and even more so the corresponding disjunctive pronouns *lui* and *elle*), ostensibly to be used for both males and masculines, females and feminines respectively, are increasingly restricted to animates, in particular to humans, to the profit of the originally 'neuter' *ce*. Thus *il est beau, lui* 'he's good-looking, him' is naturally interpreted as referring to a man, the corresponding description of a non-human masculine referent frequently being *c'est beau ça*. So far, however, *ce* has not entirely ousted *il* from another of its functions, that of 'unmarked' subject pronoun, a category necessary in French because of the absolute requirement for an overt subject even when none is semantically motivated, as for example with weather verbs, e.g. *il pleut* ('it is raining'). A further complication is that the 'non-human' conjunctive set includes a so-called 'genitive' form *en* ('of it'/'from it' etc.), which has no human counterpart, so that *je m'en souviens* (lit. 'I remind myself of it', i.e. 'I remember it') cannot, according to the rules of prescriptive grammar, have a human referent, i.e. cannot be interpreted as 'I remember him/her'. In informal registers, however, this is a possible interpretation, which in turn disrupts the long-standing parallel distribution of *en* and the 'non-human' dative *y*. To cut a long story short, *y* is now encroaching on to the 'animate' territory of *lui* and *leur*, in parallel as it were with the advance of *en*, which is simply filling a *case vide*. One final point of interest is that *ça*, which we saw earlier as the appropriate non-human disjunctive form, can also be used with a human referent, usually with a pejorative sense: *ça me dégoûte, les conservateurs* lit. 'that disgusts me, the conservatives', i.e. 'they disgust me . . .' Using only the singular forms, we may attempt to tabulate the position as in the chart of pronouns, the forms in round brackets being not as yet fully accepted, and those in square brackets being those ostensibly required for non-human referents of known gender.

French Singular Pronouns of the Third Person

	Human Male		Female		Non-human	
Nom.	il	(ça)	elle	(ça)	[il]	[elle]
					ce/ça;	il
Acc.	le		la		le/la	
Dat.	lui	(y)	lui	(y)	y	
Gen.		(en)		(en)	en	
Disj.	lui		elle		ça	

Two other points deserve brief mention. We have already seen that the Latin nominative *HOMO* 'man' gave a form *on* alongside *homme* < *HOMINEM*. This form *on* has been wholly assimilated into the personal pronoun system as a conjunctive subject form, at first with an impersonal value (*on dit* 'people say'; cf. German *man sagt*), but later as an alternative to various other subject pronouns and in particular to *nous*, which it has largely ousted in this function from the popular spoken language (*on part en voyage* 'we're off on a trip'). Note that *on* has neither an oblique nor a disjunctive form; within the immediate verb phrase, the third person reflexive form *se* is used (*on se lève de bonne heure* 'we get up early'); elsewhere, the semantically appropriate form reappears, thus *nous, on va sortir avec nos amis* (lit. 'us, one is going to go out with our friends' — note also the first person plural possessive form *nos*, to the exclusion of the third person singular form *ses*).

The relationship between *tu* and *vous* is not a straightforward singular:plural one. Since the seventeenth century, it has been normal to use *vous* in the case of singular addressees to mark 'respect', *tu* being limited to intimate contexts (e.g. within a family) or to mark a superior-inferior relationship (e.g. master to servant). *Vous* used as a 'respectful' singular shows singular concord outside the immediate verb phrase: *vous êtes content, monsieur?* (not *contents*) 'are you satisfied, sir?' As elsewhere, the 'intimate' forms are tending to gain ground in all but the most formal situations.

The demonstrative pronouns of French represent a twofold opposition of proximity, as do the corresponding determiners. In the contemporary language, this opposition is marked by the suffixes *-ci* and *-là* 'here' and 'there'), thus *celui-ci* : *celui-là* ('this' : 'that', masculine singular pronouns), *cette femme-ci* : *cette femme-là* ('this woman' : 'that woman'). There is also a genderless pair of demonstrative pronouns *ceci* and *cela*, a reduced form of the latter yielding *ça* which we have already discussed as a 'personal pronoun' and which has lost its distal value. The suffixes *-ci* and *-là* may be omitted when proximity marking is not essential, principally when the identity of the referent is immediately made clear, thus *celui que j'ai trouvé* lit. 'that that I have found' i.e. 'the one that I've found'; the omission of *-ci* and *-là* is relevant also to the discussion of determiners in French, below. It should be noted also that usage of the proximal and distal demonstratives heavily favours the latter, particularly in speech: *celui-là* may somewhat surprisingly be used both for 'this one' and 'that one' even in a context where they are juxtaposed, *celui-là-bas* 'that one over there' being used to disambiguate if absolutely necessary.

4 Syntax

The verbal system of French presents a number of interesting features. Within the indicative mood, the basic pattern is of four temporal possibilities on each of two time axes (a pattern familiar to speakers of English), with only one fully grammaticalised aspectual opposition, that between punctual and durative at the simultaneous point on the past axis. This may be represented as in figure 9.1. The reason that *a fait* appears in the table twice and that *fit* appears only in brackets is that the inherited aspectual distinction

Figure 9.1: French Verbal System

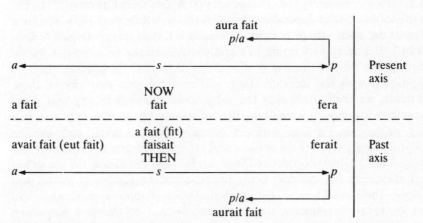

Note: *a.* anterior; *s.* simultaneous; *p.* posterior

between *faisait* 'was doing/used to do' and *fit* 'did' is now maintained in all spoken and most written registers by the use of *a fait* for *fit*, the former paradigm having taken over the functions of the latter (while retaining its own of marking a past event with present relevance) during the seventeenth and eighteenth centuries; *fit* is now restricted in effect to formal written registers. (The loss of *fit* necessarily entailed the loss of *eut fait* in the same circumstances.) The *a fait* paradigm thus corresponds both to English 'has done' and to 'did', while the original punctual:durative aspectual distinction is now maintained by *a fait:faisait*.

Synthetic forms, the 'future' (*fera*) and 'conditional' (*ferait*) paradigms, mark posterior time on each axis. However, these synthetic forms with future time reference are rivalled by analytic forms incorporating as an auxiliary the verb of motion *aller*, thus *va faire* 'is going to do' and *allait faire* 'was going to do' respectively. The present perfect *a fait* having lost its unambiguously 'present relevance' meaning, an alternative structure *vient de faire* (lit. 'comes from doing' i.e. 'has just done') is available for use, but this has not been incorporated into the system to anything like the same extent as *va faire*. Finally within the indicative mood, we should note the use of the *temps surcomposés*, ('double compound tenses') of the type *il a eu fait* (lit. 'he has had done'). These forms are used by some (but by no means all) native speakers as an optional marker of perfectivity (*quand il a eu payé...* lit. 'when he has had paid', the sense being 'as soon as he had finished paying'), thus restoring to the language the possibility of marking an aspectual distinction which had been central to the verbal system of Latin.

The subjunctive mood in contemporary French survives largely only as a conditioned variant in specifiable subordinate contexts, having been eliminated from main clauses in all but a handful of idioms (e.g. *advienne* (subj.) *que pourra* 'come what may') and the so-called 'jussive' structure (e.g. *qu'il le fasse* (subj.) lit. 'that he may do it' i.e. 'have him do it'). The use of the subjunctive in dependent clauses is partly determined by the semantic class of the main verb (e.g. verbs of 'emotion'), thus *je regrette qu'il le fasse* (subj.) 'I'm sorry he's doing so', and partly lexically (e.g. *vouloir* 'wish' requires the subjunctive but *espérer* 'hope' does not). In general, since no opposition with the indicative is possible in the vast majority of these contexts, we may doubt that the subjunctive mood is in any real sense meaningful, although a small number of minimal pairs may still be found (e.g. *de sorte que* 'so that' with the indicative marks a result, and with the subjunctive a purpose). In spoken and informal written French, only the present and perfect subjunctive (*fasse, ait fait*) are still in use, the imperfect and pluperfect (*fît, eût fait*) being restricted in the same way as the past simple. The virtual loss of semantic value by the subjunctive mood should not be taken to indicate the imminent demise of the two remaining paradigms as formal variants: they are learnt very early by children, for example, collocated with *(il) faut que* 'it is necessary that', and the present subjunctive forms of the commonest irregular verbs are very distinctive (*soit*, *ait*, *fasse*, *vienne*, *aille*, *puisse*, *sache*: 'be', 'have', 'do', 'come', 'go', 'be able', 'know').

The modal nuances previously carried by the subjunctive mood have very largely passed to the *fera* and in particular the *ferait* paradigms, noted earlier as the markers of posterior time on the two temporal axes within the indicative mood. The *ferait* paradigm can be used in main clauses (*le roi serait mort* lit. 'the king would be dead' i.e. 'the king is reputedly dead'), in apodoses (*il le ferait si . . .* 'he would do it if . . .') and in many subordinate clauses where the subjunctive is required by the rules of prescriptive grammar (*je cherche une maison qui aurait un jardin* 'I'm looking for a house that would have a garden', the precise identity or location of such a house being at present unknown). The most obvious use of the future paradigm with a modal value is in cases such as *ce sera Pierre* 'that'll (possibly) be Peter'.

One of the most interesting developments in the verbal system of at least popular spoken registers of French has been the change in status of the conjunctive subject pronouns discussed earlier. It will be recalled that four of the person-marking suffixes are homophonous in contemporary speech. Given the progressive replacement of *nous* by *on* (i.e. of *nous donnons* by *on donne* /dɔn/), only -*ez* /e/ is now distinctive, and the effective suffixal marking of the subjects of finite verbs in the case of most paradigms still in current use is a dead letter. This has not however resulted in the loss of person and number marking; rather, the appropriate conjunctive pronouns, which had become obligatory where there was no other subject by the end of the Middle French period, have become steadily more tightly bound to the verb of which they are subject, to the extent that they are found not only when a disjunctive pronoun of equivalent value is also present (*moi je pense...* lit. 'me I think...') but, in popular speech, increasingly even when there is an overt nominal subject (*mon père il dit que...* lit. 'my father he says that...'). The virtual elimination of the preverbal negative element *ne* and the widespread avoidance of inversion in interrogatives (see below) have facilitated the tendency for the sequence 'conjunctive subject pronoun + finite verb' to become indivisible, and for these pronouns to be reanalysed as bound prefixes with their semantic value unchanged. Put at its simplest, we may regard French *ils aiment* /izɛm/ 'they love' as one polymorphemic word (subject-prefix + stem) in exactly the same way as one regards Latin *AMANT* or OFr. *aiment* as one polymorphemic word (stem + subject-suffix). Parallel developments in the case of non-subject pronouns, and the interaction of all of these changes with sentential word order are discussed later.

One final word on the verb. There exists a passive structure of a familiar kind, which permits both subject deletion (*il a été écrasé* 'he has been crushed') and subject demotion (*il a été écrasé par la voiture* 'he has been crushed by the car'). When the underlying agent is human but cannot be or is not to be specified, the pronoun *on*, already discussed, is very frequently pressed into service, the voice of the verb remaining active (*on a ouvert la porte* 'someone has opened the door'/'the door has been opened'). Another strategy when the object is not human, used less than in Italian or Spanish but nevertheless not uncommon, is the pseudo-reflexive structure, that is, the use of the active forms of a verb reflexive in appearance in a 'passive' sense (*les fleurs se vendent ici le dimanche* lit. 'flowers sell themselves . . .' i.e. 'flowers are sold here on Sundays'). The original object may, as here, be promoted to subject, with appropriate verbal concord, or not, in which case an impersonal pseudo-reflexive structure is found, thus *il se pense toujours beaucoup plus de choses qu'il ne s'en dit* lit. 'it thinks itself always many more things than it says itself of them' i.e. 'many more things are thought than are said'. (Note the unmarked third person singular verb because no subject has been promoted and the empty subject pronoun *il* necessary to prevent the 'subject' slot from being left empty.)

The morphosyntax of the nominal group can be dealt with more briefly. We have seen that there are no consistent markers of gender on nouns in contemporary French (although gender is marked in the case of many adjectives) and that the sign of plurality, the suffix -*s*, is purely orthographic in the vast majority of instances. Gender and number — or, to be more accurate, gender *or* number — are nevertheless clearly phonologically indicated in the case of most noun phrases. The reason is simply that in most contexts nouns are accompanied by a determiner, and that these determiners are almost all grouped in sets of three which distinguish a masculine from a feminine in the singular and also a plural, thus *le*, *la*, *les* (the definite article), *un*, *une*, *des* (the indefinite article), *du*, *de la*, *des* (the partitive article), *ce*, *cette*, *ces* (demonstrative), *mon*, *ma*, *mes* (possessive) etc. It is true that nouns can occur without a determiner (for example in fixed phrases, e.g. *avoir faim* 'to have hunger' i.e. 'to be hungry', often after the preposition *en*, or in partitive constructions e.g. *assez de lait* 'enough (of) milk') or with a determiner that does not mark gender (*chaque* 'each', numerals) or even number (*beaucoup de fromage(s)* 'much cheese'/'many cheeses', given that final orthographic 's' is silent, reveals neither the gender nor the number of *fromage(s)*); nevertheless, the general pattern is that determiners do function in this way.

In the vast majority of cases, of course, a determiner is semantically motivated, and nothing more needs to be said. There is, however, one important consequence of the strong tendency for nouns to need an accompanying determiner. In Old French, a zero determiner was readily tolerated when the meaning of the noun in question was not to be specified in any precise way. In the contemporary language, however, this is no longer so, and the distribution of the indefinite article, and in particular the partitive article (the greatly increased use of which is a characteristic of

French) and the definite article has expanded to cover the ground where previously no determiner was required. One clear-cut consequence of this is that, out of context, *j'aime le fromage* can mean either 'I like the cheese' (the original meaning of the definite article) or 'I like cheese', a generic sense being one of those gained during the evolution of the language. As so often, however, a solution is to hand, in that whereas *ce fromage-ci* and *ce fromage-là* are utilised as demonstratives as we have seen, *ce fromage* without a suffix is often best translated as 'the (particular) cheese' rather than 'this' or 'that cheese'. Put in other words, in one, but only one, of the two senses mentioned above, that of the original definite article, *le fromage* can be and often is replaced by *ce fromage*. It may well be that, ultimately, *ce/cette/ces* will emerge as the definite article in French, leaving *le/la/les* as the unmarked or fall-back determiner used to indicate the gender and number of the relevant nominal and little else.

It is interesting to observe the striking parallelism between verb phrases and noun phrases in contemporary French, a parallelism, what is more, which reflects a complete reversal of the initial situation in Latin. In verb phrases, almost all relevant grammatical information is carried by auxiliary verbs and by clitic pronouns (bound affixes) which precede the verbal stem (and not by suffixes); in noun phrases, almost all relevant grammatical information is carried by determiners and by prepositions which precede the nominal stem (and not by suffixes). Personal pronouns and determiners are both virtually obligatory, with the result that 'unmarked' forms chosen from an identical source are needed when no pronoun or determiner is semantically motivated. The evolution and present-day structures of noun phrases and verb phrases are quite astonishingly similar.

Finally in this section, a brief glance at two other topics: sentential word order, and interrogative and negative structures. As far as the order of basic constituents is concerned, standard literary French is often said to be a canonical SVO language, that is, the subject (which is obligatory) precedes the verb which precedes the complement(s) in positive, declarative utterances. This situation has come about only since Middle French, after a period in which the language was strongly 'verb second', that is, the finite verb followed immediately after one (and only one) preceding element, whether or not this was the subject (cf. main clauses in modern German, pages 122–3). A few survivors of this verb-second structure can be found in formal styles, for instance *peut-être vient-il demain* lit. 'perhaps comes he tomorrow' i.e. 'perhaps he's coming tomorrow', but essentially SVO came to be overwhelmingly preferred, even to the extent of strongly inhibiting the use of a variant order in interrogative sentences (see below). Note that exceptionally when the complement is a conjunctive personal pronoun, it precedes the finite verb.

Alongside this SVO order, however, there is a wide variety of other possible orders, involving the dislocation of one or more of the nominal elements associated with a verb to the left and/or to the right of the core sentence. Thus alongside SVO *je déteste Marie* ('I loathe Mary'), we find, in appropriate pragmatic circumstances, *moi, je déteste Marie*; *je déteste Marie, moi*; *Marie, je la déteste*; *je la déteste, Marie*; and even double dislocations to the right, to the left or both (e.g. *je la déteste, moi, Marie*); treble dislocations of the type *je le lui ai donné, moi, le livre, à Pierre* (lit. 'I gave it to him, me, the book, to Peter') are not unknown. (The commas are conventional: the question of intonation is discussed beow.) From these examples, it will be noted that not only is the subject clitic *je* retained even if *moi* is present elsewhere in the sentence but that there is in addition a clitic coreferential with the direct object when this constituent is displaced (e.g. *je la déteste, Marie*, lit. 'I loathe her, Mary') and even with the indirect object, thus *lui = à Pierre* in the example of treble dislocation given above. In other words, the 'true' subject and/or complements can be placed, in either order relative to each other, before or after the core sentence, which remains grammatically complete because of the clitic pronouns, while the sentence as a whole normally remains unambiguous because these coreferential clitics, now effectively prefixes bound to the finite verb, make the function of each nominal clear. In this way, *je l'aime, moi, Marie* (subject before object) and *je l'aime, Marie, moi* (object before subject) both mean 'I love Mary', the 'verb' being *je l'aime*. Of course, so long as these structures remain dislocated — that is, so long as the commas correspond to a genuine intonation break — then the original word order of the core sentence is unaffected. As soon, however, as the nominal groups are felt to be reabsorbed into the core sentence, and the intonation break is lost, then we must speak of an alternative sentential word order. This is a most complex area, but in essence it seems that left-dislocated nominals generally remain outside the core sentence serving as a familiar kind of topic slot (*Marie, je la déteste*, in other words, is not (yet) an object-initial sentence), but right-dislocated nominals frequently are assimilated, so that *on y va nous à Paris* (lit. 'one there goes, us, to Paris' i.e. 'we're off to Paris') can be analysed as verb (*on-y-va*) + subject + complement. (Note the absence of commas on this occasion.) Be that as it may, we can certainly agree that popular spoken French has a highly flexible word order of the kind often called 'free', and that the device which all such languages necessarily have to avoid ambiguity is in the case of French not a set of nominal case affixes as in Latin but a complex system of preverbal affixes derived from earlier conjunctive personal pronouns.

As far as interrogative sentences are concerned, Old French made use of the fact that there were heavy restrictions on the initial placement of verbs in declarative sentences, in unmarked contexts at least, to grammaticalise subject-verb inversion as a principal mode of question forming. This structure still survives when the subject is a conjunctive pronoun (*vient-il*? 'comes he?' i.e. 'is he coming?') and in written French, in a construction known as *fausse inversion*, also when the subject is a noun, thus *le président vient-il?* lit. 'the president comes he?'. In practice, alongside the rise of SVO as the normal order in declarative sentences, interrogative inversion was progressively ousted from spoken French, questions being marked either by the use of intonation alone, or by the use of an element *est-ce que*, originally a phrase meaning 'is it (a fact) that?' but now better analysed as /ɛsk(ə)/, a question-forming particle (*est-ce que le président vient?*). When there is an interrogative word present, fronting involves inversion in the literary language (*où vas-tu?* lit. 'where go you?'): in speech, however, this can be avoided in at least four ways (*où est-ce que tu vas? où que tu vas? où tu vas? tu vas où?*). Perhaps the most interesting development in this area is that of the particle /ti/, (written *ti, ty, t'y* etc.) found in structures such as *tu viens-ti?* Still very much regarded as substandard, this particle arose through a popular reanalysis of forms such as *vient-il?* /vjɛti/ as stem (/vjɛ̃/) and interrogative marker (/ti/): thus also with *aime-t-il?* (/ɛmti/). The particle gradually detached itself from the third person, and became usable in principle with any form of the verb, thus *j'puis-t'y entrer* 'can I come in?'.

The history of negation in French shows a constant see-saw between one- and two-word patterns. The literary language currently utilises an embracing structure, requiring *ne* between subject clitic and the following constituent, and another element — pronoun, adverb or simply 'reinforcer' — after the finite verb, thus *il ne vient pas* lit. 'he not comes step', i.e. 'he isn't coming', or *il ne l'a jamais fait* 'he not it has (n)ever done', i.e. 'he has never done it'. These post-verbal elements were (with one or two exceptions) originally positive in value, thus *ne... rien* 'not... a thing', *ne ... personne* 'not... a person', *ne... pas* 'not... a step'. *Pas* has generalised in contexts where no more specific negative element was needed, though *point* is also still found in certain circumstances.

The constant collocation of words such as *rien* with *ne* has led to them becoming themselves negative in value, so that *rien, personne, jamais* and the like now carry the values 'nothing', 'nobody', 'never' (*Qui est là? Personne.* 'Who's there? Nobody'). Furthermore, the preverbal particle *ne* is now frequently omitted in spoken French, including educated speech, formal *je ne sais pas* 'I don't know' being read /ʃsepa/, i.e. *j'sais pas*. We can therefore safely argue that alongside the embracing construction, there exists an alternative structure in which the post-verbal elements, whether *pas* or a more specific item, alone carry the negative value. From this position, *pas* has become the everyday negator in virtually all other environments: thus an original *non moi* 'not me' has passed, via *non pas moi*, to *pas moi* in all but the most formal registers. Interestingly, double negation has in effect returned in the most popular registers, *je ne sais rien* passing, via *je sais rien* (see above) to *je sais pas rien*, though this is certainly regarded as non-standard. The loss of *ne* from the position between conjunctive pronoun subject and finite verb removes the only element (apart from other conjunctive pronouns) which hindered the total fusing of subject pronoun + verb as a single 'word' consisting of prefix and stem, a process discussed above in relation to the 'free' word order of contemporary spoken French.

5   Lexicon

The core vocabulary of French derives in very large measure from the Latin spoken in Gaul, the lexical items in question having in general undergone all the phonetic changes discussed briefly earlier which so often distinguish a French word so sharply from its cognates elsewhere in Romance. This Latin stock incorporated, before the linguistic fragmentation of the Romance-speaking area, a number of words from other sources, the subsequent development of which has been indistinguishable from that of their indigenous counterparts. We might mention Greek (e.g. *COLAPHUM* > *coup* 'blow', *CHORDAM* > *corde* 'rope', *PETRAM* > *pierre* 'stone'), particularly important as the source towards the end of the Empire of much specifically Christian vocabulary, some of which later greatly expanded its meaning (*ECCLESIAM* > *église* 'church', *PRESBYTER* > *prêtre* 'priest' (discussed earlier) but *PARABOLAM* 'parable', now > *parole* 'word'). Equally, among the earliest people whose territory was overrun by the Romans were the Celts, and some Celtic words — recognisable by their widespread distribution — were borrowed and assimilated into Latin very early: these included, for instance, *CAMISIAM* > *chemise* 'shirt', *CABALLUM* > *cheval* 'horse' and, more surprisingly, a very common verb *CAMBIARE* > *changer* 'to change'. The Celtic word *CARRUM* 'cart' underlies not only standard French *char* and (with a diminutive suffix) *charrette* 'cart', but also Norman French *carre*, whence English *car*, a word which has prospered not only in English but once again in French in the sense of '(motor) coach'. More specifically French, however, are the words, generally agreed to be approaching 200, which passed into the language from the local form of Celtic, Gaulish, many of them representing the names of plants, birds or other rural objects: one thinks, for instance, of *chêne* 'oak tree', *if* 'yew-tree', *alou-ette* 'lark', *soc* 'ploughshare' and *raie* 'furrow'. The word *grève*, in the sense of 'sandy river bank', is Celtic in origin: on one such bank of the Seine, unemployed workmen gathered, *en grève* thus coming to mean 'out of work' and later 'on strike'. A Celtic vigesimal counting system survives in *quatre-vingts* 'four score' i.e. 'eighty' (*huitante* and similar forms are found in many dialects: cf. *huit* 'eight').

The Roman occupation of Gaul was ended by the Germanic invasions. Although the conquerors eventually came to be French-speaking, they made a very significant impression on the language. Not only is the development of a strong stress accent, with such radical consequences on the phonological evolution of Latin words in Gaul, frequently attributed to Germanic influence, but so too are syntactic features such as the prolonged preference for a verb-second word order or the use of *on* as an alternative to the passive. While none of these claims is wholly beyond dispute, what is certain is that many words in contemporary French can be traced back either to Frankish or to less specific Germanic sources: of the 1,000 most frequently used words in contemporary French, some 35 are from this source, whether found also in other Romance languages (e.g. *guerre* 'war', *franc* 'free', *riche* 'rich', *blanc* 'white', *jardin* 'garden') or more specifically French (e.g. *bleu* 'blue', *joue* 'cheek'). The fact that so many of these words have a direct cognate in English, itself of course a Germanic language, is readily apparent.

Much the biggest influence on the French lexicon, however, is from a perhaps unexpected source, namely Latin itself (with a not insignificant admixture from Greek). This is because, from the time of the very earliest texts and even more so during and after the Renaissance, the core vocabulary inherited directly via the spoken tradition proved inadequate for the new demands made of it. This process of enrichment has yielded a very large number of 'learned' words in modern French, many of them now 'learned' only in the technical sense that they have not undergone the phonetic changes that would have affected truly 'popular' words, thus *nature*, *facile* 'easy', *imaginer*. Often indeed one finds a doublet in modern French, that is, a 'popular' and a 'learned' derivative of the same word: consider, for example, *loyal*/*légal* (< *LEGALEM*); *peser* 'weigh', *penser* 'weigh up mentally', i.e. 'think' (< *PENSARE*); *frêle*/*fragile* 'breakable'. This last pair, both derived from *FRAGILEM*, shows particularly clearly how much closer phonetically the 'learned' word will often be to its etymon.

By far the most significant present-day source of loanwords is English, reflecting at times a genuine cultural or technical innovation, but at times simply a change of fashion. During the eighteenth century, many political and legal terms (*budget*, *vote*, *jury*, *parlement*) were borrowed, reflecting admiration in France for the form of government in Britain at that time. (Note that many of these had themselves earlier been borrowed into English from (Norman) French, including all of those listed above.) During the nineteenth century, various kinds of sport were emulated, giving words such as *sport*, *golf*, *jockey*, *turf* ('racecourse', 'horseracing'), *boxe* 'boxing' etc., whereas words reflecting England's lead in the Industrial Revolution were also borrowed, particularly in the domain of the railway and textile industries. (Again, many words such as *ticket* and *tunnel* themselves had earlier passed from French to English). The twentieth century has seen many borrowings which meet a need in this way, but also many which merely reflect either the belief on the part of advertisers and others that an English name or slogan will enhance sales (*le drink pour les men* is somehow superior to *la boisson pour les hommes*) or simply the willingness of those such as pressmen constantly engaged with material in both English and French to use an English word that is readily to hand. (*Pipeline* is a much-quoted example, with the indigenous *oléoduc* now strongly favoured in its place.) Many of the borrowings take the form of blocked monosyllables, a particularly favoured phonological type in modern French as we have seen (*cross* 'cross-country race', *test*, *pull* 'pullover', *spot* 'spot-light', *star* etc.), or of polysyllables ending in *-ing* (*parking* 'car park', *dumping*) or *-man* (*rugbyman*).

Just as there has always been an exceptionally high degree of interest among educationalists and the French public more generally in the niceties of grammar, so too the present wave of Anglicisms has not passed unnoticed. Efforts have been made to staunch the inflow of such borrowings, both where they are clearly unnecessary and, more importantly, in a wide range of specialist areas where, given a little thought, a perfectly acceptable French word could become widely used and accepted. The *Office du vocabulaire français*, founded in 1957, surveys all aspects of the contemporary vocabulary, especially, but not exclusively, loanwords, and makes recommendations which, at least in written French, may at times carry the force of law.

French, then, is a language still evolving rapidly in all its aspects, particularly in respect of its grammatical system (where the gap between the classical model which is prescribed and what even educated speakers actually do is quite extraordinarily wide at times) and its lexicon. The previous very radical waves of phonetic change appear to have given way, for the time being at least, to relative stability. As a world language, French is holding its own surprisingly well in the face of constant competition from English, although only time will tell how long this can be sustained.

Bibliography

Price (1971) is an excellent survey, very readable, of the contemporary language, seen from a historical perspective. Grevisse (1980) is an outstanding descriptive/ prescriptive grammar of the modern language, with brief historical notes. A somewhat idiosyncratic but very well documented survey of certain points of interest in the modern language is given by Harmer (1954), while Frei (1929) is a fascinating analysis of how the popular language actually operates, with a wealth of illustrative material. For phonology, Fouché (1959) is a standard work on the pronunciation of contemporary French, while Tranel (1981) discusses current issues in phonological theory, clearly illustrated with French data. Von Wartburg and Zumthor (1958) is a clear and detailed survey of the syntax of the contemporary language, and Kayne (1975) is the outstanding analysis of French syntax within current grammatical theory.

Among works dealing with the history of the language, Ewert (1943) is a comprehensive but atheoretical survey, now somewhat outdated. Von Wartburg (1971) is a good general history of the language; Brunot and Bruneau (1969) is a concise and very well presented survey of the evolution of French grammar; while Pope (1952) is an exceptionally detailed historical phonology and morphology. Harris (1978) presents an analysis of French morphology and syntax within a comparative framework, diachronically with Latin and synchronically with Spanish and Italian.

Guiraud (1963) is a clear and concise survey of dialects and dialect study in France. Deniau (1983) is an excellent brief survey of the distribution and role of French in the world today, by the Président du Comité de la Francophonie; the previous standard survey, more comprehensive in its coverage, is Viatte (1969).

References

Brunot, F. and Ch. Bruneau. 1969. *Précis de grammaire historique de la langue française* (Masson, Paris)

Deniau, X. 1983. *La Francophonie* (Presses Universitaires de France, Paris)

Ewert, A. 1943. *The French Language*, 2nd ed. (Faber and Faber, London)

Fouché, P. 1959. *Traité de prononciation française*, 2nd ed. (Klincksieck, Paris)

Frei, H. 1929. *La Grammaire des fautes* (reprinted by Slatkine Reprints, Geneva, 1971)

Grevisse, M. 1980. *Le Bon usage*, 11th ed. (Duculot, Paris and Gembloux)

Guiraud, P. 1963. *Patois et dialectes français*, 3rd ed. (Presses Universitaires de France, Paris)

Harmer, L. C. 1954. *The French Language Today: Its Characteristics and Tendencies* (Hutchinson, London)

Harris, M. 1978. *The Evolution of French Syntax: A Comparative Approach* (Longman, London)

Kayne, R. 1975. *French Syntax: The Transformational Cycle* (MIT Press, Cambridge, Mass.)

Pope, M. K. 1952. *From Latin to Modern French, With Especial Consideration of Anglo-Norman*, 2nd ed. (Manchester University Press, Manchester)

Price, G. 1971. *The French Language: Present and Past* (Edward Arnold, London)

Tranel, B. 1981. *Concreteness in Generative Phonology: Evidence from French* (University of California Press, Berkeley and Los Angeles)

Viatte, A. 1969. *La Francophonie* (Larousse, Paris)

Von Wartburg, W. 1971. *Évolution et structure de la langue française*, 10th ed. (Francke, Bern)

—— and P. Zumthor. 1958. *Précis de syntaxe du français contemporain*, 2nd ed. (Francke, Bern)

10 Spanish

John N. Green

1 Introduction

Spanish is by far the most widely spoken Romance language. At a conservative estimate, there are now some 280 million native speakers, scattered through all continents, but most densely concentrated in Central and South America, where Spanish-speaking countries form a great swathe from the United States-Mexico border right to Tierra del Fuego. Spanish is the national language of 19 countries, in descending order of population: Mexico, Spain (including the Balearic and Canary Islands and the enclaves of Ceuta and Melilla on the North African coast), Argentina, Colombia, Venezuela, Peru, Chile, Cuba, Ecuador, Guatemala, Dominican Republic, Bolivia, El Salvador, Honduras, Paraguay, Uruguay, Nicaragua, Costa Rica, Panama. There are large Spanish speaking minorities in the United States (including Puerto Rico, which is predominantly Spanish-speaking), officially estimated at 10–11 million but probably much higher. Spanish is also the official language of Equatorial Guinea, and is spoken by significant minorities in the Philippines and Australia, Morocco and Western Sahara, the Balkan countries and Israel.

Like all spatially diffused languages, Spanish is subject to regional and sociolinguistic variation (some specific features are discussed in sections 3 and 4 below). Despite some well-publicised heterogeneous characteristics, the range of variation is not very great and only rarely disrupts mutual comprehensibility. Difficulties do however arise with the Spanish-based creoles of the Philippines and Colombia, and with Judaeo-Spanish, the linguistic consequence of the expulsion of Sephardic communities from Spain in 1492. *Sefardí* is reputed to have preserved numerous features of fifteenth-century usage, but the claim is exaggerated: some phonetic traits, like the preservation of initial /f-/, are indeed archaic, but *sefardí* has evolved extensively in its morphology and has assimilated large numbers of lexical borrowings.

Natural tendencies towards linguistic divergence are combatted in the case of Spanish by powerful cultural bonds and also by well-developed normative mechanisms, whose antecedents go back several centuries. (One of the earliest and best known literary examples of linguistic prejudice is the

226

criticism meted out by Juan de Valdés in his *Diálogo de la lengua*, of c. 1535, against Antonio de Nebrija's excellent *Gramática de la lengua castellana*, of 1492, on the grounds that Nebrija, as an Andalusian, could not be expected to know Castilian well enough for the task in hand!) In a puristic context, 'Spanish' almost invariably means 'Castilian' and for many speakers on both sides of the Atlantic the language can be indifferently designated *español* or *castellano*. Since 1714, when it received a royal charter, the *Real Academia de la Lengua* has had normative authority over the language. Unlike its French counterpart, the Spanish Academy is composed of linguists and philologists, with the result that its decisions, though invariably conservative, command some respect.

In matters of orthography, the Academy has steered a reasonably successful course by dint of approving fairly minor adjustments at regular intervals. Spanish orthography, though popularly reputed to be 'phonetic' (by which is meant 'phonemic'), is in fact quite highly conventionalised. The letter/sound correspondence is skewed. Once the conventions have been mastered, it is relatively easy to pronounce the written language; but transcribing from speech is altogether trickier, as attested by the difficulty Spanish schoolchildren experience with dictation exercises. The main cause is the preservation of etymological spellings. *C* and *g* have two pronunciations depending on the following vowel — *cerca* 'near' = /θerka/ or /serka/, *gigante* 'giant' = /xigante/; *h* is never sounded — *huérfano* 'orphan' = /werfano/; *b* and *v* correspond to only one phoneme and are not in the same distribution as its two allophones — *beber* 'to drink' = /beber/ [be'βer], *vivir* 'to live' = /bibir/ [bi'βir]. Words containing *b* and *v* are often misspelled, even on public notices; two recently observed in Segovia province read *se prohive aparcar* (= *prohibe*) 'no parking' and *coto pribado de caza* (= *privado*) 'private hunting'. Etymological spellings can, of course, be justified on grounds of continuity and cultural relationship, but they are not compatible with phonemic principles. If both French and Spanish were to be spelled phonemically, their visual relatedness would disappear overnight.

2   Historical Background

'Spanish' is conventionally dated to the second half of the tenth century, the date of a religious text from the monastery of San Millán in the Rioja region, whose scribe openly acknowledged the discrepancy between written Latin and spoken vernacular by including parenthetical translations of the words and phrases he knew would be unintelligible to contemporary readers. Latin had been introduced into the Iberian peninsula by Roman soldiers and colonists over a period of more than two centuries beginning during the Second Punic War (218–201 BC), when Rome was obliged to subdue the Carthaginians in Spain in order to protect its northern front, and ending in

15 BC, when a long and arduous campaign finally brought the north-west (modern Galicia and Asturias) under Roman rule. Latin took firm enough root in the regions first colonised — the Levant and the Guadalquivir valley — to produce noted centres of learning and some authors celebrated for their style, including Martial and Seneca. By the time of the first Germanic incursions in the third century AD, Latin had long supplanted the indigenous languages of Iberia, with the sole exception of Basque in the north-east. Prolonged contact with Germanic and later Arabic certainly affected its evolution, but at no time does there appear to have been a serious risk that the mass of the population would cease to be Romance-speaking.

In the tenth century there could have been little reason to suppose that Castilian, an obscure dialect of the central Cantabrian seaboard, would become a national, let alone a world, language. The history of its rise is essentially that of the Christian Reconquest, pursued with fluctuating determination and shifting alliances among the medieval kingdoms until the definitive expulsion of the Moorish rulers of Granada in 1492. Though this date is symbolic in Spanish history, the major part of the Reconquest had been achieved much earlier, the first phase culminating in the recapture of Toledo in 1085 by Alfonso VI. This was the king who banished Ruy Diaz, the Cid, and who (according to the epic) had reason to be grateful for the Cid's glorious campaigns against a new wave of Almoravid invaders who at one stage seemed likely to reverse the Christians' recent gains.

The southerly expansion of Castilian has been likened to a wedge driven between the dialects of León to the west and Aragón to the east. Castilian differed from its lateral neighbours in a number of phonological characteristics which, while not signalling any differentiation of fundamental structure, made it sound quite distinct. One of these was the loss from many words of an initial /f-/, via an intermediate stage of strong aspiration which is still preserved in the orthography; another was the tendency of the clusters /pl-/, /fl-/ and /kl-/ to palatalise; both are illustrated in the passage of *FAFLARE* 'to sniff out' to *hallar* /aʎar/ 'to find'. Castilian also affricated the medial cluster -*CT*-, as in *LACTE* 'milk' > *leche* /letʃe/, Aragonese *leyt*; but failed to diphthongise lower mid vowels before a palatal sound, as in *TENEO* 'I hold' > *tengo*, Aragonese *tiengo*. There has been intense linguistic debate on whether these and other features should be ascribed to the influence of Basque (the *f-* > *h-* change, for instance, also happens in parts of south-west France which used to be Basque-speaking). We cannot be certain. All the changes involve linguistic processes which are well attested elsewhere. The most we can safely conclude is that Basque influence would ɪ inforce some developments which could have started independently.

Castilian, which had a flourishing tradition of oral literature culminating in the epic *Poema de Mio Cid* (variously dated between c.1140 and the early thirteenth century), consolidated its national position and its international respectability in the reign of Alfonso X 'El Sabio' 'The Wise', 1252–84. The king, himself a poet and intellectual, assembled a court of international scholars and undertook the translation into Spanish of literary, historical and scientific works written in Latin, Greek, Arabic and Hebrew. Since that time, the preeminence of Castilian has never been challenged, though there have always been local norms of pronunciation (see section 3), and relations with Catalan-speaking areas along the eastern coast have not always been easy. Both Galician and Catalan, probably in reaction to years of linguistic repression during the Franco era, have received a fillip from the regional autonomy policy espoused in the late 1970s, but the position of Spanish as the national language is enshrined in the constitution and seems unlikely to be undermined in the long term.

The purely linguistic consequences of this turbulent history are fewer than one might expect. Some phonological changes, as we have seen, may be attributable to Basque; one, the velarisation of medieval /ʃ/ to /x/ in a few nouns and southern place names (*SŪCU* 'juice' > *jugo*), can probably be traced indirectly to Arabic via a medieval pronunciation of /s/ as [ʃ] in the southern dialect of Mozarabic. Some syntactic calques from Arabic survive as fossilised expressions and, more importantly, the persistence of VSO word order (which is also common in other southern Romance languages, especially Portuguese) may have been reinforced by Arabic VSO order. No inflectional morphology has been shown to derive from any source but Latin.

This leaves the lexicon (including place and personal names) as the chief repository of historical accretions. A few pre-Roman words are still in use, including *páramo* 'moor', *vega* 'river plain', *pizarra* 'slate', *manteca* 'lard' and perhaps the adjective *gordo* 'fat'; the most frequent is probably *izquierdo* 'left', which has a cognate in Basque, but may be a borrowing there too. Most of the words of Celtic origin, like *cerveza* 'beer', *camisa* 'shirt', *cambiar* 'to change', are widely distributed in western Romance, and it is therefore difficult to decide whether they are survivors of the Celtic substratum in north and central Iberia or were introduced via Latin. A significant number of Germanic words remain in regular use, nearly all shared with French, some of them having probably been diffused via Latin before the main period of invasions. They include military terminology — *guerra* 'war', *guardia* 'guard', *tregua* 'truce', *espuela* 'spur', *estribo* 'stirrup', *yelmo* 'helmet' — but also some everyday words, like *ropa* 'clothing', *falda* 'skirt', *jabón* 'soap', *ganso* 'goose', *ganar* 'to win', together with a set of common adjectives — *rico* 'rich', *blanco* 'white', *gris* 'grey' — and a few abstract concepts: *orgullo* 'pride', *galardón* 'reward' and Old Spanish *fonta/honta* 'shame'. Also Germanic are numerous place and personal names; the common suffix *-ez* of Spanish family names (*López*, *Martínez*, *González*, etc.) though Latin in origin, probably owes its diffusion to the Visigoths.

Approaching 4,000 words can be traced to Arabic, almost all nouns and a high proportion beginning with *a-* or *al-*, representing the agglutination of the Arabic definite article. An important group relates to horticulture and water management: *acequia* 'irrigation channel', *noria* 'water wheel', *aljibe* 'cistern', *aceite* 'olive oil', *alcachofa* 'artichoke', *algodón* 'cotton', *arroz* 'rice', *azafrán* 'saffron', *azúcar* 'sugar', *naranja* 'orange', *zanahoria* 'carrot'. Others concern civil administration — *aduana* 'customs', *alcaide* 'governor/ gaoler', *alcalde* 'mayor', *alguacil* 'constable' — and still others have entered international scientific vocabulary: *alcohol*, *algebra*, *cifra* 'figure/cipher', *cenit* 'zenith', *nadir* etc. For the tourist, some of the most 'typical' features of southern Spain are designated by Arabic words: *azahar* 'orange blossom', *azotea* 'flat roof', *azucena* 'lily' and *azulejo* 'ceramic tile' (so called because the basic colour was a deep blue — *azul*). In categories other than nouns, Arabic has given the adjective *mezquino* 'mean', the verb *halagar* 'to flatter' (both well adapted to Romance grammatical patterns), the preposition *hasta* 'up to' and the exclamative *ojalá* 'would that...' (literally, 'May Allah grant...').

Since the Renaissance, Spanish has borrowed extensively from other Romance languages and from Latin; from Amerindian languages spoken in its overseas colonies; and most recently from English (often American rather than British). The borrowings from Latin confront the descriptive linguist with an interesting dilemma. Many of them are related to words which have had a continuous history in the language and have undergone more extensive phonological modification than the late-comers, which were generally admitted in a hispanicised pronunciation of the original spelling. The question is whether these 'doublets' should be related by productive rules to the indigenous items. Consider the twelve examples given here, where a common noun or verb is paired with an adjective of the same root meaning but more elevated register.

hierro 'iron':	férrico	heder 'to stink':	fétido
hijo 'son':	filial	hembra 'female':	femenino
hado 'fate':	fatal	hongo 'mushroom':	fungoso
hambre 'hunger':	famélico	hormiga 'ant':	fórmico
harina 'flour':	farináceo	huir 'to flee':	fugaz
hastío 'distaste':	fastidioso	hurto 'theft':	furtivo

These give an idea of the scale of the phenomenon, being only a subgroup of those involving the phonological change $f- > h- > \emptyset$. We shall not attempt an answer, but merely observe that any across-the-board solution, whether concrete or abstract, will run foul of mixed derivational sets: *humo* 'smoke' has regular derivatives *humoso* 'smoky' and *ahumar* 'to preserve food by smoking', but is also clearly related to *fumar* 'to smoke' (of fires or of people).

We end this section on a note of optimism. Although purist hackles have been raised by the recent influx of anglicisms (as in France), the productive patterns of the language remain resolutely Romance. Spanish has at all periods created new vocabulary by suffixal derivation. The following selection, all of Latin origin, remain highly productive: the diminutives -*ito*, -*illo*, -*iño*; the augmentative -*ón*; the agentive -*dor*; the adjectivals -*oso*, -*ero*; the nominals -*aje*, -*ción*, -*miento*. Nor are derivational processes respecters of alien origin: the Germanic borrowings quoted above, *guerra* and *orgullo*, form adjectives *guerrero* and *orgulloso*, and the Arabic *halagar* forms *halagueño* — a powerful means of integrating the borrowing. Purists can take heart from new coinings like *urbanización* 'housing development', currently to be seen on builders' placards all over Spain, and composed of impeccably classical roots. Many other fairly recent inventions which might have attracted foreign labels have in fact been named by compounding indigenous roots: *parachoques* 'bumper bar', *limpiaparabrisas* 'windscreen wiper', *tallalápices* 'pencil sharpener'. Through developments of this kind, Spanish is becoming more, not less, Romance in its structure.

3   Phonology

Like other world languages, Spanish shows a good deal of internal variation. This extends to all linguistic levels but is most noticeable in the phonology. For international trade and diplomacy and for pedagogical purposes, two norms are recognised: either the educated usage of Castile (traditionally identified with Burgos, but now displaced by Madrid) or that of Bogotá, Colombia (itself increasingly eclipsed, both linguistically and culturally, by Mexico City). In the Middle Spanish period a further model was provided by Seville, which remained a flourishing cultural centre throughout the first period of colonisation of Central and South America. The fact that most of the early settlers were of Andalusian origin, and the existence of the Sevillean 'norma culta', are now generally believed to explain the present-day differences between Latin American and Castilian usage, at both popular and educated levels.

The segmental inventory of Castilian is given in table 10.1. The phonemic consonant system can be presented as neatly symmetrical, with four articulatory positions and five degrees of aperture, but this disguises some interesting irregularities in distribution. While, for instance, the absence of any point-of-articulation opposition between plosives and affricates argues for their merger, they differ in that /dʒ/ is by no means securely established in the system and neither palatal enters into syllable-initial clusters, which plosives do freely. The reintroduction of [dʒ], which was present (probably as an allophone of /ʒ/) in Old Spanish, is comparatively recent and its phonemic status remains doubtful. It represents a strengthened form of certain [j] sounds, some of them apparently determined lexically (especially the personal pronoun *yo* = [dʒo]) and others arising from an earlier weakening of palatal /ʎ/ known as 'yeísmo'. Both innovations are

Table 10.1: Segmental Sounds of Castilian

Consonants

	Bilabial	Dental	Palatal	Velar
Plosives				
[−voice]	p	t		k
[+voice]	b	d		g
Affricates			tʃ	
			(dʒ)	
Fricatives				
[−voice]	f	θ s		x
Nasals				
[+voice]	m	n	ɲ	
Laterals				
[+voice]		l	ʎ	
Vibrants				
[+voice]		r/r̄		

Vowels			Semi-vowels	
High	i	u	j	w
Mid	e	o		
Low		a		

sociolinguistically marked: while the pronunciation of *calle* 'street' as [kaje] is now very widespread in informal speech, the intermediate variant [kaʒe] is often regarded as uneducated and the affricate realisation [kadʒe] is usually stigmatised as vulgar.

The voiceless plosives are all unaspirated. The voiced series is in complementary distribution with a corresponding set of voiced spirants which occur intervocalically, thus *boca* 'mouth' [boka] but *cabo* 'end' [kaβo], *donde* 'where' [dɔnde] but *nudo* 'knot' [nuðo], *gato* 'cat' [gato] but *lago* 'lake' [laɣo]. In indigenous words neither /b/ nor /g/ occurs word-finally; orthographic -*d* is weakened to [θ] or lost completely. It has traditionally been assumed that the spirants are the subordinate members of these pairs, since the weakening of the plosives in some environments is well attested as a historical process. Recent research on language acquisition among Mexican children, however, seems to show that the spirants are acquired first and remain dominant.

The voiceless fricatives represent the remnants of a much larger set of sibilants in Old Spanish, including a phonemic voiced series; its demise is still not wholly explained. The absence of phonemic voiced sibilants now sets Spanish apart from most other Romance varieties; [z] occurs infrequently as an allophone of /s/ before voiced obstruents, but not intervocalically, thus *desd* 'from/since' [dɛzde] but *esri sa* 'wife' [ɛsposa] — compare Portuguese [ʃpozɐ], Italian [spɔːza] and French [epuz]. American Spanish and most varieties of Andalusian lack the distinctive Castilian opposition between /θ/ and /s/, as in *cima* 'summit' /θima/ : *sima* 'abyss' /sima/, *caza* 'hunt' /kaθa/ : *casa* 'house' /kasa/, *haz* 'bundle' /aθ/ : *as* 'ace' /as/. Throughout South America and in most of Andalucía, only [s] is found — a feature popularly called 'seseo'. In a few parts of Andalucía, [θ] alone is used — labelled 'ceceo'. It is probably not true that American Spanish *lost* the /θ/ : /s/ opposition; more likely it was not present in the language of the first colonists. The merger, whatever its exact date, seems to have led to some vocabulary changes in order to avoid ambiguity: the Castilian minimal pair *coser* 'to sew' /koser/ : *cocer* 'to cook' /koθer/ poses no problem in America, where *coser* is maintained, but *cocinar* /kosinar/ is the verb 'to cook'.

The three nasals contrast intervocalically, where there are numerous permutations of minimal pairs and a few triads: *lama* 'slime' /lama/ : *lana* 'wool' /lana/ : *laña* 'clamp' /laɲa/. Elsewhere, the opposition is incomplete. Word-initially, /ɲ-/ is very rare, confined to a few affective coinings and Amerindian borrowings; among Latinate items, only /m-/ and /n-/ are possible. Nasals combine freely with obstruents to form heterosyllabic clusters, in which seven or more phonetic variants can be detected, always homorganic with the following consonant and therefore neutralising the opposition — *infeliz* 'unhappy' [iɱfeliθ], *incierto* 'uncertain' [inθjɛrto], *incapaz* 'unable' [iŋkapaθ], etc. The opposition is also neutralised in word-final position, where only /-n/ occurs. A variant pronunciation, previously common in Andalucía and parts of Latin America, is now spreading rapidly in Spain though it remains sociolinguistically marked: word-final and sometimes syllable-final /-n/ is realised as -[ŋ]. Some phoneticians believe this may be the prelude to phonemic nasalisation of the preceding vowel, a development Spanish has so far resisted.

Turning to the liquids, we find /l/ is pronounced either dental or alveolar but never dark, and /ʎ/, as we noted above, is tending to lose its lateral element. /r/ and /r̄/ are unique in contrasting at the same point of articulation, but the opposition is only intervocalic — *caro* 'expensive' /karo/ : *carro* 'cart' /kar̄o/; elsewhere the two sounds are in complementary distribution. In standard Castilian the difference seems to be one of tenseness rather than length: /-r-/ is usually a flap and /-r̄-/ a full-bodied alveolar trill. But in some dialects /-r̄-/ is realised as a weaker sound with palatal friction [ɾ]. This development suggests an intriguing historical parallel with the palatals /ʎ/ and /ɲ/ which also had a principal source in Latin intervocalic geminates and appear to have evolved via a stage of tenseness.

Before passing on to vowels, we should say a few words about prosodic features, both for their intrinsic interest and because vocalic structure cannot be examined in isolation from stress and rhythm. Spanish has often been quoted as a textbook example of a syllable-timed language, with a delivery sometimes likened to a recalcitrant machine gun. A newer proposal suggests Spanish would be more accurately described as 'segment-timed' since the delivery, though perceptually regular, does not always produce isochronous syllabification *or* isochronous stress intervals. The rhythmic pattern, naturally, has implications for intonation, which tends to avoid abrupt changes and readily accommodates melodic units of ten to fifteen syllables. Castilian, whose everyday register is confined to little more than an octave, has a basic rise-fall for simple declaratives, a sustained rise for most yes-no questions, and the characteristic western Romance level or rising tone to mark enumerations and sentence-medial clause boundaries. A prominent feature of Castilian is its 'dynamic' or intensity accent, which is noticeably free from tonal modulation. Most writers also comment on the resonant quality that Castilians and northern dialect speakers impart to their everyday speech. This has been variously ascribed to an unusual articulatory setting, to the rhythmic structure, to the predominance of low, open vowels, and to the stability of vowel sounds in both stressed and unstressed positions. Though all these factors may be contributory, the principal cause must be articulatory setting, since many other regional varieties of Spanish are produced with a less marked resonant quality despite sharing the other structural features of Castilian.

As will be apparent from table 10.1, the five simple vowels form a classic symmetrical triangle. Their frequency of occurrence in running prose also follows a regular pattern: low vowels are more frequent than high, front more so than back (hence in ascending order, /u, i, o, e, a/). All five occur as independent words, with /e/ and /a/ both representing homophones. All occur both stressed and unstressed, in open and closed syllables, though /i/ and /u/ are rare in word-final position. As we noted above, there is little tendency to weakening or centralisation in unstressed syllables, a feature which sets Spanish clearly apart from its peninsular neighbours Portuguese and Catalan. Regardless of the presence or absence of stress, however, all vowels are represented by laxer variants in closed syllables; the high and mid series are lowered slightly and /a/, which in citation has a central low articulation, may be displaced forward or backward depending on the adjacent consonant: *presté* 'I lent' /pres'te/ [prɛs'te], *cortó* 'it cut' /kor'to/ [kɔr'to], *jaulas* 'cages' /'xaulas/ ['χɑwląs].

This unexceptional laxing has paved the way for a change in Andalusian and some Latin American varieties which may have far-reaching consequences for the vowel system and for plural marking. The great majority of Spanish nouns in the singular end in open /-a/, /-o/ or /-e/, but the addition of the plural marker /-s/ closes the syllable and produces the regular allophonic variation in the vowel:

hermano(s) 'brother(s)' /ermano/ [ɛr'mano] + /s/ = [ɛr'manɔs]
hermana(s) 'sister(s)' /ermana/ [ɛr'mana] + /s/ = [ɛr'manæs]
madre(s) 'mother(s)' /madre/ ['maðre] + /s/ = ['maðrɛs]

In Andalusian, syllable-final /-s/ often weakens to an aspiration [-h], so *los hermanos* becomes [lɔʰ ɛrmanɔʰ] etc. This substitution, though phonetically salient, does not affect the phonemic status of the vowels. In a more 'advanced' variety of Andalusian, however, the aspiration is lost altogether and with it the conditioning factor for the vowel alternation. Now [la maðre] contrasts functionally with [læ maðɾɛ], and we are obliged to recognise a new system of plural marking — not too different from the vocalic alternations of Italian — and with it three new vowel phonemes.

Table 10.1 shows no diphthongs or triphthongs. On the phonetic level, combinations of vowels and vowel-like elements are common, but their phonemic status has always been among the most controversial areas of Spanish linguistics. Eighteen monosyllabic combinations can be distinguished, eight with a glide onset /ja, je, jo, ju, wa, we, wi, wo/, six with an off-glide /aj, aw, ej, ew, oj, ow/ and a further four with both on- and off-glides /waj, wej, jaw, waw/ of which the last two are very rare. The analyst's task is complicated by the existence of numerous other combinations, both within and across word boundaries, of vowels 'in hiatus' — pronounced as two syllables in careful speech but readily coalescing into monosyllables in rapid or informal delivery.

To explain the controversy, we must make a brief foray into stress assignment. Stress in Spanish is usually predictable and is not used as the sole means of differentiating lexical items. Stress position is calculated from the end of the word: those ending in a consonant other than /-n/ or /-s/ are stressed on the final syllable, almost all others are stressed on the penultimate. It follows that nearly all plural forms are stressed on the same syllable as the corresponding singular. A few words, mainly borrowings, are stressed on the antepenultimate — a feature known by the convenient mnemonic of *esdrújulo*. These are not predictable (except as plurals maintaining the pattern of paroxytone singulars, like *jóvenes* 'youths'); they all have an open penultimate syllable but this is a necessary, not sufficient, condition. Stress can only move further back than the third syllable if the word is clearly compound; *entregándomelo* 'handing it to me', *fácilmente* 'easily', though the latter has a secondary stress in the expected position. This fairly straightforward account of stress is complicated when we turn to verb inflection. Here, stress operates functionally to differentiate otherwise identical forms of the same lexeme — *hablo* 'I speak' : *habló* '(s)he spoke', ¡*cante*! 'sing!' : *canté* 'I sang', *tomara* '(s)he might/would take' : *tomará* '(s)he will take'. It follows that an analysis wishing to view stress as generally predictable must make reference to morphological information. Some theories, of course, rule this out by axiom.

Returning to what we earlier labelled 'semi-vowels', we can now appreciate the problem. At first sight, [j, w] appear to be in complementary distribution with the vowels /i, u/ respectively (a pattern which holds good even for the speakers who regularly substitute [j] for /ʎ/). The economical analysis requires prior knowledge of stress position: /i/ is realised as [j] (or becomes [-syllabic] in generative terminology) if and only if it is unstressed and adjacent to some other vowel. Now, some linguists have hankered after the neatest solution, that both semi-vowels and stress assignment are predictable. Can it be done? Consider these examples:

amplio ['am-pljo] : amplío [am-'pli-o] : amplió [am-'pljo]
'ample'   'I broaden'   '(s)he broadened'
continuo [kɔn-'ti-nwo] : continúo [kɔn-ti-'nu-o] : continuó [kɔn-ti-'nwo]
'continuous'   'I continue'   '(s)he continued'

Here, the occurrence of the full vowel or glide is predictable, once stress is known. But the converse is not true: stress cannot be predicted using only the phonological information given here. Nor can it be made predictable by including general morphological conditions, since other verbs behave differently in the middle form of the series: *cambiar* 'to change' and *menguar* 'to lessen' give respectively ['kam-bjo] and ['mɛŋ-gwo] not *[kam-'bi-o] or *[mɛŋ-'gu-o]. For reductionists, the consequences are uncomfortable: neither semi-vowels nor stress assignment can be predicted on strictly phonological criteria.

An allied debate has raged around the predictability or otherwise of the verb stem alternations traditionally called 'radical changes'. The two most frequent ones involve semi-vowels and stress assignment. The verb *poder* 'to be able' has two stems: /pod-/ when the following vowel is stressed and /pwed-/ when the stem itself is stressed. This results in a heterogeneous paradigm, very striking in the present indicative, with 1 sg. *puedo* alongside 1 pl. *podemos*. Similarly, *helar* 'to freeze', has the stressed stem *hielo* /jelo/ alongside *helamos* /elamos/. Some 400 verbs follow these two patterns, far more than one would normally wish to describe as 'irregular'. In any event, the observable changes are perfectly regular once one knows the stress assignment. But the interesting question is whether membership of the radical changing pattern is itself predictable. It used to be. Most western Romance dialects inherited a seven-term vowel system /i, e, ɛ, a, ɔ, o, u/ in which the mid vowels /e:ɛ/ /o:ɔ/ were phonemically distinct. In northern Spain, /ɛ/ and /ɔ/ diphthongised when stressed. This was a regular phonological change, affecting all word classes equally and all types of syllable (in northern French, the same vowels diphthongised only in *open* syllables). So, Spanish verbs with /ɛ/ or /ɔ/ as their stem vowel were regularly subject to diphthongisation under stress, stress in turn being positioned according to the number of syllables in the inflection.

What has changed between early and modern Spanish is the loss of the phonemic opposition between the mid vowels in favour of an allophonic variation predictable from syllable structure (see above). It is no longer possible to tell, from an infinitive, whether a verb will be radical-changing or not: the stem vowel of *podar* 'to prune' is identical to that of *poder* but does not diphthongise; neither does the *e* of *pelar* 'to peel', although it is phonetically indistinguishable from that of *helar*. Some linguists, arguing that so common an alternation must be produced by regular rule, have postulated underlying vowels /ɛ, ɔ/ for radical-changing verbs and thus claim the synchronic process is identical to the historical change. Others reject this abstract analysis, but point out the alternation is 99 per cent predictable if a form like *puede* is taken as basic rather than the infinitive. Yet others believe that Spanish speakers cannot predict these alternations at all, and must learn them as inherent features of the individual verb (rather like learning the gender of a noun). This last group point to two pieces of evidence. Firstly, derivational processes have destroyed the earlier phonological regularity of diphthongisation: *deshuesar* 'to remove bones/pits' is a verb coined from the noun *hueso*, but the diphthong which regularly occurs under stress in the noun is irregular in the infinitive, where it is unstressed. Parallel examples are *ahuecar* 'to hollow out' from *hueco*, or *amueblado* 'furnished' from *mueble*. Secondly, speakers of some varieties stigmatised as non-standard, especially Chicano, regularly keep the diphthongised stem throughout a paradigm regardless of stress placement, saying *despiertamos*, *despiertáis* for standard *despertamos*, *despertáis* 'we/you awaken'. All told, it looks as though a process which at first was phonologically regular has passed through a stage of morphological conditioning and is now giving way to lexical marking on individual words. As often happens in linguistic change, this will preserve analogical relationships at the expense of phonological regularity.

4 Morphology

It is well known that the Romance languages have, over the centuries, eliminated much of the inflectional morphology that characterised formal Latin. Spanish is no exception to the general trend away from synthetic towards more analytic forms of expression. At the same time, historical accounts, by concentrating on what has been eliminated, tend to exaggerate the extent to which Spanish has abandoned inflection. True, the declension system for nouns and related forms has been radically simplified, and some extensive areas of verbal inflection (including the entire morphological passive) have been lost without trace. Nevertheless, the most frequently occurring forms of the verb remain highly synthetic in structure, and derivational patterning has always been a favoured and vigorous means of enriching the vocabulary. In consequence, Modern Spanish is far from being an isolating language: very few words consist of only one morph and the 'synthesis index' for running prose has been calculated at between 1:1.9 and 1:2.2 depending on the complexity of the register.

We begin with the simple tense-forms of the verb. Spanish verbs are traditionally said to belong to one of three conjugations, with infinitives in

-ar, *-er* and *-ir*. The *-ar* group, deriving from the Latin first conjugation in *-ĀRE*, is by far the largest and the one which accommodates almost all new coinings (compare *alunizar* 'to land on the moon' with French *alunir*). The distinction between the *-er* and *-ir* patterns is more apparent than real: aside from the future and conditional paradigms (which necessarily diverge since they take the infinitive as their stem) their endings are identical in all but four instances. We shall therefore distinguish only two basic conjugations for regular verbs, as set out in the chart given here.

The Simple Tense-forms of Regular Verbs, Showing the Stress and a Possible Morphological Analysis

	Conjugation I: tomar 'to take'		Conjugation II: comer 'to eat'	

(a) Present

Indicative	Subjunctive	Indicative	Subjunctive
tóm-Ø-o	tóm-e-Ø	cóm-Ø-o	cóm-a-Ø
tóm-a-s	tóm-e-s	cóm-e-s	cóm-a-s
tóm-a-Ø	tóm-e-Ø	cóm-e-Ø	cóm-a-Ø
tom-á-mos	tom-é-mos	com-é-mos	com-á-mos
tom-á-is	tom-é-is	com-é-is	com-á-is
tóm-a-n	tóm-e-n	cóm-e-n	cóm-a-n

(b) Imperfect

Indicative	Subjunctive		Indicative	Subjunctive	
	(1) or	(2)		(1) or	(2)
tom-á-ba-Ø	-á-se-Ø	-á-ra-Ø	com-í-a-Ø	-ié-se-Ø	-ié-ra-Ø
tom-á-ba-s	-á-se-s	-á-ra-s	com-í-a-s	-ié-se-s	-ié-ra-s
tom-á-ba-Ø	-á-se-Ø	-á-ra-Ø	com-í-a-Ø	-ié-se-Ø	-ié-ra-Ø
tom-á-ba-mos	-á-se-mos	-á-ra-mos	com-í-a-mos	-ié-se-mos	-ié-ra-mos
tom-á-ba-is	-á-se-is	-á-ra-is	com-í-a-is	-ié-se-is	-ié-ra-is
tom-á-ba-n	-á-se-n	-á-ra-n	com-í-a-n	-ié-se-n	-ié-ra-n

(c) Preterit or simple past (indicative only)

tom-Ø-é	(? = á+i)	com-Ø-í	(? = í+i)
tom-á-ste		com-í-ste	
tom-Ø-ó	(? = á+u)	com-i-ó	
tom-á-mos		com-í-mos	
tom-á-ste-is		com-í-ste-is	
tom-á-ro-n		com-ié-ro-n	

(d) Future indicative (all verbs)

Future indicative (all verbs)	Conditional (all verbs)
tom-a-r-é	com-e-r-ía
tom-a-r-ás	com-e-r-ías
tom-a-r-á	com-e-r-ía
tom-a-r-émos	com-e-r-íamos
tom-a-r-éis	com-e-r-íais
tom-a-r-án	com-e-r-ían

As in Latin, each paradigm consists of six forms representing three grammatical persons in both singular and plural. In general, all six forms are distinct, though there is some syncretism in first and third persons singular (and more in dialects which have lost final /-s/). As we noted earlier, stress operates functionally to differentiate otherwise identical forms. The unmarked paradigm is the present indicative and the unmarked person the third singular, which is the morphological shape assumed by the handful of verbs that do not accept animate subjects (*nieva* 'it is snowing', *tronó* 'it thundered'). It is useful to distinguish a 'theme vowel' after the lexical stem, /-a-/ for the first conjugation and for the second /-e-/ or /-i-/, in a rather complicated phonological distribution. It can then be seen that the distinction between the present indicative and subjunctive rests on a reversal of the theme vowel.

The order of morphemes is fixed: lexical stem + theme vowel + tense marker (sometimes including an empty morph) + person marker. Some forms, however, have fused in the course of history and a neat segmentation is not always possible. The preterit is the most difficult paradigm to analyse, since the theme vowel is sometimes indistinguishable, and segmenting the second and third person plural markers in the regular way, /-is, -n/, leaves an awkward residue which occurs nowhere else in the system. (We should perhaps add that the Latin perfect, from which this paradigm is derived, is scarcely more amenable to segmentation!) The future and conditional pose a rather different problem: both have evolved during the history of Spanish (see below) from combinations of the infinitive with either the present or imperfect of the auxiliary *haber* 'to have', and despite considerable phonetic reduction the 'endings' still contain traces of this verb's lexical stem. This secondary derivation explains the identity of the conditional endings with those of the second conjugation imperfect.

Spanish is in the unusual position of having alternative forms for the imperfect subjunctive, neither of which is a reflex of the Latin. The *-se* series derives from the Latin pluperfect subjunctive, and the *-ra* from the pluperfect indicative. In northwestern dialects and parts of Latin America, *-ra* is still used as a pluperfect. In standard Spanish, the two forms are not quite interchangeable: in the 'attenuating' sense *quisiera* 'I should like' and *debiera* 'I really ought' cannot be replaced by the *-se* counterparts, and elsewhere their distribution may be determined by considerations of symmetry or by sociolinguistic factors.

By the strictest criteria, almost 900 Spanish verbs are irregular in one or more of the simple tense-forms. This disconcerting figure contains a very few with anomalies in their endings; all the others are subject to alternations in the stem, with varying degrees of predictability. (The total, incidentally, excludes numerous other verbs which, though perfectly regular in their morphology, undergo orthographic changes and which are misguidedly classified as irregular in some manuals.) Over half the total are 'radical changing', of the types discussed above or of a minor type affecting only *-ir* verbs; some others, like *huir* 'to flee', insert a glide under predictable conditions. A significant minority retain the Latin opposition between primary and historic stems; those which do, have their preterit and both imperfect subjunctives built on a different stem from all other paradigms (see the chart of irregular verbs). Some twenty verbs of conjugation II modify their infinitival stem in the future and conditional. Finally, a handful of very frequent verbs are totally eccentric and even undergo stem suppletion.

Five Irregular Verbs Used as Auxiliaries, Given in Standard Orthography

	ser 'to be'	estar 'to be'	haber 'to have'	tener 'to have'	ir 'to go'
(a) Present indicative					
	soy	estoy	he	tengo	voy
	eres	estás	has	tienes	vas
	es	está	ha	tiene	va
	somos	estamos	hemos	tenemos	vamos
	sois	estáis	habéis	tenéis	vais
	son	están	han	tienen	van
(b) Present subjunctive (endings regular, same stem throughout)					
	sea	esté	haya	tenga	vaya
(c) Imperfect indicative (endings regular, same stem throughout)					
	era	estaba	había	tenía	iba
(d) Future indicative (endings regular, same stem throughout)					
	seré	estaré	habré	tendré	iré
(e) Preterit indicative (endings slightly irregular, same stem throughout)					
	fui	estuve	hube	tuve	fui
	fuiste	estuviste	hubiste	tuviste	fuiste
	fue	estuvo	hubo	tuvo	fue
	fuimos	estuvimos	hubimos	tuvimos	fuimos
	fuisteis	estuvisteis	hubisteis	tuvisteis	fuisteis
	fueron	estuvieron	hubieron	tuvieron	fueron
(f) Imperfect subjunctive (endings regular, same stem throughout)					
(1)	fuese	estuviese	hubiese	tuviese	fuese
(2)	fuera	estuviera	hubiera	tuviera	fuera

One class, amounting to some 200 including compounds, deserves special mention. Polysyllabic verbs which end in -cer or -cir preceded by a vowel, like *conocer* 'to know' or *relucir* 'to flaunt', have an extra velar consonant before non-front vowels, *conozco* being pronounced [ko-'nɔθ-ko] in Castilian and [ko-'nɔs-ko] in 'seseo' districts of Andalucía and throughout Latin America. The intriguing question is: where does the velar come from? Is it part of the underlying stem but lost before front vowels? Or is it epenthetic, and if so under what conditions? The first answer is historically correct: all these verbs contain an originally inchoative infix -*ISC*- whose velar regularly palatalised before a front vowel and assimilated to the preceding sibilant. But it seems unlikely that contemporary speakers recapitulate this process to produce the less frequent of the two alternants. If the velar is regarded as epenthetic (though phonetically unmotivated), it remains predictable in Castilian but only by reference to the phoneme /θ/. In 'seseante' dialects which lack the /θ:s/ opposition, the alternation is unpredictable: speakers cannot know from the phonological structure that *reconocer* 'to recognise' [re-ko-no-'sɛɾ] requires [-k-] while *recoser* 'to sew up' [re-ko-'sɛɾ] does not. They must, in other words, learn the alternation as an inherent lexical feature of the verb. Castilians, too, may do this; but they appear to have a choice.

In addition to its simple paradigms, Spanish is particularly well endowed with compound or periphrastic forms, more so than any other standard Romance language. Usually, these consist of an inflected auxiliary followed by a non-finite form of the lexical verb (an infinitive or participle), but more complex combinations are also possible. Virtually all are Romance creations, though some embryonic models are attested in Latin. The most far-reaching innovation was the compounding of *HABĒRE*, originally meaning 'to possess', with a past participle. *HABEO CĒNA(M) PARĀTA(M)* first meant 'I have the supper here, already prepared', but with increased use and a change of word order, it soon came to mean simply 'I've prepared the supper'. The new construction provided a powerful model: in principle, any paradigm of *HABĒRE* could be combined with the past participle to make a new tense-form. This remains true in Modern Spanish: all eight simple paradigms of *haber*, including the rare future subjunctive, can be compounded (their meanings are discussed in section 5). Although the compounds were flourishing in Old Spanish, they could only be used with transitive verbs, a direct consequence of their etymology. Intransitives were conjugated with *ser*, rather as in Modern French. It was only at the end of the fifteenth century that *haber* ousted *ser* for all verbs, and the past participle became invariable. In Spanish, *tener* can also be used as an auxiliary: *tengo preparada la cena*, with agreement, means the same as the Latin expression from which we set out.

The chart of irregular verbs, detailing the most common auxiliaries, shows two verbs 'to be', a notorious difficulty for foreign learners of Spanish. At some risk of oversimplification we shall say that *ser* is the normal copula, denoting inherent qualities, while *estar* focuses on resultant states; compare *la pimienta es picante* 'pepper is hot' (inherently) with *la sopa está fría* 'the soup's cold' (because it's cooled down). Both verbs can be used as auxiliaries, in conjunction with a past participle, to make analytic passives. This results in a plethora of forms, since any paradigm of *ser* or *estar* can be used, including those which are already compound. Nor are the two passives synonymous: *ser* denotes the action or process, as in *el dinero ha sido robado (por un atracador)* 'the money has been stolen (by a gangster)', whereas *estar* denotes the subsequent state, as in *la tienda está abierta* 'the shop's open' (because it has been opened). *Estar* also combines with a present participle to create a range of progressive forms. In turn, these may combine with other compounds, without grammatical restriction. Nevertheless, three-term compounds like *había estado andando* 'I'd been walking' are not frequent, and monsters like *ha estado siendo construído* 'it's been being built' are usually avoided in compassion for the listener.

By comparison with the verb, the Spanish noun and its related forms have a very simple inflectional structure. This is mainly due to the complete elimination of the Latin declension system, from a very early date and well before the emergence of vernacular texts in the tenth century. Nonetheless, as we hinted earlier, the effect of vigorous derivational processes has been to create large numbers of nouns whose overall morphological structure, while reasonably transparent, can hardly be described as simple. An abstract nominal like *desaprovechamiento* 'negligence' probably consists of six synchronic morphemes, with a further historical division fossilised in the root *-pro(-vech)-*. The majority of nouns consist of at least two morphemes, a root and gender marker, to which a plural marker is affixed if need be.

The categories of number and gender inherited from Latin are for the most part overtly marked on determiners, demonstratives, pronouns and adjectives of all kinds, as well as nouns. In Castilian, all plural substantives and determiners end in /-s/, though the derivation of plurals from singulars is not quite so straightforward as this implies, since a sizable minority adds the full syllable /-es/ and a few already ending in /-s/ remain unchanged. We have already seen the drastic effect on plural marking in those dialects which have lost final /-s/. Modern Spanish has only two genders, which normally respect the sex of animate beings, but must be regarded as inherent and semantically arbitrary for inanimate nouns. The Latin neuter was eliminated from substantives, usually in favour of masculine, before the Old Spanish period, but faint traces of it persist in the pronoun system. Thanks to the frequency of the markers *-a* (overwhelmingly feminine) and *-o* (almost exclusively masculine) the gender of a high proportion of nouns is immediately apparent, though predictability for other endings is much lower. Curiously, *-a* and *-o* derive from Latin suffixes whose primary purpose was to mark not gender, but declension membership, from which gender was in turn partly predictable.

The demonstratives form a three-term system which correlates with grammatical person: *este* 'this (of mine)' : *ese* 'that (of yours)' : *aquel* 'yonder (of his/hers/theirs)'. One set of forms doubles up for adjectives and pronouns (the latter take an orthographic accent) and the system is essentially identical to its Latin forerunner, though with different exponents. In European Spanish, person is undoubtedly a three-term system if approached via verbal inflection, but there are in fact twelve pronouns to distribute among the six inflectional endings, and it is the third person that proves obligingly polysemous. Since the end of the Middle Spanish period, the physical distance encoded in the person category (and in demonstratives) has been exploited metaphorically as a marker of social distance. Thus the 'polite' address forms *usted/ustedes* colligate with third person endings, emphasising the differential status accorded by the speaker to the addressee. The minor semantic clash of second person referent with third person verb is resolved in West Andalusian and Canary Island dialects by colligating *ustedes* with second person morphology: *ustedes sois*, etc. In Latin America, the position is more complicated. *Vosotros*, the familiar plural form, has given way to *ustedes*, used with third person inflection, as a generalised plural. *Vos*, which in medieval Spanish had been used as a polite singular (just as Modern French *vous*), has taken over in many varieties as the generalised singular, colligating with inflections which are historically both singular and plural, sometimes even blends. 'Voseo' is not a recent phenomenon; its roots must be sought in the colonial period, and recent archival research has revealed that it was well established in educated Buenos Aires usage by the beginning of the last century.

5   Syntax

Spanish has sometimes been described as having free, or relatively free, word order. Without qualification, this is misleading. What is usually meant is that subject noun phrases are not fixed by grammatical requirements at a particular point in the sentence. This is a salient characteristic, one which differentiates Spanish from French (in its formal registers) and more so from the major Germanic languages, but which is less unusual among the southern Romance group. At the same time, Spanish has strong constraints on word order *within* the main syntactic constituents and even the theoretical freedom available elsewhere is subject to pragmatic conventions. As a general rule, themes precede rhemes and new information is located towards the end of the utterance.

To characterise the purely syntactic constraints, we must recognise the categories of subject, verbal unit, object and complement (abbreviated as S, V, O, C). Within the simple declarative sentence, object and complement phrases follow the verb: *Elena compró un coche* 'Helen bought a car', *el libro parecía interesante* 'the book seemed interesting'. In everyday language, the VO/VC order is fixed; objects cannot precede their verbs — **Elena un coche compró*. It is certainly possible to topicalise an object consisting of a definite noun phrase or proper noun by moving it to the front of the sentence, but when this happens there is an intonation break after the topic, and an object clitic is obligatorily inserted before the verb: *el coche, lo compró Elena* '(as for) the car, Helen bought it'. The result is no longer a simple sentence; *lo compró Elena* is a complete structure in its own right.

Subject phrases are harder to pin down. Because of the marked tendency for the topic to coincide with the grammatical subject in spoken language, SVO/SVC order is very frequent, especially where the subject consists of a single proper noun or very short phrase. So *?compró Elena el coche* would sound very odd, and *compró el coche Elena* would tend to be reserved for contradiction or contrast — 'it was Helen (not Jane) who bought the car'. Nevertheless, in more formal registers VSO order is common, and in all registers unusually long or 'heavy' subject phrases appear to the right of the verb: *han llegado todos los transeuntes de la Compañía X* 'all passengers travelling with Company X have now arrived'. VS order is the norm in many types of subordinate clause even when the subject consists of a single word: *no vi lo que leía Juana* 'I didn't see what Jane was reading'. VS is also obligatory in existentials, *viven gitanos en las cuevas* 'there are gypsies living in the caves', and in questions beginning with an interrogative word: *¿qué quieren ustedes?* 'what would you (pl.) like?', but not **¿qué ustedes quieren?* Interrogatives of this kind should not be assumed to entail syntactic inversion since VS, as we have seen, frequently occurs in statements and conversely yes-no questions may show either VS or SV order, relying entirely on the intonation to differentiate questions from corresponding statements.

On most of the criteria favoured by typological theory, Modern Spanish is a consistent VO language. Briefly: in simplex sentences VO/VC order is obligatory; noun phrase relationships are expressed exclusively by prepositions; genitives follow their head noun; the standard follows the comparative; most adjectives and all attributive phrases and relative clauses follow their head noun; most adverbs follow the verb they modify; auxiliaries are frequent and always precede the lexical stem; quantifiers and negatives precede the item they qualify and have only forward scope; interrogative words are always phrase-initial. Needless to add, there are some complications. Among the adjectives, some of the most common always precede their noun, most others may precede if used figuratively, and a few are polysemous according to position: *un pobre pueblecillo* 'a miserable little town', *un aristócrata pobre* 'an impoverished aristocrat'. Adverbs acting as sentential modifiers are usually the first word, *desgraciadamente*, ...'unfortunately, ...'; adverbs modifying adjectives almost always precede whereas those modifying verbs just as regularly follow, so that scope (for manner adverbials at least) is pivotal.

The most serious discrepancy for VO typology, however, is the vigour of suffixal inflection in the verb system, a feature little modified by the development of auxiliaries, since auxiliaries themselves are both frequent and highly inflected. Verbal inflection has two important syntactic functions. In conjunction with the concord system (see below) it guarantees the freedom of movement of subject phrases. It also tends to preserve the optionality of subject pronouns, permitting many grammatical sentences of V(S)O form with no overt subject nominal. Spanish, as we have seen, shows little syncretism in its inflections and, unlike French, rarely needs subject pronouns to avoid syntactic ambiguity, though they are regularly used for emphasis and contrast. At the same time, any move to increase the use of personal pronouns (and there is some evidence this is happening in colloquial registers) would undermine the necessity to preserve verbal inflection.

Spanish has a fully explicit concord system which marks number and gender on all modifiers within the noun phrase, and number and person (and occasionally gender too) between the subject and verb. There is no concord between verb and object. In most cases, concord unambiguously assigns a subject to a verb, and any ambiguity arising in this relationship (if, for instance, both subject and object are third person singular) is usually resolved by syntactic differences between subjects and objects. They differ in two important ways, both connected with specificity. The first is illustrated in *el hombre compra huevos* 'the man is buying (some) eggs'. The subject phrase in Spanish — whether definite, indefinite or generic — requires a determiner, but the object does not. In this respect Spanish differs considerably from Latin, which had no articles and did not require determination of either subjects or objects, but has evolved less far than French, which requires both. The second distinction is illustrated in *vi a tu hermana* 'I saw your sister', where the specific, animate object is introduced by the preposition *a* (popularly known as 'personal *a*'). At first sight, this looks like a nominative:accusative opposition, and it may indeed represent a remnant of the defunct case system. In fact, the opposition is between particularised animate beings and all other object phrases (with a little latitude for metaphorical extension). Moreover, this distinction is preserved at the expense of another: since *a* is also the preposition used to introduce datives, there is no overt difference between the majority of direct and indirect objects. Whether the categories have genuinely fused or are merely obscured by surface syncretism is hard to say. Most Latin American varieties preserve a distinction between third person direct and indirect pronominal objects, but this too has been lost in much of Spain.

Curiously, voice is the verbal category with which pronominals have been most closely linked during the history of Spanish. The connection, brought about by cliticisation of part of the pronoun system, seems likely to result in the evolution of a new set of medio-passive paradigms. Whereas Latin pronouns were free forms not necessarily positioned adjacent to the verb, in most Romance varieties they have become clitic, sometimes resulting in differentiated sets of free and bound forms. In Spanish, clitics may appear alone or supported by a corresponding free form, but the converse is not true: *te vi* 'I saw you', *te vi a ti* 'I saw **you**', but not **vi a ti*. Enclisis, which was frequent in older stages of the language, has been virtually eliminated from contemporary spoken Spanish, where clitics 'climb' from a lower clause to the front of the main verb — compare formal *tiene que traérmelo* 'he must bring it for me' with colloquial *me lo tiene que traer*. As we noted earlier, clitics show a direct:indirect opposition only in the third person, and not always there. Reflexivity is distinguished, if at all, only in third person *se*, which neutralises not only direct:indirect, but also number and gender.

Recently, *se* and its congeners in other Romance languages have been the focus of intense linguistic debate. The problem is whether *se* should be treated as one single morpheme or a set of homophonous forms. Traditional accounts distinguish three or four functions: a true reflexive pronoun — *se lavó* 'he washed himself'; a passive marker — *el congreso se inauguró* 'the congress was opened'; an impersonal marker — *se habla inglés* 'English spoken'; and a substitute form of *le/les* when used with another deictic pronoun — *se lo dio* 'she gave it to him', not * *le lo dio*. (The latter usage is peculiar to Spanish and is known to have a different historical origin from the others.) These four functions, however, seem to be semantically compatible, yet Spanish never permits more than one *se* per verb phrase. Combinations of, for instance, an 'impersonal' *se* with a 'reflexive' verb are ungrammatical — * *se se esfuerza por* …'one struggles to …' — as are many other apparently reasonable pairs. If *se* were only one morpheme, the problem would not arise; but can such disparate meanings be reconciled? Two accounts are now available which solve most of the problems. In one, *se* is viewed as a pronoun with very little inherent meaning ('third person, low deixis'), which acquires significance from contextual inferences. In the other, *se* is seen as part of a new medio-passive paradigm, its third person impersonal use paralleling that of Latin: *VĪVITUR* = *se vive* = 'one lives'. In neither treatment is *se* a reflexive pronoun!

If Spanish is indeed creating new inflectional morphology, it would not be the first time. The clearest example is the new future paradigm we mentioned above, a compound of the lexical verb plus *HABĒRE* (/kantar + 'abjo/ > /kanta're/ etc.), which originally expressed mild obligation 'I have to sing' and whose component parts were still separable in Old Spanish. Another example would be the adverbials in *-mente*, compounded from the ablative of the feminine noun *MĒNS* 'mind/manner' with a feminine adjective, thus *STRICTĀ MĒNTE* > *estrechamente* 'narrowly' (notice the Latin adjective position); here the two components remain separable. But is Spanish really in need of a new passive when it already has a plethora of compound forms with *ser* and *estar*? All we can reply is that they have discrete functions: only the 'reflexive' passive is used in an inchoative sense — *se vio obligado a* …'he became compelled to …'; only the *ser* passive is acceptable to most speakers with an explicit agentive phrase. But the major difference is one of register: *ser* passives, though common in journalistic and technical writing, have been virtually ousted from speech and from literary styles to the advantage of the clitic forms, which may eventually generalise to all contexts.

We have so far said little on the verbal categories of tense, aspect and mood, and will devote our remaining space to them. The first two are inextricably bound up with the evolution of auxiliaries, in which Spanish is particularly prolific. Auxiliaries usually derive from full lexical verbs whose semantic content is progressively weakened as they become 'grammaticalised'. By the strictest definition — a verb with no independent lexical meaning — Spanish has only one auxiliary: *soler* as in *Juan suele madrugarse* 'John habitually gets up at dawn'. *Haber*, *ser* and *estar* come close behind, having only remnants of lexical meaning: *yo soy* 'I exist', *Ana no está* 'Anne's not ᵗ home'. After that comes a continuum of more than fifty verbs, ranging from *tener* and *ir* which have important auxiliary functions, to those like *cam..nar* 'to walk/journey' which in expressions like *camina enlutada* 'she goes about in mourning' contrive to support the past participle while preserving most of their lexical content. True auxiliaries carry tense and aspect information for the main verb and this is clearly one reason for the grammaticalisation of *HABĒRE*. The Latin system opposed three time values to two aspects, imperfective and perfective, giving a six-cell structure; but one paradigm, usually called 'perfect', was bivalent between present perfective and past punctual meaning. The development of *HABĒRE* compounds not only preserved the morphological marking of aspect (previously perfective was signalled by a stem alternation) but also resolved this bivalency, *VĪDĪ* in the sense of 'I have seen' being replaced by *HABEO VĪSU(M)* > *he visto*, leaving the original to mean 'I caught sight of'. In the 'core' system of Modern Spanish this opposition is maintained, though in Castilian the perfect *he visto* is beginning to encroach on contexts previously reserved for the preterit *vi*. It is not yet clear whether Spanish is moving towards the pattern of Modern French (see pages 215–16, for details), but certainly the elimination of the preterit paradigm would provoke a major realignment of functions.

All varieties of Spanish preserve a vigorous subjunctive mood (see the charts of regular and irregular verbs for the morphology). Opinion is divided, however, on whether the subjunctive — which does not occur in declarative main clauses — should be viewed as a 'mere' marker of subordination or as a meaningful category. In many contexts, its use seems to be grammatically determined; *querer* 'to want', for instance, when followed by a clause always takes a subjunctive — *quiero que lo hagas/ *haces* 'I want you to do it'. In others, the conditioning is more subtle: *busco a un amigo que puede ayudarme* 'I'm looking for a (particular) friend to help me' alternates with *busco un amigo que pueda ayudarme* 'I'm looking for a (=any) friend to help me', but the subjunctive may still be grammatically conditioned by the indeterminacy of the object noun phrase. There are a few instances, however, where a genuine alternation is possible: *¿crees que vendrá?* and *¿crees que venga?* can both be translated as 'do you think he'll come?', but the first is neutral in implicature while the second conveys the speaker's belief that he won't. If such examples are taken as criterial, the 'grammatical marker' hypothesis cannot be maintained. In any event, the complementiser *que* is a much more efficient marker of subordination, and most complement clauses dependent on verbs of saying, thinking or believing require an indicative rather than a subjunctive. Nevertheless, it remains very difficult to find a single, uniform meaning for the subjunctive, the traditional suggestions of 'doubt' or 'uncertainty' being only partially accurate. The most we can say is that the 'meaningful' uses of the subjunctive, though rather few, are Romance creations and appear to be increasing rather than decreasing.

Bibliography

The best reference grammar of (American) Spanish is Bello (1981), while Real Academia Española (1973) is the draft version of the new normative grammar, completely revising the unsatisfactory edition of 1931. Modern descriptions include. Marcos Marín (1980), an introduction to linguistic analysis very fully exemplified from Spanish, with an excellent bibliography; and Whitley (1986), a comprehensive contrastive grammar of Spanish and English. Harris (1983) is an application of metrical theory to Spanish phonology, superseding the author's earlier classic on the subject; it can usefully be supplemented by the five articles on the interface of phonology and morphology in Nuessel (1985). The most reliable dictionary of modern Spanish usage is Moliner (1982).

For the history of the language, Lapesa (1980) is the classical external account paying special attention to literary sources; a reliable, if rather technical, treatment of internal changes in phonology and morphology can be found in Lloyd (1987). An excellent etymological dictionary is Corominas and Pascual (1980–8). For regional variants, Zamora Vicente (1967) is a historical description of peninsular dialects with shorter sections on Spanish outside Spain. For Latin America, Sala (1982) is a useful general survey of vocabulary, while Canfield (1982) is a brief but authoritative guide to pronunciation arranged by country. Amastae and Elías-Olivares (1982) is a collection of 18 articles on sociolinguistic variation, Chicano, and aspects of language policy in the USA. For Judaeo-Spanish, Sala (1976) provides a good survey and bibliography.

References

Amastae, J. and L. Elías-Olivares (eds.) 1982. *Spanish in the United States* (Cambridge University Press, Cambridge)
Bello, A. 1981. *Gramática de la lengua castellana*, critical edition by R. Trujillo. (Instituto Universitario de Lingüística, Tenerife)
Canfield, D.L. 1981. *Spanish Pronunciation in the Americas*, 2nd ed. (University of Chicago Press, Chicago)
Corominas, J. and J.A. Pascual 1980–8. *Diccionario crítico etimológico castellano e hispánico*, 6 vols. (Gredos, Madrid)
Harris, J.W. 1983. *Syllable Structure and Stress in Spanish* (MIT Press, Cambridge, Mass.)
Lapesa, R. 1980. *Historia de la lengua española*, 8th ed. (Gredos, Madrid)

Lloyd, P.M. 1987. *From Latin to Spanish* (American Philosophical Society, Philadelphia)

Marcos Marín, F. 1980. *Curso de gramática española* (Cincel-Kapelusz, Madrid)

Moliner, M. 1982. *Diccionario de uso del español*, 2 vols. (Gredos, Madrid)

Nuessel, F.H. (ed.) 1985. *Current Issues in Hispanic Phonology and Morphology* (Indiana University Linguistics Club, Bloomington)

Real Academia Española. 1973. *Esbozo de una nueva gramática de la lengua española* (Espasa-Calpe, Madrid)

Sala, M. 1976. *Le judéo-espagnol* (Mouton, The Hague)

—— 1982. *El español de América, 1: Léxico* (Instituto Caro y Cuervo, Bogotá)

Whitley, M.S. 1986. *Spanish/English Contrasts* (Georgetown University Press, Washington D.C.)

Zamora Vicente, A. 1967. *Dialectología española*, 2nd ed. (Gredos, Madrid)

11   Portuguese

Stephen Parkinson

1   Introduction

Portuguese, the national language of Portugal and Brazil, belongs to the Romance language group. It is descended from the Vulgar Latin of the western Iberian Peninsula (the regions of Gallaecia and Lusitania of the Roman Empire), as is Galician, often wrongly considered a dialect of Spanish.

Portugal originated as a county of the Kingdom of Galicia, the westernmost area of the Christian north of the peninsula, the south having been under Moorish rule since the eighth century. Its name derived from the towns of Porto (Oporto) and Gaia (< *CALE*) at the mouth of the Douro river. As Galicia fell under Castilian rule, Portugal achieved independence under the Burgundian nobility to whom the county was granted in the eleventh century. Alfonso Henriques, victor of the battle of São Mamede (1128), was the first to take the title of King of Portugal. Apart from a short period of Castilian rule (1580–1640), Portugal was to remain an independent state.

The speed of the Portuguese reconquest of the Moorish areas played an important part in the development of the language. The centre of the kingdom was already in Christian hands, after the fall of Coimbra (1064), and many previously depopulated areas had been repopulated by settlers from the north. The capture of Lisbon in 1147 and Faro in 1249 completed the expulsion of the Moors, nearly 250 years before the end of the Spanish reconquest, bringing northern and central settlers into the Mozarabic (arabised Romance) areas. The political centre of the kingdom also moved south, Guimarães being supplanted first by Coimbra, and subsequently by Lisbon as capital and seat of the court. The establishment of the university in Lisbon and Coimbra in 1288, to move between the two cities until its eventual establishment in Coimbra in 1537, made the centre and south the intellectual centre (although Braga in the north remained the religious capital). The form of Portuguese which eventually emerged as standard was the result of the interaction of northern and southern varieties, which gives Portuguese dialects their relative homogeneity.

For several centuries after the independence of Portugal, the divergence of Portuguese and Galician was slight enough for them to be considered variants of the same language. Galician-Portuguese was generally preferred to Castilian as a medium for lyric poetry until the middle of the fourteenth century. Portuguese first appears as the language of legal documents at the beginning of the thirteenth century, coexisting with Latin throughout that century and finally replacing it during the reign of D. Dinis (1279–1325).

In the fifteenth and sixteenth centuries the spread of the Portuguese Empire established Portuguese as the language of colonies in Africa, India and South America. A Portuguese-based pidgin was widely used as a reconnaissance language for explorers and later as a lingua franca for slaves shipped from Africa to America and the Caribbean. Some Portuguese lexical items, e.g. *pikinini* 'child' (*pequeninho*, diminutive of *pequeno* 'small'), *save* 'know' (*saber*), are common to almost all creoles. Caribbean creoles have a larger Portuguese element, whose origin is controversial — the Spanish-based Papiamentu of Curaçao is the only clear case of large-scale relexification of an originally Portuguese-based creole. Brazilian Portuguese (BP), phonologically conservative, and lexically affected by the indigenous Tupi languages and the African languages of the slave population, was clearly distinct from European Portuguese (EP) by the eighteenth century. Continued emigration from Portugal perpetuated the European norm beside Brazilian Portuguese, especially in Rio de Janeiro, where D. João and his court took refuge in 1808. After Brazil gained its independence in 1822, there was great pressure from literary and political circles to establish independent Brazilian norms, in the face of a conservative prescriptive grammatical tradition based on European Portuguese.

With over 160 million speakers, Portuguese is reckoned to be the fifth most widely spoken language in the world. It is spoken by 10 million people in Portugal and approaching 150 million in Brazil; it remains the language of administration of the former colonies of Angola, Mozambique, Guiné-Bissau, S. Tomé-Principe and the Cape Verde Islands (where it exists beside Portuguese-based creoles) and is spoken in isolated pockets in Goa, Timor, Malaysia, Macao and in emigré communities in North America.

The standard form of European Portuguese is traditionally defined as the speech of Lisbon and Coimbra. The distinctive traits of Lisbon phonology (centralisation of /e/ to /ɐ/ in palatal contexts; uvular /ʀ/ in place of alveolar /r/) have more recently become dominant as a result of diffusion by the mass media. Unless otherwise stated, all phonetic citation forms are of European Portuguese.

Of the two main urban accents of Brazilian Portuguese, Carioca (Rio de Janeiro) shows a greater approximation towards European norms than Paulista (São Paulo). While the extreme north and south show considerable conservatism, regional differences in Brazilian Portuguese are still less marked than class-based differences; non-standard, basilectal varieties show considerable effects of creolisation, with drastic simplifications of inflectional morphology and concord.

2 Phonology

Portuguese orthography (summarised in table 11.1) is phonological rather than narrowly phonemic or phonetic, assuming knowledge of the main phonological and morphophonemic processes of the language. It also uses a variety of devices to indicate word stress. Final stress is regular (i.e. orthographically unmarked) in words whose final syllable either (a) contains an oral diphthong, one of the nasal vowels /ã õ ĩ ũ õĩ/ or orthographic *ão, i, u, ãe* (as opposed to *am, e, o, em (en)*, which indicate unstressed final syllables); or (b) ends in *r, l* or *z* (but not *s*, which generally indicates

Table 11.1: Portuguese Orthography

a	/a ɐ/*	lh	/ʎ/
á	/a/ (stressed)*	m (final)	nasality of preceding vowel*
ã	/ẽ/	(elsewhere)	/m/
â	/ɐ/ (stressed)*	n (final)	nasality of preceding vowel*
ãe	/ẽĩ/	(elsewhere)	/n/
ão	/ẽũ/	nh	/ɲ/
b	/b/	ó	/ɔ/ (stressed)*
c (+a, o, u)	/k/	ô	/o/ (stressed)*
(+i, e)	/s/	o	/o ɔ u/*
ç	/s/	ou	/o/
ch	/ʃ/	õe	/õĩ/
d	/d/	p	/p/
e	/e,(ɐ),ɛ,ə, i/*	qu (+a, o)	/kw/
é	/ɛ/ (stressed)*	(+i, e)	/k/
ê	/e/ (stressed)*	r	/r, ʀ/*
f	/f/	rr	/ʀ/
g (+a, o)	/g/	s (final)	/z ʃ ʒ/*
(+i, e)	/ʒ/	(intervocalic)	/z/
gu (+a, o)	/gw/	(elsewhere)	/s/
(+i, e)	/g/	t	/t/
h	silent (but cf. ch,lh,nh)	u	/u/
		v	/v/
i	/i,j/*	x	/ʃ (ks,gz,z)/
j	/ʒ/	z (final)	/z ʃ ʒ/*
l	/l/	(elsewhere)	/z/

Note: This table represents European Portuguese pronunciation. * marks points (including Brazilian Portuguese variants) explained in the text. ai, au, ei, éi, eu, éu, iu, oi, ói, ui represent falling diphthongs. k,w are only found in foreign words. final = word- and syllable-final.

inflectional endings). Otherwise, penultimate stress is regular. Any irregular stress pattern, including all cases of antepenultimate stress, is marked by a written accent. These accents also indicate vowel quality (often redundantly). The circumflex accent ˆ indicates closed vowels [ɐ e o], while the acute accent ´ indicates open vowel qualities [a ɛ ɔ] and is also used to mark stress on *i*, *u*, which are deemed to have no 'closed' phonetic values. In a few cases these two accents are still used to indicate vowel quality in regularly stressed words (e.g. *três* 'three', *pôde* '(s)he could' vs. *pode* '(s)he can', *pó* 'dust') and to distinguish stressed monosyllables from clitics, e.g. *dê* [de] 'give (3 sg. pres. subj.)' – *de* [də] 'of'. The grave accent has a very limited use to indicate unreduced atonic vowels (usually /a/). Nasality is indicated either by the til ˜ or by a nasal consonant following the vowel.

Brazilian and Portuguese orthographies have been progressively harmonised by agreements between the respective governments and academies, latterly in 1971 decrees in both countries, in which the distinctively Brazilian convention of marking unpredictable closed mid vowels with the circumflex was abandoned, as part of a rationalisation of the use of accents. The orthographic differences that remain reflect phonological differences between European and Brazilian Portuguese.

The vowel system of Portuguese (tables 11.2 and 11.3) is one of the most complex of the Romance family. Portuguese is rich in monophthongs and (falling) diphthongs, as a result of two developments which set it off from Castilian. There was no diphthongisation of Vulgar Latin /ɛ ɔ/, (compare Cast. *nueve*, Ptg. *nove* < *NOVEM* 'nine', Cast. *diez*, Ptg. *dez* < *DECEM* 'ten') with the result that the seven-vowel system inherited from Vulgar Latin remains complete. Intervocalic /l/ was effaced, and /n/ fell after nasalising the preceding vowel: these two processes, in addition to the deletion of intervocalic /d g/, resulted in Old Portuguese being characterised by large numbers of sequences of vowels in hiatus: e.g. *BONUM* > *bõo* 'good', *MALUM* > *mao* 'bad', *MOLINUM* > *moĩo* 'mill', *PEDEM* > *pee* 'foot'. Many of these hiatuses were resolved as monophthongs or falling diphthongs: *pee* > *pé*; *bõo* > *bõ*; *mao* > *mau*. Nasal vowels in unresolved hiatuses were denasalised (*BONAM* > *bõa* > *boa* 'good (f.)'; **PANATARIUM* > *pãadeiro* > *paadeiro* > *padeiro* 'baker') except for the sequences [ĩo], [ĩa] where the hiatus was broken by a palatal nasal glide [j] which subsequently developed into the nasal [ɲ], e.g. *moinho* [mu'iɲu] < *moĩo*. The effacement of intervocalic /l n/ has been morphologised, in the inflection of nouns and adjectives with root-final /l/ e.g. *azul* 'blue', plural *azuis*, and in derivational morphology, partly as the result of the introduction of unevolved forms: *céu* 'heaven, sky' (< *CAELUM*) corresponds to *celeste* 'heavenly'; *fim* [fĩ] 'end' (< *FINEM*) to *final* 'final'; beside *irmão* 'brother' there is a familiar form *mano* (borrowed from Castilian *hermano*).

The phoneme /ɐ/ is only found in the European Portuguese system, and

Table 11.2: Portuguese Vowels

Monophthongs

i	ī			u	ū	High
		(ə)				
e	ē			o	õ	High mid
ε		(ɐ)ẽ		ɔ		Low mid
		a				Low

Diphthongs	Front		Central	Back		
	iu				ui	ũĩ
	eu	ei	ẽĩ	(ou)oi		õĩ
	εu	εi	(ɐi)	ɔi		
		ai	ẽĩ au	ẽũ		

Note: sounds enclosed in brackets are distinct phonemes in only some varieties.

there in a marginal role. In Brazilian Portuguese, [ɐ] is an allophone of /a/, in post-tonic position and in nasal contexts; in European Portuguese, [ɐ] is likewise tied to atonic and nasal contexts, but the exclusion of [a] from the same contexts is not absolute, leading to occasional contrasts not found in Brazilian Portuguese, e.g. *nação* [nɐ'sẽu] 'nation' – *acção* [a'sẽu] 'action'; *a* (preposition, f. sg. def. art.) [ɐ] vs. *à* (*a* + *a*) [a]; *-amos* (1 pl. pres. indic., 1st conjug.) -['ɐmuʃ] vs. *-ámos* (ibid., pret.) -['amuʃ]; *casa suja* ['kazɐ'suʒɐ] 'dirty house' – *casa azul* ['kaza'zul] 'blue house'. In Lisbon, /ɐ/ is found preceding the palatal consonants [ʃ ʒ ʎ ɲ], where other accents have /e/, and the diphthongs /ɐi/ and /ẽĩ/ correspond to /ei/ and /ẽĩ/ in other accents.

Of the large inventory of phonemic diphthongs (ignoring those phonetic diphthongs arising by vowel contraction) most have a limited distribution. /ũĩ/ is found only in *muito* 'much, many' (and is often realised as [wĩ]); /iu/ is only found in preterit forms of third conjugation verbs; /εu/, /εi/, ẽĩ/, /ẽũ/, /ẽĩ/, /ui/, /õĩ/ and /ɔi/ are found almost exclusively in stem-final position, and are closely associated with inflectional patterns. /ẽĩ/ (Lisbon /ɐ̃ĩ/) is a word-final variant of /ẽ/, as can be seen from the doublet *cento* 'hundred' [sẽtu], *cem* 'hundred' [sẽĩ], and also occurs preceding inflectional -*s*: *nuvem* 'cloud' [nuvẽĩ] plural *nuvens* ['nuvẽĩʃ]. (The orthographic change of *m* to *n* is without phonetic significance.) In most dialects there is a distinction between /ẽĩ/ and the relatively uncommon /ẽĩ/: *quem* 'who' /kẽĩ/ vs. *cães* 'dogs' /kẽĩʃ/. In Lisbon the centralisation of /ẽ/ eliminates the distinction by realising all cases of /ẽĩ/ as /ɐ̃ĩ/. Some dialects retain the diphthong /ou/ distinct from /o/ (European Portuguese has evidence for a morphophonemic /ou/, in cases of unreduced atonic /o/). In Brazilian Portuguese, the vocalisation of postvocalic /l/ creates a new series of falling diphthongs, e.g. *sol* 'sun' [sou] (BP), [sɔl] (EP).

The vowel system is further complicated by a regular alternation of high vowels (/i u/), low mid vowels (/ɛ ɔ/) and high mid vowels (/e o/) inside verbal paradigms. The alternation is found in the second and third conjugations, where root-final mid vowels are realised as /e o/ (2nd conjug.) or /i u/ (3rd conjug.) in the first person singular present indicative, and the whole of the present subjunctive (which always takes its stem form from the first person singular present indicative) but as /ɛ ɔ/ in the remaining root-stressed forms of the indicative (2 sg., 3 sg., 3 pl.). Thus *meter* 'put' (see the chart of verb forms) has present indicative forms ['metu] (1 sg.), |['mɛtə] (3 sg.), and *fugir* 'flee' ['fuʒu] (1 sg.), ['fɔʒa] (3 sg.). This alternation is known as 'metaphony' in token of its origin in an assimilation of the open root vowel to the theme vowel in the first person singular, where the theme vowel was semi-vocalised and lost, e.g. *FUGIO* > **fogjo* > *fujo*. The process has long been morphologised, but can still be analysed as an assimilation in a relatively abstract morphophonemics. It was extended by analogy to some third conjugation verbs where the root vowel was originally a high /i u/ e.g. *fugir* 'to flee'. Vowel alternation is found in a more restricted domain in adjectives and nouns, where it is less easily explicable as assimilation. Adjectives with stem-final /o/, particularly those ending in *-oso* (f. *-osa*) have a closed /o/ in the masculine singular form and open /ɔ/ elsewhere, e.g. *formoso* 'beautiful' [fur'mozu], f. sg. *formosa* [fur'mɔzɐ], pl. [fur'mɔzuʃ], [fur'mɔzɐʃ]. A similar alternation is found in a restricted set of nouns such as *ovo* 'egg', sg. ['ovu], pl. ['ɔvuʃ].

Nasal vowels are in contrast with the corresponding oral vowels in open syllables (medial and final): e.g. *mudo* ['mudu] 'dumb' – *mundo* ['mũdu] 'world'; *ri* [ʀi] 'laugh' – *rim* [ʀĩ] 'kidney'. There is no contrast between nasal vowels and sequences of vowel + nasal consonant in this position, nasal vowels being very frequently followed by a more or less consonantal nasal off-glide, e.g. ['mũdu] = ['mũndu], so that it is frequently argued that nasal vowels can be analysed phonologically as vowel + nasal consonant sequences. (This analysis is problematic because it cannot easily accommodate nasal diphthongs, and is not easily reconciled with morphophonemic rules relating nasal vowels and nasal consonants.) There is a general phonetic tendency for nasal consonants to cause nasalisation of preceding and following vowels; in Brazilian Portuguese the resulting nasality can be as strong as phonemic nasality. (Historical progressive nasalisation accounts for the nasal vowels of *mãe* 'mother' (< *MATREM*); *muito* (< *MULTUM*); *mim* 'me' (< *MIHI*), *nem* 'nor' (< *NEC*) and for the palatal nasals of *ninho* 'nest' ['niɲu] < *nĩo* < **nio* < *NIDUM* and *nenhum* 'no, not any' < *nẽ ũu* < *NEC UNUM*.)

The open vowels /a ɛ ɔ/, absent from the nasal series, are also excluded from contexts where a nasal consonant follows. This restriction is absolute in Brazilian Portuguese; in European Portuguese it is overridden by morphophonemic processes leading to open vowels (notably metaphony) and by antepenultimate stress. A verb such as *comer* 'eat' shows metaphonic alternations in European but not in Brazilian Portuguese; BP *tônico* 'tonic' corresponds to EP *tónico*.

The morphophonemics of nasal vowels were complicated by a series of changes resulting in the syncretism of the word-final nasal vowels -[ã], -[õ], with -[ãũ] (>[ẽũ]), leading to alternations such as *cão* (sg.) 'dog' (< *cã*) – *cães* (pl.); *razão* (sg.) 'reason' (< *razõ*) – *razões* (pl.); *fala* (3 sg. 'speak') – *falam* ['falẽũ] (3 pl.). This phonological change was effectively morphologised when it was obscured by the subsequent reintroduction of final *-õ* and *-ã* by the contraction of *-õo* and *-ãa*: *bom* < *bõo*, *irmã* < *irmãa* in the fifteenth century.

Stress, (or more precisely, lack of stress) is a major conditioning factor in vowel quality, the range of atonic vowel contrasts being systematically limited, as shown in table 11.3. There is large-scale neutralisation of vowel

Table 11.3: Atonic Vowel Systems

	EP		BP	
Final (including clitics)	ə	u	i	u
	ɐ		a (=[ɐ])	
Non-final	i ə u		i	u
	(o)		e	o
	(ɛ) ɐ (ɔ)			
	(a)		a	

quality contrasts in the front and back vowel series, most of all in final syllables, where each series is represented by a single vowel: the front vowels by EP [ə], BP [i], the back vowels by /u/. (In European Portuguese atonic final [i] is very rare, and can usually be replaced by [ə]: *táxi* 'taxi' ['taksi], ['taks(ə)].) As in English, EP [ə] is a 'neutralisation vowel' rather than an independent phoneme. In European Portuguese (and to a lesser extent in Brazilian Portuguese) the rules relating tonic and atonic systems are the source of widespread allomorphic variation in inflectional and derivational morphology: e.g. *casa* ['kazɐ] 'house', *casinha* [kɐ'ziɲɐ] 'little house', *mora* ['mɔrɐ] '(s)he lives', *morara* [mu'rarɐ] (BP [mo'rarɐ]) '(s)he had lived', *bate* ['batə] '(s)he hits', *bater* [bɐ'ter] 'to hit', *peso* ['pezu] 'weight', *pesar* [pə'zar] (BP [pe'zax]) 'to weigh'. In some accents of Brazilian Portuguese similar effects result from a rule of vowel harmony by which pretonic /e o/ are raised to /i u/ when a high vowel (usually /i/) follows, e.g. *dormir* [dux'mix] 'to sleep', *medir* [mi'dix] 'to measure'. In European Portuguese there are many 'irregular' forms in which pretonic /a o ɛ ɔ/ appear (hence their appearance in parentheses in table 11.3). Most are explicable as originating in vowel sequences or diphthongs which were not subject to atonic vowel reduction

(as diphthongs and nasals are still exempt): e.g. *pregar* 'preach' [prɛ'gar] <
preegar < *PREDICARE*; *corado* 'red, blushing' [kɔ'radu] < *coorado* <
COLORATUM; *roubar* 'steal' [ʀo'bar] (EP), [xou'bax] (BP) < OPtg.
roubar. Other cases of pretonic /ɛ ɔ a/ occur in syllables closed by plosives
e.g. *secção* [sɛk'sẽũ], *optar* [ɔp'tar] 'to choose', where Brazilian Portuguese
has open syllables.

Atonic vowels are also involved in a major feature of phrasal phonetics,
the contraction of vowels across word boundaries. This most typically takes
the form of the fusion of word-final atonic vowels or clitic articles with word-
initial vowels or clitics, and results in a wide range of diphthongs and
monophthongs: *o uso* 'the custom' /u uzu/, [u:zu]; *uma amiga* 'a friend' /umɐ
ɐ'migɐ/, [uma'migɐ]; *é o Pedro* 'it's Pedro' /ɛ u 'pedru/ [ɛu'pedru].

Like English, Portuguese is nominally a free-stress language, with stress
being nonetheless predictable in the majority of words, by a complex of
grammatical and morphophonological factors. Stress generally falls on the
penultimate syllable (or the final syllable, if it is strong, that is, closed by any
consonant except inflectional /z/ or containing as its nucleus a diphthong or
nasal vowel); in verbs (simple forms) stress falls on the final vowel of the
stem, unless this vowel is word-final, when penultimate stress is the rule. It
should be noted that the (morpho)phonological regularities of stress
placement do not always agree with the orthographic rules previously given.
European Portuguese is a clear case of a stress-timed language. Atonic
syllables are considerably shorter than tonic ones, the vowels being
centralised and raised; [ə] and [u] are frequently effaced or reduced to
secondary articulation of preceding consonants. Brazilian Portuguese has
considerable reduction of atonic final vowels, but otherwise is mainly
syllable-timed. This difference in timing is related to syllable structure.
Brazilian Portuguese tends towards a simple consonant-vowel structure,
allowing few syllable-final consonants, weakening syllable-final /l r/, and
breaking medial clusters by vowel epenthesis, e.g. *advogado* 'lawyer' EP
[ɐdvu'gadu], BP [adivo'gadu]. The epenthetic vowels are often counted as
full syllables for metrical purposes. European Portuguese allows more
syllable-final consonants (compare EP *facto* 'fact' ['faktu], BP ['fatu]; EP
secção [sɛk'sẽũ], BP *seção* [se'sẽũ]) and freely uses them in acronyms (e.g.
CUF [kuf] *Companhia União Fabril* compared to BP *PUC* ['puki] *Pontifícia
Universidade Católica*); large numbers of clusters and syllable-final
consonants result from the effacement of European Portuguese atonic [ə].

The consonant system, displayed in table 11.4, is less complex. As in
Spanish the contrast between the two 'r' phonemes is neutralised in all
except intervocalic position. Elsewhere, /r/ is always found in syllable-initial
position; in many Brazilian Portuguese accents /ʀ/ also fills syllable-final
positions, invariably filled by /r/ in European Portuguese. This is closely
connected to the phonetic realisations of /ʀ/. In European Portuguese /ʀ/ is a
strong uvular or postalveolar trill, its distribution following a well known

Table 11.4: Portuguese Consonants

	Bilabial (and Labio-dental)	Dental	Palatal (Palato-alveolar)	Velar	Uvular
Plosives	p	t		k	
	b	d		g	
Fricatives	f	s	ʃ		
	v	z	ʒ		
Nasals	m	n	ɲ		
Laterals		l	ʎ		
Vibrants		r [r]			ʀ
Semi-vowels	(w)		(j)		

Hispanic pattern of strengthening of sonorants in 'strong' syllabic contexts; in Brazilian Portuguese /ʀ/ is realised as a fricative or frictionless continuant, the range of phonetic variants including [h x χ ʁ], and thus occupies the 'weak' syllable-final contexts originally filled by /r/. In both languages syllable-final *r* is subject to further weakening; EP /r/ may be an approximant [ɹ], while BP /ʀ/ is frequently effaced.

The sibilants /s z ʃ ʒ/ are only in contrast intervocalically (inside the word) and word-initially (where /ʃ/ derives mainly from palatalised plosive + lateral clusters, e.g. *chama* 'flame' < *FLAMMA*, *chuva* 'rain' < *PLUVIA*); elsewhere they are subject to complex distributional (or morphophonemic) rules. Before a voiceless consonant or pause, only /ʃ/ (EP) or /s/ (BP) is found; before a voiced consonant only /ʒ/ (EP) or /z/ (BP); before a word-initial vowel only /z/ (EP and BP). Northern dialects of European Portuguese retain an apico-alveolar series of fricatives (the '*s* beirão') which was originally distinct from the dental and palato-alveolar series. In all except the most northerly dialects this three-way contrast has been reduced to a binary contrast, between dentals and palato-alveolars in the south and between apico-alveolars and palato-alveolars in the centre, together with the loss of the contrast between palato-alveolar affricate [tʃ] and the corresponding fricative [ʃ]. Northern dialects show their affinity to Galician by having no contrast between /b/ and /v/.

In many Brazilian Portuguese accents the dental plosives /t d/ are realised as palato-alveolar affricates [tʃ dʒ] when followed by /i/: *o tio Dino vende um lote* 'Uncle Dino sells a piece of land' [u tʃiu dʒinu vẽdʒi ũ lɔtʃi].

The semi-vowels /j w/ are marginal phonemes. In most cases [j w] result from the semi-vocalisation of atonic /i u/ in hiatus: *diário* ['djarju] (=[di'ariu]) 'daily', *suar* 'to sweat' [swar] (=[su'ar]), except for a few borrowings (e.g. *iate* 'yacht' ['jatə]) and /kw gw/ (in *quando* 'when' ['kwẽdu], *guarda* 'policeman' ['gwardɐ]) which are perhaps best analysed as labialised velars /kʷ gʷ/.

3   Morphology

The basic morphological structure of Portuguese simple verb forms is stem + tense/aspect/mood + person/number. For the present, imperfect and pluperfect indicatives, and the future subjunctive and (regular) imperfect subjunctive, the stem is made up of the root and the theme (conjugation class) vowel (first conjugation /a/; second /e/; third /i/ subject to some morphophonemic variation); the present subjunctive has the same structure with mood indicated by reversed theme vowels (first conjugation /e/, second/ third /a/); the remaining tenses employ special stem forms (basic stem + r for the future group; suppletive stem forms for irregular preterits) and idiosyncratic person-number morphs. (It is possible, but not always plausible, to devise abstract underlying forms of a uniform morphological structure for all synthetic forms). There is a nucleus of irregular verbs resisting easy incorporation in any conjugation; *ser* 'to be', *ir* 'to go', which incorporate forms from more than one Vulgar Latin verb, and *ter* 'to have', *vir* 'to come', *pôr* 'to put', (OPtg. *têer* < *TENERE*, *vīir* < *VENIRE*, *põer*, *poer* < *PONERE*) which incorporate nasal root vowels with a variety of realisations. Regular and irregular paradigms of the types described are displayed in the chart of verb forms, tentatively segmented.

Alongside the synthetic past tenses (imperfect, preterit, pluperfect) there exists a series of analytic forms, made up of the auxiliary *ter* and the past participle: perfect, pluperfect and future perfect tenses (indicative and subjunctive) are formed using the present, imperfect and future tense forms of *ter*. (*Ter* has replaced *haver* (< HABERE) not only as auxiliary but also as the verb of possession; in Brazilian Portuguese even the existential *há* 'there is', *havia* 'there was', etc. has been taken over by forms of *ter*: *tem* (present), *tinha* (imperfect).) Only in the pluperfect are the synthetic and analytic forms equivalent (though the former is rarely used in colloquial registers). The (synthetic) preterit is aspectually complex. It is a non-durative past tense, in opposition to the durative imperfect; it can also have the value of a present perfect (*o que se passa? — perdi a caneta* 'what's the matter? — I've lost my pen') because the (analytic) perfect tense represents only continued or repeated action in the near past (*tenho tomado banho todos os dias* 'I've been bathing every day'). The perfect subjunctive, however, is a genuine present perfect: *não é possível que ele tenha feito isso*, 'he cannot have done that' (lit. 'it is not possible that he has done that'). The perfect and pluperfect subjunctives have no synthetic form. There is a wide range of periphrastic verbal expressions (which traditional grammar does not clearly distinguish from verb complementation structures) expressing temporal, modal and aspectual values: *estar + -ndo* (present participle) (progressive); *ir + infinitive* (future); *haver de + infinitive* (predictive/ obligative); *ter que + infinitive* (obligative); *ficar + present participle* (resultative). In European Portuguese the constructions with the present

Portuguese Verb Forms

Regular verbs

	falar 'speak'		*meter 'put'*		*partir 'depart'*	
Present						
indicative	fal-o (a+u)	fala-mos	met-o (e+u)	mete-mos	part-o (i+u)	parti-mos
	fala-s	(fala-is)	mete-s	(mete-is)	parte-s	(partís (i+i))
	fala	fala-m	mete	mete-m	parte	parte-m
Imperfect						
indicative	fala-va	falá-vamos	meti-a	metí-amos	parti-a	partí-amos
	fala-vas	etc.	meti-as	etc.	parti-as	etc.
Pluperfect						
indicative	fala-ra	falá-ramos	mete-ra	meté-ramos	parti-ra	partí-ramos
	fala-ras	etc.	mete-ras	etc.	parti-ras	etc.
Imperfect						
subjunctive	fala-sse	falá-ssemos	mete-sse	metê-ssemos	parti-sse	partí-ssemos
	etc.		etc.		etc.	
Present						
subjunctive	fal-e (a+e)	fal-emos	met-a (e+a)	met-amos	part-a (i+a)	part-amos
	fal-es	(fal-eis)	met-as	(met-ais)	part-as	(part-ais)
	fal-e	fal-em	met-a	met-am	part-a	part-am
Future						
subjunctive	fala-r	fala-rmos	mete-r	mete-rmos	parti-r	parti-rmos
	fala-res	(fala-rdes)	mete-res	(mete-rdes)	parti-res	(parti-rdes)
	fala-r	fala-rem	mete-r	mete-rem	parti-r	parti-rem
Infinitive	falar	falar-mos	meter	meter-mos	partir	partir-mos
	falar-es	(falar-des)	meter-es	(meter-des)	partir-es	(partir-des)
	falar	falar-em	meter	meter-em	partir	partir-em
Future	falar-ei	falar-emos	meter-ei	meter-emos	partir-ei	partir-emos
	falar-ás	(falar-ais)	etc.	etc.		
	falar-á	falar-ão	etc.	etc.		
Conditional	falar-ia	falar-íamos	etc.	etc.		
Present						
participle		fala-ndo		mete-ndo		parti-ndo
Past						
participle		fala-do		meti-do		parti-do
Preterit						
(regular)	falei (a+i)	fala-mos	meti (e+i)	mete-mos	parti (i+i)	parti-mos
	fala-ste	(fala-stes)	mete-ste	(mete-stes)	parti-ste	(parti-stes)
	falou (a+u)	fala-ram	mete-u	mete-ram	parti-u	parti-ram

Irregular verbs

	estar 'be'		*dizer 'say'*		*poder 'be able'*	
Preterit	estive	estive-mos	disse	disse-mos	pude	pude-mos
	estive-ste	(estive-stes)	disse-ste	(disse-stes)	pude-ste	(pude-stes)
	esteve	estive-ram	disse	disse-ram	pôde	pude-ram
Pluperfect	estive-ra	estivé-ramos	disse-ra	dissé-ramos	pude-ra	pudé-ramos
Future						
subjunctive	estive-r	estive-rmos	disse-r	disse-rmos	pude-r	pude-rmos
	etc.		etc.		etc.	
Imperfect						
subjunctive	estive-sse	estivé-ssemos	disse-sse	dissé-ssemos	pude-sse	pudé-ssemos
	etc.		etc.		etc.	

participle are interchangeable with constructions with *a* + infinitive.

The future and conditional still retain a mark of their origin in analytic forms incorporating the auxiliary *(h)aver*; clitic pronouns are mesoclitic — affixed between stem and ending — e.g. *amar-me-á* '(s)he will love me'. (This feature is not found in Brazilian Portuguese, where either the pronoun is proclitic to the whole verb form or an alternative verb form is used.)

Two noteworthy morphological peculiarities of Portuguese are the retention of a future subjunctive form and the appearance of an infinitive inflected for person/number. (In neither is it unique in the Romance sphere: Old Castilian had the former, and Sardinian is reported to have the latter. Only in Portuguese do both appear, with a close link between them.) In regular verbs the forms are identical (though possibly of different structure, cf. the chart of verb forms). In irregular verbs the future subjunctive uses the strong preterit stem, instead of the infinitive stem, betraying its origin in the Latin future perfect indicative (*FABULARINT* > *falarem*: *DIXERINT* > *disserem*). The origin of the personal infinitive is less clear: its form derives from the Latin imperfect subjunctive (*FABULARENT* > *falarem*, *DICERENT* > *dizerem*), but its use (see section 4) is a Galician-Portuguese innovation.

Gender and number are the only two grammatical categories relevant to noun and adjective inflection. Singular number is unmarked; plural is marked by *-s* (morphophonemic /z/ realised as /s z ʃ ʒ/ according to the sibilant system) with a number of consequent stem alternations in roots with final consonants (e.g. *flor – flores* 'flower(s)'; *raiz – raizes* 'root(s)'; *sol – sóis* 'sun(s)'; *pão – pães* 'loaf, loaves'). Nouns are classified by gender as masculine or feminine, grammatical gender usually correlating with natural gender, with a few exceptions, e.g. *cônjuge* (m.) 'spouse'; *criança* (f.) 'child'. Stem-final /u/ usually corresponds to masculine gender, stem-final /a/ to feminine; other endings can correspond to either gender, e.g. *amor* (m.) 'love', *cor* (f.) 'colour'; *rapaz* (m.) 'lad', *paz* (f.) 'peace'; *estudante* (m. and f.) 'student'. Similar patterning is found in adjectives, except that the lack of a gender suffix is more frequently a mark of masculine gender, in opposition to the regular feminine suffix /a/: e.g. *inglês – inglesa* 'English', as it is in animate nouns, e.g. *professor – professora* 'teacher'. (There is a tendency to extend this pattern to nouns ending in *-e*: in popular speech the feminine counterpart of *estudante* is *estudanta*, following the pattern of *monge* (m.) 'monk' – *monja* (f.) 'nun'.)

The determiner system includes definite and indefinite articles (the former identical to weak direct object pronouns (see the chart of pronouns), the latter, *um*, f. *uma* identical in the singular to the numeral *um* '1') and a three-term demonstrative system, *este* 'this' (first person) *esse* 'that' (second person) *aquele* 'that' (third person) parallel to the adverbs *aqui*, 'here', *aí*, 'there', *ali* 'over there'. The indefinite inanimate demonstrative pronouns (*isto*, *isso*, *aquilo*) are the nearest thing to a morphological neuter.

The Portuguese pronoun systems are displayed in the chart given here. Modern Portuguese distinguishes weak (clitic) pronouns from strong pronouns: the former are used as verbal objects, the latter as subjects or prepositional objects. The pronoun system has been radically affected by the development of the address system.

Portuguese Pronouns

	Strong Pronouns		Weak Pronouns	
	Subject	Object	Dir. Obj.	Indir. Obj.
1 sg.	eu	mim (OPtg. mi)	me	me
2 sg.	tu	ti	te	te
3 sg.	ele (m.), ela (f.)	ele, ela	o (m.), a (f.)	lhe
(address)	você	você, si		
	o senhor (etc.)	o senhor		
1 pl.	nós	nós	nos	nos
(2 pl.	vós	vós	vos	vos)
3 pl.	eles, elas	eles, elas	os, as	lhes
(address)	vocês	vocês, si		
	os senhores	os senhores		

Portuguese maintains a highly structured system of address forms which has been compared to the honorific systems of oriental languages. Second person plural forms are no longer used except in a religious or highly formal ceremonial context (and accordingly appear in parentheses in the charts of verb forms and pronouns). Second person singular forms are used for familiar address in European Portuguese (and conservative Brazilian Portuguese dialects); otherwise, third person verb forms are used for all address in Brazilian Portuguese, and formal (and plural) address in European Portuguese, with the pronoun *você* or (in EP) the partly pronominal *o senhor* (m.), *a senhora* (f.). In addition, a wide range of titles can be used as address forms e.g. *o pai* 'father', *o senhor doutor* 'Doctor', *a avó* 'grandmother' etc., with third person verb forms. Accordingly, third person object pronouns *o(s)*, *a(s)*, have also acquired second person reference. Brazilian Portuguese has been resistant to this: there is a tendency for *lhe*, exclusively used as an indirect object in European Portuguese, to be used for second person functions. Alternatively, the second person object pronoun *te* is used even where the corresponding subject pronoun and verb forms are missing, or else weak forms are avoided altogether: *eu vi ele* 'I saw him', *eu vi você* 'I saw you'.

4 Syntax

The basic word order of Portuguese simplex sentences is subject–verb–object (SVO): *o gato comeu a galinha* 'the cat ate the hen'.

(All of the features of VO typology identified in the chapter on Spanish — page 254 — are equally applicable to Portuguese.) In the absence of any morphological case marking, word order indicates grammatical subjects and objects, and is little varied. The order VS is very common with intransitive verbs, especially those of temporal or locative content: *chegou o domingo* 'Sunday came'; *apareceu um homem no jardim* 'a man appeared in the garden', reflexives, *libertaram-se os escravos* 'the slaves freed themselves' (or 'the slaves were freed'), and in sentences with heavy subject clauses, *entraram dois homens gordos e um rapaz loiro* 'two fat men and a fair-haired boy came in'. This is closely related to the principle of thematic organisation which specifies that new information is placed at the end of sentences for maximum prominence. Noun phrases may be dislocated for the purposes of topicalisation: *comeu a galinha, o gato* (VOS), though objects cannot be preposed without a pronoun copy (cf. the discussion in the chapters on French and Rumanian, pages 219–20 and 305): *a galinha, o gato comeu-a* (OSVPron), *a galinha, comeu-a o gato* (OVPronS). Topicalisation is more usually by varieties of cleft or pseudo-cleft constructions: *foi a galinha que o gato comeu, foi o gato que comeu a galinha* (clefting); *o que comeu a galinha foi o gato*; *o que o gato comeu foi a galinha* (normal pseudo-cleft); *o gato comeu foi a galinha* (elliptical pseudo-cleft) including the emphatic use of *é que*: *o gato é que comeu a galinha*.

Word order changes are not greatly used for other grammatical functions. Interrogation is by intonation (*o seu pai está aqui?* lit. 'your father is here?'), by tag question (*o seu pai está aqui, não é?* 'your father is here isn't he?'), or by means of *é que: é que o seu pai está aqui?* lit. 'is it (true) that your father is here?'. In non-polar questions inversion is the rule after non-pronominal interrogatives: *quando morreu o seu pai?* lit. 'when died your father', *onde mora você?* 'where live you?' (the same order being possible in non-interrogative subordinate clauses: *quando morreu o seu pai, o que é que você fez?* 'when your father died, what did you do?'); normal SVO order can still be preserved by use of the *é que* periphrasis: *quando é que o seu pai morreu?* As the interrogative pronouns *quem* 'who(m)', *o que* 'what' have no case marking, inversion is avoided and the *é que* form used in object interrogation: *o que (é que) matou a galinha?* 'what killed the hen?', *o que é que o gato matou?* 'what did the cat kill?'. Replies to yes-no questions take the form of an echo of the main verb: *(você) tem lume? — tenho (sim)* / *não tenho*, 'do you have a light?' – '(yes) I have' / 'no I have not' (the appropriate response to an *é que* question being *é* or *não é*.)

The principal means of negation is the negative particle *não* inserted before the verb (or the auxiliary, in the case of an analytic form). Multiple negation occurs with additional negative elements following the verb: when they precede it, *não* is not inserted: *não veio ninguem = ninguem veio* 'nobody came'; *não fiz nada = nada fiz* 'I did nothing'. The indefinite *algum* 'some' may be used as an emphatic negative; *não vi nenhum homem* 'I didn't see any man', *não vi homem algum* 'I didn't see any man whatsoever'. (*Nada* is rarely used as a subject, and may be used as an adverb *não gostei nada da comida* 'I didn't like the meal at all'.)

Aspectual contrasts are behind the distinction between the copular and auxiliary verbs *ser* and *estar* (see the chapter on Spanish, pages 241–2). *Ser* (< *ESSERE/SEDERE*) is used in non-progressive (stative) expressions and *estar* (< *STARE*) in progressive expressions (including its use as the auxiliary for progressive verb forms). In the majority of cases the aspectual value is expressed by (or inherent in) the context, so that the choice of verb is conditioned rather than contrastive: *o João é bombeiro* 'João is (**ser**) a fireman', *o Pedro está zangado* 'Pedro is (**estar**) angry'; *o João é um desempregado* 'João is (permanently) unemployed', *o Pedro está desempregado* 'Pedro is unemployed'; *o João é esquisito* 'João is an awkward person', *o Pedro está (sendo) esquisito (hoje)* 'Pedro is (being) awkward (today)'. For expressing location, the aspectually neutral verb *ficar* is more often used: *onde fica o Turismo?* 'where is the Tourist Office?'.

Ser functions as auxiliary for the passive construction: *a casa foi construída por J. Pimenta*, 'the house was built by J. Pimenta'. There is a good case for analysing the passive as a copula + adjective (passive participle) construction. The alternative copula can be used to form passives, *a casa está cercada por soldados* 'the house is surrounded by soldiers'. Where verbs have two forms of the past participle, e.g. *prendido*, *preso* from the verb *prender* 'to arrest', the strong form is usually used as passive participle and the weak form as an active participle. Frequently used alternatives to the passive are the reflexive passive (common in the Romance languages), *aqui alugam-se quartos* 'rooms are let here', and the impersonal construction using *se* as marker of an indefinite subject, with third person singular verb forms, *aluga-se quartos aqui* (cf. the discussion in the chapter on Spanish, page 246).

The extensive set of verb forms outlined in section 3 is rarely utilised in spoken forms of Portuguese. The present indicative is used in place of the future (*se tiver tempo, falo com você* 'if I have time I (will) talk with you'). The imperfect indicative replaces the conditional both in temporal and modal functions: *eu disse que vinha* ...'I said I would come', *eu queria perguntar*...'I would like (lit. 'wanted') to ask...'.

As in Spanish, the subjunctive mood occupies a less central position, especially in spoken registers. Its use is determined by a complex of grammatical and semantic factors, so that any attempt to define its 'meaning' must come to terms with the fact that it is rarely independently meaningful. The subjunctive is used to the exclusion of the indicative in a wide range of subordinate clauses: *se ele viesse, não o cumprimentaria* 'if he came, I would not greet him', *que os meninos bebam vodka não me aflige* 'I'm not worried about the children drinking vodka', *chamei para que ela me ajudasse* 'I called for her to help me', *grito sem que me ouçam* 'I shout without them hearing me'. The indicative only appears in subordinate clauses expressing real events: the subjunctive has thus been characterised negatively as the mood of suspension of reality. Only in a few rather recondite cases, however, does the context permit a contrast of indicative and subjunctive, so that the subjunctive form can carry all the connotations of irreality. Contrasts like *gritei de maneira que me ouviram* 'I shouted so that they heard me' vs. *gritei de maneira que me ouvissem* 'I shouted so that they should hear me' are not the stuff of normal colloquial speech. In spoken Portuguese the present subjunctive is frequently replaced by the indicative.

The most vital subjunctive form is the one whose use is most restricted, namely the future subjunctive. It is used in temporal or conditional clauses with future reference (not necessarily expressed by a main verb in the future tense): *quando vier o pai, teremos comida* (future)/ *avisa-me* (imperative)/ *vou-me embora* (present), 'when Father comes we will have some food/tell me/I'll go away'. In some registers it is the only non-past verb form used with *se* and *quando*.

One of the main functions of the personal infinitive is to circumvent problems of mood. Being a verb form marked only for person/number it is used where contrasts of tense and mood are (or can be) neutralised, but where the non-identity of the subjects of the main and subordinate clauses would otherwise require a finite verb form (and the selection of an appropriate tense/mood). Many of the preceding examples can be recast using the personal infinitive: *não me aflige os meninos beberem vodka*; *chamei para vires*; *grito sem me ouvirem*; *gritei de maneira de eles me ouvirem*. The usage of the personal infinitive (vis-à-vis the plain infinitive) cannot be precisely defined because of a tendency to use personal and impersonal infinitives indiscriminately with overt subjects, following the widespread belief that extensive use of the personal infinitive is a mark of good style. (The fact that in the first and third persons singular the forms are identical is an additional problem for description.)

Subject pronouns are duplicated by verb inflection (except in basilectal Brazilian Portuguese where there is a tendency for verbs to be invariable) and are frequently omitted, especially in the unambiguous first and second person forms. Third person forms are more ambiguous. The use of third person grammatical forms as the main form of address restricts the omission of pronouns to clear cases of anaphora or address. Otherwise, subjectless third person verbs are interpeted as having indefinite subjects *é horrível* 'it is terrible', *dizem que é proibido* 'they (people) say that it is forbidden'.

Weak object pronouns are usually enclitic to the verb in European Portuguese and proclitic in Brazilian Portuguese: *o pai deu-me um bolo* (EP), *o pai me deu um bolo* (BP) 'Father gave me a cake'. In written Brazilian Portuguese, as in European Portuguese, sentence-initial clitics are excluded, but this does not hold for spoken Brazilian Portuguese. In both varieties the clitic will invariably precede the verb if any item except a lexical subject noun phrase precedes; negatives, subordinating conjunctions, notably *que*, relative pronouns, interrogative pronouns and (in literary language) preposed adverbs all trigger clitic attraction, e.g. *não me deu o bolo* 'he did not give me the cake', *se me der o bolo* 'if he gives (fut. subj.) me the cake', *quero que me dê o bolo* 'I want him to give me the cake'.

5 Lexicon

The main body of the Portuguese lexicon is predictably of Latin origin, either by direct transmission through Vulgar Latin or as a result of borrowing at some stage of the language's history. The same Latin etymon can thus surface in several different phonetic and semantic guises: *ARTICULUM* was the source for OPtg. *artelho* 'ankle', modern *artigo* (< *artigoo*) 'article' and *artículo* 'joint'; in the fifteenth century *flor* 'flower' was reborrowed to replace the older *frol* and *chor* (< *FLOREM*).

Portuguese shows a typical Iberian conservatism of vocabulary, preserving Latin terms which French and Italian replaced: *queijo* 'cheese' < *CASEUM* (cf. Castilian *queso*, Rumanian *caş*); *uva* 'grape' (cf. Fr. *fromage*, *raisin*). Portuguese is alone in maintaining unchanged the old Christian denominations of days of the week: after *domingo* 'Sunday', first day of the week, come the weekdays numbered two to six: *segunda-feira* (< *FERIAM SECUNDAM*), *terça-feira*, *quarta-feira*, *quinta-feira*, *sexta-feira* until *sábado* ushers in the weekend. (The weekdays are often reduced to their number, *chegará na quinta* 'he will arrive on Thursday'.)

Portuguese shares the common Romance and Ibero-Romance heritage of pre-Roman Celtic and post-Roman Germanic vocabulary: *barro* 'mud', *veiga* 'plain', *manteiga* 'butter' are Celtic terms shared with Castilian; *guerra* 'war', *guardar* 'guard', *roubar* 'steal', *branco* 'white' are common Germanic items. The Arabic adstrate of the South contributed some 1,000 words to Portuguese, such as *alface* 'lettuce', *arroz* 'rice', *armazém* 'store', *azulejo* 'glazed tile', and many placenames, e.g. *Alfama*, *Algarve*.

The African element is fairly strong in Brazilian Portuguese, particularly in those areas of popular culture and belief with strong African roots: *macumba* 'voodoo ritual', *samba*, *marimba*; *cachimbo* 'pipe' has passed into common European Portuguese usage. Tupi contributes a large vocabulary of Brazilian Portuguese flora and fauna: *maracujá* 'passion-fruit', *piranha* 'piranha fish'. Contacts with the Far East contributed *chá* 'tea' (borrowed from Mandarin: English *tea* is the Min form); *mandarim* 'mandarin' from Malay *mantri* contaminated by Ptg. *mandar* 'to order'.

Portuguese makes extensive use of derivational suffixes. As well as the common stock of noun- and verb-forming suffixes derived and borrowed from Latin (e.g. *-izar* (verb-forming), *-ismo*, *-ista* (noun-forming), *-ção* (< *-TIONEM*) (nominalising)) there is a large stock of productive and semi-productive suffixes with semantic (rather than grammatical) content, frequently involving emotive as well as referential meaning. Prominent among these are diminutive and augmentative suffixes. The most productive diminutives are *-(z)inho* (feminine *-(z)inha*) and *-(z)ito* (*-(z)ita*): *pedra* 'stone', *pedrinha* 'pebble', *pedrazinha* 'small stone'; *casa* 'house', *casita* 'little house'. These diminutives have connotations of endearment or disparagement (according to situational context) which become prominent when they are applied to humans: *mulher* 'woman', *mulherinha* 'scheming woman'; *avó* 'grandmother', *avozinha* '(dear old) granny', and especially when used to modify adverbs or interjections: *adeus* 'goodbye', *adeusinho* 'bye-bye' (familiar), *devagar* 'slowly', *devagarinho* 'little by little'. Augmentative suffixes have strong pejorative overtones: *mulher* 'woman', *mulherona* 'stout woman'.

A further set of suffixes has a very wide range of meanings (including augmentatives, collectives and instrumentals) such that the suffix can only be taken as signalling the morphological link between the derived form and the base, while the precise meaning of the word is an independent lexical unit: the suffix *-ada* is identifiable in *palmada* 'slap' (*palma* 'palm of hand'); *colherada* 'spoonful' (*colher* 'spoon'); *rapaziada* '(gang of) kids' (*rapaz* 'boy'); *marmelada* 'quince conserve' (source of Eng. *marmelade*) from *marmelo* 'quince'; *noitada* 'night out' (*noite* 'night').

In those suffixes with alternative forms incorporating the augment *-z-* (e.g. *-(z)inho*), the unaugmented variant functions as an internal suffix, forming a complex stem which is stressed like simple forms, while the augmented suffix functions as an external suffix, forming compounds in which the base and the suffix both have gender and number markers (the latter being overt only when plural number is realised by stem mutations as well as suffixes, e.g. *pãozinho* 'bread roll', plural *pãezinhos*) and are both stressed. (Similar structure is found in the adverbs formed with *-mente* e.g. *novamente* [nɔvɐˈmẽtə] 'recently, newly' where the suffix is affixed to the feminine form of the adjective *novo* 'new' and the base vowel quality is preserved.) The augmented suffixes thus give a morphological transparency, which is matched by a semantic transparency: forms incorporating internal suffixes are more likely to have unpredictably restricted meanings, e.g. *folha* 'leaf, sheet of paper', *folhazinha* 'small leaf', *folhinha* 'calendar'.

Bibliography

Cámara (1972) is a synchronic and diachronic description by the principal Brazilian linguist. Among reference grammars, Cuesta and Luz (1971) Cunha and Cintra (1984) and Teyssier (1984) are reliable, the latter two with greater coverage of Brazilian Portuguese, while Mateus et al. (1983) is a modern linguistic account, mainly concerned with syntax. For phonology, Viana (1973) contains the collected articles of the great nineteenth-century phonetician, including the standard descriptions of European Portuguese; Mateus (1982) is the first and most complete generative phonological study of European Portuguese, though needing some revision to modify the excesses of abstract morphophonemics. Thomas (1969) is a thorough study of differences between written and spoken varieties of Brazilian Portuguese.

Teyssier (1982) is a concise history of the language.

References

Câmara, J. Mattoso. 1972. *The Portuguese Language*, translated by A.J. Naro. (University of Chicago Press, Chicago)

Cuesta, P. Vázquez and M. Luz. 1971. *Gramática portuguesa*, 3rd ed., 2 vols. (Gredos, Madrid)

Cunha, C.F. and Cintra L.F.L. 1984. *Nova gramática do português contemporâneo* (João Sá da Costa, Lisbon)

Mateus, M.H.M. 1982. *Aspectos da fonologia portuguesa*, 2nd ed. (INIC, Lisbon)

—— et al. 1983. *Gramática da língua portuguesa* (Almedina, Coimbra)

Teyssier, P. 1984. *Manuel de langue portugaise (Portugal-Brésil)*, 2nd ed. (Klincksieck, Paris)

—— 1982. *História da língua portuguesa* (Sá da Costa, Lisbon)

Thomas, E.W. 1969. *The Syntax of Spoken Brazilian Portuguese* (Vanderbilt University Press, Nashville)

Viana, A.R. Gonçalves. 1973. *Estudos de fonética portuguesa* (Imprensa Nacional, Lisbon)

12 Italian

Nigel Vincent

1 Introduction

'Italy', in the words of Count Metternich, 'is a geographical expression'. He might with equal truth have added that Italian is a linguistic expression. While there is now, almost a century and a quarter after political unification, a fair measure of agreement on the grammar and the morphology and, to a lesser extent, on the phonology and lexis of the standard language as used in the written and spoken media and as taught in schools and to foreigners, it is still far from being the case that Italians speak only, or in many instances even principally, Italian. It is appropriate, therefore, to begin this chapter with a general survey in two dimensions, historical and geographical.

Historically, Italian is clearly one of the modern-day descendants of Latin, but the line of descent is not altogether direct. With the dismemberment of the Roman Empire, the spoken Latin of everyday usage — what has come to be called Vulgar Latin — gradually split into a series of regional vernaculars, whose boundaries are identifiable by bundles of isoglosses in a linguistic atlas. The most important of these, which separates Western (French, Spanish, Portuguese etc.) from Eastern (Italian, Rumanian etc.) Romance, cuts right across peninsular Italy to form the so-called La Spezia-Rimini line. Dialects to the north of the line are divisible in turn into Gallo-Italian (Piedmontese, Ligurian, Lombard and Emilian) and Venetian, with the latter sharing some of the properties of other northern dialects and some of the properties of Tuscan. Typical northern traits include the loss of final vowels (*pan* vs. st. It. *pane* < Lat. *PANEM* 'bread'), often with devoicing of the resultant final obstruents and velarisation of a nasal; lenition or even loss of intervocalic stops (*-ado* or *-ao* vs. *-ato* < *-ATUM* 'past participle suffix'); palatalisation of *-kt-* clusters (*lač* vs. *latte* < *LACTEM* 'milk'), and of *Cl-* clusters (*čatsa* vs. *piazza* < *PLATEAM* 'square'); development of front rounded vowels (*čöf* vs. *piove* < *PLUIT* 'it rains'), frequent use of subject pronouns, usually derived from the Latin accusative; loss of the synthetic preterit in favour of the present perfect periphrasis; a two-term deictic system; etc. These dialects, then, are often structurally closer to French and Occitan than to the dialects south of the line. The latter may in turn be further subdivided into Tuscan, Central (Umbrian and the dialects of northern Lazio and the Marches) and Southern dialects (Abruzzese, Neapolitan, Pugliese, Calabrese, Sicilian). Relevant Southern features here are NC > NN (*monno* vs. *mondo* < *MUNDUM* 'world', *piommo* vs. *piombo* < *PLUMBUM* 'lead'); characteristic patterns of both tonic and atonic vowel development; use of postposed possessives (*figliomo* vs. *mio figlio* 'my son'); extensive use of the preterit; etc. A number of features mark off Tuscan from its neighbours: absence of metaphony (umlaut); -V*ri*V- > -V*i*V- (*IANUARIUM* > *gennaio*, cf. *Gennaro*, patron saint of Naples); fricativisation of intervocalic voiceless stops — the so-called *gorgia toscana* 'Tuscan throat' — which yields pronunciations such as [la harta] *la carta* 'the paper', [kaɸo] *kapo* 'head', [lo θiro] *lo tiro* 'I pull it'; etc.

Such divisions reflect both geographical and administrative boundaries. The La Spezia-Rimini line corresponds very closely both to the Appennine mountains and to the southern limit of the Archbishopric of Milan. The line between Central and Southern dialects approximates to the boundary between the Lombard Kingdom of Italy and the Norman Kingdom of Sicily, and to a point where the Appennines broaden out to form a kind of mountain barrier between the two parts of the peninsula. The earliest texts are similarly regional in nature. The first in which undisputed vernacular material occurs is the Placito Capuano of 960, a Latin document reporting the legal proceedings relating to the ownership of a piece of land, in the middle of which an oath sworn by the witnesses is recorded verbatim: *sao ko kelle terre, per kelle fini que ki contene, trenta anni le possette parte Sancti Benedicti* 'I know that those lands, within those boundaries which are here stated, thirty years the party of Saint Benedict owned them'. The textual evidence gradually increases, and by the thirteenth century it is clear that there are well-rooted literary traditions in a number of centres up and down the land. These are touched on briefly by the Florentine Dante (1265–1321) in a celebrated section of this treatise *De Vulgari Eloquentia*, but it is the poetic supremacy of his Divine Comedy, rapidly followed in the same city by the achievements of Petrarch (1304–74) and Boccaccio (1313–75), which ensured that literary, and thus linguistic, pre-eminence should go to Tuscan.

There ensued a centuries-long debate about the language of literature — *la questione della lingua* 'the language question', with Tuscan being kept in the forefront as a result of the theoretical writings of the influential Venetian (!) Pietro Bembo (1470–1547), especially his *Prose della volgar lingua* (1525). His ideas were adopted by the members of the Accademia della Crusca, founded in Florence in 1582–3, which produced its first dictionary in 1612 and which still survives as a centre for research into the Italian language. Meanwhile, although the affairs of day-to-day existence were largely conducted in dialect, the sociopolitical dimension of the question increased in importance in the eighteenth and nineteenth centuries, assuming a particular urgency after unification in 1861. The new government appointed the author Alessandro Manzoni (1785–1873) — himself born in Milan but yet another enthusiastic non-native advocate of Florentine usage — to head a commission, which in due course recommended Florentine as the linguistic standard to be adopted in the new national school system. This suggestion was not without its critics, notably the great Italian comparative philologist, Graziadio Ascoli (1829–1907), and a number of the specific recommendations were hopelessly impractical, but in any case the core of literary usage was so thoroughly Tuscan that the language taught in schools was bound to be similar. Education was, of course, crucial since the history of standardisation is essentially the history of increased literacy. On the most conservative estimate only 2½ per cent of the population would have been literate in any meaningful sense of the word in 1861, although a more recent and more generous estimate would go as high as 12½ per cent. The figure had increased to about 91½ per cent by 1961, the centenary of unification and the thousandth anniversary of the first text. Even so, there is no guarantee that those who can use Italian do so as their normal daily means of communication, and it was only in 1982 that opinion polls recorded a figure of more than 50 per cent of those interviewed claiming that their first language was the standard rather than a dialect. Yet the opposition language/dialect greatly oversimplifies matters. For most speakers it is a question of ranging themselves at some point of a continuum from standard Italian through regional Italian and regional dialect to the local dialect, as circumstances and other participants seem to warrant. Note too that the term dialect means something rather different when used of the more or less homogeneous means of spoken communication in an isolated rural community and when used to refer to something such as Milanese or Venetian, both of which have fully-fledged literary and administrative traditions of their own, and hence a good deal of internal social stratification.

Another significant factor in promoting a national language was conscription, first because it brought together people from different regions, and second because the army is statutorily required to provide education equivalent to three years of primary school to anyone who enters the service illiterate. Indeed, it is out of the analysis of letters written by soldiers in the First World War that some scholars have been led to recognise *italiano popolare* 'popular Italian' as a kind of national substandard, a language which is neither the literary norm nor yet a dialect tied to a particular town or region. Among the features which characterise it are: the extension of *gli* 'to him' to replace *le* 'to her' and *loro* 'to them', and, relatedly, of *suo* 'his/her' to include 'their'; a reduction in the use of the subjunctive in complement clauses, where it is replaced by the indicative, and in conditional apodoses, where the imperfect subjunctive is replaced by the conditional, and the pluperfect subjunctive is replaced by either the conditional perfect or the imperfect indicative (thus standard *se fosse venuto, mi avrebbe aiutato* ('if he had come he would have helped me') becomes either *se sarebbe venuto, mi avrebbe aiutato* or *se veniva, mi aiutava*, the latter having an imperfect indicative in the protasis too; the use of *che* 'that' as a general marker of subordination; plural instead of singular verbs after nouns like *la gente* 'people'. Some of these uses — e.g. *gli* for *loro*, the reduction in the use of the subjunctive and the use of the imperfect in irrealis conditionals — have also begun to penetrate upwards into educated colloquial usage, and it is likely that the media, another powerful force for linguistic unification, will spread other emergent patterns in due course. Industrialisation, too, has had its effect in redrawing the linguistic boundaries, both social and geographical.

In addition to the standard language, the dialects and the claimed existence of *italiano popolare*, there are no less than eleven other languages spoken within the peninsula and having, according to one recent but probably rather high estimate, a total of nearly 2¾ million speakers. Of these, more than two million represent speakers of other Romance languages: Catalan, French, Friulian, Ladin, Occitan and Sardinian. The remaining languages are: Albanian, German, Greek, Serbo-Croat and Slovene. Amidst this heterogeneity, the Italian national and regional constitutions recognise the rights of four linguistic minorities: French speakers in the autonomous region of the Valle d'Aosta (approx. 75,000), German speakers in the province of Bolzano (approx. 225,000), Slovenian speakers in the provinces of Trieste and Gorizia (approx. 100,000), Ladin speakers in the province of Bolzano (approx. 30,000). Yet French (and Occitan — approx. 200,000) and German speakers outside the stated areas are not protected in the same way. Nor paradoxically are the ½ million speakers of Friulian, very closely related to Ladin, the two in turn being sub-branches of the Rhaeto-Romance group. The recognised linguistic minorities are, not surprisingly, in areas where the borders of the Italian state(s) have oscillated historically. In contrast, the southern part of the peninsula is peppered with individual villages which preserve linguistically the traces of that region's turbulent past. It is here that we find Italy's 100,000 Albanian, 20,000 Greek and 3,500 Serbo-Croat speakers, as well as a number of communities whose northern dialects reflect the presence of mediaeval settlers and mercenaries.

Sardinia too contains a few Ligurian-speaking villages and 15,000 Catalan speakers in the port of Alghero as evidence of former colonisation. More importantly, the island has almost 1,000,000 speakers of Sardinian, a separate Romance language which has suffered undue neglect ever since Dante said of the inhabitants that they imitated Latin *tanquam simie homines* 'as monkeys do men'. What he was referring to was the way in which Sardinian, both in structure and vocabulary, reveals itself to be the most conservative of the Romance vernaculars. Thus, we find a vowel system with no mergers apart from the loss of Latin phonemic vowel length;

an absence of palatalisation of *k* and *g*; preservation of final *s* (with important morphological consequences); a definite article *su*, *sa*, etc. which derives from Latin IPSE rather than ILLE. Old Sardinian also maintained direct reflexes of the Latin pluperfect indicative and imperfect subjunctive, and the language is one of the few not to retain a future periphrasis from Latin infinitive + *HABEO*, using instead of reflex of Latin *DEBERE* 'to have to', e.g. *des essere* 'you will be'. On the lexical side we have *petere* 'to ask', *imbennere* 'to find' (cf. Lat. *INVENIRE*), *domo/domu* 'house', *albu* 'white', etc. (contrast It. *chiedere*, *trovare*, *casa*, *bianco*).

The presence of Italian outside the boundaries of the modern Italian state is due to two rather different types of circumstance. First, it may be spoken in areas either geographically continuous with or at some time part of Italy, as in the independent Republic of San Marino (population 13,000), enclosed within the region of Emilia-Romagna, and in Canton Ticino (population approx. 250,000), the entirely italophone part of Switzerland. Both have local dialects, Romagnolo in San Marino and Lombard in Ticino, as well as the standard language of education and administration. Elsewhere, the historical continuity is reflected at the level of dialect, but with the superimposition of a different standard language. Thus, in Corsica (population approx. 200,000) the dialects are either Tuscan (following partial colonisation from Pisa in the eleventh century) or Sardinian in type, but the official language has since 1769 been French. The same situation obtains for those Italian dialects spoken in the areas of Istria and Dalmatia now part of the state of Yugoslavia.

The second circumstance arises when Italian, or more often Italian dialects, has been carried overseas, mainly to the New World. In the USA the 3.9 million Italian speakers constitute the second largest linguistic minority (after Hispano-Americans). They are concentrated for the most part either in New York, where they are mainly of southern origin and where a kind of southern Italian dialectal koine has emerged, and in the San Francisco Bay area, where northern and central Italians predominate, and where the peninsular standard has had more influence. Italian language media include a number of newspapers, radio stations and television programmes. The current signs of a reawakening of interest in their linguistic heritage amongst Italo-Americans are paralleled in Canada and Australia, each with about half a million Italian speakers according to official figures. There were also in excess of three million emigrés to South America, mostly to Argentina, and this has led, on the River Plate, to the development of a contact language with Spanish known as 'cocoliche'. If Italian in the Americas and Australia had its origins in the language of an underprivileged and often uneducated immigrant class, in Africa — specifically Ethiopia and Somalia and until recently Libya — Italian survives as a typical relic of a colonial situation. Ethiopia also has the only documented instance of an Italian-based pidgin, used not only between

Europeans and local inhabitants but also between speakers of mutually unintelligible indigenous languages. The position of Italian in Malta is similarly due to penetration at a higher rather than a lower social level. Research is only now beginning into the linguistic consequences of the post-war migration of, again mainly southern, Italian labour as 'Gastarbeiter' in Switzerland and West Germany. Finally, two curiosities are the discovery by a group of Italian ethnomusicologists in 1973 in the village of Štivor in northern Bosnia of a community of 470 speakers of a dialect from the northern Italian province of Trento, and the case of a group of emigrés from two coastal villages near Bari in Puglia, who settled in Kerch in the Crimea in the 1860s and whose dialectophone descendants have only died out in the last decade.

2 Phonology

One of the consequences of the chequered and fragmented linguistic and political history outlined in the previous section is that at the phonetic and phonological level there has been even less uniformity of usage than at other levels. The conventional starting point for any treatment of Italian phonology is the speech of educated Florentines. Incidentally, most of the letters of the Italian alphabet correspond closely to the IPA value of that symbol, but the following exceptions should be noted: -gl- = /ʎ/, -gn- = /ɲ/, sc(i) = /ʃ/, s = /s/ or /z/ (see below on the status of /z/), z = /ts/ or /dz/, c, g = /k, g/ before a, o and u, and /tʃ, dʒ/ before i and e. The digraphs ch, gh represent /k, g/ before i, e, and ci, gi represent /tʃ, dʒ/ before a, o and u. No orthographic distinction is made between /e/ and /ɛ/ or between /o/ and /ɔ/, although in stressed final position /e/ is represented normally by é and /ɛ/ by è. Stress is marked only when final, usually by a grave accent (except on /e/); other accent marks used in this chapter are for linguistic explicitness and are not part of the orthography.

Table 12.1 sets out the consonant phonemes usually recognised in the Florentine system. Some comments on points of detail are in order. First, note that for the vast majority of speakers [s] and [z] do not contrast: in initial position before a vowel all speakers have [s], including after an internal boundary as in ri[s]aputo 'well known' — cf. [s]aputo 'known'; [s]taccato[s]i 'having detached oneself' — cf. [s]taccare 'to detach' and [s]i '3rd pers. refl. pron.'. Preconsonantally the sibilant takes on the value for voicing of the following segment. Intervocalically, when no boundary is present, northern speakers have only [z] and southern speakers only [s]. However, in parts of Tuscany, including Florence, it is possible to find minimal pairs: chie[s]e 'he asked' vs. chie[z]e 'churches'; fu[s]o 'spindle' vs. fu[z]o 'melted'. The opposition between /ts/ and /dz/ is also somewhat shaky. In initial position, although both are found in standard pronunciation — /ts/ in zio 'uncle', zucchero 'sugar', and /dz/ in zona 'zone', zero 'zero', there is

Table 12.1: Italian Consonant Phonemes

	Bilabial	Labio-dental	Dental	Alveolar	Palato-alveolar	Palatal	Velar
Stop	p b		t d				k g
Affricate				ts dz	tʃ dʒ		
Fricative		f v		s (z)	ʃ		
Nasal	m			n		ɲ	
Lateral				l		ʎ	
Trill				r			

an increasing tendency due to northern influence for /dz/ to be used in all words. Medially, the two sounds continue to exist side by side, and a few genuine minimal pairs can be found, e.g. *ra*[tts]*a* 'race' vs. *ra*[ddz]*a* 'ray fish'. /ts, dz/ share with /ʃ, ʎ, ɲ/ the property of always occurring long intervocalically, an environment in which for all other consonants there is an opposition between short and long (or single and double): e.g. *copia* 'copy' vs. *coppia* 'couple'; *beve* 'he drinks' vs. *bevve* 'he drank'; *grato* 'grateful' vs. *gratto* 'I scratch'; *vano* 'vain' vs. *vanno* 'they go'; *serata* 'evening' vs. *serrata* 'lock-out'; etc.

The vowel system is displayed in table 12.2. /i, u/ have allophones [j, w] in non-nuclear position in the syllable: *più* ['pju] 'more', *può* ['pwɔ] 'he can'.

Table 12.2: The Vowels of Italian

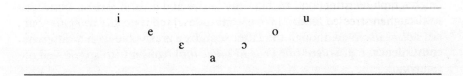

The oppositions /e~ɛ/ and /o~ɔ/ are neutralised outside stress, but even allowing for this their status is problematic, since, although most speakers have the four sounds, the lexical classes and phonological rules which govern their distribution vary widely.

Another important type of neutralisation in Italian phonology is that which affects nasals before consonants and ensures that the whole cluster is homorganic. This is only reflected orthographically in the case of bilabials — hence *campo* 'field', *impossibile* 'impossible' etc., but labio-dentals, dentals etc. are always spelt *n*C: *inferno* [iɱfɛrno] 'hell', *indocile* [iṇdɔtʃile] 'unmanageable', *incauto* [iŋkauto] 'incautious'. The same process also operates across word boundaries in a fully productive manner: *con Paolo* 'with Paul' [..mp..] vs. *con Carlo* 'with Charles' [. .ŋk. .], etc. A morphophonemic process of more limited applicability is the synchronic residue of Romance palatalisation, which is revealed in alternations such as *amico* 'friend (m. sg.)' with *c* = [k] and *amici* 'friends (m. pl.)' with *c* = [tʃ], and *vin*[k]*o* 'I win' but *vin*[tʃ]*i* 'you win'. Note that the *e* which marks feminine plural (< Latin *AE*) does not trigger this process nor does plural *-i* in most nouns, and hence the spellings *amiche* 'friends (f.)', *buchi* 'holes'. *e* as a thematic vowel (see p. 279), a direct reflex of the Latin thematic *e*, does; thus *vincere* 'to win', *vince* 'he wins', *vinceva* 'he was winning', all with [tʃ]. The same patterning is also found with the voiced congeners of [k, tʃ], namely [g, dʒ], in the paradigm of a verb such as *volgere* 'to turn'. A further synchronic residue is observable in what are traditionally called *dittonghi mobili* 'mobile diphthongs', as in *buono* 'good' but *bontà* 'goodness', *viene* 'he comes' but *venire* 'to come'. They are the result of a historical process causing the diphthongisation of Latin *Ĕ*, *Ŏ* in stressed, open syllables. The pattern is, however, being gradually eroded away by analogical generalisations in both directions, e.g. *suono* 'I play' had a past participle *sonato* but one now more commonly finds *suonato*, whereas *provo* 'I try' has replaced an earlier *pruovo*.

Italian words may consist of one or more syllables and are subject to a general constraint that they be vowel-final. Exceptions to this are certain loanwords (*sport*, *boom*, *slip*, *camion* etc.), a handful of Latinisms (*lapis* 'pencil', *ribes* 'blackcurrant') and an increasing number of acronyms (*Agip*, *Fiat*). Some grammatical words — e.g. the masculine singular of the definite article *il*, the prepositions *in*, *con*, *per*, the negative particle *non* — have final consonants, but the rules of the syntax will never allow them to appear in sentence-final position. Similarly, there is a vowel truncation rule which deletes final /e/ after /l, r, n/, but only between words in a close syntactic nexus: *volere dire* 'to mean' (lit. 'to want to say') may become *voler dire* but not *volere dir*, even though the latter sequence is possible with a different constituency, e.g. *volere (dir bene di qualcuno)* 'to want (to speak well of someone)'.

Words may begin with either a consonant or a vowel. A word-initial single consonant may be any of those given in table 12.1, though initial /ɲ/ is rare (*gnomo* 'gnome', *gnocco* 'a kind of dumpling' and a few others) and initial /ʎ/ non-existent in lexical words. However, since the form *gli* /ʎi/ occurs both as the masculine plural of the definite article before vowel-initial nouns (*gli amici* 'the friends') and as the masculine singular dative unstressed pronoun (*gli dissi* 'I said to him'), /ʎ/ in utterance-initial position is very common.

Apart from in borrowings and in technical terms, two-member initial clusters are limited to the following types:

(i) /p b t d k g f/ + r
(ii) /p b k g f/ + l
(iii) s + /p b t d k g tʃ dʒ f v l r m n/

(Note that /s/ is realised as [z] before voiced consonants — hence not just [zb] in *sbagliare* 'to make a mistake' or [zdʒ] in *sgelo* 'thaw', but also [zl] in *slitta* 'sledge', [zn] in *snello* 'slim', etc. It should also be noted that purists do not admit [stʃ], but it is regularly heard in words where there is a clear morphemic boundary, e.g. *scentrato* 'off centre'.)

Three-member clusters can only consist of /s/ plus any of the possible two-member clusters under (i) or (ii). A non-final syllable may end in /l, r, s/ or a nasal. Examples of such clusters can be created productively by juxtaposing forms such as *il*, *per*, *bis*, and *in* with a noun or an adjɛ ɩive, although only a subset of the possible clusters generated in this fashion are attested internally in existing lexical items. An intervocalic cluster may also consist of a geminate consonant, with a syllable boundary between the two: *piop-po* 'poplar', *gof-fo* 'clumsy', *cad-de* 'he fell', *bel-lo* 'beautiful'. Indeed, the evidence of syllable division is one of the principal reasons for treating them as geminates rather than long consonants. Note that in such groups, if the first member is a stop or affricate, it is unreleased, hence such transcriptions as [pat-tso] for *pazzo* 'mad', [fat-tʃa] for *faccia* 'face'.

Tautosyllabic vowel sequences all conform to the pattern of a nuclear vowel followed or preceded, or both, by [j] or [w]: *piano* 'flat' [pjano], *sai* [saj] 'you know'. Otherwise, vowel sequences involve a hiatus between two syllables: *teatro* 'theatre', *poeta* 'poet'. We have both in *laurea* 'university degree' ['law-re-a].

Primary or lexical stress is not predictable on phonological grounds alone, hence such minimal pairs as *princìpi* (plural of *princìpio* 'principle') and *prìncipi* (plural of *prìncipe* 'prince'), or *càpito* 'I turn up', *capìto* 'understood', *capitò* 'he turned up'. There are, however, a number of morphological cues to stress. A third person singular preterit verb form is always final-stressed, while all second person plural forms are penultimately stressed. Such patterns are best described by distinguishing in the morphology between stress-neutral and stress-attracting suffixes. The lexical bases which receive these suffixes may be either penultimately or antepenultimately stressed: *cànta* 'sing' vs. *fàbbrica* 'make'. A stress-neutral suffix attached to the latter produces stress four syllables from the end: *fàbbricano* 'they make'. If clitics are attached post-verbally, stress may be made to appear even farther from the end of the word: *fàbbricalo* 'make it', *fàbbricamelo* 'make it for me', *fàbbricamicelo* 'make it for me there'. Underived words, however, can only have stress on one of the last three syllables: *ànima* 'soul', *lèttera* 'letter', *perìodo* 'period'; *radìce* 'root', *divìno* 'divine', *profòndo* 'deep'; *virtù* 'virtue', *caffè* 'coffee', *velleità* 'wish'. Final-stressed words are either loanwords, often from French, or the results of a diachronic truncation: *virtù* < Old Italian *virtude* < Lat. *VIRTUTEM*. Secondary stress is not in general contrastive, but is assigned rhythmically in such a way as to ensure that (a) the first syllable, if possible, is stressed; (b) there are never more than two unstressed syllables in sequence; (c) there are never two adjacent stressed syllables. Apparent minimal pairs have, nonetheless, been adduced such as: ˌauto-reattòre 'auto-reactor' vs. auˌtore-attòre 'author-actor' (contrasting position of secondary stress); procùra 'he procures' vs. ˌpró-cùra 'for-care' (two stresses vs. one).

Stress interacts with vowel length and the distribution of geminate consonants. Vowels are always short if not primarily stressed, or if followed by a consonant in the same syllable. They are long, therefore, in stressed, open syllables: ànima ['aː-ni-ma], lèttera ['lɛt-te-ra], divino [di-'viː-no], profondo [pro-'fon-do]. Final vowels are always short, so that if stressed and in close nexus with a following word, they ought to create a violation of our previously stated principle. Such a situation, however, is avoided by so-called raddoppiamento sintattico 'syntactic doubling', whereby the initial consonant of the following word is geminated: parlò chiaro 'he spoke clearly' [par-'lɔk-'kjaː-ro]. The double consonant here also seems to act as sufficient barrier to permit two adjacent main stresses. It has recently been pointed out that in the north, where the doubling effect is not found, the first of the two stresses is retracted instead. This doubling also takes place after a number of words which have lost the final consonant they had in Latin: tre 'three' < Lat. TRES, a 'to' < Lat. AD, though again this effect is only found south of the La Spezia-Rimini line. Raddoppiamento, then, is typical of central and southern speech, and the failure of northern speakers to adopt it mirrors its absence from their own dialects, and explains their tendency to produce only those geminates which the orthography indicates. Indeed, it can be argued more generally that there is emerging in Italy a kind of standardised spelling pronunciation based on the interaction of northern phonetic habits and an orthography which reflects the Florentine origin of the standard language.

3 Morphology

In morphology Italian exhibits a typically Indo-European separation of verbal and nominal inflection, the latter also encompassing pronouns, articles and adjectives.

3.1 The Noun

Nouns inflect for gender — masculine and feminine — and number — singular and plural — according to the following patterns:

Singular	Plural	Gender	
-o	-i	m.	libro 'book'; exception mano f. 'hand' (< Lat. MANUS f.)
-a	-e	f.	casa 'house', donna 'woman'
-e	-i	m. or f.	monte m. 'mountain', mente f. 'mind'
-a	-i	m.	problema 'problem' and other words of Greek (sistema, programma, etc.) or Latin (artista, poeta, etc.) origin.

Such a system of plural by vowel alternation rather than by suffixing of *-s* is one of the features which marks Italian off from Western Romance languages such as French, Spanish and Portuguese. Nouns which in the singular end in *-i*, e.g. *crisi* 'crisis', in stressed vowels, e.g. *città* 'town', *tribù*, 'tribe' and in consonants, e.g. *sport*, *camion* 'lorry', are unchanged in the plural. A small class of nouns — e.g. *dito* 'finger', *uovo* 'egg', *lenzuolo* 'sheet' — distinguish between a collective and a non-collective plural: *osso* 'bone', *le ossa* 'bones (together, as in a skeleton)', *gli ossi* 'bones (scattered)'. The synchronically unusual *-a* in the collective plural is a residue of the Latin neuter plural. Note that articles and adjectives going with such nouns are masculine in the singular and feminine in the plural.

Adjectives fall into two principal classes, having either four forms: *buono*, *-i*, *-a*, *-e* 'good' or two: *felice*, *-i* 'happy' (with a few like *rosa* 'pink' that are uninflected). The four-form pattern also shows up in the unstressed pronoun system: *lo/la/li/le*. In Old Italian these were also the forms of the definite article, but the modern language has a more irregular pattern: m. sg. *lo* only before /ʃ/, *s* + consonant, and certain other groups, *il* elsewhere; m. pl. *gli* corresponding to *lo* and *i* to *il*; f. sg. *la*; f. pl. *le*. In the case of both articles and pronouns the vowels of the singular forms commonly delete before an initial vowel in the following word.

3.2 The Verb

The chart of verb forms represents the paradigmatic structure of three typical regular verbs exemplifying the three traditional conjugations, each of which is marked by a characteristic thematic vowel, *a*, *e* or *i*. The chart is organised in such a way as to bring out the four classes of elements in the verbal structure — stem, thematic vowel, tense/aspect/mood markers and person/number markers — whose linear relations are schematically displayed as: STEM + TV + (T/A/M) + P/N. The use of curly brackets seeks to highlight some of the patterns of overlap between the traditional conjugations (at the expense of some non-traditional segmentations), and the numbers here and throughout this section refer to the six grammatical persons, three singular and three plural.

However, a classification of this kind is inadequate in two apparently contradictory respects. On the one hand, it does not allow for a number of further classes which seem to be necessary, for instance to distinguish between two types of *e*-verb according to whether they have stem or ending stress in the infinitive: *crèdere* 'to believe' and *vedère* 'to see' do not rhyme. Historically, in fact, the stem-stressed verbs have in some cases even undergone loss of the theme vowel in the infinitive with attendant consonant deletion or assimilation: Lat. *PONERE*, *DICERE*, *BIBERE* > It. *porre*, *dire*, *bere*. We also need to recognise two types of *i*-verb, one with the stem augment *-isc-* in persons 1/2/3/6 of the present and one without: *capisco* 'I understand' but *servo* 'I serve', and *partisco* 'I divide' as against *parto* 'I

Finite Forms of Italian Regular Verbs

	1	2	3	4	5	6
Present indicative	{cant / tem / sent} -o	-i	canta / {tem~sent} -e	{cant / tem / sent} -iamo	{canta / teme / senti} -te	canta-no / {tem~sent} -ono
Imperfect	{canta / teme / senti} -v -o	-v -i	-va -ø	-mo	-te	-no
Present subjunctive	{cant / tem / sent} -i / -a	-i / -a	-i / -a	{cant / tem / sent} -iamo	-iate	{cant / tem / sent} {-i / -a} -no
Preterit	{canta / teme / senti} -i	-sti	cantò / temè / sentì -e	{canta / teme / senti} -mmo	-ste	-rono
Past subjunctive	{canta / teme / senti} -ss -i	-i	-e	-imo	-ste	-ss -ero
Future	{canter / temer / sentir} -ò	-ai	-à	-emo	-ete	-anno
Conditional	-ei	-esti	-ebbe	-emmo	-este	-ebbero

leave'. These latter two verbs have a number of homophonous forms elsewhere in the paradigm: *partiamo*, *partire*, *partivo*, etc. On the other hand, a basically tripartite classification fails to capture the generalisation that *e*- and *i*-verbs are a good deal more similar to each other morphologically than either is to *a*-verbs (which constitutes the main open class for new coinings and borrowings). This relationship is particularly noticeable in forms 3/6 of the present indicative, and in the reversal effect whereby the present subjunctive vowel is -*i*- for *a*-verbs and -*a*- for *i/e*-verbs. Hence a better representation of Italian conjugational structure might be as in figure 12.1.

Figure 12.1: A Model of Italian Conjugation Structure

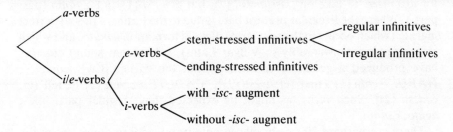

In addition to these finite forms, each verb has a past participle (*cant-a-to*, *tem-u-to*, *sent-i-to*) and a gerund (*cant-a-ndo*, *tem/sent-e-ndo*), which are used both independently and in a number of verbal periphrases (see section 4 for details of these and of the grammar and meaning of the various finite forms). The present participle formation (-*a/e/ie-nte*) is of more equivocal status since the possibilities for its use are grammatically very circumscribed.

As in any language, there are a number of verbs which fail to conform to the schemata established above, but it would be neither possible nor helpful in the present context to list all such idiosyncrasies. It is, however, of interest to note the ways in which patterns of irregularity intersect with the regular verb paradigms. For example, no verb has any irregularity in the imperfect (except *essere* 'to be', which seems to stand outside all such generalisations), and, again excluding *essere*, only *dare* 'to give' and *stare* 'to be, stand' have irregular past subjunctives (*dessi*, *stessi* for the expected **dassi*, **stassi*). Discrepancies in the future and the conditional (and no verb is irregular in one without having the same irregularity in the other) are due either to the verb already having an exceptional infinitive — *porrò*, *dirò*, *farò* — or to the historical effects of syncope on the periphrases from which they derive: *VENIRE + HABEO > verrò*, *VOLERE + HABUIT > vorrebbe* etc.

By far the largest number of exceptions, however, are to be found in three parts of the paradigm: the present (indicative and subjunctive), the preterit and the past participle. Of these, the latter two are closely related: very few verbs have an irregular preterit and a regular past participle, and even fewer have an irregular past participle and a regular preterit. The characteristic perturbation in both cases is a reduced stem, which appears in persons 1/3/6 and the participle: e.g. for *prendere* 'to take', we have *preso* (past part.) and *presi* (1), *prese* (3), *presero* (6) vs. *prendesti* (2), *prendemmo* (4), *prendeste* (5). The patterns are best accounted for by assuming a base form with no theme vowel (hence no stress on the ending) but in its place a sigmatic preterit marker (ultimately of Indo-European origin but considerably generalised in its applicability in Vulgar Latin). This form, *prend-s-i* etc., can then be converted into the surface forms by a set of phonotactically motivated rules of consonant cluster reduction and assimilation. The sigmatic form in the participle (e.g. *preso*) is less common, but the regular suffix *-to* will trigger the same effects if not preceded by a theme vowel: e.g. for *assumere* 'to take on', *assumesti* (2), but *assunsi* (1) and *assunto* (past part.). Where the irregular preterit base is due to the Latin *-u-* [u~w] perfect marker (which occurs in the regular participial formation *temuto*, and which also extended considerably in Vulgar Latin), subsequent sound changes have produced a geminate consonant from the earlier [Cw] sequence: *HABUI > ebbi* (1) 'I had' (cf. *avesti* (2)), **CADUIT > cadde* (3) 'he fell' (cf. *cadesti* (2)). Such verbs, as might be expected, have regular participles: *avuto*, *caduto*.

There are perhaps 200 verbs whose only irregular formations are in the preterit and the past participle, almost without exception members of the class of *e*-verbs. On the other hand, there are less than 50 which are irregular in the present, and they are spread throughout the conjugation classes. We cannot characterise all the patterns here, but once again it is worth noting how the incidence of stress was one of the principal determining factors for these alternations in the diachronic perspective (we have added the accent marks for clarity here, although the normal orthography does not use them). Thus, we find *uscire* 'to go out' has *èsco* (1), *èsci* (2), *èsce* (3), *èscono* (6), and *èsca(no)* (subj.), but *usciàmo* (4), *uscìte* (5) and *uscìvo* (imperf.), *uscìi* (pret.) etc. For *avère* 'to have', we find (and the *h* here is purely orthographic) *hò* (1), *hài* (2), *hà* (3), *hànno* (6), but *àbbia(no)* (subj.), *abbiàmo* (4) and *avète* (5) *avèvo* (imperf.). Notice too how a verb like *andàre* 'to go' may be suppletive in the stem-stressed forms: *vàdo* (1), *vài* (2), *và* (3), *vànno* (6), *vàda(no)* (subj.), but almost entirely regular elsewhere: *andiàmo* (4), *andàte* (5), *andàvo* (imper.), *andài* (pret.) *andàto* (past part.) — but note the minor irregularity in the future and conditional: *andrò*, *andrei* etc. This is also a good example of the way in which a verb may be irregular to the point of suppletion in the present and show few or no ill effects elsewhere in its paradigm.

A number of other exceptional formations involve the morphophonemic processes of diphthongisation and palatalisation discussed in section 2.

Thus, *sedère* 'to sit': *sièdo* (1), *sièdi* (2), *sième* (3), *sièdono* (6) vs. *sediàmo* (4), *sedète* (5); *morìre* 'to die': *muòio* (1), *muòri* (2), *muòre* (3) *muòiono* (6) vs. *moriàmo* (4), *morìte* (5) exhibit clearly the effects of the so-called *dittonghi mobili*. Palatalisation is to be seen in *dico* 'I say' where *c* = [k] vs. *dici* 'you say' where *c* = [tʃ].

The conjugation of *essere* is as follows: Present 1 *sono*, 2 *sei*, 3 *è*, 4 *siamo*, 5 *siete*, 6 *sono*. Imperfect 1 *ero*, 2 *eri*, 3 *era*, 4 *eravamo*, 5 *eravate*, 6 *erano*. Present subjunctive 1, 2, 3 *sia*, 4 *siamo*, 5 *siate*, 6 *siano*. Preterite 1 *fui*, 2 *fosti*, 3 *fu*, 4 *fummo*, 5 *foste*, 6 *furono*. Past subjunctive 1, 2 *fossi*, 3 *fosse*, 4 *fossimo*, 5 *foste*, 6 *fossero*. Future 1 *sarò*, etc. Conditional 1 *sarei*, etc. Present participle *essendo*. Past participle *stato*.

Finally with regard to the verb, mention must be made of the system of address. Like many languages, Standard Italian distinguishes between a familiar and a polite style. The former is expressed through the use of the second person singular forms *tu*, *ti*, *tuo* and the imperatives *canta*, *temi*, *senti* (note again the formal overlap of the *i/e*-verbs). The latter requires the deferential pronoun *Lei*, which is grammatically third person singular and is therefore accompanied by clitic *si* and possessive *Suo*. In lieu of the imperative the present subjunctives *canti*, *tema*, *senta* are used. The use of *Lei* goes back to Late Latin, and became widespread due to Spanish influence in the Renaissance. Until quite recently the same distinction could be regularly maintained in the plural with *voi*, *vi*, *vostro* for familiar usage and *Loro* (lit. 'they') as the polite form. The latter is becoming increasingly rare and is now only used in the most formal circumstances — otherwise *voi* serves both functions. *Voi* as a polite singular, on the other hand, is still common in parts of southern Italy, particularly amongst older speakers.

3.3 Suffixes

Italian has an unusually rich range of affective suffixes relating to the size and the speaker's (dis)approval of the object in question. Thus, from *ragazzo* 'boy', we have *ragazzino*, *ragazzetto*, *ragazzuccio* 'little boy', *ragazzone* 'big lad', *ragazzaccio* 'nasty boy, lout', *ragazzotto* 'sturdy lad'. The chief analytical problem is that not all suffixes combine with all nouns, yet no clear rules are discernible for predicting the possible combinations: *-ello* is a diminutive but **ragazzello* cannot be used for 'little boy'. Sometimes too a noun plus suffix has acquired independent status as a lexical item: *pane* 'bread', *panetto* 'small loaf', *panino* 'bread roll' and *panettone* (etymologically containing two contradictory suffixes *-ett-* 'small' and *-one* 'large') refers to a special kind of fruit cake eaten at Christmas. This process is reminiscent of the way certain items of Italian vocabulary are derived from Latin diminutives — e.g. Lat. *AURIS* 'ear', but It. *orecchio* < *AURICU-LUM*. These suffixes are most commonly attached to nouns, but can also be used with other categories: adjectives — *facile* 'easy', *facilino* 'quite easy', *caro* 'dear', *caruccio* 'quite expensive' (but note *carino* 'pretty'); adverbs —

bene 'well', *benone* 'very well', *benino* 'quite well'; verbs — *dormire* 'to sleep', *dormicchiare* 'to snooze', *sputare* 'to spit', *sputacchiare* 'to splutter'.

---

4 Syntax

We shall concentrate here on aspects which either seem to typify Italian as opposed to other languages, or which have aroused interest amongst syntactic theorists, the two naturally not being unconnected.

4.1 The Nominal Group

Nouns in Italian may be accompanied by articles, definite or indefinite, numerals and quantifiers, demonstratives, possessives and adjectives. Of these, demonstratives and articles have parallel distribution and may be united in a single class of determiners. It is worth noting that only a two-term deictic opposition survives in modern usage, *questo* 'this' vs. *quello* 'that'. The often cited third term, *codesto* 'that by you' (cf. Spanish *ese*), is now limited to Tuscany, and is archaic even there. Possessives behave distributionally more like adjectives than determiners and, except in the case of nouns for close members of the family, never occur unaccompanied by an article or demonstrative: *mio zio* 'my uncle', *la mia macchina* 'my car', *un tuo cugino* 'one of your cousins' (lit. 'one your cousin'), *questi suoi libri* 'these books of his' (lit. 'these his books'). Quantifiers such as *alcuni* 'some', *parecchi* 'several', *pochi* 'few' may also precede the possessive: *parecchi nostri amici* 'several (of) our friends'. This class includes some words which in a different sense follow the noun as independent adjectives: *certe persone* 'a certain number of people' and *certi miei colleghi* 'some of my colleagues', but *persone certe* 'people who are certain', *diversi tuoi professori* 'several (of) your teachers' but *due caratteri diversi* 'two different characters'.

Examples such as these in turn raise one of the central issues of the syntax of the noun phrase in Italian: the function and position of the adjective. It is clear that there are independent pre- and post-nominal positions: *una breve visita* 'a short visit', *una visita turistica* 'a sightseeing visit', *una breve visita turistica* 'a short sightseeing visit'. Three questions arise: are there any constraints on how the two positions may be filled? Can a systematic meaning be attached to each position? Is one position dominant, such that it would make sense to say that Italian had noun-adjective order, say, in the way that typological cataloguing seems to require? Note first that although there is a small class of adjectives where a change of position corresponds to a quite discernible change of meaning, cf. the above examples and others: *un semplice soldato* 'a mere soldier' vs. *un soldato semplice* 'a private soldier', *numerose famiglie* 'many families' vs. *famiglie numerose* 'large families', most adjectives can occur in either position. Nor is length a decisive factor: the heptasyllabic *interessantissimo* 'very interesting' frequently precedes the noun in the speech of the more gushing interviewers and journalists! What distinguishes the two positions rather is the function of the adjective: if it is used in a distinguishing or restrictive sense, it follows; if the use is descriptive, rhetorical, emphatic or metaphorical, it precedes. *Pietre preziose* are 'precious stones' as opposed to ordinary ones, but one would refer to *i preziosi gioielli della contessa* 'the countess's precious jewels', where the value is taken for granted. Similarly, courtesy would require one to thank a friend for *il suo prezioso aiuto* 'his valuable help'. Hence, whether an adjective precedes or follows will depend on how easily its inherent meaning lends itself to one or other or both types of use. Adjectives of place and nationality are normally contrastive and therefore tend to follow: *i turisti inglesi* 'English tourists', *l'industria settentrionale* 'northern industry'. To distinguish Florentine literature from that of Rome or Venice one would talk of *la letteratura fiorentina*, but since everybody knows that 'The Divine Comedy' is by a Florentine, the adjective has a more rhetorical function and precedes in *la fiorentina Divina Commedia*. A postposed adjective would suggest Dante had a rival elsewhere!

We are, then, required to say that Italian has two equal but different adjective positions. The opposition having thus been grammaticalised, the typological parameter of adjective-noun order in such a language is rendered irrelevant.

4.2   The Verbal Group

We begin with some remarks on the meaning and use of the verbal forms set out in section 3, paying particular attention to mood, aspect, valency and voice.

The subjunctive mood is clearly identifiable both in terms of its morphological marking and its grammatical and semantic role. The latter emerges perhaps most evidently in pairs of the following kind: *Pietro vuole sposare una ragazza che ha* (indic.)/*abbia* (subj.) *studiato l'astrofisica* 'Peter wants to marry a girl who has (indic./subj.) studied astrophysics'. The indicative verb tells us there is a particular girl, one of whose attributes is that she has studied astrophysics; with the subjunctive we know only what Peter considers to be the desirable quality in a future wife, but not whether such a person exists. The function of the subjunctive, then, is to deny, put in doubt or suspend judgement on the question of the independent existence of the state of affairs referred to in the relevant proposition. Hence it is mandatory in the complement clauses of verbs which express attitudes towards possible, desired, feared etc. situations rather than assert that such situations actually obtain: *voglio/temo/spero che il treno sia* (subj.) *in ritardo* 'I want/fear/hope that the train is late'. With other verbs a contrast emerges: *se pensi che ha* (indic.) *soltanto dodici anni* 'if you think (= bear in mind) that he is only twelve' vs. *se pensi che abbia* (subj.) *soltanto dodici anni* 'if you think (= believe) that he is only twelve'. Likewise, the subjunctive is also appropriate after a negated verb: *capisco perché l'ha* (indic.) *fatto* 'I understand why he did it' but *non capisco perché l'abbia* (subj.) *fatto* 'I don't understand why he did it'; and after conjunctions that introduce an element of doubt or futurity: *prima che il gallo canti* (subj.) 'before the cock crows', *benché Giorgio sia* (subj.) *partito* 'although George has left', *lavora sodo perché lo si paga* (indic.) *bene* 'he works hard because they pay him well' vs. *lavora sodo perché lo si paghi* (subj.) *bene* 'he works so that they will pay him well'. Similar factors are involved in the use of the subjunctive with *se* in conditionals, but space prohibits even a cursory treatment of this complex area. Nor indeed has it been possible to survey all other uses of the subjunctive, but the foregoing should suffice to demonstrate that the category is semantically productive in the modern language. We may note finally that the subjunctive is less widely used in some colloquial registers, including so-called *italiano popolare*, and in some regions. On the other hand, in Sicilian and some other southern dialects where a conditional verb form has not emerged historically, the subjunctive has an even wider range of functions.

The central issue regarding aspect is the relation between the imperfect (*cantava*), the preterit (*cantò*), and the present perfect (*ha cantato*) (see section 3 for a full list of forms). The conventional view is that the first of these expresses an incomplete or a habitual action — 'he was singing' or 'he used to sing' — while the latter two refer instead to single completed actions. The difference between them in turn involves the recentness and the relevance of the events described to the current situation. Hence, in native grammatical terminology, *ha cantato* is dubbed the *passato prossimo* 'near past' and *cantò* the *passato remoto* 'distant past'. However, the imperfect is often found, particularly with verbs of mental state — *non sapeva cosa dirmi ieri* 'he didn't know what to say to me yesterday' — and in journalism and less formal writing where traditional usage might require one of the other two forms. Hence it has recently been argued that the imperfect is the unmarked past tense, deriving its precise value from the context, whereas both the perfect and the preterit have an inbuilt aspectual value. One advantage of this view is that it more easily accommodates the common, though by no means obligatory, progressive periphrasis *stava cantando* (cf. the present *sta cantando* 'he is singing'). In the case of the preterit and the present perfect, the issue is further complicated by the fact that spoken usage varies considerably up and down the peninsula. Northern speakers rarely utter the preterit, so the perfect subsumes both functions (cf. the discussion of French on pp. 215–16), while southern speakers often use only the preterit, reserving the reflex of the Latin HABEO + past participle periphrasis for a sense more like that in English 'I have the letter written'. The traditional distinction lives on in Central Italian (including Florentine and Roman) speech, but northern influence is strong even here and may eventually come to predominate.

One question not treated in the preceding discussion concerns the choice of auxiliary verb in constructing the perfect periphrasis. There are four possibilities: (a) some verbs always take *avere* 'to have' — *ho pensato* 'I have thought', *ha viaggiato* 'he has travelled', *abbiamo letto il libro* 'we have read the book'; (b) others always take *essere* 'to be' — *è uscita* 'she has (lit. is) gone out', *è morto* 'he has died'; (c) some take either auxiliary, but with more or less discernible differences of sense — *hanno aumentato il prezzo* 'they have increased the price', but *è aumentato il prezzo* 'the price has gone up'; *ha corso* 'he has run (= done some running)' vs. *è corso* 'he has run (= gone by running)'; (d) a very small number of verbs, particularly weather verbs, take either auxiliary with no difference of meaning — *è/ha piovuto* 'it has rained'. Crucial to an understanding of the process of auxiliary selection is an appreciation of the semantic relation between the subject and the verb. If the subject is the agent or experiencer (for a verb of mental state), then the auxiliary is *avere*; hence type (a) regardless of whether the verb is transitive or intransitive. If the subject is more neutrally involved in the activity or state defined by the verb — in traditional terms a patient, then the auxiliary is *essere*. Such verbs will by definition be intransitive — *andare* 'to go', *salire* 'to go up' (contrast *arrampicare* 'to climb' with *avere*), *morire* 'to die', *ingiallire* 'to turn yellow, wither'. If a verb can take two different types of subject — *aumentare* 'to increase', *correre* 'to run', *crescere* 'to grow', *procedere* 'to proceed' (with patient subject and *essere*) vs. *procedere* 'to behave' (with agent subject and *avere*), then it can take both auxiliaries. If the distinction between agent and patient is not valid for certain types of activity/state, then either auxiliary may be chosen indifferently — *piovere* 'to rain', *vivere* 'to live'. A final point to note here is that if the infinitive following a modal verb would independently take *essere*, then by a process of auxiliary attraction the modal itself, which would normally take *avere*, may take *essere*: either *ho dovuto uscire* or *sono dovuto uscire* 'I had to go out'.

Patient as subject not only identifies *essere*-taking verbs but is of course the time-honoured way of characterising the passive voice, and it is not coincidental that *essere* is also the auxiliary in passive constructions — *gli svedesi vinceranno la battaglia* 'the Swedes will win the battle', *la battaglia sarà vinta dagli svedesi* 'the battle will be won by the Swedes'. In fact, if we regard the subject of *essere* as itself being a patient (i.e. having a neutral role as the person/thing/etc. about which predications are made), then we can achieve a unified explanation of why (a) it takes *essere* as its own auxiliary; (b) it is the active auxiliary of the appropriate subclass of intransitives and the passive auxiliary of all transitives; (c) the other two verbs which enter into passive periphrases are also patient subject verbs. The first of these is *venire* 'to come', which may be regularly substituted for *essere* to distinguish an 'action' from a 'state' passive. Thus, *la bandiera veniva/era issata all'alba* 'the flag was hoisted at dawn', but only *essere* in *in quel periodo la bandiera era issata per tutta la giornata* 'at that time the flag was hoisted (i.e. remained aloft) all day'. The second is *andare* 'to go', which combines with the past participle to express the meaning 'must be V-ed', e.g. *questo problema va risolto subito* 'this problem must be solved at once'. One interesting morphosyntactic restriction is that neither *andare* nor *venire* can occur in these functions in their compound forms, whereas *essere* of course can. Curiously, *andare* does occur as a compound auxiliary in *la casa è andata distrutta* 'the house was (lit. is gone) destroyed', but then there is no sense of obligation and the construction is limited to verbs of loss and destruction.

Essere is also the auxiliary for all reflexives: *Maria si è criticata* 'Mary criticised herself'. Since a reflexive is only a transitive verb where agent and patient happen to be identical, one might expect to find *avere*, as indeed one sometimes does in Old Italian and in some, notably southern, dialects. However, another very frequent use of the reflexive construction is as a kind of passive. Thus, in *le finestre si sono rotte* 'the windows got broken' (lit. 'broke themselves') the sentence is formally reflexive but the subject is patient rather than agent (contrast the non-reflexive in *Giorgio ha rotto le finestre* 'George has broken the windows'). Furthermore, since patient-subject verbs and constructions in Italian frequently have post-verbal subjects (see below), we also have the possibility of *si sono rotte le finestre*, a structure which is susceptible to an alternative analysis, viz.: *si* (su.) V *le finestre* (obj.). Evidence that such a reanalysis has taken place comes from the fact that, colloquially at least, such sentences often have a singular verb: *si parla diverse lingue in quel negozio* 'several languages are spoken in that shop', and from the extension of the construction to intransitive verbs of all kinds: *si parte domani* 'one is leaving tomorrow', *si dorme bene in campagna* 'one sleeps well in the country'. Indeed, it is even possible to have the so-called impersonal *si* in combination with a reflexive verb: *ci si lava(no) le mani prima di mangiare* 'one washes one's hands before eating' (where *ci* is a morphophonemic variant of *si* before *si*).

These two *si*s (impersonal and reflexive) take different positions in clitic sequences: *lo si dice* 'one says it', *se lo dice* 'he says it to himself' (*se* for *si* before *lo* is a consequence of a regular morphophonemic adjustment), and hence with both present we find *ce lo si dice* 'one says it to oneself'. Notice too that if *si* in impersonal constructions is taken as subject, then examples like *si rilegano libri* 'one binds books' have to be construed as involving object agreement on the verb. Subject *si* is also unusual in that in predicative constructions while the verb is singular, following adjectives, participles and predicate nominals are plural: *si è ricchi* (m. pl.) 'one is rich', *si è usciti* 'one has gone out', *quando si è attrici* (f. pl.) 'when one is an actress'. Compare in this regard the plural with other impersonal verbs; *bisogna essere sicuri* 'it is necessary to be safe'. On the other hand if impersonal *si* is found with a verb which normally requires *avere*, the auxiliary becomes *essere*, as with reflexive *si*, but the past participle does not agree; *si è partiti* 'one has left' vs. *si è detto* 'one has said'.

As the preceding examples have shown, one feature of the Italian verbal group is the possible presence of clitic pronouns, whose categories and basic order are set out in the following table:

1st sg.	3rd sg. dative	2nd pl.	2nd sg.	1st pl.	Refl.	3rd sg./pl. accusative	Imp.	Partitive
mi	gli (m.) le (f.)	vi	ti	ci	si	lo (m. sg.) la (f. sg.) li (m. pl.) le (f. pl.)	si	ne

Note, however, that combinations of *ne* and the third person accusative forms are rare, but when they do occur, *ne* precedes: *ne la ringrazierò* 'I'll thank her for it'. In clitic clusters there is a morphophonemic adjustment of /i/ to /e/ before sonorants. Hence *me lo*, *te ne*, etc. Standard too in such clusters is the replacement of *le* 'to her' by its masculine congener *gli*, so that *gliene* translates as 'of it to him/her'. *Gli* for *le* in isolation is becoming increasingly common, but is still regarded as non-standard. Much more acceptable is *gli* for *loro*, the latter being anomalous in occurring post-verbally: *ho detto loro* 'I said to them'. Likewise, *suo* 'his/her' is extending ground to replace *loro* 'their' in the possessive. In *italiano popolare* and in many dialects the whole system *gli/le/loro* merges with the neuter *ci*, which thus becomes an omni-purpose indirect object clitic. Note that, whereas in modern Italian, unlike in earlier stages of the language, the past participle in the perfect does not normally agree with its object, clitic objects do trigger agreement: *ho trovato Maria* 'I found Mary' vs. *l'ho trovata* 'I found her'. *Ne* also causes agreement (contrast French *en*): *ne hanno mangiati tre* 'they have eaten three of them'.

A further complication arises in the rules for placement of the clitics or clitic clusters. The general principle is that they precede finite verb forms but follow non-finite ones: *me lo darà* 'he will give it to me', *deve darmelo* 'he must give it to me', *avendomelo dato* 'having given it to me'. Certain verbs, however, which take a dependent infinitive allow the latter's clitics to 'climb' and attach to the governing verb: *vuole parlarti* or *ti vuole parlare* 'he wants to speak to you', *volendo parlarti* or *volendoti parlare* 'wanting to speak to you'. Such clitic-climbing is obligatory with the causative *fare*: *me lo farà dare* 'he will have it given to me', even if this formally converts the causative into a reflexive and provokes an attendant auxiliary change: *si è fatto dare un aumento di stipendio* 'he got himself given a rise'. Furthermore, if the clitics climb (and in a cluster they must all move or none), then the phenomenon of auxiliary attraction mentioned earlier becomes obligatory: *non ho/sono potuto andarci* 'I couldn't go there' but only *non ci sono potuto andare*.

4.3   The Sentence
We conclude with some brief remarks relating to overall sentence structure,

beginning with the question of word order. Assuming a traditional division of the sentence, we find both the orders subject-predicate and predicate-subject attested: *Pietro fumava una sigaretta* 'Peter was smoking a cigarette', *è arrivato il treno* 'the train has arrived'. To understand what distinguishes the two orders we need to add the concepts of theme (= what is being talked about) and rheme (= what is said about the theme), and the ordering principle 'theme precedes rheme'. In the unmarked case, a subject which identifies the agent-experiencer of the activity/state expressed by the verb will constitute the theme, and will accordingly come first. The rheme will consist of the verb plus, where appropriate, an object whose interpretation follows directly from the meaning of the verb, what we have earlier called a patient. Thus, S V (O) is a natural order for sentences with any transitive and some intransitive verbs in Italian. If we extend the notion object to include the sentential complements of verbs of saying, thinking etc. and also allow for indirect objects and prepositional objects, we can say that the rheme consists of the verb followed by its complement(s). If, however, the subject is rhematic with respect to its verb, as it will be if its semantic role is patient, then it will normally follow. Hence the characteristic post-verbal subjects in the *essere*-taking constructions discussed above: *verrà Giorgio* 'George will come' (taking the 'mover' as patient with a verb of motion), *domani saranno riaperti il porto e l'aeroporto* 'tomorrow the docks and the airport will be reopened', *si svolgeva il dibattito* 'the debate took place'. In appropriate circumstances and with suitable intonation the basic patterns can be reversed, but that does not alter the fact that the position of the subject in Italian is not fixed but depends on its semantic relation to the verb. Moving the object from its post-verbal position is, by contrast, less easy and normally requires a pronominal copy: *quel libro, non lo legge nessuno* 'that book nobody reads'. Similarly, it is rare and decidedly rhetorical for the subject to be interposed between verb and object. Adverbs and subcategorised adjectives on the other hand regularly separate verb and noun: *parla bene l'italiano* 'he speaks Italian well', *il professore ha fatto felici gli studenti* 'the teacher made the students happy'.

The possibility of post-verbal subjects with *essere*-taking verbs and the general optionality of pronominal subjects have been linked in the recent generative literature with another detail of Italian syntax, namely the fact that sentences such as *chi credi che verrà?* 'who do you think will come?' are grammatical (contrast the ungrammaticality of the literal English rendering *who do you think that will come?*). If such an example was derived from an intermediate structure like *credi che verrà chi*, then Italian and English both agree in being able to extract from a post-verbal position (cf. English *who do you think that Fred saw?*), but differ in what may occupy such a position. The preverbal subject is treated throughout as a dummy category licensed by the putatively universal Empty Category Principle (ECP), and languages like Italian have thus become known as pro-drop or null-subject languages. In addition to the properties already mentioned, such languages are claimed to have rightward agreement of the copula (*sono io* 'it's me'), so-called 'long' *wh*-movement of the subject (*l'uomo che mi domando chi abbia visto* 'the man that I wonder who he saw' cf. the ungrammaticality of the English translation) and the possibility of an empty resumptive pronoun in embedded clauses (*ecco la ragazza che mi domando chi crede che vincerà* vs. English '*there's the girl that I wonder who believes that she will win'). Unfortunately, there is not room here to examine in more detail these fascinating insights into Italian syntax.

Bibliography

Lepschy and Lepschy (1988) is an excellent general manual which is refreshingly up-to-date and unprescriptive in its approach to points of grammar. Muljačić (1982) is a very handy one-volume bibliographical guide.

Among descriptive grammars, Fogarasi (1983) is a comprehensive, if rather conservative, reference grammar; nine of a projected twelve volumes of Brunet (1978–) have so far appeared, an exhaustive compilation of modern usage with relatively little grammatical analysis or commentary; Schwarze (1983–) — projected to be in three volumes, of which two have appeared — provides a series of excellent and detailed studies of modern usage. Chapallaz (1979) is a good traditional account of the phonetics of the standard language; Muljačić (1972) is a useful survey of work done on Italian phonology from a variety of theoretical viewpoints; Bertinetto (1981) is an excellent study of the suprasegmental phonology of Italian. Rizzi (1982) is a collection of articles by one of the leading figures in the investigation of Italian in the light of recent generative theory.

Rohlfs (1966–9) is a classic historical grammar with very generous attention to the dialects; Tekavčić (1980) is an indispensable manual combining factual detail on the history of the language and largely structuralist methods of analysis and interpretation. Migliorini and Griffith (1984) is the best external history of the language.

De Mauro (1983) is the standard account of the changes in the linguistic situation in the peninsula since unification in 1861. Two volumes out of four have so far appeared of Cortelazzo (1969–), one of Italy's leading dialectologists; unfortunately, we still await the main descriptive volume. Albano Leoni (1979) is a wide-ranging set of conference proceedings which give a clear picture of the current linguistic complexity of the peninsula.

Acknowledgement

I am grateful to Joe Cremona, Martin Harris, Giulio Lepschy, Žarko Muljačić and Donna Jo Napoli for their comments on an earlier version of this chapter.

References

Albano Leoni, F. (ed.) 1979. *I dialetti e le lingue delle minoranze di fronte all'italiano*, 2 vols. (Bulzoni, Rome)
Bertinetto, P. M. 1981. *Strutture prosodiche dell'italiano* (Accademia della Crusca, Florence)

—— 1986. *Tempo aspetto e azione nel verbo italiano*: il sistema dell'indicativo (Accademia della Crusca, Florence)

Berruto, G. 1987. *Sociolinguistica dell'italiano contemporaneo* (La Nuova Italia Scientifica, Rome)

Brunet, J. 1978–. *Grammaire critique de l'italien*, 9 vols. (Université de Paris VII, Vincennes)

Burzio, L. 1986. *Italian Syntax* (Reidel, Dordrecht)

Chapallaz, M. 1979. *The Pronunciation of Italian* (Bell and Hyman, London)

Cortelazzo, M. 1969–. *Avviamento alla dialettologia italiana*, 4 vols. (Pacini, Pisa)

De Mauro, T. 1983. *Storia linguistica dell'Italia unita*, 8th ed. (Laterza, Bari)

Fogarasi, M. 1983. *Grammatica italiana del Novecento*, 2nd ed. (Bulzoni, Rome)

Lepschy, A. L. and G. C. 1988. *The Italian Language Today*, 2nd ed. (Hutchinson, London; Italian edition: *La lingua italiana*, Bompiani, Milan, 1981)

Migliorini, B. and T. G. Griffith. 1984. *The Italian Language*, 2nd ed. (Faber and Faber, London; translation and adaptation of B. Migliorini, *Storia della lingua italiana*, 5th ed., Sansoni, Florence, 1978)

Muljačić, Ž. 1972. *Fonologia della lingua italiana* (Il Mulino, Bologna)

—— 1982. *Introduzione allo studio della lingua italiana*, 2nd ed. (Einaudi, Turin)

Rizzi, L. 1982. *Issues in Italian Syntax* (Foris Publications, Dordrecht)

Rohlfs, G. 1966–9. *Grammatica storica della lingua italiana e dei suoi dialetti*, 3 vols. (Einaudi, Turin; translation and revision of *Historische Grammatik der italienischen Sprache und ihrer Mundarten*, 3 vols., Francke, Bern, 1949–54)

Schwarze, C. (ed.) 1983–. *Bausteine für eine italienische Grammatik*, 2 vols. (Gunter Narr, Tübingen)

Tekavčić, P. 1980. *Grammatica storica della lingua italiana*, 2nd ed., 3 vols (il Mulino, Bologna)

13 Rumanian

Graham Mallinson

1 Introduction

The relative neglect of Balkan Romance by linguists in favour of the Western Romance languages is attributable in part to the geographical isolation of the country where most Rumanian speakers live. The Socialist Republic of Rumania has a population of well over 20 million, of which some 90 per cent have Rumanian as their first language. There are some speakers of Rumanian in the border areas of neighbouring countries, including over 2½ million speakers of the Moldavian dialect in the Moldavian Soviet Socialist Republic (formed from areas annexed by the Soviet Union during the course of the twentieth century). This failure of linguistic and national borders to coincide reflects the fluid political history of the Balkans. Rumania itself is host to several minority language groups, including German-speaking Saxons (over half a million) and Hungarians (at least one million and perhaps over two million). Both these minorities are concentrated in Transylvania, the presence of so many Hungarian speakers resulting from the acquisition by Rumania of the province from Hungary at the end of the First World War.

A number of features at all linguistic levels serve to highlight the differences between Rumanian and the Western Romance languages, many being attributable to its membership of the Balkan Sprachbund. In each of the four main sections which follow, reference will be made to such features in describing the divergence of Rumanian from mainstream Romance evolution.

The form of Balkan Romance to be discussed is Daco-Rumanian, so named because it is associated with the Roman province of Dacia, on the north bank of the lower Danube (part of the Empire for a relatively short period from the first decade of the second century to AD 271). The wider term Balkan Romance includes three other varieties: Arumanian, spoken in northern Greece, Albania and southern Yugoslavia; Megleno-Rumanian, spoken in a small area to the north of Salonika; Istro-Rumanian, spoken in the Istrian peninsula of western Yugoslavia. All four varieties are deemed to have a common origin, with the initial split dating from the second half of the first millennium. Because the earliest extant Rumanian texts date from as

late as the beginning of the sixteenth century, the history of Balkan
Romance involves a great deal of speculation (compare the dates of early
extant texts for Old French).

Besides the question of dating the breakup of Common Rumanian, other
controversies include the problem of whether the original centre of
dispersion was north of the Danube in Dacia, or south of the Danube in
Moesia; also, whether Arumanian, Megleno- and Istro-Rumanian are
dialects of Rumanian or constitute separate languages. In the latter case,
one can say that the four varieties are very closely related but that the three
minor varieties have each been heavily influenced by the national languages
of the countries in which they are spoken. Mutual intelligibility between
Daco-Rumanian and Arumanian would be at a very low level on first contact
but would increase dramatically in a very short period. However, in this area
of Europe it is extra-linguistic factors such as nationalism that are more
pertinent to the perception of linguistic identity (compare the discussion in
the chapter on Serbo-Croat about the relations between Serbian and
Croatian). In the case of Balkan Romance I will leave this sensitive question
open, since I will be concentrating on Daco-Rumanian (henceforth simply
'Rumanian'), the national language of Rumania.

Map 13.1

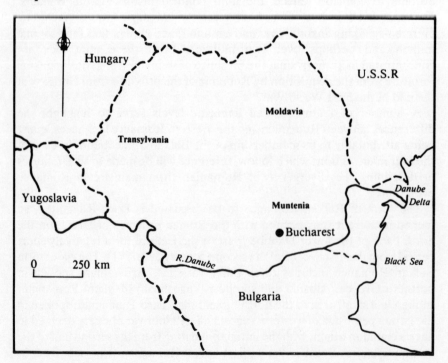

Finally, Rumanian is also spoken by a considerable number of immigrants to the New World. Even in Australia there are enough Rumanian speakers to warrant a weekly one-hour programme in both Sydney and Melbourne on ethnic radio, though not enough to have given rise to discernible, institutionalised features of Antipodean Rumanian such as one finds in the larger Italian and Greek communities.

Rumanian proper can be divided into several (sub)dialects. The major forms are Moldavian and Muntenian, spoken in the former principalities of Moldavia (northeast) and Muntenia, or Wallachia (southeast), though several other minor dialects can be discerned within present-day Rumania. These are spoken in the north and west of the country, including much of Transylvania. Despite its political history in relative isolation from the two principalities, it is, however, inaccurate to speak of a Transylvanian dialect as such. Both Moldavian and Muntenian cover parts of Transylvania, and there is, as one would expect, overlap between dialects spoken in adjoining regions.

During the course of the nineteenth century, Muntenian was gradually adopted as the national and literary standard, the final step in this process being the union of the principalities in 1859 as an independent state with Bucharest as the capital. The use of Muntenian as the point of entry into Rumanian of Western Romance vocabulary and morphosyntactic innovations over the last 150 years (a period marked at times by what has been described as 'Gallomania') has served to set this dialect off from the others. However, communication and education in modern society have allowed many innovations to filter through and dilute other dialects, including the original spoken Muntenian on which the national standard is based and which was itself left behind by the developing literary language.

Even so, spoken Muntenian was already somewhat more innovative than the other spoken dialects. For example, it showed a greater tendency to fricativise voiced dental plosives before front vowels: Lat. $D\bar{I}CO > zic$ /zik/ 'say', compared with Moldavian affrication in /dzɨk/. Muntenian has also gone further towards complete elimination of the high, back vowel /u/ from Latin words ending in $-o(+C)$ and $-u(+C)$: $AM\bar{A}RU- > amar$ /amar/ 'bitter', compared with Moldavian /amar^u/. Both /dz/ for /z/, and final /u/ are also typical of Arumanian.

The 'reromancing' tendency of the last two centuries has gone some way towards countering the specifically Balkan character of earlier Rumanian development. Such Western Romance influence was by no means accidental, however, and groups of writers during the late eighteenth and early to mid-nineteenth centuries made positive efforts to import French- and Italian-based vocabulary to fill gaps in the native lexical stock. The Transylvanian School made the first real attempt to replace the Cyrillic orthography with a Roman one, as well as engineering Rumanian vocabulary to substitute Romance for Slavonic. However, they had only limited success in each case, their main fault being an overzealous desire to hark back to the Latin origins of the language. Their etymological spelling system (that rendered /tʃintʃ/ 'five' by *quinqui* — compare the modern spelling *cinci*) could serve only to confuse the populace whom they wished to educate.

It was the mid-nineteenth-century writers of Muntenia, with their less extreme attitude towards renewing the language, who had the greatest influence in resurrecting its Romance character. Yet one should point out also that political developments helped to bring to prominence the dialect in which they wrote. One can only speculate on the likelihood of some Transylvanian-based form of Rumanian having come to the fore had that province not been isolated from the two principalities. And if some other dialect had been adopted as the national standard, one might also ask how great a difference there would have been today between the other three varieties of Balkan Romance and a national language of Rumania based on a more conservative form.

2   Orthography and Phonology

The Cyrillic writing system was introduced into the area occupied by the modern language when Old Church Slavonic became the medium for religious texts. Given the absence of contact between Rumanian and Latin in medieval times (compare the situation in the west of Romania), it was inevitable that when Rumanian words and names of places and people began to appear sporadically in Old Church Slavonic texts from the thirteenth century, they too should be written in Cyrillic script. The first extant texts wholly in Rumanian merely followed this tradition so that a non-Roman alphabet was dominant for the greater part of the four and a half centuries since then.

Two clear factors led to dissatisfaction with this system and thus to the eventual adoption of a Roman script: the practical problem of adapting the Cyrillic system to match phonemes found in Rumanian and those introduced with Romance loans from the west; and the growing feelings of national awareness that increased as contact with the Western Romance languages grew and brought widespread recognition of linguistic ties with Latin, Italian and French. Nevertheless, it was not until the union of the principalities in the late nineteenth century that the Cyrillic system was finally replaced by a Roman one. During the last century, various attempts were made to adapt the Roman alphabet to Rumanian, including systems of a transitional nature with a largely Roman alphabet but with Cyrillic symbols for those sounds not represented orthographically in Western Romance — for example, the middle vowel /ə/ was represented by ъ and the post-alveolar fricative /ʃ/ by ш.

Today Rumanian is written and printed in a wholly Romanised alphabet with three diacritics, though the Moldavian spoken in the Moldavian SSR is represented by an adaptation of the Russian Cyrillic alphabet. Because it is a relatively short time since the current Rumanian alphabet was instituted, there has been little opportunity for the spoken and written languages to diverge. For this reason, Rumanian examples will normally be given in their orthographic form. The phonemic values of the letters are shown in table 13.1, with some oddities discussed in the remarks which follow it. One value of using the orthography is that, as with French, it provides some insight into the history of the language, because of the method used for representing final palatalised consonants.

Among the vowel symbols, *â* is an archaic form of *î* and is normally reserved for words representing the name of the country and its people and language: *România* 'Rumania', *românesc/român* 'Rumanian', *românește* 'Rumanian language'. A limited number of words beginning with *e-* are pronounced /je-/, this ioticisation apparently a Slavonic inheritance. More recent loans from Western Romance are unaffected, giving rise to the occasional doublet: *era* /éra/ 'the era' but *era* /jerá/ 'was'. Initial *i-* before another vowel is also pronounced /j-/: *iute* /jute/ 'quick'; *iar* /jar/ 'again'. Final *-i* normally represents palatalisation of the preceding consonant: *lup* /lup/ 'wolf' but *lupi* /lupʲ/ 'wolves'. However, this does not apply when the preceding consonant cluster is consonant+liquid: *tigri* /tigri/ 'tigers'. Final *-ii* represents a full /i/ and so the system allows for the differentiation of some masculine nouns into three forms. Thus, the singular *lup* /lup/ 'wolf' is made plural by the palatalisation of the final plosive: *lupi* /lupʲ/ 'wolves', and

Table 13.1: Orthographic System of Modern Rumanian

a	/a/	m	/m/
ă	/ə/	n	/n/
b	/b/	o	/o/
c (+h)	/k/	p	/p/
c (+i/e)	/tʃ/	r	/r/
d	/d/	s	/s/
e	/e/	ş	/ʃ/
f	/f/	t	/t/
g (+h)	/g/	ţ	/ts/
g (+i/e)	/dʒ/	u	/u/
h	/h/	v	/v/
i	/i/**	# w	/v/ or /w/
î/â	/ɨ/	x	/ks/
j	/ʒ/	y	/j/
k	/k/	z	/z/
l	/l/		

Note: **i* is the most troublesome orthographic symbol in Rumanian. The phoneme equivalent given here relates to full vowels. See the text for comments on other values. # Used for common international terms only, e.g. *weekend*, *watt*.

definite plural by addition of a full /i/: *lupii* /lupi/ 'the wolves'. This can be
alarming when the stem of the noun ends in *-il*. The noun *copil* 'child' has a
plural *copii* /kopi/ 'children' (the final /l/ is palatalised out of existence) and a
definite plural *copiii* /kopiʲi/ 'the children'. The three major diphthongs /ea/,
/oa/ and /eo/ are represented by their starting and finishing points — *ea*, *oa*
and *eo*. The sequence *au* is pronounced as two separate vowels, as normally
is *ău* too.

Among the consonant symbols, *k* is a comparative rarity (being reserved
for international terms such as *kilogram, kilometru*) and the voiceless velar
plosive is represented by *c* (*ch* before front vowels). Similarly, the voiced
velar plosive is represented by *g* (*gh* before front vowels). The post-alveolar
affricates /tʃ/ and /dʒ/ are also represented by *c* and *g*, but by the digraphs *ci*
and *gi* (sometimes *ce* and *ge*) before back and middle vowels (see Italian,
page 274). The fronting of velar plosives before front vowels is a
characteristic Rumanian shares with Western Romance, and is discussed
later in this section.

Standard Rumanian has 32 phonemes (or more, depending on the method
of phonological analysis employed — the series of palatalised consonants
being treated either as a distinct set or as the non-palatal series plus a
recurring palatal off-glide). The neatest system identifies 7 simple vowels,
3 diphthongs and 22 consonants, which include two semi-vowels. The
number of diphthongs is increased substantially if the semi-vowel /j/ is
treated as a vowel unit rather than as a consonant (thus /je/ would be a
diphthong, but is treated here as a consonant-vowel sequence). The
phoneme inventory is set out in figures 13.1 and 13.2, and table 13.2.

Figure 13.1: Vowels   **Figure 13.2: Diphthongs**

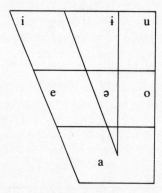   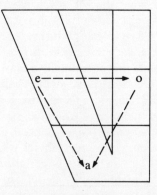

The two back vowels are rounded,   All three diphthongs are rising,
the remainder are unrounded.   with stress on the second element.

Table 13.2: Consonants

	Bilabial	Labio-dental	Dental	Post-alveolar	Palatal	Velar	Glottal
Stops	p b		t d			k g	
Affricates			ts	tʃ dʒ			
Fricatives		f v	s z	ʃ ʒ			h
Nasals	m		n				
Liquids			l r				
Semi-vowels	w				j		

There is some symmetry within the consonant system, most obstruents being in voiced/voiceless pairs. Voiced and voiceless plosives alike are unaspirated. Unpaired are the glottal fricative /h/ (often pronounced with audible friction) and the dental affricate /ts/ — though in more conservative dialects this too is matched with the voiced equivalent /dz/. There are only two nasals, the gap in the system being the velar nasal, which occurs only as an allophone of /n/ before velar plosives. There are two liquids, /r/ being a lingual flap or light roll, and the dental lateral /l/ being consistently clear.

As mentioned earlier, Rumanian has followed the normal Romance path of fronting velar plosives before front vowels, giving rise to the post-alveolar affricates. However, /k/ and /g/ also occur slightly fronted as an allophonic variation before front vowels: *chema* 'call' and *ghetou* 'ghetto'. The failure of the velar plosives to front all the way to post-alveolar affricates in many words reflects the distinct treatment of words inherited directly from Latin and those borrowed from other languages at later dates, e.g. from Slavonic: *chilie* '(monk's) cell' (from *kelija*) or from Hungarian: *chip* 'face, facial expression' (from *kép*).

Among consonants also attributable to contact with other languages is /ʒ/. This derives from Latin *-di-* sequences: *DEORSUM > jos* 'down'; *ADJŪTO > ajut* 'help'; but also from Latin *j* + back vowels: *JUGUM > jug* 'yoke'; *JOCUM > joc* 'game'. Its presence in Slavonic-based words (*grajd* 'stable'; *jar* 'live coals') testifies to its reinforcement through contact with Southern Slavonic if it is not actually a Slavonic-induced development.

The glottal fricative /h/ has an uncertain history, some linguists claiming it was reintroduced after its loss in Vulgar Latin in order to bring symmetry back to the plosive/fricative system (thus: p~f; t~s; k~h). Again this development was reintroduced, if not necessarily induced, by languages Rumanian came into contact with: from Slavonic, *duh* 'soul' and *hrană* 'food, fodder'; from Hungarian, *hotar* 'border' and *hîrdău* 'bucket'; from Turkish, *hamal* 'porter' and *huzur* 'leisure'.

A substratum influence from Dacian/Thracian has been suggested for some distinctive phonological developments in Balkan Romance, though this is highly speculative, given the dearth of extant material from such a substratum. Comparison with Albanian shows some parallels: /ə/ from unstressed /a/ is found in both Rumanian and Albanian, as well as Bulgarian; Rumanian /ɨ/ from /a/ before nasals in closed syllables: Latin *CAMPUM* > *cîmp* 'plain', but not in open syllables: Latin *ANNUM* > *an* 'year' (-*nn*- appears to have become a long, rather than geminate, consonant and was grouped with the following vowel); labialisation of velars in velar+dental clusters: Latin *COXAM* > *coapsă* 'thigh' (Albanian *kofshë*). Treatments like this last one also provide useful patterns for comparison between Balkan and Western Romance:

Latin	Rumanian	French	Italian	Spanish
FACTUM	fapt	fait	fatto	hecho
LACTEM	lapte	lait	latte	leche

Like Italian, however, Rumanian inherits vowel-final plurals from Latin, with loss of final -*s*: *FLŌRES* > *flori* 'flowers' (though, of course, final -*i* now represents palatalisation of the final consonant).

In some instances there was substitution of one liquid for the other: *CAELUM* > *cer* 'sky'; *MELLEM* > *miere* 'honey'; *SALEM* > *sare* 'salt'. Later loans from Western Romance thus gave rise to doublets: *ceresc~celest* 'celestial/of the sky'. Sixteenth-century texts of the north Transylvania area of Maramureş also show evidence of rhotacism, with intervocalic /n/ becoming /r/: *lumiră* for *lumină* 'light'; *tire* for *tine* 'you'. This is a feature also of Istro-Rumanian: *plıră* for *plınă* 'full'; *lıră* for *lınă* 'wool'.

Consonant clusters also show differences between Rumanian and Western Romance. Matching the voiceless /str/ and /skl/ are the voiced /zdr/ and /zgl/; /zb/ and /zg/ match /sp/ and /sk/; /zv/ matches /sf/; /zm/ and /zl/ also occur; while the presence of post-alveolar /ʃ/ leads to the existence of clusters such as /ʃt(r)/ and /ʃp (l~r)/. While all these clusters fill natural gaps in the Romance system, phonotactically much more unexpected are: /hl/, /hr/, /ml/ and /mr/ as well as word-initial /kt/.

Finally, stress is free and variable, giving rise to doublets: *módele* 'the fashions' but *modéle* 'models'; *cíntă* 'sings, sing!' but *cîntắ* 'sang'. Rumanian orthography does not regularly mark stress but it will be marked here whenever it is relevant to the discussion.

3 Morphology

As in Western Romance, the Latin declension system for nouns and adjectives was reduced in Balkan Romance through phonetic attrition. However, Rumanian is more conservative to the extent that it retains three distinct case forms: nominative/accusative, genitive/dative, vocative. It has also reintroduced what has been described as a neuter gender. This diversity of case forms is most evident among feminines, but also with masculines

Nouns

(a) some typical masculine nouns

(i) lup 'wolf'

		Sg.	Pl.
Nom./acc.	-def	lup	lupi
	+def	lupul	lupii
Gen./dat.	-def	lup	lupi
	+def	lupului	lupilor

(ii) arbore 'tree'

		Sg.	Pl.
Nom./acc.	-def	arbore	arbori
	+def	arborele	arborii
Gen./dat.	-def	arbore	arbori
	+def	arborelui	arborilor

(iii) codru 'forest'

		Sg.	Pl.
Nom./acc.	-def	codru	codri
	+def	codrul	codrii
Gen./dat.	-def	codru	codri
	+def	codrului	codrilor

Some further sg./pl. alternations: *om-oameni* 'man'; *împărat-împăraţi* 'emperor'; *băiat-băieţi* 'boy'; *cal-cai* 'horse'; *fiu-fii* 'son'; *brad-brazi* 'fir tree'.

(b) some typical feminine nouns

(i) casă 'house'

		Sg.	Pl.
Nom./acc.	-def	casă	case
	+def	casa	casele
Gen./dat.	-def	case	case
	+def	casei	caselor

(ii) stea 'star'

		Sg.	Pl.
Nom./acc.	-def	stea	stele
	+def	steaua	stelele
Gen./dat.	-def	stele	stele
	+def	stelei	stelelor

(iii) cîmpie 'plain'

		Sg.	Pl.
Nom./acc.	-def	cîmpie	cîmpii
	+def	cîmpia	cîmpiile
Gen./dat.	-def	cîmpii	cîmpii
	+def	cîmpiei	cîmpiilor

Some further sg./pl. alternations: *basma-basmale* 'kerchief'; *viaţă-vieţi* 'life'; *carte-cărţi* 'book'; *fată-fete* 'girl'; *dovadă-dovezi* 'proof'; *bară-bări* '(metal) bar'.

(c) some typical 'neuter' nouns

(i) studiu 'study(ing)'

		Sg.	Pl.
Nom.acc.	-def.	studiu	studii
	+def	studiul	studiile
Gen./dat.	-def	studiu	studii
	+def	studiului	studiilor

(ii) oraş 'town'

		Sg.	Pl.
Nom./acc.	-def.	oraş	oraşe
	+def	oraşul	oraşele
Gen./dat.	-def	oraş	oraşe
	+def	oraşului	oraşelor

(iii) deal 'hill'

		Sg.	Pl.
Nom./acc.	-def.	deal	dealuri
	+def	dealul	dealurile
Gen./dat.	-def	deal	dealuri
	+def	dealului	dealurilor

Some further sg./pl. alternations: *tablou-tablouri* 'picture'; *nume-nume* 'name'; *templu-temple* 'temple'.

when the noun is definite. A characteristic that Rumanian shares with Bulgarian and Albanian is the use of suffixes to mark definiteness: Latin *HOMO ILLE* > *omul* 'the man', with fusion of the demonstrative (compare the normal pattern in the West from *ILLE HOMO*). Indefinites follow the normal Romance pattern: *un om* 'a man'.

The representative sample in the chart of nouns demonstrates the greater variation in form within the feminines in the non-definite paradigms. Vocatives are discussed separately, as they are irregular and relatively infrequent. It will be seen that morphologically the neuters are masculine in the singuar and feminine in the plural. They have also been described as *ambigeneric* for this reason. Syntactically, it is difficult to choose between the two labels, the only relevant data, involving the agreement between adjectives and conjoined nouns of different genders, being highly unreliable.

The examples in the chart of nominal paradigms show that masculines and neuters are invariable without the definite suffix, in both singular and plural paradigms. In the indefinite system it is only feminines that show a distinction between nominative/accusative and genitive/dative, the feminine genitive/dative singulars normally coinciding in form with the plural. It is the suffixal nature of the definite marker that has contributed most to the apparent conservative nature of the Rumanian case system.

The vocative case is defective, being reserved mainly for animates, especially humans. It also usually occurs in the definite form: *om* 'man' → *omule* 'o man'; *cumătru* 'godfather' → *cumătrule* 'o godfather' (but also *cumetre* — the use of kin terms without possessives or definite determiners being common in Rumanian, as in other languages).

Proper names also occur as vocatives, the use of the definite suffix depending on the stem termination: *Radu* → *Radule* but *Gheorghe* → *Gheorghe* (not *Gheorghele*); *Ana* → *Ana*, *Anǎ* or *Ano*.

The vocative is under very heavy pressure and is likely to disappear. Its occurrence in the modern language, as limited as it is, is felt to be a Slavonic legacy — in particular, feminines in *-o* (*Ano; vulpe* 'vixen' → *vulpeo* 'o vixen' — though this latter is admittedly rare). This directly reflects a Slavonic termination and cannot readily be accounted for by normal evolution from the Latin vocatives.

Adjectives follow the same morphological pattern as nouns, with which they agree in gender, number and case. There are some less variable adjectives which do not distinguish masculine and feminine in the indefinite form of the nominative/accusative: *mare* 'big' (m./f. sg.) ~ *mari* 'big' (m./f. pl.), but genitive/dative feminine singular follows the same pattern as the nouns in matching the plural forms: *unui om mare* 'of/to a big man', *unei fete mari* 'of/to a big girl'. Normal adjectives inflect like the noun they agree with: *om bun* 'good man', *fată bună* 'good girl'; feminine/neuter plural adjectives take the *-e* form, not *-uri*. Finally, it is also possible for adjectives to take definite suffixes: *omul bun* 'the good man' and *bunul om* 'the *good* man'.

The personal pronoun system derives directly from Latin. The chart of personal pronouns shows cliticised and free forms for nominative, accusative and dative.

Personal Pronouns

		1st sg.	2nd sg.	3rd sg. (m.)	3rd sg. (f.)	1st pl.	2nd pl.	3rd pl. (m.)	3rd pl. (f.)
Nominative	Cliticised								
		eu	tu	el	ea	noi	voi	ei	ele
	Free								
Accusative	Cliticised	mă	te	îl	o	ne	vă	îi	le
	Free *pe* +	mine	tine	el	ea	noi	voi	ei	ele
Dative	Cliticised	îmi	îți	îi	îi	ni	vi	le	le
	Free	mie	ție	lui	ei	nouă	vouă	lor	lor

Note: The cliticised forms are the full forms. Syncope takes place depending on environment: for example, *îmi dau cadoul* 'they give the present to me' but *mi-l dau* 'they give it to me'.

The preposition *pe* is an accusative marker — its distribution is dealt with in section 4.

There are from three to five verb conjugations, depending on how strong is the linguist's desire to relate them to the clasical Latin system. The infinitive and present indicative and subjunctive of the different types, together with *have* and *be*, are given in the chart of verb forms. The greatest controversy is whether verbs like *vedea* 'see' (from Latin second conjugation verbs like *VIDĒRE* and *MONĒRE*) are in the process of being absorbed into the larger pattern represented by *face* 'do, make'. Following the chart there is some discussion of the forms of the various tenses, moods and voices, with comments on their origins.

The future in Rumanian is periphrastic, and appears to have been so throughout its history. The more literary form is *voi cînta*, deriving from Vulgar Latin forms of *VOLEO* 'wish' (*voi, vei, va, vom, veți, vor*) + infinitive. The selection of 'wish' as the auxiliary is characteristic of Balkan languages. Periphrastic too is the spoken future: *am să cînt* (lit.) 'have to sing' — formed from the auxiliary 'have' from *HABEO* + subjunctive; the invariable particle *o* also occurs in a similar structure: *o să cînt* 'I will sing', *o să cînți* 'you will sing'.

The imperfect is a direct development from Latin *-BAM* forms: *cîntăm, cîntái, cîntá, cîntám, cîntáți, cîntáu* 'I etc. was singing/used to sing'. The perfect derives from the Latin perfect: *CANTĀVĪ* > *cîntái, cîntáși, cîntă,*

Present Indicative and Subjunctive

	Type I (a) cîntá 'sing'	Type II vedeá 'see'	Type IV (a) **dormí 'sleep'	Type V (a) omorí 'kill'	Irregulars aveá 'have'
1 sg.	cínt	vắd	dórm	omór	ám
2 sg.	cínţi	vézi	dórmi	omóri	ái
3 sg.	cíntă	véde	dóarme	omoáră	áre
1 pl.	cîntắm	vedém	dormím	omorím	avém
2 pl.	cîntáţi	vedéţi	dormíţi	omoríţi	avéţi
3 pl.	cíntă	vắd	dórm	omoáră	áu
3 subj.	să cínte	să vádă	să doármă	să omoáre	să aíbă

	Type I (b) lucrá 'work'	Type III fáce 'make/do'	Type IV (b) **zidí 'build'	Type V (b) urí 'hate'	fi 'be' Indicative	Subjunctive
1 sg.	lucréz	fác	zidésc	urắsc	sínt	să fíu
2 sg.	lucrézi	fáci	zidéşti	urắşti	éşti	să fíi
3 sg.	lucreáză	fáce	zidéşte	urắşte	é(ste)	să fíe
1 pl.	lucrắm	fácem	zidím	urím	síntem	să fím
2 pl.	lucráţi	fáceţi	zidíţi	uríţi	sínteţi	să fíţi
3 pl.	lucreáză	fác	zidésc	urắsc	sínt	să fíe
3 subj.	să lucréze	să fácă	să zideáscă	să uráscă		

Note: Stress is shown on all forms, though it is normally unmarked in written Rumanian. Comparison between types II and III shows that type II has stress on the termination in 1 and 2 plural; in type III, stress is consistently on the stem.
** Orthography is irregular here — consistent system would show full vowel value of -i by -ii.

cîntárăm, cîntáráţi, cîntáră 'I etc. sang'. However, this is normal only in Oltenia, the western region of Muntenia (as well as in Arumanian, where its use matches that of the Greek aorist). Normally in Rumanian the compound perfect is used: am, ai, a, am, aţi, au cîntat 'I etc. sang/have sung' (based on HABEO + past participle). Conversely, in Rumanian the compound pluperfect does not exist, the synthetic forms deriving from Latin pluperfect subjunctives: cîntásem, cîntáseşi, cîntáse, cîntáserăm, cîntáseráţi, cîntáseră 'I etc. had sung' (while in Arumanian, Greek contact is again reflected in the use of a compound pluperfect).

Morphologically, the present subjunctive has been all but neutralised with the indicative being differentiated from the present indicative only in the third person, except for the irregular fi. The remaining forms of the verb paradigm are periphrastic, with combinations of voi (future marker), să (subordinating particle) or aş (conditional particle) followed by the BE infinitive fi and then either the past participle (chemat) or the gerundive (chemînd). That is:

$$\left. \begin{matrix} \text{voi} \\ \text{să} \\ \text{aş} \end{matrix} \right\} \qquad \text{fi} \qquad \left\{ \begin{matrix} \text{chemat} \\ \text{chemînd} \end{matrix} \right.$$

for example: *să fi chemat* (perfect subjunctive); *aş fi chemînd* (conditional presumptive).

Most notable of the periphrastic forms is the conditional: *aş, ai, ar, am, aţi, ar cînta* 'I etc. would sing'. This seems to represent the unusual process of a synthetic form being reinterpreted diachronically as an analytic construction, i.e. from original *cîntareaş*, the *-re* termination having been lost after the periphrastic form came about, in line with the general loss of the *-re* termination on all infinitives.

The morphological material on which the numeral system is based is predominantly Latin (with the exception of *sută* 'hundred', from Old Slavonic *sŭto*). There has, however, been a calquing on the Slavonic pattern for the teens and multiples of ten: *QUATTUOR SUPER DECEM* > *patrusprezece* 'fourteen'; *QUATTUOR + DECEM* > *patruzeci* 'forty'. Arumanian is more conservative in retaining the Latin 'twenty' (/jingits/, from *VĪGINTI*), but less conservative in following the Slavonic pattern for 'twenty-one' to 'twenty-nine' as well as for 'eleven' to 'nineteen' (/patrusprejingits/ 'twenty-four').

4   Syntax

The basic order of major constituents is: subject–verb–object (SVO), though variations occur under a variety of circumstances. Yes-no questions are normally represented by a change in intonation but inversion of subject and (part of the) verbal complex is an option, and normal with *wh*-questions: *cînd a venit Ion?* 'when did Ion come?'. Heavy constituents also may result in a change of word order, with long noun phrases containing embedded clauses being extraposed: *Merită să fie notate în această ordine încercările scriitorului de a găsi un echivalent sunetelor ă şi î* lit. 'deserve to be noted in this respect the attempts of the writer to find an equivalent for the sounds *ă* and *î*'. Pronouns also complicate discussion of word order. They can occur in different positions as clitics from their full noun phrase equivalents: *bărbatul a dat carnetul copilului* 'the man gave the notebook to the child', but *(el) i l-a dat* lit. '(he) to him it gave'. Along with most other Romance languages Rumanian subject personal pronouns can be dispensed with, there being sufficient morphological differences between the personal verb forms to make them redundant, except for emphasis or contrast.

OVS is also a common alternative to SVO, as in other Balkan languages such as Greek. The ability to distinguish subject from object morphologically increases the incidence of this reversed order. The preposition *pe* (normally 'on') acts as an accusative marker for all pronouns but also for full noun phrases high in animacy (and thus to some extent corresponds to Spanish *a* — see page 255). It can thus decode noun phrase–verb–noun phrase structures and is assisted in this by the use of reduplicative pronouns. *Ion a văzut-o pe Maria* lit. 'Ion saw her Maria' occurs as an alternative to *Ion a văzut Maria* 'Ion saw Maria', but both *pe* and the clitic must appear when the order is OVS: *pe Maria a văzut-o Ion* lit. 'Maria saw her Ion'. Resumptive pronouns also occur as a cross-reference for lower items on the animacy hierarchy when these occur as initial objects (though *pe* is not obligatory under these circumstances): *singura menţiune a acestei părţi de cuvînt o găsim în...* lit. 'the only mention of this word part (we) it find in...'; and in relative clauses, a relativised object must be represented by both decoding methods: *acesta e carnetul pe care l-am furat* lit. 'this is the notebook which (I) it stole'.

Variability in the use of *pe* as an object marker (it is a feature more of formal than of informal language) leads to hypercorrection. The Rumanian linguist Graur notes examples such as: *îmi trebuie pe cineva care...* lit. 'to me is necessary someone who...', where speakers have treated the grammatical subject *cineva* as an object.

Within noun phrases the normal order is:

(a) Determiner   –   Noun   –   Adjective
    Un/acest   copil   bun
    'A/this good child'

(b) Noun+def   –   Demonstrative+def   –   Adjective
    Copilul   acesta   bun
    'This good child'

(c) Adjective+def   –   Noun
    Bunul   copil
    'The good child'

Thus, indefinite determiners precede the noun, while adjectives (and relative clauses) follow it, except for contrastive use, as in (c); when demonstratives follow the noun (as in (b)), both are marked for definiteness.

Definiteness on nouns is unmarked when the noun is part of a prepositional phrase (*cu* 'with' is an exception), unless the noun is further modified: *masă* 'table'; *masa* 'the table'; *sub masă* 'under the table'; *sub masa pe care ai construit-o* 'under the table that you constructed (it)'. This phenomenon provides a useful method of distinguishing restrictive and non-restrictive relative clauses. Compare the following *non*-restrictive example, where the head noun is *not* marked for definiteness: *sub masă, pe care ai construit-o* 'under the table, which you constructed (it)'.

Rumanian retains the reflexive *se*, but with an increase in its use. In addition to its true reflexive sense (*se bate* 'beat oneself'), it has semi-fossilised to form verbs without a reflexive interpretation (*se duce* '(he) goes, to go'); it is used as an impersonal (*se spune* 'it is said') and as a passive (*aici se vînd cărţile* 'here are sold books').

Features shared with other Balkan languages include the periphrastic future, with 'wish' as the auxiliary; the use of a suffixal definite marker (found not only in Rumanian and Albanian, but also in Bulgarian/ Macedonian, unusual among the Slavonic languages in having the equivalent of the definite article in English); the use of cliticised resumptive pronouns (these occur in Western Romance but are usually part of a dislocated structure); and a severe decline in the use of the infinitive.

Like Western Romance, Rumanian inherited an infinitival complement clause structure in addition to indicative and subjunctive structures. However, where French and Italian would now use an infinitive Rumanian is more likely to use a subjunctive: Fr. *je veux chanter*; It. *volo cantare*; Rum. *vreau să cînt* 'I want to sing'. Within the auxiliary system one can see retention of the short infinitive: *voi cînta* 'I will sing'; *aş cînta* 'I would sing'. Many speakers also use *pot cînta* for *pot să cînt* 'I am able to sing'. Given the modal value of verbs representing ability or possibility, such an option is not surprising — the short infinitive can be seen as a stem form of the verbal complex and *pot* straddles the boundary between main verb and auxiliary verb.

The decline of the infinitive appears to be relatively recent. It is used as a complement clause marker in regular alternation with the subjunctive in a mid-eighteenth century grammar: *se cuvine a păzi/se cuvine să păzească* 'it is proper to be on guard'. Hand in hand with the reduction in use of the infinitive went its truncation (by loss of its Latin *-re* termination). In the modern language, *-re* forms are now clearly established as nominals and correspond closely to gerunds or derived nominals in English: *se întoarce* 'to return, he returns' → *întoarcerea lui neaşteptată* 'his unexpected return'.

Despite these Balkan characteristics, there has been some tendency during the last 150 years for the language to move towards the mainstream Romance pattern in syntax. The infinitive has begun to appear more regularly as a complement clause marker, and the periphrastic passive has made great inroads into the area occupied by the reflexive passive: *a fost furat* lit. 'was stolen' is more common than *s-a furat* lit. 'stole itself'. The regional use of a preposition to mark possession or indirect objects has found some currency in the spoken standard language, rather than the genitive/dative case marking. A much-cited example of a prepositional indirect object marking is : *dă apă la vite* instead of *dă apă vitelor* 'give water to the cattle'; and street vendors in Bucharest were noted between the wars as using the prepositional *planul de Bucureşti* in place of *planul Bucureştiului* 'plan of Bucharest'. In Arumanian it is normal to find the *la* 'to' + nominative/accusative structure with full noun phrases instead of the dative case, since Greek also has a prepositional construction: *ðíno ta práɣmata stin yinéka* 'I give the things to the woman'.

It is, of course, impossible to predict how far this reromancing tendency will go in morphosyntax but it is certainly the case that in some areas of structure change is unlikely. Thus, while there has been a resurgence in the use of the infinitival future (*voi cînta*) rather than the subjunctive alternative (*o să cînt*) in literary texts, it is hard to imagine Rumanian adopting a future based on infinitive + 'have' in line with Western Romance. Indeed, it would appear that in Western Romance a periphrastic future is also on the increase.

5   Vocabulary

Since vocabulary is more readily borrowed than other linguistic features, it is in its lexical stock that Rumanian has shown the greatest tendency to reromance during the last 150 years. For the same reason, however, the language had also had its original Latin lexical base diluted by contact with other languages in the Balkans, not least Slavonic. The total Slavonic element in Rumanian has been put as high as 40 per cent, though recent borrowings of international vocabulary have reduced this overall proportion considerably. It is in any case misleading to give a single figure for the language as a whole, since no speaker will use, or even know, all the words in the language. In everyday conversation the proportion of words from one source may well differ from the overall proportion in the language of material from that source. Using a basic 100- or 200-item word list relating to everyday life, it can be shown that Rumanian has a Latin lexical base of well over 90 per cent.

Nevertheless, the overall Slavonic element in Rumanian cannot be ignored, even if the Romance structure of the language has been left relatively unaffected. For the remainder of this section I give a brief résumé of the various lexical influences Rumanian has undergone, with examples from the major sources.

There is little evidence of substratum influence in Balkan Romance. Latin appears to have replaced the local Thracian language to such an extent that only a few words can even be considered Thracian in origin. Some of these are cognate with Albanian words and it is possible that they represent the remains of some Thraco-Illyrian language base. The following words are possible candidates, though it cannot be ruled out that they are indigenous Albanian words borrowed from Albanian by Rumanian: Rum. *abure* 'steam' (Alb. *avull*); Rum. *brad* 'fir' (Alb. *bredhi*); Rum. *mal* '(river) bank' (Alb. *mal*); Rum. *vatră* 'hearth' (Alb. *vatrë*).

Slavonic vocabulary in Rumanian can be divided into two main groups: popular, borrowed from the time of earliest contact between Balkan Romance and South Slavonic (approximately from the sixth century onwards); and technical or literary borrowings, from the thirteenth century onwards. This gave rise to doublets: from Old Slavonic *sŭvŭršiti* came popular *sfîrşi* and literary *săvîrşi* 'finish, complete'. Borrowing was not always direct and calques can be found. One much-cited example: on the basis of the two meanings of the South Slavonic *svĕtŭ* 'light' and 'world', Latin *LŪMEN – LŪMINIS* 'light' had two derivations in Rumanian — *lume* 'world' and *lumină* 'light'.

Much religious vocabulary in Rumanian has a Slavonic character — as pointed out in section 2, Old Church Slavonic was the official language of the Orthodox church in what is now Rumania. When the vernacular became the norm, much of the Old Church Slavonic terminology was taken over. At the same time, it should be appreciated that an original source of much of this vocabulary was Greek, Old Church Slavonic merely being the vehicle for its transfer to Rumanian. The word *chilie* 'cell' attributed in section 2 to Slavonic was in fact borrowed originally by Old Church Slavonic from Greek *kéllion*. It is partly for this reason that Greek influence on Balkan Romance was much greater than on Western Romance. Greek words also found their way into Rumanian via popular Slavonic language: *broatec* 'toad' derives via Slavonic from Greek *brotachos*, with cognate forms in Albanian and Arumanian. However, the early borrowing *drum* 'way, road' via Bulgarian from Greek *ðrómos* is not found in the Arumanian of present-day Greece, where a derivative of Latin *CALLEM* 'track' is used instead (Arumanian /kale/; Rum. *cale* does exist but has a more restricted sense than the general word *drum*).

During the Phanariot period (1711–1821), when the principalities of Moldavia and Wallachia were administered for the Turks by Greek princes, many words were borrowed from Greek by Rumanian, though it has been calculated that of the more than 1,200 words borrowed in this period only 250 are left in the modern language (e.g. *stridie* 'oyster' from *stríði*; *aerisi* 'air, ventilate, fan' from the aorist of *aerízo*). During this period too, Turkish words found their way into Rumanian but many of these have also disappeared from use. Perhaps three per cent of Rumanian vocabulary is Turkish in origin, and relatively common words include: *duşman* 'enemy' (Tk. *duşman*) and *chior* 'one-eyed' (Tk. *kör*).

Over the last 200 years the influence of Western Romance and Latin on Rumanian has been substantial. The Transylvanian School began importing Western Romance loans from the late eighteenth century, but interest was more in the Latin origins of the language than in Romance relationships. Consequently, not only did they etymologise their writing system (see section 1), but they also set about purging the language of Slavonic loans and creating new Latin-based vocabulary. Some portmanteau words were created: from Slavonic-based *război* 'war' and Latin *BELLUM* was created *război*, which has not survived into the modern language; on the other hand, the combination of Slavonic-based *năravuri* 'customs' and Latin *MÕRES* gave *moravuri* 'customs, morals', which is in common use today. The desire to 'improve' and 'purify' Rumanian on the part of the Transylvanian School has complicated considerably the already difficult task of carrying out research on the origins of Rumanian vocabulary.

It was the rise of France and French as cultural models during the nineteenth century that did most to change the overall pattern of the Rumanian word stock. French became the source of much new vocabulary but also the vehicle for the entry of words from other languages. For example, a modern dictionary attributes *miting* '(political) meeting' and *dumping* '(trade) dumping' to 'French (from English)'. On the other hand, some French vocabulary entered Rumanian via Russian. As Russian influence increased during the second half of the nineteenth century, military and administrative terms were introduced: *infanterie* 'infantry', *cavalerie* 'cavalry', *parlament* 'parliament' and *administraţie* 'administration' all appear to have followed this route.

There were two distinct attitudes among writers of the Muntenian school towards the treatment of Romance loans. There were those who, like the Transylvanian School, wanted to modify considerably in line with what were felt to be normal Rumanian developments. This gave rise to linguistic terms such as *obiept* and *subiept* in place of *obiect* and *subiect* (though the *-pt-* form reflects the $CT > pt$ pattern discussed in section 2, it was the *-ct-* form that survived). Other writers took a more realistic approach and, while only using words for which there was not already an adequate native Rumanian equivalent, embraced the imported vocabulary without amendment. Nevertheless, the lack of a clear relationship between French spelling and pronunciation has meant that, for example, Fr. *réveillon* is rendered in Rumanian today as both *reveion* and *revelion* 'New Year celebration'. Finally, French loans also gave rise to doublets as Latin-based words came face to face again. In addition to the example in section 2, *sentiment* was imported alongside the more native *simţămînt* 'feeling, sentiment'.

Today, the effect of American economic power and technological growth can be felt in the importing of many English technical and commercial terms into Rumanian, their fate regulated to some extent by the Rumanian Academy, which began to unify the treatment of neologisms (choosing, for example, the appropriate gender and plural forms) from 1940 onwards. The irony is of course that much of this new vocabulary from English has itself Latin and Romance origins, thus adding yet another layer onto what was already a very complex foundation.

Bibliography

Much of the material produced on the language is inaccessible, being either published in Rumania or written in Rumanian. A thorough reference grammar in English has been prepared by this author for the Croom Helm Descriptive Grammars series.

Agard (1958) is a short volume in structuralist mould, concentrating on phonology and morphology, while Lombard (1974) is a detailed structural description, fuller than Agard but more difficult to find one's way around. Deletant (1983) is a very good introduction to the language for those wishing to speak it. The Academy grammar, Graur et al. (1963), is very thorough and better than many academy grammars, though it has the usual slightly prescriptive bias. Sandfeld and Olsen (1936–62) is a full description of the syntax of the written language, with many examples, in the style of Lombard; a transformational description of the major syntactic structures, in the framework of Chomsky's Standard Theory, is provided by Vasiliu and Golopenția-Eretescu (1969).

For the history of the language, Rosetti (1968) gives a wealth of detail on the development of the language from Latin and its contact with other languages, and is well worth the effort for those with an interest in Romance languages; Rosetti (1973) is a brief summary of this magnum opus. Close (1974) is an excellent discussion of the rise of the Muntenian dialect as the standard language, with great detail on the nineteenth-century vogue for Romance and particularly French linguistic culture.

References

Agard, F.B. 1958. *Structural Sketch of Rumanian* (Linguistic Society of America, Baltimore)

Close, E. 1974. *The Development of Modern Rumanian — Linguistic Theory and Practice in Muntenia 1821–1838* (Oxford University Press, Oxford)

Deletant, D. 1983. *Colloquial Romanian* (Routledge and Kegan Paul, London)

Graur, Al. et al. 1963. *Gramatica limbii romîne*, 2 vols. (Academy of Sciences, Bucharest)

Mallinson, G. 1986. *Rumanian* (Routledge, London)

Rosetti, Al. 1968. *Istoria limbii române de la origini pînă în secolul al XVII-lea* (Bucharest)

—— 1973. *Brève histoire de la langue roumaine des origines à nos jours* (Mouton, The Hague)

Sandfeld, Kr. and H. Olsen. 1936–62. *Syntaxe roumaine*, 3 vols. (Droz, Paris)

Vasiliu, E. and S. Golopenția-Eretescu. 1969. *Sintaxa transformațională a limbii române* (Bucharest; also available in an irritatingly poor English translation, *The Transformational Syntax of Romanian*, Mouton, The Hague, 1972)

Language Index